THE SIGHT OF SOUND

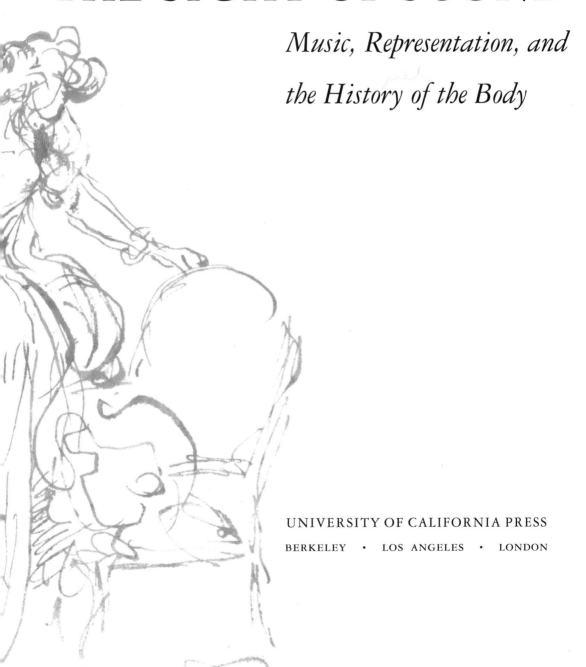

Richard Leppert

THE SIGHT OF SOUND

Music, Representation, and

the History of the Body

UNIVERSITY OF CALIFORNIA PRESS

BERKELEY · LOS ANGELES · LONDON

This publication has been supported by a subvention
from the American Musicological Society.

The publisher gratefully acknowledges the contribution
provided by the Art Book Endowment Fund of the
Associates of the University of California Press, which
is supported by a major gift from the Ahmanson Foundation.

University of California Press
Berkeley and Los Angeles, California
University of California Press, Ltd.
London, England
© 1993 by
The Regents of the University of California
Printed in the United States of America
9 8 7 6 5 4 3 2 1

Library of Congress Cataloging-in-Publication Data

Leppert, Richard D.
    The sight of sound : music, representation, and the history of the body /
Richard Leppert.
        p.   cm.
    Includes bibliographical references and index.
    ISBN 0-520-08174-9
    1. Music—Social aspects.   2. Music—Philosophy and aesthetics.
3. Music—Physiological aspects.   4. Music—History and criticism.
5. Social sciences—Philosophy.   I. Title.
ML3800.L6   1993
781'.11—dc20   92-39075
                                                        MN

The paper used in this publication meets the minimum
requirements of American National Standard for
Information Sciences—Permanence of Paper for Printed
Library Materials, ANSI Z39.48-1984. ⊗

FOR ANN, MY WIFE · FOR JOHN, MY BROTHER

CONTENTS

ILLUSTRATIONS

ACKNOWLEDGMENTS

I AM GRATEFUL FOR the research assistance rendered by Barbara Engh, who pointed me toward materials I would not otherwise have known and provided invaluable guidance in judging what was central, what peripheral. The critical readings offered by Philip Brett, Wayne Franits, Jamie Kassler, Lawrence Kramer, Simon Miller, Derek Scott, and Ruth Solie were invariably stimulating; I owe each of them many thanks. My friend Jeanne Long helped prepare parts of the manuscript, and quite apart from her boundless energy and professionalism I enjoyed her good humor and benefited from her patience. I also wish to acknowledge my editors at the University of California Press, Doris Kretschmer and Stephanie Fay, for their considerable effort and support.

I am indebted to the staffs of several research libraries: the Witt Library, Courtauld Institute of Art, University of London; Interlibrary Loan Services and Special Collections, O. Meredith Wilson Library, University of Minnesota; J. Paul Getty Center for the History of Art and the Humanities, Santa Monica; The Thomas J. Watson Library, and the Department of Musical Instruments, both of The Metropolitan Museum of Art. Christie's and Sotheby's auction houses in London, as always, were generous with their time and photographs. Linda Hammerbeck, Fine Art Photographs, London, was especially helpful in locating reproductions of a number of obscure Victorian paintings and watercolors. I am grateful to the many private collectors and public institutions that granted permission to reproduce the objects illustrated in this study.

I wish to acknowledge financial support received from the National Endowment for the Humanities and the University of Minnesota Graduate School.

My wife, Ann, and our children, Adam and Alice, deserve my final and most heartfelt thanks.

The chapters of this book first published elsewhere, as listed below, appear here in revised and corrected form. Chapters 2 and 6, in particular, are considerably expanded. I acknowledge with gratitude those who have granted permission to reprint this material. Chapter 1 appeared as "Music as a Sight in the Production of Music's Meaning," in *Metaphor: A Musical Dimension,* ed. Jamie C. Kassler (Sydney: Currency Press, 1991). Chapter 2 appeared as "Vision and the Sonoric Construction of Reality (Private Pleasure and Social Order)," in *Musica Privata: Die Rolle der Musik im privaten Leben: Festschrift für Walter Salmen,* ed. Monika Fink, Rainer Gstrein, and Günter Mössmer (Innsbruck: Helbling, 1991). Chapter 3 appeared as "Music, Representation, and Social Order in Early Modern Europe," *Cultural Critique* 12 (Spring 1989). Chapter 5 appeared as "Music, Domestic Life, and Cultural Chauvinism: Images of British Subjects at Home in India," in *Music and Society: The Politics of Composition, Performance, and Reception,* ed. Richard Leppert and Susan McClary (Cambridge: Cambridge University Press, 1987). Chapter 6 appeared as "Sexual Identity, Death, and the Family Piano," *19th-Century Music* 16 (Fall 1992).

Richard Leppert
Minneapolis, October 1992

THE SIGHT OF SOUND

CONCERNING MUSIC:

All music, any organization of sounds is then a tool for the creation or consolidation of a community, of a totality. It is what links a power center to its subjects, and thus, more generally, it is an attribute of power in all its forms.

> Jacques Attali,
> *Noise: The Political Economy of Music*

CONCERNING REPRESENTATION:

When power wants to make people *forget,* music is ritual *sacrifice,* the scapegoat; when it wants them to *believe,* music is enactment, *representation.*

> Jacques Attali,
> *Noise: The Political Economy of Music*

CONCERNING THE BODY:

The love-hate relationship with the body colors all more recent culture. The body is scorned and rejected as something inferior, and at the same time desired as something forbidden, objectified, and alienated. . . . In man's denigration of his own body, nature takes its revenge for the fact that man has reduced nature to an object for domination, a raw material.

> Max Horkheimer and Theodor W. Adorno,
> *Dialectic of Enlightenment*

INTRODUCTION: MUSIC, REPRESENTATION, AND THE SCANDAL OF THE BODY

In 1971 THE ROCK CRITIC Lester Bangs remembered the Troggs and their 1966 hit "Wild Thing" ("And as for what else I did before I began to get balled, well, I used to fill my days with huddling by the record player digging music that fed my nascent sense of sexual identity, like the Troggs"[1]). His memory triggered by the tune, Bangs shared his high school daydreams about the girl sitting at the desk in front of him. "Wild Thing"—short on melody, mostly just rhythm punctuated by crashing guitar chords—sonorically inscribed the necessarily veiled sexual allusions of the lyrics: sound and the body, music and sex, the discursiveness of the nonverbal; it encoded what could not be spoken. Bangs's concern was sonority that defined a boy's musically induced fantasies about the body and its suspect pleasures. The conjunction of music and the body, especially the function of musical practices as representations through which the history of the body is produced, constitutes the subject of this book.

The body is a sight, in essence a sight of sights. It is also a site, a physical presence that is biologically empowered to see at the same time it is being seen. The body is a terrain, a land, as it were, both familiar and foreign; as such it can be mapped. The geography of the body has both topography and interiority, surface and depth, and all its levels are meaningful. The body, simultaneously site, sight, and possessing sight, is an object of tactile sensation and an aural phenomenon. The body *sounds:* it is audible; it hears. Sound constitutes the atmosphere supporting and confirming life on and in the terrain of the body. The ether of aurality is vital; it is constitutive of noise, language, and music. The body is a sight and a sound (and more, but these two are my concerns); the body is sighted and hears; the body sees and makes audible. Indeed, throughout much of Western musical history, a virtual homology existed between these two human senses, producing mutual semantic mediation, though this is not the case today given the plethora of possibilities for separating sound from the sight of its production via electronic technologies. Thus historically musicians were hidden from view—in late medieval mystery plays, Italian Renaissance pastorals, Elizabethan masques, and finally Wagnerian music dramas at Bayreuth—to achieve particular effects (magic and mystery) by the socially abnormal rupture of sound from sight.[2] For much of Western history, at the most fundamental levels of human perception, the sound *is* the sight, and the sight *is* the sound.[3]

The body is more than a living, biological, phenomenon. It is also a history beyond the flesh, blood, and bones that form it, little of which long survives the cessation of breathing—the exceptions are notable: Lenin's body, for example, though his corpse is remarkable for the degree to which, ironically, it constitutes a representation of itself. If we seek the history of the body, we must look to the body's image (here painting and drawing), for that is what lasts beyond biological death. The body is real, but its reality is produced, by cognition, as a representation. It is a product of multiple discourses constructed via the body's sensory capacities. We "know" our bodies through the "languages" about and of the body. The body as a sight and site, we know as a representation, even when we fix our gaze on the three-dimensional breathing body of the self or the other, in that we "consider" the data recorded by the retina via language, whether spoken or silent, and language is, perforce, representation (and not reality).

The body produces music, often from the depths of its interiority, as with singing and the exhalation of breath into wind-driven instruments. Whatever else music is "about," it is *inevitably* about the body; music's aural and visual presence constitutes both a relation to and a representation of the body. Nonetheless, the connection between music and the body throughout Western history is highly problematic and contradictory, the product of deep socio-cultural anxieties and antagonisms. Throughout this book, I consider some of the social causes and consequences of this troubled link, focusing especially on the gendered body because the singular difference between feminine and masculine (neither the same as nor coterminus with female and male) is the constitutive element of every other conceivable relation as regards music's connection to the body.

My concern with vision focuses on the physicality of music making itself (the sight of the body's labors to produce sound), and on the irony that the "product" of this activity—musical sonority—lacks all concreteness and disappears without a trace once the musician's "physical labors" cease (acoustic decay). Precisely because musical sound is abstract, intangible, and ethereal—lost as soon as it is gained—the visual experience of its production is crucial to both musicians and audience alike for locating and communicating the place of music and musical sound within society and culture. I am suggesting, in other words, that the slippage between the physical activity to produce musical sound and the abstract nature of what is produced creates a semiotic contradiction that is ultimately "resolved" to a significant degree via the agency of human sight. Music, despite its phenomenological sonoric ethereality, is an embodied practice, like dance and theater. That its visual-performative aspect is no less central to its meanings than are the visual components of these other performing arts is obvious in musical theater—opera, masque, and so forth (though this linkage is little discussed in musicological literature)—but the connection between sight and sound in other sorts of art music remains untheorized.

My interest in the sight of music focuses on music's representation in visual art, rather than on eyewitness written accounts of musical performances. My reasons for subordinating written accounts are several. First, and less important, *detailed* written accounts of (nontheatrical) musical events, especially prior to the public concerts of the nineteenth century, are rare, though this rarity presents only a practical problem, not a theoretical one. Few of the eyewitness accounts, moreover, are concerned to relate sonority to the sight of its production (my topic), though these narratives depend for their existence on both eyes and ears. Second, written eyewitness accounts of musical activity transliterate the retinal action of the eyes through the process of language. The "image" of the activity is reproduced in the "mind's eye" of the reader of that account: the reader's eyes confront words, which in turn produce *linguistic* images. The representation of musical activity in art, by contrast, remains specifically visual, "translating" the three-dimensional and sonoric world into a two-dimensional and silent "argument" for and about the world—though this is not to deny the fundamental role that language plays in "processing" the image.

Music's effects and meanings, which in performance are produced both aurally *and* visually, in painting must be rendered visually only. The way of seeing hence incorporates the way of hearing: the artist must produce images in such a way that their meanings will be congruent with those produced by sight and sound together in the lived experience of the original and intended viewer. To render visually meaningful the *acoustic* phenomenon of music, the artist engages semiotic codes that operate *as a sight* when music is actually made in real life. The artist does not invent a visual code entirely divorced from life practice, for the simple reason that there is no point in doing so. If artists failed in their endeavor, if their envisioning confused viewers, musical subjects would not have been painted in the West for many centuries in such abundance as survives. The issue is not that artists were unproblematically bound to reproduce in paint what "is" in life; it is instead that life practice and artistic conventions engage in a mutually mediating relation despite the functional specificity and history of art practice itself—the painter is not the precursor of the camera, after all.

The visual code functions through the human body in its efforts to produce and receive music. When people hear a musical performance, they see it as an embodied activity. While they hear, they also witness:[4] how the performers look and gesture, how they are costumed, how they interact with their instruments and with one another, how they regard the audience, how other listeners heed the performers. Thus the musical event is perceived as a socialized activity. Visual representation in effect encapsulates more or less all of the embodied activity, not as a "disinterested" record of events, but as a coherent and discursive, commonly dialectical, vision of the varied relations within whose context sound occurs and hence, I shall argue, sound means.[5] Visual art cannot replicate musical acoustics, but it can provide an invaluable hortatory account of what, how, and why a given society heard and hence in part what the sounds meant. I should add that visual representations, except perhaps those that include decipherable musical inscriptions, tell us nothing specific about particular pieces of music; instead they suggest the range of semiotic possibilities for specific compositions performed under conditions similar to those represented.

I want to draw attention briefly to the changing "histories" of seeing and hearing in post-medieval Western Europe, since these may further help explain the significance of sight to the hearing of music. I am borrowing from the work of Donald Lowe,[6] which traces the relation of human sensing to the organization of communications. Lowe points out that in oral cultures, where information is passed on by word of mouth (e.g., in the West in the Middle Ages), where knowing cannot be separated from the knower's own memory, hearing enjoys a privileged position in the hierarchy of sensing. By contrast, in chirographic cultures (e.g., in the West predominantly in and after the Renaissance), because knowledge exists in writing, it can be separated from the memory of a particular human subject—though prior to the development of typography such knowledge is nevertheless highly restricted. With the printing press, knowledge can be separated from the person who knows (e.g., the author) and relocated in the (mass-produced) book. Whereas in oral culture hearing (and touching) predominate over seeing in the transmission of knowledge,[7] in typographic culture—the culture of reading, not listening—sight gains priority over other senses. My concern is with the period when sight is the prime means by which Western European culture accounted for reality. If Lowe's thesis about the change in the hierarchy of sensing is accurate, it strengthens my argument that sight is important to the production of acoustic meaning in life practice and that visual art is thus a means by which to reconstruct this meaning.

FIG. 1   Marcellus Laroon the Younger, *A Musical Conversation* (c. 1760), oil on canvas,
66 × 78.4 cm. New Haven, Yale Center for British Art, Paul Mellon Collection.

MUSICAL BODIES, LIFE AND DEATH

Let us look to Marcellus Laroon, an eighteenth-century "musician, singer, professional soldier and man of pleasure"[8] and a painter and drawer of "musical conversations" (Fig. 1), depictions of musical "speakers" and listeners—producers
and consumers of musical discourse. Conversation—dialogic speech—is *of* the
body, an abstract and ethereal breathing outward—like singing, like flute playing—meant to connect to the body of the other so as to represent, to account for.
There are two conversations in Laroon's picture, and their duality is made an issue.

On the left is the conversation of the (nonmusical) speech act, characterized as
being of and about the body. The pairs of speaker-listeners are couples, men and
women, conventionally represented as spouses or lovers—even the two seated
women who whisper together also touch. On the right is another conversa-

tion—musical—partly texted (a man sings) but mostly not of or about words but about sounds as such. The bodies in this instance do not pair off; all the musicians are men, apart from the harpsichordist. Yet their discourse is about love, hence the body. How do we know this? Laroon organizes his picture around a meeting, a coming together at the center of the painting, framed by the archway. A man and a woman meet, bow, touch; they engage. Their gestures semiotically shade into the opening moves of physical contact associated with social dancing, itself a ritual form of lovemaking, a rehearsal of bodies organizing their sensualities and desires, guided by musical sonorities that give form to their practices.

On the back wall are landscapes, geographies of land and sea. These are the terrains of self and other; a place to be, a place to want; a map and a representation. All this in the background, while in the foreground is something odd—to which I shall return at the end of the book in regard to a different Laroon painting. It is a storage case for a musical instrument lying atop music books. There is a negative aesthetic quotient to this dark, unattractive utilitarian object, yet its presence is asserted by the painter. Its excuse for "being" lies in its meaning.

The music case is like a coffin. It protects something precious at the same time its protection confirms loss. Both a casket and the case allude to vitality, to sound, to breath, though only by announcing death and silence. The music case, however, differs from the coffin. The coffin protects the corpse from the worms, if only figuratively, but it also shrouds survivors from the look, and perhaps the stench, of decomposition. It is a frame marking the permanent dissolution of the body it contains. The music case, on the contrary, protects something that "sleeps" and might be awakened. The awakening, as in the fairy tale, comes from the touch—of fingers, mouth, tongue—of the player who, like a lover, embraces the instrument and brings it to life, makes it "speak." Laroon's is a painting of promise centered around the body, young and old, desired and desiring. The musical conversation is ultimately one about the possibility of life itself, involving shared, embodied interiorities.

Laroon repeatedly sketched and painted similar musical conversations; the scene seems to have captivated him. On one occasion, however, he approached the topic in a radically different manner, in a bizarre, unquestionably theatrical drawing (Fig. 2).[9] With its architectural setting, it looks like a scene from a play, though to my knowledge no such connection has been determined. No matter. This is not a scene about love (though perhaps the figures on the balcony at the left, shocked witnesses to the carnage below them, suggest a disruption of lovers). The scene is, however, a "conversation" (perhaps an anti-conversation) to the extent that a fight, whether verbal or physical, constitutes a discourse. What interests me are its implied sounds and silences and the bond between seeing and hearing. As in Laroon's utopian musical conversation (Fig. 1) this distopian image

FIG. 2   Marcellus Laroon the Younger, *A Fight* (c. 1770), reed pen and brown ink over pencil with wash, 45.1 × 70.5 cm. Oxford, Ashmolean Museum.

separates its characters—here all male—into two groups, each penetrated by the other. The two groups are distinguished by their slight physical separation, but since everyone is fighting, it is obvious that the opposing forces interact and that a desperate anarchy ensues.

In the center, town waits look on, huddling together while presumably trying to find safe passage through the fighting men, illuminating their way with lanterns. This detail tells us that the scene occurs at night, that what we see clearly the waits can see only dimly. They do not see, they *hear*. We see them, as it were, hearing. That Laroon frames them between the two fighting groups grants them special function. In effect the waits are the ears to our eyes. What is it they hear? Audible to them—but not to us—are the cries, shouts, and agonized screams of men afraid and in pain. These sounds encode dissolution, devolution, and perhaps death. What the waits cannot see—and what we can—are the tools of the violence: musical instruments used as bludgeons, except for the swords of two men at the left, whose weapons convey the seriousness of the event.

At the front and center of the fight Laroon employs an emblematic musical device that is semiotically the reverse of the one used in Figure 1. This time, he shows us, not a musical instrument case, but a broken violin with its bow alongside what seems to be a recorder. The musical "body" is broken; there is nothing for its case to protect. No further possibility of musical sonority exists. The end result of the noise being produced is music silenced, men fallen: symbolic death. In our own century, war has been theorized by the Futurists, among others, in sensual, even erotic, terms, as something vital. Closely related is the metaphorical locating of the mortal enemy in wars of this century in the female body,[10] the rage against which is transferred to one's male opponent. With these ideas in mind—the anachronism of the intervening centuries notwithstanding—it may be appropriate not only to read Laroon's allegory as the silencing of music by an overwhelming noise, produced by musical instruments used as weapons, but also to postulate that the "conversation" between these men involves simultaneously the problem of the sensate, sensual, and gendered body, on the one hand, and the *production* of that body in the representations of musical sonority, on the other. This seems to be a fight to the bitter end, between men, over what it is to be a man, a fight whose stakes are mapped on musical instruments. Laroon's allegory depends on a basic and ancient division in music, between strings, activated by bowing and plucking, and winds, activated by breathing and exhaling. In the first the action is external and public; in the second it is more personal and private. In Greek understanding the music of strings was Apollonian, civilized, in a word, manly, whereas that of winds was internal, sensual, sexual, Dionysian, and potentially *un*manly, that is, excessive, womanly—the unspeakable force encoded in the negative prefix "un-." Laroon thereby *genders* musical sound and then breaks its back, silences all of it, making us his witnesses.

We see but cannot hear; the waits hear but cannot see. All that is solid melts into air. The nothingness of music is radically confirmed. Yet in the confirmation of this eternal negative, Laroon nonetheless affirms that without music no theory of human sociability can be formulated. He imagines that the end of music is the end of life, the death of the body. The absolute outcome of the skirmish he represents is uncertain—only one man has fallen. But clearly the war over sonority is the war over society—in his time, as in ours, controlled mostly by men—whose antagonisms are mapped on the terrain of gender difference, where gender difference marks everything, notably including music. The body is sonorous; the body is threatened.

My subject is the body as a palimpsest in musical practices—the discourse of the historical, gendered body in the visual representation of sonority. That is, I shall be concerned with the sight of the sound-producing body and the discourses of power, knowledge, desire, and identity that the musical body encodes.[11] The historical frame is roughly 1600 to 1900, with three chapters on the seventeenth century (Chapters 1–3); two on the eighteenth (Chapters 4–5), and four on the nineteenth (Chapters 6–9). The territory encompassed involves the Low Countries (Chapters 1–3), England (Chapters 4, 6–9), and India under British colonial rule (Chapter 5). The social class discussed is bourgeois; the related antagonisms of class and race are given direct attention in three instances (Chapters 1, 2, and 8 for class; Chapter 5 for race). Each chapter confronts its own set of theoretical issues, thereafter worked through with respect to specific practices and their representations. Thus the theory underlying my research unfolds only gradually throughout the text.

In Chapter 1, "Music as a Sight in the Production of Musical Meaning," I outline a theoretical basis for delineating how sight acts as an organizer of musical semantics, and how the sight of music's performance connects abstract sonoric phenomena with the social. My concern is to locate the sight of music within the corpus of shared experiences from which people both produce and draw their perceptions of reality. I have organized this discussion around an allegorical marriage portrait, wherein music serves as the primary organizing principle, the governing metaphor for marital fidelity, and, in a larger sense, male-female relations, gender hierarchy, class distinction, and social order itself, all of which are mapped on the terrain of the physical body.

In Chapter 2, "Desire, Power, and the Sonoric Landscape (Early Modernism and the Politics of Musical Privacy)," I take up the implications of social class difference in the tensions between the public and the private in music, and between high culture and low. The discussion plays on the links between desire, pleasure, power, and the production of meaning in what I term the sonoric landscape: the discursive, experiential, and political parameters of heard sound.

In Chapter 3, "The Poetics of Anguish, Pleasure, and Prestige (Hoarding Sound in a Culture of Silence)," I consider the sight of music as an agent of prestige formation at court in France, Germany, and the Spanish Netherlands in the sixteenth century and, especially, the seventeenth. I posit that the increasingly sharp post-Renaissance distinctions between musics high and low, elite and popular, secular and sacred, and so forth not only reflect similar distinctions between social levels but also mediate social organization and the accompanying intersubjective human experience. The discussion centers on two hyper-decorated musical instruments and several paintings representing large inventories of instruments. My purpose is to understand how musical practices—and by implication the sonorities of art music—function as socio-political conceits, in which the sounds (agonies) associated with state terrorism, war, and the politics of colonialism are all cast as the necessary predecessors and producers of peace—in sonoric terms as art music.

In Chapter 4, "Social Order and the Domestic Consumption of Music (The Politics of Sound in the Policing of Gender Construction)," my concern is music's agency in shaping female identity and subjectivity within the social patterns governed by domesticity, and in conjunction with domesticity's relation to the production of nationhood. In its essentials, the story of music's domestic role involves the sonoric inscription of male authority, but that tells only half the story. I will be concerned as well to recount the resistance to the narrow ideology of domesticity, precisely as it is organized by women (and men) around music, on the one hand, and pleasure, on the other. This part of the story demands attention to the question of what one consumes in consuming music. In the end, my topic becomes music's semantic slipperiness in its complex relation to the body and its desires.

Chapter 5, "Music, Domesticity, and Cultural Imperialism," focuses on images, especially portraits in oil, of British residents in India in the eighteenth and nineteenth centuries that include notable reference to music. By this means, and also by a discussion of the ideological functions of musical instruments in domestic gender relations, I suggest the function of music in the economic and social colonization program carried out by the English in India. I read the "texts" and "subtexts" of these images in conjunction with archetypal examples of European Enlightenment music theory treatises, which, in their dual appeal to nature and reason—explicitly valorizing a mental account of music over the embodied and experiential—make tonality appear both universal and objectively superior to any other kind of musical system. My purpose is to demonstrate immanent political and ideological agendas motivating the claim to autonomy in music and disguised in both the gentility of portraits and the apparent theoretical abstraction of music theory treatises.

Chapter 6, "Sexual Identity, Death, and the Family Piano in the Nineteenth Century," concerns Victorian piano case design and decoration, though I begin with seventeenth-century harpsichords whose cases carry printed mottoes. My concern is to treat the decorated cases as "texts" that provide a discursive gloss on whatever music was played on them. The chapter focuses on a series of extraordinary eighteenth- and nineteenth-century instruments whose painted cases represent two contrary, but in my view explicitly related, subjects: first, battles and sieges (warfare) and hunting scenes (blood sport); second, women, in particular dead—or about to be dead—women. My purpose is to read these instruments, and several related pictures, against the increasingly complex and contradictory social position in the nineteenth century of both art music itself and its female (and male) practitioners.

In Chapter 7, "The Piano, Misogyny, and 'The Kreutzer Sonata,'" I locate the piano as sign in an effort to understand its related agency in social construction to stabilize another, more important, sign: "woman." I consider the cultural characterization of (art) music as feminine under the conditions of patriarchy, at once the hated other and the desired. My interest centers on music, sexuality, and physical desire and involves the discussion of an extraordinary corpus of Victorian painting, principally English but Danish and Italian as well, explicitly connecting women to the piano—no surprise—and music itself via the piano to the agency of the sexual body and women's purported ability, according to Victorian fears (expressed in disciplines as disparate as philosophy and medicine), to control and enervate men. "The Kreutzer Sonata" in the chapter title is both Tolstoy's novella and Beethoven's Opus 47 sonata for solo violin and piano, discussed in the contexts just enunciated. (Tolstoy's story centers on a husband's murder of his wife brought about when she performs the composition with the musician her husband supposes is her lover.)

Chapter 8, "Male Agony: Awakening Conscience," focuses on the famous Victorian painting by William Holman Hunt identified in the chapter subtitle. My story, as regards this image, is about a woman's body—especially her face—and the twin powers of her sexuality and music in relation to a panoply of bourgeois male anxieties surrounding love, morality, and the loss of time. In the end, this essay is about song and singing, speech and authority, and the impossibility of certainty in a culture obsessed with certainty. It concerns the felt need to stabilize the meanings of the body of woman, whose semantic excess was metaphorically identified as musical and socially designated as pernicious.

Chapter 9, "Aspiring to the Condition of Silence (The Iconicity of Music)," takes up "song" again, first Mendelssohn's "Lieder ohne Worte" and thereafter "implied" song in several late-Victorian paintings. I address the extent to which musical semantics, marked feminine, are located in and on the body, an object at once of love and hate, like music itself. In the end my subject is the crisis of music and musical meaning at the close of the nineteenth century, in the moment of aestheticist art's self-separation from society (the valorization of "being" over meaning, in which form becomes content). In musical terms, sonority produced under these rules is semantically silent, its "universality" enshrined in the stillness of social death. This is a musical culture personified in fin-de-siècle visual representation via the male body, ironically at once phallic and emasculated, dead in life.

Discipline produces subjected and practised bodies, "docile" bodies. Discipline increases the forces of the body (in economic terms of utility) and diminishes these same forces (in political terms of obedience). In short, it dissociates power from the body; on the one hand, it turns it into an "aptitude," a "capacity," which it seeks to increase; on the other hand, it reverses the course of the energy, the power that might result from it, and turns it into a relation of strict subjection.

Michel Foucault,
Discipline and Punish

MUSIC AS A SIGHT IN THE
PRODUCTION OF MUSICAL MEANING

Some years ago *A Music Party* (1633; Fig. 3), by the Dutch artist Jan Miense Molenaer, was the subject of an important essay by the art historian P. J. J. van Thiel,[1] whose ideas I want to summarize before providing my own reading. Van Thiel argued that the picture constitutes a marriage portrait allegorizing, and highly valorizing, marital fidelity.[2] Music provides the interpretative key to the picture, musical *mesure* standing in visually as a referent for order, regulation, temperance, and fidelity—stressed most notably by the woman sitting in the middle holding a partbook, at once singing and marking time with her right hand. Her self-restrained gesture keeps together an ensemble that includes a lutenist and a cellist. Van Thiel draws particular attention to the male figure standing directly behind the woman who holds the partbook. In a spectacular, indeed preposterous, gesture borrowed from a contemporaneous print representing the virtue of Temperance, he pours water from a jug held above his head into a wineglass at his side. The semiotic importance of this detail is evident not only from the singularity of the man's action but also from the compositional location of the pitcher at the upper center of the picture. It casts its significance over everything and everyone beneath it.

Van Thiel argues that the painting is formally organized around a thesis (marital temperance) set against a subsidiary antithesis (intemperance). Antithesis is shown in two vignettes: one in the background at the extreme left, where two men in small scale stab each other with knives, represents anger (*ira*); and one in the foreground at lower left, where a chained monkey ridiculously embraces a cat, represents enslavement to the senses and to pleasure—in a word, lust, the cat being a common symbol of libidinous temperament. The cat and monkey are

FIG. 3   Jan Miense Molenaer, *A Music Party* (*Allegory of Fidelity in Marriage*) (1633), oil on canvas,
99.7 × 141 cm. Richmond, Virginia Museum of Fine Arts, the Adolphe D. and Wilkins C.
Williams Collection.

offset by the dog (*fides*, fidelity)—not coincidentally male—standing guard by
the newlyweds. Van Thiel comments that the picture is a "mirror of virtue" for
the husband and wife alike, a "key to an harmonious married life."[3]

I wish to pursue the semiotics of this painting beyond the analysis provided
by van Thiel so as to suggest two additional points closer to my own concerns.
First, moderation or temperance is articulated as a class issue. Moderation is a
possibility for and the obligation of the upper classes. It is the peasants who are
violent and who behave with anarchical excess; hence, they are threats to themselves and to the social order whose calm they disturb. The painting's sights en-
gender sounds in opposition: the sounds of art music versus the sounds of brutality, for fights are punctuated by animal-like grunts and groans and often by cries
of pain. The painting invites, perhaps even compels, its viewers to *envision* and to
hear the difference between chaos and order, the antisocial and the social.

But the issue is not quite so simply articulated. In the main part of the image, where the musical performance takes place, sonority as such is accorded privilege—even though we cannot actually hear any sound—on account of the visually commanding presence of the instruments, the lute and violoncello. They are striking objects in a painting where every object has been carefully chosen; and they occupy considerable, and compositionally "prestigious," pictorial space. By contrast, the peasants, whose fighting would doubtless greatly overpower and upset the musical tranquillity of the main scene, command attention only by their visual incongruity; even in a detail, their inclusion is striking—and purposely worrisome. They possess what the well-to-do burghers had to surrender in exchange for their status and their art: physicality. The peasants' movements are spontaneous and unpredictable, whereas those of their betters are planned and constrained. Indeed, the spatial logic enshrined in the paved terrace on which the central characters stand helps emphasize the opposite of spontaneity.

My second point, one I must address in detail before returning to questions about music, is that the moderation valorized in this image is visually gendered. It is made the responsibility of the woman more than the man, an inequality that relates to the larger issue of gender hierarchy in marriage. Here my view diverges from van Thiel's. Marriage portraits were characteristically ordered by husbands. Thus the marriage portrait might be a husband's gift to his wife, but it was a gift with strings attached, for it informed her of his expectations of her in all the permanence of the picture's visibility. Not for nothing does the husband wear garb for the outdoors—the hat, cape, and boots: he is not always, or even commonly, going to be around. The burgher's domain is extra-domestic. Thus the famous Dutch poet, Jacob Cats: "The husband must be on the street to practice his trade/ The wife must stay at home to be in the kitchen."[4] The painting will be prominently displayed in the dwelling as a surveillance, intended to address the prime anxiety of the absent husband: his wife's sexual fidelity,[5] which in Dutch culture was the cornerstone of domestic *and* social order.[6] It is not going too far, then, to suggest that the painting's musical metaphor stands in for the very possibility of Dutch culture itself. And the metaphor incidentally helps clarify the importance in musical life of access to, and sanctioned understanding of, the "right" kind of music.

The newlyweds at the extreme right are posed differently from each other, and for a purpose.[7] The lady is statuesque, virtually immobilized in drapery; from the waist down she is almost leaden.[8] Her husband, lithe by contrast, is not only ready to move but actually taking a step that would lead him into the space occupied by the viewer outside the picture; and he will move gracefully, unlike the fighting peasants posed in spread-legged brutishness. That the wife is the lesser of the pair, physically and metaphorically, is emphasized by the husband's proximity to the picture plane, which further increases his apparent stature at her expense. His body also cuts off part of hers. He gestures to move; she stands stock still. More-over, she demands even less visual attention than the woman in the center with the partbook—an invidious comparison that cannot be made of the husband and the male musicians, since the husband, although off to the side, is painted so as to look physically larger than either of these other men, and his bright red outfit captivates us more than that of any other figure in the painting, male or female. Indeed, his importance as a person is visually affirmed by Molenaer's striking way of painting his doffed hat; its darkness takes up space and powerfully draws the viewer's eyes toward the husband, away from the woman with the partbook, the painting's putative central figure. More accurately, the viewer's eyes, denied a stable locus, shift back and forth between the woman musician and the husband. By producing this visual instability, Molenaer brilliantly encodes into the viewer's act of looking a reminder that the painting functions ideologically as a surveil-lance;[9] and as I have suggested, the ideal viewer for the image is the wife herself, who as a viewer must watch herself being watched.

Something about the wife's look—or *where* she looks—interests me. It is compositionally obvious that music provides the painting's central event. Yet Mo-lenaer focuses the newlyweds' eyes elsewhere. The man appears to look outside the picture, as if toward where he is heading, out into the world, as it were; the woman, by contrast, looks inward. She stares slightly downward, though not, I think, specifically at anything, such as the cat-monkey vignette. Hence as regards the musical ensemble around which the image is constructed, what the viewer (ideally, the wife looking from outside the picture in at herself) *sees* within the picture she (only) *hears*. She does not look; she listens. In other words, *for the characters inside the painting music accrues meaning as a sonoric phenomenon, whereas from outside the painting, for the viewer, who can see but cannot hear the events represented, music means as a sight.* For the one intended and ideal viewer, the wife, the two elements of the semiotic equation—sight and sound—converge.

MUSIC AS VISUAL METAPHOR

Why is music such an apparently important visual metaphor for driving home such extra- or nonmusical ideas? What does Molenaer's image feed on? Despite its musical "look," what has it to do with music? The vignettes of watering down wine, of the monkey and cat, and of the dog are fundamentally emblematic.[10] Their function in this image is hence clear; and on precisely that account it is easier for us to "read out" the semiotic function of the musical details. Yet the meaning of music is not related specifically to emblems but to a praxis fully congruent with emblematic allegory. The emblems present themselves to the viewer as allegorical because something about each of them simultaneously registers a visual slippage from lived experience and appears to participate in a narrative. Watering wine in the manner represented in reality would produce a mess; monkeys and cats do not embrace; dogs, of course, do stand guard, like Molenaer's, but his painted dog, with its exaggerated stiffness, takes on symbolic character. The same cannot be said for any of the central human subjects, though again there is a rupture between the upper-class figures and the profiled iconic servants behind the musicians at the left. The three musicians have semiotic functions to carry out, just like the emblematic vignettes, though the image's consummate naturalism and the apparently mundane activities they engage in would seemingly deflect such a reading—except for one crucially important detail, their compositional placement, which looks "wrong." The difficulty hinges on the identification of the musicians, in particular their social class status, and, in relation to class status, the gender of the dominant figure in the musical ensemble, the woman seated in the painting's center who holds the partbook.

Who are these musicians? Molenaer renders them ambiguous. They could be family members or hired professionals (in family portraits of the time it was conventional for all adult men present to wear hats, though to our eyes this might signal the presence of outsiders). The lutenist and cellist are dressed expensively; in fact they are overdressed—more elegantly attired than the husband, overshadowing him, as is best seen by looking at the lutenist, since none of his body is blocked off. Most noteworthy are his shoes, which, by comparison with the husband's boots, are at once conspicuous and impractical—qualities common enough in Dutch life of the time but consistently condemned by Calvinism and rather out of place, it would seem, given the seriousness of the picture. The same may be said of the lutenist's rakish pose, taken directly from the conventions of the often bawdy Merry Company paintings of the period. Similarly, the dress of the seated woman overshadows that of the wife; in particular, compare the collar and cuffs. The somber facial expressions of all three musicians suggest a family connection; but sartorial inconsistencies—with negative moral associations in a patently moralistic image—may indicate outsiders. The real point is that the musicians are functionally nonpersons, despite the naturalism of their representation: their role is metaphoric.

Given the normal circumstances of a wedding celebration, the musicians would be hired professionals, except that a female professional would be extraordinarily unusual and certainly unacceptable as a character—a central character—in a marriage portrait, because female professional musicians at the time were déclassé. Yet in Molenaer's painting it is the woman who, by marking time with her hand, keeps in tow the two male musicians, both of whom are young, dashingly costumed, and invested with erotic energy; they register the extra-domestic sexual danger against which the wife must guard.[11] Perhaps this is the point. In posing the woman, Molenaer makes an otherwise curious choice, which can be explained, I think, only if she functions with the ambiguity I have implied. I refer to her right foot, protruding from under her voluminous drapery, made visible by being placed atop a foot warmer. With one foot raised, her pose formally echoes that of the lutenist beside her; the formal relationship in turn links her visually to him. And the pose itself endows her with a sensuality akin to his own much more obvious sexuality because it emphasizes the outline of both her legs and the separation between them. Her lifted leg, in art of the period suggestive in itself, allows the fabric of her dress to fall between her legs, showing them to be apart.[12] Nevertheless, as the man standing behind her and watering down his wine most clearly indicates, it is her responsibility to maintain *mesure*. The woman concentrates dutifully on her partbook—literally a text, the *word,* so to speak, by which her metaphorical (musical, temperate) duties are *pre*scribed. Her duty is to control her sexual drives, which are visually acknowledged and even fore-grounded. Word and image, in other words, conspire to define her duties, just as the terrace beneath her feet delineates a black and white regularity, a predict-ability.

Molenaer could only have employed this musical motive for the larger pur-poses of the painting if actual musical practices of the same sort (potentially) car-ried complementary meaning—meaning that would affect the sound as well as the sight of the music. Were that not the case, the painting could not make sense to its original and ideal viewer. This is not to say that only "one" meaning was possible; indeed, contrary meanings attended musical imagery, as Molenaer was well aware. Such imagery could not be used unproblematically, simplistically; its semantic "surface" encompassed potential ruptures and ambiguities—some of which, like the relation of musical sound to social class, theological belief, and gender hierarchy, must of social necessity be handled gingerly—no less in the seventeenth century than in our own.

In the Low Countries in the seventeenth century, as elsewhere, art music was a suspect practice among the upper classes on two grounds. First, there was grow-ing uncertainty that music making, whether solitary or social, was appropriate to this social class, especially men. Indeed, art music was well on its way to being classified as a female activity, though this cultural principle would not gain full precedence for another century. Second, and closely related, art music (indeed, all secular music) was viewed suspiciously in Calvinist theology, though the extent of that suspicion has often been overstated. While in one sense, then, the practices of art music registered themselves as exercises of sonoric order mirroring social order, in another they signaled precisely the opposite, a threat to that order. The reasons this is so depend on two competing sets of criteria. As order, a desideratum whose terms were defined by the dominant classes, the sonorities of art music could only mean in opposition to the music of the lower classes, the Dutch peasantry. Lower-class music, directly or indirectly, was theorized as disorder, a sonoric and social threat *from outside* (I will return to this idea later). Art music as disorder, by contrast, located the enemy as a threat *from inside;* its terms were no longer those of class difference but became those of gender distinction within the upper social strata. Music was potentially effeminizing; it was a specific threat to masculine identity. And worse, when confined to women's practice, its specific relation to physicality and to sexual arousal was perceived as a challenge to husbands' authority.[13]

All this being so, why employ a musical motive at all in the painting? Why not try for a less conflicted practice to drive home the same point about fidelity? I think there are two reasons. First, music's association with love *and* sexuality was entirely enshrined in the culture and had been for many centuries. Marriage was the approved locus for sexuality and for the sexual availability of the woman. Music as an expression of desire, and as a well-practiced device for the production of desire, was fully theorized and valorized. Ribald song texts, not to mention the literary feast of Dutch proverbs, preserve such references in abundance, just as numerous published Calvinist diatribes condemned them and the practices they described.[14] Molenaer's painting, in other words, walks a fine line. To satisfy his male patron, the husband, Molenaer instructs the wife to be sexually temperate and sexually active. Art music is *the* metaphor by which to delineate this desideratum; after all, its several socio-cultural roles were commonly conflicted. It served as the sonoric simulacrum for order and disorder, arousal and calm, mind and body, and so forth. Sound in its abstraction is by itself semiotically difficult to control, though socially and culturally it is essential to control as it is those of any other form of human expression and communication. The semantic ambiguity of music can never be totally overcome, but reference to the sight of musical practices can often channel it sufficiently to connote acceptable meanings. In this respect, specific visual reference to music's semiotic ambiguity is ideologically more useful than denying the existence of dichotomy, for acknowledging it both identifies the problem and presents the solution. The musical problem is inevitably important in this regard because it stands in for larger questions about the construction and maintenance of society.

The second reason, I think, has to do with class difference. The practices of art music in the Low Countries during the seventeenth century were emerging as an important component of class distinction in a world rapidly changing from a feudal order to a mercantilist, precapitalist order. Medieval economic stasis was being replaced by economic dynamism, by the building of new fortunes. But many of

the cultural implications of these changes were being invented as the socio-
economic changes occurred, following the successful separation from the rigidly
feudal political hegemony of conservative Spain during the religious wars of the
late sixteenth and the early seventeenth century.[15] Dutch culture was middle-class
in the ways that historically determined what that term meant in the West generally. Dutch culture created for itself the challenge of class self-definition. It is
not surprising that the habits it adopted included conspicuous consumption, in
which it effectively aped the European aristocracy, even though the price paid was
enormous guilt.[16]

Music was a prime component of the new habits—visually, in the form of
expensive musical instruments; sonorically, in the music that was played: it was
increasingly sophisticated and complex, inevitably composed and notated, and
collected in printed form. Expensive musical instruments made with precious or
rare materials (exotic woods, ivory, silver), were clear signs of excess wealth. Because they did not "do" anything except produce sound, they were perfect signs of
social position, the very ethereality of what they "produced"—sound—assuring
the correct reading. Indeed, sermons condemning music during the seventeenth
and eighteenth centuries in Holland and elsewhere commonly stress this point: to
make music well takes much time, yet music made well is nothing—simply air.[17]
Thus the ubiquitous vanitas still-life paintings of the period commonly include
musical instruments, usually those associated with art music. Although as vanities
instruments are condemned—for example, by visual reference to life's brevity via
an hourglass, a burned-down candle, and so forth—they are visually celebrated,
along with other consumer goods, as objects of class pedigree and cultural accomplishment (Fig. 4), to an extent that undercuts the didactic function of such paintings.[18] Still-life paintings thus feed, and feed off, the desires and pleasures of scopophilia. More to the point, vanitas paintings do not sort out the conflicts I am
delineating but only affirm their existence.

The musical sonorities that can be assumed in Molenaer's painting stand in
silent opposition to the noise[19] judged characteristic of the music making of peasants. David Teniers the Younger, a contemporaneous Flemish painter whose work
ideologically complements Dutch images from the same period,[20] specialized in
arch representations of peasants in paintings obviously produced for the upper,
especially urban, social strata. One musical scene that he produced in several versions shows peasant listeners belittling peasant players behind their backs, as if to
assure the viewer that even they know the stuff stinks.[21]

In calling their music noise, I do not mean that peasant musicians played
poorly or that their instruments were incapable of producing pleasing sounds.
Indeed, the opposite was undoubtedly true, though few instruments have survived
on which to base a judgment. The issue is not circumscribed by the skills of

FIG. 4   Dutch School (17th Century), *The Yarmouth Collection* (*Vanitas*), oil on canvas,
165 × 246.5 cm. Norwich, U.K., Castle Museum. Photo courtesy of Norfolk Museums Service.

players or instrument makers. It develops instead from the ideological necessity
to differentiate, according to principles that delineate *socio-political* superiority, the
sounds of one class from those of the other, as established by the particular group
enjoying power. The sounds of the lower classes are associated with anarchy, registered visually as vulgar physicality and drunkenness (Fig. 5) and as leering sexuality (Fig. 6). By contrast, the sounds of the upper classes are associated with a
high degree of order, registered visually as physical self-control, as in the case of
Molenaer's painting, one among many similar representations.

I need to comment further on Figure 6, for like Molenaer's painting it (ironically) concerns a new marriage. Being a peasant affair, it provides Teniers with the
opportunity for caricature.[22] The visual argument, and the sonoric one on which
it depends, reverse the discourse employed by Molenaer. Teniers places the newlyweds beside a bagpiper and, like Molenaer, moves them to the edge of the image.
The bagpipe is the location of sexual energy,[23] since its chanter pipe and windsack
together replicate the male genitalia, a likeness noted in contemporaneous proverbs.[24] Further, the bagpipe is decorated with the head of Pan, whose lechery and
fertility go hand in hand. The husband's coarse arousal is captured in his face; the

FIG. 5   David Teniers the Younger and Lucas van Uden, *Peasants Dancing*, oil on canvas, 119 × 215 cm. Dublin, National Gallery of Ireland. Photo copyright A.C.L., Brussels.

FIG. 6   David Teniers the Younger, *A Village Wedding* (1648), oil on canvas, 76.5 × 114 cm. Vienna, Kunsthistorisches Museum, Gemäldegalerie. Photo copyright A.C.L., Brussels.

bovine stupidity and incomprehension registered by his bride's profile is made more ludicrous by the conventional bride's crown she wears.

The visual differences between Molenaer's and Teniers's images could hardly be more extreme. And the same holds for sonoric distinctions. The sounds of Molenaer's ensemble are soothing, easy on the ear. Those of Teniers's bagpipe are raucous, especially with the instrument blaring virtually into the ears of the whispering lovers, who under the circumstances could not have heard each other. But that does not matter. For in this image marriage is not temperate—the union does not depend on the prescribed order-giving "word" of Molenaer's woman's partbook. It merely follows the guidance of biological rhythm, whereby the peasantry are reified as little more than animals whose irresponsibility it is the noblesse oblige of the upper classes to control and their right to belittle. And it is the *noise* of peasants' music that provides their degraded identity and subjectivity, much as the non-noise of Teniers's and Molenaer's patrons distinguishes their class. The political difficulty here, of course, is that only one side is empowered to represent these judgments in historical memory by preserving the image of the social order of sound long after the sounds themselves have decayed.

It should be clear that the pleasure of music is not an issue in Molenaer's painting. Indeed, nothing in the picture seems to produce the slightest joy: the uncanny seriousness of all the participants in the wedding celebration conflicts with what we know of the historical reality in Dutch culture, as in virtually any other. But for Molenaer's presumed patron, the absence of pleasure is useful for underscoring a fact of social organization: that the personal, including the personally pleasurable, is political, that politics is inevitably a serious business, and that "entertainment" and politics do not exist in separate spheres.[25] The arts, music included, discursively "transliterate" the political process into an aesthetic chronicle.[26] That music's pleasure or pain can only be experienced as a sonoric account of the world, causes confusion because of the effort, throughout our history, to mystify music's social relations, most notably via philosophical aestheticization. It is ironic but hardly surprising that the connection of music to politics has been presented most insistently in the theories of those who condemn music, or certain music, on precisely this account, for example, the ancient ruminations of Plato[27] and the recent panicked diatribe against rock by Allan Bloom.[28]

The concatenation of pleasure and politics is evident in the history of musical notation, which contains an anxiety about meaning as well as about preservation. The only purpose in preserving—making replicable—sounds is that they mean something; and their meaning helps mediate the social and cultural order in which they are born. It is no accident that the early history of notation coincides with the codification (regularization for ideological and political purposes) of the liturgy in the medieval Church. It is no accident that musical manuscripts were often elaborate, visually stunning productions or that much of the printed art music of the nineteenth century carried dedications to rich patrons. The issue of dedications goes beyond the mere economic gain hoped for by impoverished composers. It begs the question why the commission of manuscripts and dedications in printed music might matter to patrons. The value implied exceeds that of physically possessing notated music, which cannot, like a painting, be hung up and looked at. The value instead comes with the faith, sometimes *not* justified, that the experiential sonoric phenomena promised by the score have transliterated a particular world order into the properly aestheticized aural form.

Molenaer emphasizes the stakes of the issue, that order must be defined and specified if *mesure* is to result. In his picture, the partbook occupies the exact center of the composition because by the seventeenth century the life that art music ideally replicated was itself a "scored" experience, not an "improvisatory" one. The woman holding the partbook, who is at once Madonna and whore,[29] encompasses in her body—torn between "reason" and desire—both the reward promised for observing this order and the cost of gaining it: society, constructed according to a set of rules not wholly, or even particularly, in her interest.

History exists where there is a price to be paid.

Michel de Certeau,
The Practice of Everyday Life

DESIRE, POWER, AND THE SONORIC LANDSCAPE

(Early Modernism and the Politics of Musical Privacy)

WHEREAS WESTERN MUSIC HISTORY is written on the complex grid of relations between the public and the private, Western musicology remains focused on
public musical life, as filtered through the institutions of state, church, concert
hall, opera theater, and the semipublic court. The history of private musical life
remains largely unwritten.[1] I want to speculate and to theorize about the social
and cultural "problem" of the public and private spheres in relation to each other.
My purpose is to suggest some implications of the tension between the public
and private in music as a product of discursive practice intimately tied to socio-
cultural relations, constructions of the human subject, and human subjectivity.
Hence, I shall suggest something about the alliances between human desire, on
the one hand, and the manipulation of power, on the other, as these entities are
played out on the field of activities I shall call sonoric landscapes over stakes that
are in every sense always already political.

The phrase "sonoric landscapes" embeds the following observations and as-
sumptions, some obvious, other perhaps not: (1) that sounds surround us, helping
to construct us as human subjects and to locate us in particular social and cultural
environments; (2) that sounds produced or manipulated by humans result from
conscious acts and hence carry a semantic and discursive charge; (3) that all
sounds—even those not produced by humans but "merely" heard by them—can
be read or interpreted; and (4), drawn from the preceding three, that sounds are a
means by which people account for their versions of reality: as it was, is, and/or
might be. That is, people do not employ sounds arbitrarily, haphazardly, or unin-
tentionally—though the "intentionally" haphazard may itself constitute an important sort of sonoric discourse.

A number of musicologists have begun the awesome overdue task of reconsidering how music means and how its meanings help produce both society and culture. A few of them have attempted—often in the face of considerable opposition—to reopen issues of musical semantics that were taken out of musical discussion by a deadly combination of nineteenth-century hard-line aesthetics and twentieth-century humanistic pseudo-science borrowed from the social sciences, which in turn borrowed, in lamentably nonscientific fashion, from the "hard" sciences. One notable result of this combination is what now constitutes mainline music theory: nothing if not rigorous, profoundly similar to literary New Criticism, where the only questions asked—indeed, the only questions that can be asked, given the "methodology"—involve the notes in relation to the notes. And whereas literary New Criticism has been on life-support in English Departments for well over a decade, slowly fading with faculty retirements, the analogue in musicology and music theory is anything but threatened. It continues to overshadow and marginalize all other research.

In the past decade a few scholars have examined music as a discursive practice.[2] This is not the place to survey their work, but I want to draw attention to the opening chapter of Lawrence Kramer's *Music as Cultural Practice, 1800–1900*, "Tropes and Windows: An Outline of Musical Hermeneutics."[3] Here Kramer lays out his case for musical criticism organized largely according to post-structuralist, especially deconstructive, cultural theory. The strength of his proposal lies precisely in his insistence that the hermeneutics he undertakes is located in the musical text. His criticism combines social groundedness, historicity, and the generic specificity of musical discourse—all elements of post-structural practice and all argued for nearly thirty years ago by Theodor W. Adorno, whose work indeed articulated several facets of post-structuralism, at least in generative form, via a systematic examination of music.[4] Kramer and, among others, Susan McClary and Rose Subotnik, organize research on *particular* musical texts. This is altogether necessary. My purpose is to offer an "even more than this" to these scholars' conceptions about the discursive practices of music.

The part of music-as-discourse and musical hermeneutics I address is differentially embedded or encoded in any particular musical text at the same time that it both *exceeds* the text and exists *prior* to it, either as an unrealized but notated composition or as a performance. This "it" has at least two antecedents, or referents: the first is a spoken and unspoken, conscious and unconscious relation of people in a given social unit to music in general and to different sorts of music in particular as well as the relation of music, in its phenomenological ubiquity, to everything nonsonoric. In other words, prior to *and* simultaneous with any given musical text and/or its performance are the relations of music to lived experience. This notion, "lived experience," identifies the second antecedent for my "it": the human body—not just the ears but also the eyes and the effect of seeing and hearing on emotion, physicality, and consciousness (in his introductory chapter, Kramer identifies music's connection to the body in passing).

My point is this: musical discourse necessarily both precedes and exceeds the semantic quotient of any particular musical text. Musical discourse operates, in other words, even in silence, a fact brilliantly articulated years ago by John Cage, who made specific use of human sight as the problematizing agent of "musical" silence—you had to "be" there and to "see" the silence to know that what was happening was nonmusically musical. If musical discourse functions even in silence, can the meaning of this "silent precedent" be demonstrated? How?

In a tentative, exploratory way, and by moving into a relatively distant pre-electronic, prephotographic past, I hope to get at these issues via a few paintings, whose *topoi* do not, however, privilege music as primary subject matter. I have intentionally picked examples where music is compositionally somewhat ancillary yet where its visual representation is nonetheless semantically crucial to a proper understanding of the image. I argue for an understanding of music's discursive power as a sight and for music's ubiquitous presence—paradoxically always prior to and simultaneous with any particular musical event—in people's readings of reality.

THE SONORIC LANDSCAPE, REPRESENTATION, AND EMBODIMENT

The seriousness and intensity of debate over sonoric meaning is notable in the histories of musical codification, virtually all of which focus on the different social and cultural consequences of authorized and unauthorized sounds. Indeed, so significant is the need to exert control over sonority, I would suggest, that the history of the West itself could profitably be rewritten as an account of sonoric difference: from Plato to the Parents' Music Resource Center, I doubt there is a generation that has escaped the deeply self-conscious concern for ordering the world sonorically.[5]

The landscape, as opposed to the earth as a physical entity, is a perception, a specific and ultimately confined view of a portion of the land that seems "worth" viewing because it is somehow noteworthy. Thus landscape is the different within the same; it is what draws attention to itself. What we define, and separate out, as a landscape appears in our consciousness as something at once "itself" and a representation of itself. That is, when a portion of land is raised in our consciousness to the status of land*scape*, the physical entity is reconstituted in our minds as something in excess of the factual. This excess is experienced as a representation—and as such is discursive. By the phrase "sonoric landscape" I wish to evoke the ubiquity of sonority—a sweep of sound as broad as the land itself. But I also wish to evoke the particularity of *musical* sonority in the larger agglomeration of sounds and the particularities of different musical sonorities.

Sonoric landscapes are both heard and seen. They exist because of human experience and human consciousness. Music (the part of the larger sonoric landscape that interests me) connects to the *visible* human body, not only as the receiver of sound but also as its agent or producer. The human embodiment of music is central to any understanding of music's socio-cultural agency. The semantic content of music—its discursive "argument"—is never solely about its sound and the act of hearing. It is instead about the complex relations between sound and hearing as these are registered and as they mediate the entire experience of being. That experience is physical; intellectual, in the broad meaning of the word; and spiritual, though hardly restricted to the religious or the mystical. But it is especially to be understood as the result of mediations between the ear and the eye. The sonoric landscape is peopled and hence interactive. It is external to the human subject yet internalized by its sight and sound.

The terms *power* and *desire* in my chapter title foreclose the discursive particularities that can be explored in a single essay. I did not choose this pair arbitrarily. After all, to argue that musical discourse possesses agency is to raise questions about power. Yet I do not mean any and all power, but power operating at the level of social and cultural organization—power, that is, in its most obvious connection to the political, narrowly defined. Since music, especially art music, so often these days seems removed from power (one of aestheticism's more peculiar "accomplishments," though an utterly false consciousness if ever there was one), then arguably I should try to relocate it precisely in this more "difficult" space. The category "desire" provides me entry into the *embodied* relations between the private and the public, which, through music, act to shape individual human subjects as well as classes of subjects.

SOUND AND SOCIAL ORDER

In 1607 the Antwerp painter Abel Grimmer produced a small panel representing spring, one of the four seasons (Fig. 7). The image represents a feudal hierarchy and the beneficent prosperity it presumably provided. The subject is poignant given the historical circumstances, namely, the end of a period of bloody conflict between the Spanish Netherlands and its overseers in Spain.[6] Embedded in European representations of the seasons—popular from the Middle Ages onward—are ideals of recurrence, predictability, and the banishment of chaos as well as antago-

FIG. 7   Abel Grimmer, *Spring* (1607), oil on wood panel, 33 × 47 cm. Antwerp, Koninklijk Museum voor Schone Kunsten. Photo copyright A.C.L., Brussels.

nisms and anxieties about nature and culture and the roles they assigned to people. Spring located the dialectical relation between nature and culture in human desire and sexuality, expressions of hope for new life and general social fecundity. What especially interests me is the role that certain kinds of music play in the representation.

The painting frames a society that is coherent, ordered, hierarchical, static, and peaceful. Hierarchy is evident in the differences between persons, notably between the landed nobility and the peasants who work the land. Stasis, represented perhaps less obviously, is the quality most directly tied to peacefulness. This is not "Spring 1607"; it is "Every Spring" or, more accurately, the visualization of a desire for, and possibly a confidence in, perpetual recurrence.

The cycle of time encoded by definition into representations of the seasons is as integral to agricultural societies as images encapsulating the loss of a day-to-day relation to nature are to our own society—the calendar imagery of endangered species, the Public Television specials on the destruction of the Amazon rain forest, and so forth. To perceive the cycles of time does not eliminate anxiety over the powers that operate in a seasonal spiral. The cycle of all life is biologically established, but any particular life, however its experiences may be constrained by the individual's position in the social hierarchy, is nonetheless lived actively, dynamically, and consciously. Before taking these issues up in detail, I need to describe the picture.

In Grimmer's *Spring* the château of a feudal lord looms in the background, emphasizing his formal garden, probably an herb garden, with all that suggests about medicine and healing. The area under cultivation is laid out geometrically but has none of the statuary or fountains appropriate to a purely decorative garden. Workers prepare the beds, turning soil, raking the earth, seeding, planting slips, spreading fertilizer, watering. Just outside the garden enclosure two men prune a tree, and two women shear sheep. They are all either servants or peasants. Those for whom they labor disport themselves on the grass (Fig. 8) in a bower, where musicians play while the listeners drink or embrace, as well as above the bower, beneath a topiaried shrub, where several more people, sketchily painted, enjoy

FIG. 8   Abel Grimmer, *Spring* (detail). Photo copyright A.C.L., Brussels.

social intercourse. Some of them appear to make music, though it is hard to be certain of this. Nearby a couple alone embrace in a small boat on the river, within earshot of the music making. On the horizon, behind a forest, rooftops and a tower stand in for a town or city. In sum, the image's primary details are those of land-scape architecture (the beds), intense horticulture (topiary), and architecture proper (not only buildings but also such details as the fencing), though the whole is not rationalized to the degree found in later bourgeois art.[7]

The painting's composition is simultaneously medieval and early modern, its form confronting the changing social constructions in the region during the early seventeenth century. Its modernity locates itself in the strong, off-center diagonals of the garden bed that direct our eyes toward the aristocrats under the bower. Its medieval character, but a conflicted one, locates itself in the activities of the fore-ground, where our eyes cannot rest on any one figure but wander from person to person, vignette to vignette. A medieval harmony asserts itself in the full social hierarchy represented; I have said as much already. But the stasis necessary for this hierarchy is flawed.

The first flaw, an especially dangerous one, is evident even before we sort out the picture's narrative. It locates itself in the painting's compositional vanishing point, though it is not so neatly established as it will be in later art—is it the castle tower, the town tower, or the meeting of land and sky between the two? The vanishing point is nothing if not a conception of *dynamic,* not static, space. The far horizon establishes difference; it is neither town, nor castle, nor cultivated land, and its ownership is ambiguous. Yet the horizon is made visually relevant once it is incorporated into the composition by means of the vanishing point. Its status rises; the far away means something to the near at hand. Its emptiness, which draws us, is powerful. Like something repressed, it returns; indeed it in-trudes. Without the vanishing point, what matters is the world "as shown." Once our eyes are drawn to the distant by means of the vanishing point, the world "as shown" is at once "enriched"—literally and metaphorically deepened—and made more terrestrial, less philosophical. But it is also made relative, part of something else, hence inadequate and unfinished. The guarantee of stasis is undercut. The horizon is a threat whose semantic power acts within the dimension of time, guar-anteeing change; it makes space a problematic category, a discursive terrain. Land is no longer a static, unproblematic category for representation; it is instead a depth, a space, a distance: a more-than-this. Land ownership becomes visually fetishized once the land one possesses (here the space close up) is differentiated from what one has not (distant, unconvincingly "claimed" space). Thus this paint-ing incorporates and problematizes the perception of space and time central to the formation of the modern world. To perceive these elements as dynamic was at once to challenge feudalism and to mark the prerequisites for capitalism.

I ask indulgence for an apparent detour, for this history is fundamental to my discussion of music. The connection I seek to establish is this: music, like no other medium of discursive practice, acts simultaneously in space and in time. Although theater does too, it does so differently, because its predominant "text" is words, whereas music's is sonorities as such, even when words are present (worded music). Music is simultaneously more and less than the concrete: it is abstract, yet it is inevitably made and experienced as embodied. Music, unlike theater, has a mystical substance; as an "embodied abstraction" it simultaneously is and is not. It fills space but cannot be measured; and it disappears as absolutely as a shadow once light fades.

Music bears relation to the shadow: it is the *is not* of that which is; it is the account of the real that itself is both real and not real. In no other human practice does agency depend so specifically on being and not being; in this respect music relates to spirituality. This much is true of music throughout human history. What is different and additional at the moment of *Spring, 1607*, is that now and for the first time representationally, hence experientially, the dimensions of time and space in which music operates were severely problematized in Western European experience. The comparatively static and cyclical feudal world, which had been slowly dying for more than a century, was being subsumed under the dynamism of mercantilism and soon-to-be capitalism. Space and time were becoming the dimensions through which human dynamism and agency were understood to operate most fruitfully, in the process giving rise to modern conceptions of the human individual and the activities of individualism. Cycle was about to disappear in favor of vector. Music's history could be read as the prophet. But the feudal and proto-capitalist sides of this history would necessarily read the prophecy differently, each according to its own interests. The ideal audience for this image would find its visual pleasure in a reading premised on feudal continuance, even though the representation itself could not but acknowledge feudalism's decline.

In the center foreground of *Spring* a man bends to his shovel. He and a companion at the extreme left, also holding a shovel, occupy more picture space than other figures and far more than any of the nobility. Our interest in them develops not from any individuality, for they have none, but from their roles as workers and their proximity to our own space. Their faces are not shown; what matters is their strength, marshaled to a task. If we shift our focus to the other workers, men and women alike, we see that they too are mostly faceless and that those whose faces are represented betray not individuality so much as the hardness of their labors (the woman at the extreme left foreground), their contentment (the woman farthest right poking seeds into the ground), and even a kind of lumpish stupidity (the men raking and casting seeds). I say "lumpish" advisedly, for the painter consistently represents the workers as low to the ground, their bodies, shaped like

swelled turnips, differentiating them from the two women of superior class looking on at the right side of the garden and giving instructions. The workers' bodies
also contrast with those of their social superiors under the bower, notably the male
lutenist stretched out comfortably on the ground and his servant who pours wine:
long-legged, far from the ground, so to speak.

Yet the nobility themselves are little more than dashes of color; they too are
essentially "faceless," so small that we can do little more than call them by their
social type. But we see enough, because difference is the key, and difference is
unquestionably and unambiguously established. Faces or portraits are not at issue.
The scene is a bit of Flanders—as though Flanders were the whole world, except-
ing again the difficulty with the vanishing point. That *represented* world—I am
not arguing about the "real" world of Flanders, only the pictorial one—is type-
cast, and only the roles matter, not who fills them. So long as the roles hold,
everything else matters less and can be made to fit the general scheme. The aristocracy's certainty of position and authority is visually enhanced by its retreat into
the background to pursue its pleasures. In later bourgeois images the self-image
is foregrounded, openly asserted, and such retreats seldom occur; even in Grimmer's painting, however, prebourgeois anxiety about social position may be evident in both the revelers' proximity to their fortress and the river-as-moat that
separates them from their work force.[8]

CONTEMPLATION AND THE BODY

The image is structured by three related differences: work from leisure, peasant
from aristocrat, and *silence from music.* I am not arguing that the painting's foreground—the nonmusical portion—strikes us as "literally" silent, for the memory
traces it activates in viewers do include sound. Sheep, for example, commonly
bleat when being sheared, not liking to be held for shearing and often being
nicked. And workers are hardly silent in all their labors. Gardeners may hum to
themselves, making their own music while engaged in light labor like scattering
seeds, if not during more taxing jobs like spading earth. But for the most part the
sounds their labors suggest are not musical. More to the point, the painter offers
us no encouragement to "see" the laborers singing, whereas he requires us to acknowledge the music of the nobility.

Thus the painting represents two landscapes and two soundscapes. In the foreground is a formal garden, of the sort that would reach its apogee and richest
discursive manifestation at Versailles roughly two centuries later. In the background, at the vanishing point to the right of the château, is a forest in an apparently primeval state. The forest is a privileged space, both legally and symboli-

cally. (Poaching game carried severe penalties in forested lands held as private hunting preserves, where the authorized killing of game served not only to supply the princely table with exotic meats but also to signal the princely power of life and death within the domain.) The soundscapes register themselves by simultaneous presence and absence: music fills the air under the bower, opposing the putative silence of the foreground. Expressed via Saussurian semiotics, the *is* (music) defines itself by means of the *is not* (silence, or nonmusic) and vice versa. As such, music—a particular kind of music—represents itself as the sonoric simulacrum of one sort of life, private life, with *private* conflated with privilege and prestige. Private music, ironically represented "in public" so that privacy as such can be visually valorized, is the sonoric overlay that gives meaning to the entire scene, both for the revelers and for the laborers who may overhear sounds that define what they themselves are not.

The immediate function of the music under the bower is love. Those for whom that music is played are the couple with their backs to us between the men playing viol and lute, the couple in the boat, and the couple standing and embracing in dark recess. But overriding the music's amatory function is its role as an agent of social order, manifested in the contemplation of the couple listening between the two instrumentalists. That is, music's pleasure is "purposeful" and not merely something in the air, like the chirpings of birds. It invites conscious audition, of sufficient seriousness that the one couple turn their backs to us to hear. What they listen to and for—by definition—is a sonoric discourse, probably one that interpolates them less in the present, which after all is momentarily uncontested to the extent that it simply *is,* than in the future, which more than ever before is up for grabs, not only because feudalism is dying but also specifically because Flanders was experiencing upheavals at the moment of the painting's production.

The incorporation into the image of "art music" and its audition as the central "event" among the nobility establishes an opposition between contemplation (thought) and physical labor (in essence, nonthought). Such music is self-conscious, intentional, inherently and necessarily "rational." It is not spontaneous but planned, so as to sanction and articulate sonorically a meaning of the physical events transpiring not only under the bower but also in the painting's foreground. To the extent that this music is listened to, it is a passive engagement; but because passivity functions here as a sign of social division, it is a means of valorizing social difference. Not accidentally, it recapitulates the ancient Boethian precedence of the critic/auditor over the producer.

It is well known that opera houses, well into the nineteenth century, were the locus for conversation and other activities as much as for listening and that audiences commonly quieted down en masse only to hear favorite musical bits. It is also established that the gradual silencing of talk and the increasing expectation that audiences attend to musical performance in both opera theater and concert hall developed with the middle class's enshrinement of symphonic instrumental music. Attentiveness to music—what Adorno termed contemplation—may of course be explained as a laudable enhancement of high art, but it is neither that simple nor entirely benign.

The problematics of contemplation, a "mental" activity, emerge the moment mind intersects with body. The etiquette of "contemplation" is, before anything else, a controlling of the body in time, a working against the body, whether self-imposed or imposed by others (like parents who discipline their squirming children). And it is an etiquette that turns music from an inherently participatory activity into a passive one in which the listener maintains physical stasis by exerting the cultural force of will against the body's desires. The auditor may move toes in time to the beat but not hum, stomp feet, sway the torso, or bob the head: bodily reaction to music in the concert hall must be neither audible nor visible. To give oneself over to any of these reactions invites rebuke.[9]

I will not sort out here the full complexities and ramifications of this etiquette, but will instead identify just one facet that applies most directly to my concerns, namely, that the etiquette invokes, mirrors, and replicates macrocosmic mechanisms for establishing social order. The etiquette of physical passivity, simultaneously imposed and self-imposed, reflects the achievement of social hegemony in part through cultural practice. "Consent" is manufactured, gradually learned and internalized, rather than imposed by raw force, as Antonio Gramsci pointed out many years ago.[10] Further, a socially required passivity of reception becomes a simulacrum of the socially correct meaning of the performance itself. Both the sonorities heard and the act of performance itself are disciplines.[11] The music being contemplated draws attention to itself, raises the stakes of its presence, specifically as an "activity" whose valorization is organized by rendering the body static. Music in this guise acts as a sonoric surveillance on the body, holding it captive to contemplation with the social proscription of physical reaction.[12] Not incidentally, whether the auditor actually contemplates is perfectly irrelevant to the demand.

MUSIC AND DIFFERENCE

In *Spring* music possesses and creates prestige by imposing its presence in relation to lived, *linear* time, this despite the typically cyclical experience of time in agricultural societies. I want to connect this matter first to erotics, then to music. One common feudal articulation of linear time occurs in the mythology of courtly love.

Though the "literary practice" of courtly love predates by several centuries the period of my concern, the courtship central to it occupies the group under the bower. Courtly love, as idealized and theorized by Andreas Capellanus in the twelfth century,[13] valorized relationships whose intensity depended on the indefinite postponement of the physical. The lover's platonic suffering could be enjoyed for many years; indeed, the longer the wait, the sweeter the agony. Any reader of *The Romance of the Rose,* the best known verse account of chivalric love, is aware that delay—prolonged through tens of thousands of lines—articulated desire and was itself an object of desire worthy of intense contemplation. Delay and desire are premised on a grid of time. And that grid, on which one plays out one's life by willfully waiting, charts an excessive control over time, one that enables the lover to wait in a world where the ability to wait establishes status.

In the painting time is valorized in an equation, whose product is prestige, that depends on our witnessing simultaneous but opposing events confirming that while some must work, others must not and that if one kind of work is physical, the other is overtly and actively mental: contemplative listening. Contemplative listening is not philosophically removed from the world, as later aesthetic theory would have it; it is instead the sign of one's control and domination of the world. Music, as a phenomenon that acts through time, when heard contemplatively stops all other activities. As such, it *is* an exercise of power, a political act. It is worth noting that "contemplative" sensual desire, that odd privilege of "doing without," is explicitly opposed to the sensual archaeology of the lower social strata, as characterized in endless numbers of contemporaneous representations, where the order of the day is rampant physical groping in an uncertain, unstable time frame. For the peasantry, the sensual is formulated temporally as instantaneous, the mythology of chivalric love disappearing in the lunge of bodies striving to copulate.[14] Nonetheless, as regards the private music making represented in *Spring,* an irony has to be faced. To account for the political capital of privacy, the sonoric-visual signs of that privacy, music making and lovemaking together, have to be made visually public, have to be voyeuristically displayed. In *this* sense representation, whether visual or sonoric, is the simulacrum not of strength but of weakness, an acknowledgment that culture is process and that all process incorporates the promise of change.

Music is a possession to be paraded before Grimmer's laborers, and before viewers outside the picture frame, as the sight and sound of difference. But since music itself is "simply air," what it encodes of power is the power over time. For some, the world can be made to stop while the air is filled with music's emptiness. Music's power, according to this formulation, *is* its emptiness, which constitutes itself ironically as a sign of fullness and excess. It can be no wonder that with the advent of the bourgeois world, but with notable recourse to Plato, so much anxiety was manifested about music as a waste of time. That the emergent bourgeoisie were so consistently reproachful about musicians in their ranks, especially male musicians, is hardly surprising given both the class's hatred for the perquisites and discursive practices of the nobility and its ironic fetishization of time as money. Nor can it be surprising that the bourgeoisie themselves quickly figured out how music—to be sure, music of their "own sort"—could be engaged sonorically to represent their interests.

Representations of the seasons are visual idealizations of feudal ideology, feudal hierarchy, and feudal consciousness. They are mental projections, visually articulated, about a future that continues and perfectly realizes the present. They are less the world as it truly is than the world as it is desired, but with desire seamlessly constructed out of present circumstances. Not incidentally, therein lies the inherent anxiety of representation: "A visual image, so long as it is not being used as a mask or disguise, is always a comment on an *absence*. The depiction comments on the absence of what is being depicted. Visual images, based on appearances, always speak of *dis*appearance."[15] As for music, the representation does not, strictly speaking, address the reality of performance practices. But that is not to suggest that musical images like Grimmer's bear no relation to musical life. Grimmer's musicians and their audience must relate closely to the functions of music in the society represented; if not, their presence would be nonsensical: discursive practice disallows "empty decoration."

Grimmer, in deciding to organize his image around the full social spectrum, had to face the issue of what he would have the nobility *do*. Apart from warring and hunting, the nobility ordinarily conveyed their rank by an absence of physical activity. But in an image whose subject—spring—requires an orderly presentation of peace (no warring) and growth or new life (no hunting), the nobility nonetheless need to be shown *using* the time they supposedly controlled, over which no power is so absolute as that of appearing to do nothing while others do for you. Music is the ideal activity to make the point clear. One can make music oneself with a minimum of physicality, like the lounging lutenist, or one can pay someone else, like the violist, to make it in one's presence; the result is something at once beautiful *and* produced. It is something cultural, not natural; the manifestation of another level of power, it is nevertheless *nothing*. The power of music making is not only the power to control time through the expenditure of leisure; it is also the license to waste time. Music is visually extravagant. (The possibility that music, as a productless entity, was trivial has troubled philosophers, moralists, and politicians throughout Western history, though these concerns only reached their zenith in post-Renaissance Europe.)[16]

Music's pleasures and relevance have virtually never been denied. Indeed, music's most virulent enemies have often condemned music, or some music, precisely for the pleasures it provides and the effects of its audition on the social fabric. Even when judged a trivial pursuit, in other words, music retains its relevance, a negative one. Throughout history music has existed in conflict with what, sonorically, it is its purpose to define. Music is condemned, if not interdicted, as much as it is praised and supported. It is necessary to realize that debates about music are not about nothing. The disputes in any age between ancients and moderns concern the sonoric portion of the social order and the identity of the human subject, especially the sensual subject, therein. That is why Grimmer, ultimately responsible to the interests of his patrons—who might sit under a bower but would not wield shovels—represented the only music possible, just as music itself is very nearly the only "activity" ideologically and politically available to project ideological "correctness."

There is a complementary way of expressing this point. *Spring* is a narrative that strives visually for closure, doubly postulated as a successful ending, a nonchallenge, and an account sealed off from the outside. Any narrative not only produces a world but also, by that very act, necessarily excludes as well. The activities of including and excluding are never innocent, accidental, or semantically void. They betray an interest—stakes. Moreover, the concern with closure in representation incorporates a gendered response to storytelling, a characteristic of male psycho-sexual efforts to gain and maintain control.[17]

In hierarchical societies there cannot be one undifferentiated body of music. The musics that exist must be classified, and their differences must be articulated *in words*. Unclassified sound, soundscape without the registration of difference, is the sonoric allowance of either democracy or anarchy. Valorization must occur; sound as a dimension of human activity and human agency cannot be left out of the socio-cultural equation. The Platonic metaphor conflating musical harmony and world harmony was not accidental, as Plato himself makes clear in his diatribe on listening—however abstract his conception and nonscientific his "astronomy." Musical classification for Plato is essential because sonoric control is one guarantee of the utopia he envisions.

ENVELOPMENT

In human sensing, whereas sight distances, hearing envelops.[18] Envelopment counted for everything in feudal society's understanding of itself, even in its late stages of decay. Envelopment meant mutuality. At the social apex it incorporated noblesse oblige; indeed, the war between Spain and the Spanish Netherlands, in truce at the moment of Grimmer's painting, was in part waged over the deterioration of that fundamental principle. Society was neither held together by raw coercive power nor even conceived in terms of it.

A painting that represents the hierarchy of the social totality, like Grimmer's, thus incorporates a problem. To the extent that sight distances us from the world, providing a primary means by which we measure and classify, the medium of painting becomes socially and politically problematic to the self-representation of feudal society. This is so because the world the painting represents is made silent. As such, the image stands off, separates itself from us like something to be studied. It is a medium easily given over to the clinical.

Sound, by its enveloping character, brings us closer to everything alive. Hearing musical sound, with or without words, makes us especially aware of proximity and thus connectedness. Parents sing lullabies to their infants, and their infants respond: this is music at its most enveloping, for it connects the baby's consciousness to the parent's body via the parent's warm, moist breath, the sonoric articulation of life itself. Music fills breath with substance, fleshes it out, so to speak, and doubly touches the body of its infant auditor, whose ears hear and whose skin feels the breathy imprint. The reassurance is formed by a bond at once utterly abstract and profoundly embodied.

Sight can accomplish none of this, though not for want of trying: "Sight as a drive attaches itself to pleasure-giving, or anxiety-alleviation. Objects become symptoms, referring back to the psyche, as it robs them of their true nature as material things and gives them a new meaning and significance."[19] But sight nonetheless holds us at arm's length—even when we embrace our lovers. Sight distracts lovers in embrace; eyes close to erase sight's distancing; we close our eyes, and the eye-produced classifications shouting out our separateness disappear. We become one. Sight reminds us of difference but also of the promise of loss. Feudal society's structural connectedness—its metaphoric familial linkage—is severely strained in this painting's raw articulation of extreme social difference. This tension must be overcome.

Of all human activities only music can reproduce the breath of connectedness in painting, because the visual trace of its activity insists on its operation. Music is there only because it must be; it cannot be done without. And it exists in thousands of paintings because its function is central to lived experience. Music is the "argument" that the spring idealized in Grimmer's painting is still possible.[20]

OWNERSHIP, FAMILY, AND
THE PROMISE OF DOMESTIC PRIVACY

A half century after Grimmer's *Spring,* two Flemish painters, Guilliam van Schoor and (perhaps) Gillis van Tilborgh, collaborated on a representation of the Nassau mansion in Brussels (Fig. 9). The canvas, over six feet wide, commanding by itself, depicts a commanding architectural and quasi-agricultural enclosure in which

FIG. 9   Guilliam van Schoor and Gillis van Tilborgh (?), *Nassau Mansion at Brussels* (1658), oil on canvas, 123.5 × 206 cm. Brussels, Musées Royaux des Beaux-Arts de Belgique. Photo copyright A.C.L., Brussels.

open land is as abundant as it is scarce in the city that abuts the estate on the right. In this representation the prestige of the Nassau family depends on the vastness of the open space they control in a larger, crowded, geography. The power fueling prestige is horticulture, both the garden plantings and the lack of plantings. There is space within the enclosure for a nonfunctional formal garden—the sections closest to the château—whose geometries delineate nothing so much as the imposition of mathematical, hence intentional, order on nature. In the middle distance are an herb and perhaps a kitchen garden, where individual plants are accorded fallow space. The lower right quadrant of the enclosure closest to the viewer is entirely fallow, a radical spatial excess in an urban setting. There are only two or three workers but more than a dozen aristocratic observers. The activities of the aristocrats, to the extent they can be discerned, are contemplative, leisured, and, with reference to the five figures in the right foreground, familial and musical.

The man and woman at the extreme right are posed as icons of *mesure,* metaphoric agents and living microcosms of everything else visible in the enclosure. In one sense the guitarist provides the imaginative sonoric completion of what is visible, eliciting in the viewer's memory sounds that trace the universalizing, politically totalizing tendency asserted alike by the order of the ornamental garden design, the physically imposing dwelling that towers over the rest of the visible city, and indeed the land itself.

Lest we react to the musical event as a pictorially "innocent" *tranche de vie,* the painter reminds us that it counts for more. Perched atop the guitar's neck is an exotic bird, apparently a parrot, a perfect visual substitute, because of its exotic coloration (not because of its own "voice") for the music we cannot hear. Visually excessive, the bird is precisely on that account both functional and essential in a discourse about, and an argument for, a particular way of life. (Such pets were a common badge of prestige among the upper classes in the Low Countries, together with various small primates.) On the surface, it might seem that the painters could have filled that corner of the picture's space with anything or anyone, or perhaps with nothing. To have chosen a musical vignette, and to have added to it the detail of a bird, one whose color draws our eyes to the guitarist, was a rhetorical act.[21]

This rhetorical gesture would seem useless if we did not understand the significant role of sonority in social organization, one that I can articulate in two ways. First, the guitarist's placement near the wall at her back helps define her act as private. The wall forms the boundary between the private and the public, privilege and the lack of privilege. The painters show the distinction by means of a raised perspective, a quasi–bird's-eye view, that allows us to see over the wall to the other side. The space within the garden wall, and the activities occurring there, gain meaning as the viewer sees differences outside the enclosure. Second, the horticultural emptiness of the front-most garden plot, although it encodes prodigality, is nonetheless pictorially "dangerous," taken by itself, to the extent that it might be read as lack; in an image where cultivation is the visible analogue to power, noncultivation is ambiguous. This ambiguity is stabilized by twin components: family (the couple with the child) and music (the guitarist and her male companion). Together these two groups form a human and sonoric "garden," where art is cultivated rather than vegetables and where the fallow earth serves as a visual frame.

The painting contains few distractions; it fetishizes not people but a building. Its compositional lines invariably pull toward the mansion, whose inhabitants at the front picture plane seem to wait almost helplessly for our glance to leave them so as to focus on the mortar and brick icon of their identity. The walls of their garden are merely extensions of the architecture, in that they guarantee a privacy almost as complete as that afforded by the walls of the château. This is not a trivial matter, and it has consequences for the history of music. In the half century that passed between Grimmer's *Spring* and this picture's execution, the role of music had changed. Music's social circumstance now approaches the bourgeois ideal of a private sphere totally separate from the public. The music of the nobles in *Spring,* performed in a quasi-agricultural setting, where a river physically separates it from the laboring peasants, nonetheless carries to their ears. By contrast, the urbanites on the other side of the wall in the later painting could hear little of the guitar. The wall limits both sound and sight.

Earlier, in sixteenth-century Flanders, townsfolk commonly heard the public music of the town pipers performing in municipal towers, their playing a sonoric promise of social order and shared municipal vitality. It was shawm and sackbut music, meant to be heard—indeed, a music not to be denied. What goes on, musically or otherwise, behind the walls of the Nassau mansion, however, depends on access; to see and hear one must first be admitted. That difference—between private and public—becomes a driving force in the history of modern society; it also becomes a fundamental distinction in the history of music. The enclosed garden of the Nassau mansion is the prototype of the concert hall, which delineates a physical space for a certain kind of music, whose sonorities are the acoustic signs of a certain privileged group of people.

NOISE

David Teniers the Younger repeatedly painted the lower and upper classes together in scenes that commonly incorporate musical activity (Fig. 10).[22] His *Landscape with Shepherds, Swineherds, a Harvest, and a Genteel Couple at Music* exudes fecundity, its soil supporting an ample harvest gathered by peasants and its grasses the fatness of sheep and pigs and the swelling of cows' udders. It is a specific landscape in that the distant city towers resemble those of Mechlin and Antwerp. There is labor in the background, business in the center foreground, and intimations of love among the couples on the left and right. Abundance is shared; there are tables at either extreme from which sustenance is enjoyed. Human subjects of different classes are separated spatially, with the hierarchy established by a sweeping movement of the eyes from left to right, the aristocratic couple and their servant occupying, in effect, half the pictured landscape, the crowd of peasants the remainder.

The two other fundamental distinctions that mark difference and prestige involve the implied aurality of the image. On the right half is noise of activities both necessary and mundane: the squeals of pigs being captured and the discourse of money or business. On the left, in sharp contrast, a contemplative and cultured "discourse" ensues between the socially elevated couple: she reads; he plays the violin. The vignette creates the impression of serenity, but the man and his violin also replicate the effect of Orpheus charming the animals; this was a pictorial subject much in evidence in seventeenth-century Flanders, against which Teniers's painting necessarily resonates (Fig. 11) and to which I will return. Even though

FIG. 10 David Teniers the Younger, *Landscape with Shepherds, Swineherds, a Harvest, and a Genteel Couple at Music* (1677), oil on canvas, 180 × 270 cm. Cologne, Wallraf-Richartz-Museum and Museum Ludwig. Photo: Rheinisches Bildarchiv, Cologne.

FIG. 11 Roelant Savery, *Orpheus Charming the Animals* (1617?), oil on wood panel, 62 × 131.5 cm. The Hague, Mauritshuis Museum. Photo copyright A.C.L., Brussels.

the man's noble status required that he remain aloof from peasant tasks such as animal husbandry, that social "rule" is momentarily violated for a higher purpose, though the violation is not likely to be noticed. What I mean is that the man's violin playing pulls the sheep, lambs, and even cows to his side, as though he were their attendant.

This "violation" or license nonetheless serves a purpose. Orpheus charming the animals, after all, is a subject organized to represent a man who commands all nature as the measure of all things. The Orpheus story locates virtually magical powers in a single individual; it aestheticizes his power into music and poetry; and it promises an Edenic order as the result of that power. Where Orpheus plays, the world is at peace (thus the appeal of the story during this period of Flemish history). The political dimension of the subject, obvious and incontestable, is that a particular music—Apollonian, or art, music—commands the world, and at the same time confirms the propriety of the man's position. Music closes a sonoric circle around the man, marking and authorizing his identity and providing the source of his power. The potential stakes of music's ability to sanction one's identity, it seems to me, were what Beethoven registered in removing the original title page of the "Eroica" carrying his dedication to Napoleon.

Teniers's landscape is a soundscape as well as a blatant, even heavy-handed, visualization of smugly managed power. His aristocrat may appear a bit too much a farmer and not enough a cousin of Orpheus for our taste, but that ultimately matters little when even the tree under which he sits bends to envelop him in a compositional acknowledgment of who he is and what he can do—incidentally in perfect union with the original story where even the trees and rocks were moved by the sounds of Orpheus's lyre.

The violin in the seventeenth century was a popular instrument among the lower classes, who used it principally to accompany dance.[23] It is an instrument thus commonly associated with intense physicality, frenetic movement. Yet there is no invitation to the dance here; indeed, no movement whatever is suggested save that of the bow across the strings. Therein lies the point: music itself is tamed (and an actual "taming" occurred during this century in northern Europe as the violin was slowly adopted by the upper classes for art music). The noble couple, stationary, are bearers of status. They remind us of an essential distinction in music between the physicality of the popular (noise, nonart) and the comparative passivity of the aristocratic (art).

Teniers accords his aristocratic sitters status by emphasizing the striking incongruity of his compositional arrangement. In effect, he poses the couple and their servant as if they were in private chambers, complete with basic furniture and accessories—table, tablecloth, wine glasses, and serving tray. He translates an interior enclosure into the outdoors, with the protective shade of the tree under which the couple sits as architecture: chamber music in a chambered landscape. The charge of prestige the image carries is constructed in visual and aural terms that are the opposite of those that make prestige possible. That is, prestige here accrues from physical inaction, or as close to that as possible, although in reality it depends on physical actions, typically, to be sure, those of dependable others under one's charge. Leisure as culture, in other words, is the mask for the action against nature by which culture is achieved. In the nature-culture equation, disharmony is the constant, but its presence must be neither seen nor heard.

SURVEILLANCE AND JUDGMENT

An alternate means by which artists of the period incorporated sonority's trace into paintings was to look to the other end of the social spectrum and represent the music of the lower classes. Two examples will suffice, the first, by Theodoor van Thulden, probably representing a wedding feast (Fig. 12), the second, one of a seemingly endless number of so-called kermis scenes or peasant celebrations painted by Teniers the Younger (Fig. 13).[24] Both depict the two extremes of the social hierarchy within a single pictorial frame.

Wedding Feast (Fig. 12) is composed like a stage set. The bridal couple sit at a table beneath a temporary canopy hung from an outside wall. The building itself, hyper-picturesque, is also like a theater flat with one outside wall removed so we can look in on events. The crowd scenes are distributed throughout the canvas as vignettes; many concern lovemaking and peasant drunkenness. An entrance onto this "stage," already overburdened with actors, is in progress; at the lower left, an aristocratic couple have emerged from their coach (compositionally framed by the poles supporting a lean-to shed). Their costumes are very different from the peasants', and that difference is heightened by a noteworthy detail: the woman in the foreground, wearing the painting's most elaborate costume, is masked. She is hardly rendered incognito to her audience by this gesture. The painting's inhabitants would know exactly who she was, for it was the role of the feudal aristocracy to honor peasants by appearing at major rituals like weddings. The mask does not disguise; it establishes identity, difference, and distinction. It marks presence and the simulacrum of absence.

An additional compositional detail makes clear the separateness of social spheres. Near the standing aristocratic couple is another pair of the same class. They are seated and also elevated physically; compositionally, they rise above the peasant couple near the painting's center who head a dance line. The aristocrats are observers, not participants, an audience for a play-within-a-play that we also witness. We as viewers—and originally this "we" must have constituted people

FIG. 12   Theodoor van Thulden, *Wedding Feast,* oil on canvas. Brussels, Musées Royaux des Beaux-Arts de Belgique. Photo copyright A.C.L., Brussels.

similar in social rank to the feudal lords—are twice removed from the events that occupy the bulk of the picture's space. The only justification for painting the small rise of land on which to seat the nobility is visually to increase the distance between social ranks otherwise made evident by costume. But there is more, and here I will state my point.

The scene's action is governed by music, specifically by a man at the right who stands on a barrel and plays the bagpipe. As the Flemish instrument most characteristic of peasant life, it figured in countless sixteenth- and seventeenth-century paintings. It provided, in life, the sonoric accompaniment to village fairs, weddings, and the like. (As to weddings, a popular proverb made clear the visual similarity of the instrument to the male genitalia—windpipe and windsack together—and, indeed, some peasant wedding subjects of the period refer to male sexuality; see Fig. 6). The bagpiper is a kind of pied piper: he calls the tune. How his audience of peasants visually reacts to the sound is crucial. In painting the only way to establish that reaction is through the body.

As one might expect, the music sets people dancing. But the point is how they dance, and how their physical movements are embodied differently from those of the aristocrats who view them. It is crucial that van Thulden connect the viewer visually to the two couples on whom the matter turns; hence he not only places the standing lord and his wife near the couple at the head of the dance line, but he also has them look at one another. Moreover, the peasant couple "perform" for their masters. The peasant man doffs his hat, the characteristic gesture of deference. And, most important, he lifts his leg high in the exaggerated dance step of the *Hoppaldei*.[25] This gesture is almost certainly the most eye-catching, prominent detail in the painting. It is a movement of intense physicality, visually contrasted with the extreme reserve of the noble couple.

The painting's naturalism is severely curtailed. Everything is too posed; the buildings are too stagey; the break between foreground and background is too clear. But ideologically it is entirely correct. It is a representation not of an event as such but of a social ideal where there is no uncertainty and nothing is challenged. The lives of the peasantry are inevitably public. Their space can be entered and witnessed. It is clear that the nobility's entrance is unexpected, for nearly all the peasantry nearby engage in activities—drunkenness and groping lovemaking—ordinarily inappropriate to the decorum and deference superior rank demands.

This is Bakhtin's carnival.[26] That is, the wedding celebration is a bracketed event, where the momentary suspension of normal activities is structured into a long season of a religious and political Lent.[27] There is an unmistakable sign reminding us of this fact. In the lower foreground, directly in front of the peasant whose dancing leg is suspended so high, lies an upturned rake. It visually connects to the barn at the back of the scene filled with gathered hay. These two details frame the celebration and provide its "excuse": the peasant "time-out" occurs after work is finished. The rake and the hay in the barn, in their relation to human events, problematize the dimension of time. Equally important and closely related, these details establish the character actors as "good" peasants.[28]

Sonorically associated with intense physical labor, hence encoding silence, the rake and the hay are visual antidotes to the bagpiper and the dancers. The bagpipe is a profoundly sonoric instrument, its ability to pierce silence nearly unparalleled. The only exclusively aristocratic instruments that could match it were trumpets and kettledrums, employed as the celebratory and signaling instruments of the exclusively aristocratic cavalry. (The right to play trumpets and kettledrums was tightly, even violently, controlled, and extreme pageantry accompanied the performance, sight and sound merging in the representation of the sign.[29] Apart from kettledrums and trumpets, the only "loud" instruments of the period were the shawms and sackbuts played by those in the employ of Flemish towns, musically representing the interests of the urban trade centers in a social space between the

FIG. 13   David Teniers the Younger, *Kermis,* oil on canvas, 157 × 221 cm. Brussels, Musées Royaux des Beaux-Arts de Belgique. Photo copyright A.C.L., Brussels.

nobility and the peasantry.) The "private" instruments of the nobility were of the *bas,* or soft, variety. All this being true, the peasant bagpipe is a sonoric simulacrum of and for difference. It is not accidental that the painterly conventions of the period (late sixteenth century to nearly the end of the seventeenth) manifest concern over peasant activities in representations of peasants' musical practices.

In van Thulden's painting, just as in Teniers's (Fig. 13), the immanent threat peasants posed to aristocrats is in part diminished by a heavy dose of the picturesque. But that cannot silence the sonority of the bagpipe, because the bagpipe's sound was ubiquitous in Flemish life. It penetrated vast space, especially by comparison with that of the bowed strings and soft winds (for example, recorders) favored by the aristocracy. Sonorically, it represented the social majority whose lives it helped define and order at events like fairs, tavern gatherings, and weddings. Its insistence was public, just as the "soft" music of the upper social orders was largely private. The opposition between outside (public) and inside (private) is crucial, even at this early stage of modernism. It looks forward to the troubled fetishization of privacy in nineteenth-century domesticity that I shall take up later in this volume.

Tenier's version of this subject (Fig. 13), although similar to van Thulden's, divides more neatly into two halves. On the right are the bagpiper, a high-stepping dancing couple, and their peasant auditors. At the left the local lord and his spouse enter, having arrived in their coach. Directly above the coach stands their château, informing us whence they came. It is closed off, only its towers and battlements visible through the trees; it is identifiable on account of its defensive function. Everything on the left side of the picture is serene, reserved, private, and *silent*. What lies within its precincts can only be imagined. It is for neither seeing nor hearing.[30]

NATURE AND WORD

Among the more curious pictorial subjects popular in seventeenth-century Flanders were so-called bird concerts (Fig. 14). These are the most imaginary of natural and sonoric landscapes; they gather birds, both local and exotic, from climates hot and cool, dry and moist. Bird concerts are analogous to contemporaneous still-life

FIG. 14   Jan van Kessel the Elder, *Bird Concert*, oil on canvas, 53 × 72 cm. Private collection. Photo copyright A.C.L., Brussels.

paintings of flowers that incorporate the ordinary with the unusual, the governing factor being visual splendor (flowers are placed together that bloom at different times of the year, an arrangement achievable, if at all, only through forcing in hothouses). In this aviary, whose inhabitants come from the Old World and the New, predator birds commingle with their putative prey in an Eden without humans—but not without the trace of humans.

The ordinarily violent intra- and interspecies relations are held in a suspension that allows the Australian ostrich to be sighted with the new-world parrot and the ostrich and parrot with the European swan. That suspension is music—not the natural "music" of the birds, for their sounds are not in fact musical—but the music of men, inscribed on the choir book propped on the ground around which the birds gather like a schola cantorum. What can this mean if not the control of nature by the Word, wherein text is accorded privileged status over the things of this earth? Yet the Word is more than text; it is texted music.

This subject demarcates the visual beginnings of aesthetics, wherein music as a practice and music as a metaphor for society meet in a self-conscious and problematic relation. Music in this instance is problematized in a "society" of birds not only as a sonoric, texted suspension in which geographical impossibilities and violent instincts are held (and held in check) but also as a practice that draws attention to itself as something separate and momentary. The music governing the birds' song is a music of unison (that much is clear, though not much else, in the notation). The birds are "asked" to sing what humans have given them. We classify them; they are ours. Their very naturalness is an affront to our status, and as such it is subsumed in the Word. This is a dialectic of enlightenment wherein nature, simultaneously the enemy, the tool, and the resource "given" us to exploit, comes to us only at the cost of splitting the body, our "nature," from the mind.[31]

It is also the dialectic into which music is culturally located *as* music, and not as mere sound or noise. Music is not "in the air" like the natural sounds of birds or, for that matter, the sounds of people generally;[32] it is instrumentalized, understood as a behavior to be defined, characterized, rationalized, made purposeful and useful. The music of the bird concert, that is, does not define the birds; instead, it violates them by misrepresenting their nature. The pleasure of their "music" is not theirs, but ours. Their pleasure is no longer innocent in its purposelessness. It is coerced. It is no longer Orpheus who charms the animals but man's rule that classifies them. I would go so far as to suggest that the musical text at the base of the tree, on the banks of a river, is more than a little akin to the passenger list for the Old Testament Ark; it is hardly accidental that most of the birds are shown in pairs. Music is charged with providing the aestheticized cover for what is metaphorically the determinate text for survival.

So in the end this is pretty serious business—Platonic metaphors of music of the spheres, expressed in explicitly terrestrial terms, to be sure, nonetheless define the terms for life itself. That music organizes the terms provides ample evidence for what is otherwise disguised in the visual splendor of the painting's rich colors. Aesthetics is never passive and music is never drained of meaning. In aesthetics and music alike, purposelessness is only a mask or a sweetener for something deemed more important, namely, the shape of society and the human subjects within it. Pleasure is never without consequences. It is a component of history and comes with a price to be paid.

Every work of art is an uncommitted crime.

Theodor W. Adorno,
Minima Moralia

THE POETICS OF ANGUISH, PLEASURE, AND PRESTIGE

(Hoarding Sound in a Culture of Silence)

THE NOTATED, HENCE SURVIVING, music produced in Western Europe from the sixteenth century to the eighteenth responded primarily to the needs of two groups: those in charge of organized and largely hegemonic religions (essentially but not exclusively the Roman Catholic church and the several main Protestant sects) and the hegemonic social classes (initially the aristocracy and the educated bureaucratic class that served their needs while coveting their class privileges, and later the bourgeoisie proper). The music itself came into existence because the powerful individuals of both groups perceived its role in maintaining their power and the modes of self-definition on which it depended. Music was an acknowledged means of establishing caste: it was a nonverbal, emotive vehicle for establishing and preserving a level of prestige sufficient to authorize and therefore help stabilize position.

Prestige was related to sonority through hierarchies that effectively encompassed all musical sounds characteristic of the culture. (Here, to save time, I am lumping together the western regions of Europe, though, to be sure, regional cultural differences existed.) In the early-modern period of European history, music was clearly and increasingly differentiated from nonmusic, so that many of the sonorities regarded as music in the Middle Ages were increasingly labeled noise.[1] In fact, I have stated the issue backward, for in the Middle Ages the definition of what was music—and what was not—in the sounds people produced seems not to have been the burning issue it became in and after the early Renaissance. (The most notable exception was the Frankish church, which forced the codification of what we know as Gregorian chant in response to the political need of Frankish

43

rulers, beginning with Pepin and Charlemagne, "to strengthen their relationship with the Church of Rome."[2])

Prior to the Renaissance, the codification of music (the development of music theory, methods of composition, and performance practices) had been the concern of ecclesiastical writers and musicians. Now, however, codification became a concern in elite secular society as well. What for churchmen had been an issue of orthodoxy, in elite secular society was increasingly one of differentiating self and class. Music, that is, could help stabilize and authorize hierarchical social position and the various means by which it was gained and held. With the articulation of separate musics—especially by the codification of a distinct secular art music—the Platonic theory about the place of musical sound on the continuum of order-disorder was reinvigorated: the wrong kind of music, which would make you into the wrong kind of person, also carried no status; the right kind of music set you apart.[3] This equation, in which sound was one means by which society constructs itself, was applied in efforts to colonize music so as to produce only those meanings deemed supportive of one group's (and not the community's) aspirations.[4]

Among the lower social orders in Europe, by contrast, music seems to have existed, not as a separate sonoric entity, but as a ubiquitous phenomenon that benefited communities by defining and stabilizing their socio-cultural locus and intersubjectivity. I mean to suggest, not that sixteenth-century peasants failed to recognize the difference between the bagpipe and the bleating of their sheep, but that music, like bleating, was simply in the air. It was not art but life: musical sound was as important to peasants as the sounds their animals made, a reassurance of life and of both individual and communal identity.[5] Once those who maintained the primary means of social control had problematized music—by *systematically* separating it out from "noise" (or sound in general),[6] by categorizing it, for example, into amateur and professional varieties,[7] by separating art from craft, and especially by self-consciously articulating and valorizing music along class lines—the equation necessarily changed for everyone in the society.[8]

The socio-political question of art music thus centers on its differentiation from all other music and its absolute valorization. Art music as a genre was theorized and nurtured by Renaissance humanists as a sonoric homology of themselves; its socio-political role was to identify a particular type of person with itself.[9] To succeed at that, its sonoric equivalents necessarily had to encode two opposing principles that characteristically operate in such Western formulations: nature and culture (here a code word for social order). That is, the sonorities had to seem "natural" in their appropriateness to the class whose interests they represented. It was not enough for these sounds to be identified with a particular class; they had to be heard, essentially, as the only sounds possible. By this I mean that their "fit" with the ideal listener needed to be perfect, without ruptures, with no aural challenge to the listener's identity. These sounds thus had to represent order—that is, a highly particularized social order—as a sine qua non justification for the sound's existence. Nature and order: a circle needed to be squared.[10]

This chapter focuses on musical sonority as a sight (and site) for the construction of prestige in visual artifacts that represent music (and noise).[11] In the examples I discuss, actual music is silenced, rendered audible, if at all, only via memory. What is left is the visual assertion that sounds—or authorized sounds—are homologous with power where power itself is utterly aestheticized and where sound and power and the visible together conspire to mediate the production of prestige. I can be clearer about these homologies by moving to a discussion of a hybrid art form, the hyper-ornamentation of musical instruments.

THE MUSICAL GAZE AND THE TERRAIN OF SURVEILLANCE

During the sixteenth, seventeenth, and eighteenth centuries the viola da gamba (or bass viol) was played by professional musicians and aristocratic amateurs alike.[12] As a ubiquitous instrument of the highest social circles it seemed often to demand an ostentatious physical presence, and as such it was a favorite instrument for expensive manufacture and elaborate decoration. One such example is by the Hamburg master Joachim Tielke (Fig. 15). This is an instrument as important to see as to hear; indeed seeing it—without hearing it played—may produce in the viewer a response as powerful as that of the instrument's actual sound. (Tielke's many surviving viols are noted for their excellent sound, though the ideological need for elaborately decorative instruments challenged a maker's skill to preserve the full musical potential of the instrument.) In Tielke's viol, the viewer can witness musical perfection even without any sound; thus a musical sight occupies equal ground with musical sonority. This in turn confirms the political success of the exclusive use of certain kinds of music (and the appropriate instruments on which to make this music) to construct and maintain the courtly prestige always closely tied to power. Expressed in crass political terms, that is, the visual "threat" of music (the sight of it) is here as semiotically effective and unambiguous as that encoded in musical sound itself.

The instrument is made, not from European species of spruce and maple, as would typically be the case, but from rosewood, often imported from Brazil, and ivory, the quintessential exotic substance that—like rosewood—was a trophy of European expansionism. That is, the instrument's very materiality is a mute signifier of political subjection, just as its physical beauty is a disguise worn by subjection, to both construct and authorize prestige. This happens because of the raw materials from which it is fashioned and the degree to which they are worked,

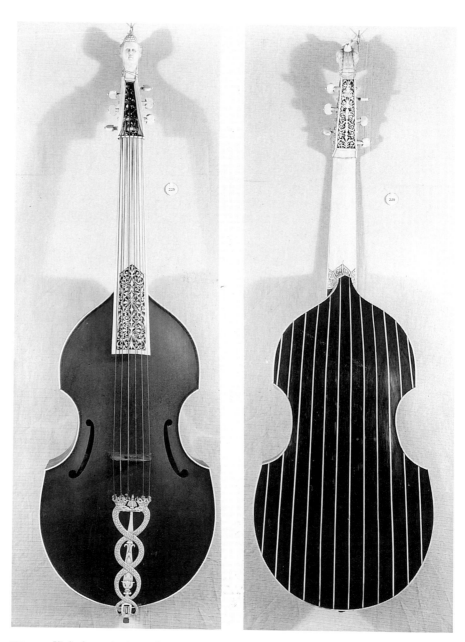

FIG. 15   Viola da gamba (1701) by Joachim Tielke. Brussels, Conservatoire Royal de Musique, Musée Instrumental. Photo copyright A.C.L., Brussels.

often with tortuous exactness and delicacy, as in the pierced ivory fingerboard and pegbox, the crowned-serpent tailpiece, and the ivory fillets paralleling one another across the back of the instrument. The worked surfaces encode an exponential expenditure of physical labor, skill, and artisanry (far surpassing that expected for instruments of lesser status), thus silently affirming the power of social control that makes possible the sonorities the viol actually produces.

The implications for the construction and maintenance of prestige suggested by this instrument are more directly characterized by another, equally famous but earlier, example of the luthier's art, a viola da gamba made by Gaspar Tieffenbrucker for King Henry II of France (r. 1547–59), probably around 1555, when Henry acknowledged Tieffenbrucker as "*nostre cher et bien amé*" (Fig. 16).[13]

When the instrument is played, held between the legs of the performer, the sight it provides, with its decorated front, is simultaneously natural and exotic: blooming plants, butterflies, and birds perched in laurel are paired with an oriental motif. The sounds made by the viol are thus preconstituted to some extent as a sight, without regard either to the specific piece of music being played or to the location of the performance. The viol's sonorities are predetermined as benign and harmonious, the ether of an exotic and utopian Platonic vision.[14]

But the benign and the harmonious, as aristocratic categories of hegemonic self-confirmation, are underwritten by more than their mere assertion as a sound and sight. While the listener-viewer experiences the double articulation of peaceful order, via sight and sound, the animal head surmounting the pegbox also listens and watches—or, more accurately, listens to the music but looks penetratingly at us. The spectator-listener, in other words, is being observed. On the back side of the pegbox a woman's head is set with equally attentive eyes and preposterously cocked ears that provide a salute to the sonorities being produced (two lions and a satyr playing panpipes are also represented). Like the pronounced stare of the decorative head on the front of the pegbox, however, the cocked and enlarged ears on the back signify more than the human sense of hearing; they encode surveillance. But here the surveillance is directed backward, that is, toward the performer, toward the expectation and confirmation of order inscribed in socioculturally authorized musical sonorities. Music here is articulated, not as an activity of calm leisure, a momentary, pleasurable escape from heavier responsibilities, but as an organized experience that reconstitutes worldly responsibilities into an aesthetics of eternal vigilance.

This helps explain the otherwise apparently comic use of similar gigantic ears in period engravings, where what is at stake is not merely hearing but what is heard (Fig. 17).[15] The grotesque reification of hearing in the blind head in the center foreground of Abraham Bosse's engraving has gigantic ears that seem at

FIG. 16 Viola da gamba (c. 1555) by Gaspar Tieffenbrucker. Brussels, Conservatoire Royal de Musique, Musée Instrumental. Photo copyright A.C.L., Brussels.

FIG. 17   Abraham Bosse, *Hearing* (c. 1635), engraving. Paris, Bibliothèque Nationale. Photo: Bibliothèque Nationale, Paris.

once to hear *and* to see (for they are attached close to the eyes' normal position). What they hear (and what we see) is an ensemble at art music: peaceful, orderly, and familial—domesticated, elegant women, and worldly, cultivated men (their worldliness inscribed by their hats). Yet this chamber-music inscription of an aestheticized sonoric-social order is more than itself. It is a by-product of something else, simultaneously acknowledged and disguised. That is, it depends on the visual representation, in the tapestries on the back wall, of war and conquest, activities sonorically defined in each tapestry by the noise of the aristocratic cavalry trumpet. These images-within-the-image make the claim that Culture (advisedly uppercase) both comes from struggle and authorizes struggle even as it translates struggle into calm. The violence on the outside, in other words, makes possible the peace on the inside. Moreover, the refinement of the chamber-music scene is backed up not only by armed combat but by the redundancy of a key signifier, the fortress-château, replicated three times in the background: in each of the tapestries, as a two-dimensional "symbol," and as the "real thing" in a "three-dimensional" reference visible through the central window behind the sitters. The reiteration of the fortress-home as the site and sight of social, cultural, and domestic order is, in other words, the self-conscious articulation of the "peace" over which armed struggle occurs and which art music and class privilege simultaneously define and justify.

That the chamber-music scene disguises what it nevertheless acknowledges as its source is clarified in the engraving's two textual glosses, which together establish an alibi for the struggle on which the music depends. The languages are Latin and French, one ancient, the other modern, across whose histories civilization marched from the classical world to the early-seventeenth-century present. The Latin text at the left reads: "The lyre plucked by my nimble fingers delights me wonderfully, and the nightingale enraptures me with its sweet songs. But to me no harmony is ever more pleasing than the one that sings my praises with skillful art." The French text at the right reads: "Considering the infinite sweetness of musical sounds and their various harmonies, it is not without reason said that the harmony of the spheres sustains the universe." The Latin text builds to an acknowledgment of personal glory via nature imagery, while the citation's Latin verse inscribes Roman authority; and the French verse in its linguistic modernity nevertheless authorizes culture around the ancient Platonic ideal. The ideal modern world and the ideal ancient world are thus presented as interchangeable and built on models of cosmic (that is, universal) control.

But to return to Tieffenbrucker's viol, it is the scene on the back of the instrument that particularly interests me. As on the front, there is nature, namely the sword lily (fleur-de-lis), the attribute at once of the French royalty, the Holy Trinity, and the Virgin Mary. This is nature as politics, a conflation of church and state, though this conflation is more aptly established by looking at the decorative scheme as a whole. At the top are the characteristically ambiguous figures—both sacred and secular—of angels heralding with trumpets but functioning as attributes of worldly fame. They serve as a visual frame and a compositional pointer, helping to establish in the viewer's mind the importance of what is represented. (Precisely what they herald is unclear—St. Luke in the middle with the ox, his attribute,[16] floating on a cloud over the city of Paris, or both the man and the city?)

The presence of Luke, the gentle physician, provides mute testimony to the moral authority claimed by Henry II; at the same time, Luke's presence utterly transforms Henry's political actions. Although Henry II was in fact a rabid, bigoted Catholic and a political absolutist, ruthless, like many rulers of his time, toward his enemies, the absolutism ascribed to him here is paternal, civilized, even studious. The bookish contemplation of St. Luke runs directly counter to the acts of cruelty recorded during Henry's reign,[17] just as his alignment with the church was a means of helping him secure and maintain power.

The ground over which this figure looms—labeled Paris—is really the Île-de-France, the territories of the king together with his capital, all mapped, ordered, rationalized. The question is, how can one explain this seemingly crazy concatenation of a bird's-eye view and the musical instrument on which the scene is inscribed—the ultimate instrument of sixteenth- and seventeenth-century courtly art music?

Without question the image was neither accidental nor inappropriate in the eyes of its intended owner. The musical sounds that emanate from the viol, given its standard repertory during the period, were those that harmonized the power relations exercised by the courts. The wealth necessary to produce prestige was celebrated in such instruments, as in the importation of foreign musicians and composers to Europe's courts (the human analogue to the desire for and acquisition of precious rosewood and ivory); musician-composers were among the most traveled citizens of early-modern Europe. A particular conception of music played in metaphorical ensemble with the various combinations of wealth, power, and prestige: art music as order, as highest nature, as the aesthetization of political authority and action.

The two important visual constants in the decorations of the viol might be termed redundancy and excess. Regarding both, the meanings I have just suggested are oversubscribed, ingrained with such oversufficiency that they may not be questioned. This is evident in the profound materiality of the mapping of Paris and its environs, in its incredible detail of individual streets and buildings (more than two hundred are represented, some individualized) and of the cultivated fields outside the city's walls.[18] (What matters here is not the map's accuracy but rather its convincing appearance because of its overload of detail: it looks right, as opposed to being right. This effect is strengthened by the scene's being, not painted, but incorporated into the surface of the instrument as marquetry, a technical tour de force signifying the owner's command over those with specialized skills and his access to the rare and exotic materials from which the image is pieced together—access, in other words, to markets.) Perhaps more important to my line of argument, the impact of excess is further heightened by the conceit of locating the map on the back of a musical instrument. The singularity of placement manufactures prestige, even though decorations on the back of the instrument are almost always invisible, whether the instrument is being played or hung on a wall. In other words, the seeming illogic of producing an image that can rarely be seen has use value as an agent of prestige: it is another manifestation of excess, an invisible-visible metaphor of sound as the manifestation of the peaceable kingdom replicated in the map.

Redundancy is implicit in the label—Paris—suspended in the sky above the cityscape, for no contemporaneous European of consequence could ever doubt that identification. But here enters a central problematic of prestige: its maintenance against the inevitable, ubiquitous threat of time; and here, once again, music itself enters. The dialectics of prestige that inhere in music are highly troubling. Music *is* order, and that plays to the good. But music is also time, which threatens music's own decay and disappearance, all the more in a nonelectronic age. Musical sound (order) can be maintained only by constant physical action. When the bow stops, the strings cease vibrating and the sound stops; the instrument becomes a hollow, mute—but not meaningless—shell. "Paris" on the viol's back is an acknowledgment of fear created by the consciousness of time. The peasantry may have labored and played in the cycle of seasons; the aristocracy, by contrast, lived with a split consciousness at once circular and frighteningly linear. "Paris" is an epitaph to the survival of one's memory, once one's only trace is in the mind of one's successors. "Paris" is the accidental acknowledgment of death, an ironic acknowledgment of temporality, just as the celestial St. Luke encodes the hope of timelessness. Music confirms that humanism's victories played out in the arena of European power politics—order from staged disorder—are a doomed triumph set in the surviving competing dialectic of Christian conceptions of life in preparation for afterlife.

Indeed, the dialectic between earthly power, commonly attained through violence (usually more physical than metaphorical), and power's temporality, hence impermanence and failure, is incorporated deeply into the structure of this instrument. Between the instrument's front and back is the airspace of the resonating chamber. It is from this chamber that sound (and sonoric meaning) issue and from which sound (which means differently by its disappearance) disappears. This airspace is the symbolic locus, in other words, of that for which men strive. The visual assertions inscribed on the instrument's front and back rest, in effect, on nothing more solid than air. Nevertheless, these images are inscribed there precisely to render more permanent the socio-cultural meaning of art music once its sounds cease: seeing, in other words, takes over when there is nothing left to hear.

INVENTORIES OF SONORIC PLENTY
IN A CULTURE OF STARVATION

To pursue in greater detail art music's connection to power, I move to a painting by Jan Brueghel the Elder ("Flower" Brueghel, 1568–1625), an allegorical representation of the sense of hearing (Fig. 18), a subject this artist, and later his son, Jan the Younger (1601–1678), treated in similar fashion a number of times.[19] Jan

FIG. 18 Jan Brueghel the Elder, *Hearing* (c. 1617/18), oil on wood panel, 65 × 107 cm. Photo copyright Museo del Prado, Madrid.

Brueghel was the second son of Pieter Brueghel the Elder. He was admitted into the Antwerp painters' guild, the Guild of St. Luke, in 1597, when he was twenty-nine years old. As a painter he seems to have led a charmed life, rather like his friend and sometime collaborator Rubens. Indeed, he enjoyed considerable fame in his own lifetime, and he attained real wealth (he had owned six houses in Antwerp by about age fifty, and even the first was large). Much of his financial success lay in his appointment as painter to Archduke Albert and Archduchess Isabella beginning in 1609. His court privileges provided tax forgiveness and exemption from duties on paintings he sent abroad. So close was his relationship with Albert and Isabella that the archduchess herself was named godparent to Jan's youngest daughter.[20]

Brueghel's painting *Hearing* was produced near the end of the Twelve Years' Truce that interrupted more than forty years of religious and political warfare in the region—wars waged by the Spanish government, its puppets in Brussels, and its armies of occupation (Spanish and mercenary). These conflicts brought devastation to the southern region, now part of Belgium, and there is no question that the general population, or what was left of it, was thoroughly traumatized by the experience.[21] My interest in Brueghel's image has to do with the relationship between socio-political history and the visual representation of musical practices and musical sonorities.

The painting is a striking visual conceit built on an encyclopedic inventory of musical instruments set in an elaborate interior. In a side room modern-day musicians perform, while in the center foreground a nude woman plays the lute. Paintings-within-the-painting represent a concert of Muses, Orpheus charming the animals, and so on. (The stag makes allegorical reference to the sense represented, given the animal's acute hearing.)

My interest here, however, is chiefly the musical instruments, or, more precisely, their accumulation and placement. Most were used for contemporaneous art music, though some were just coming into fashion (in particular the various larger members of the violin family), and others were approaching decline (the lira da braccio in the center foreground). There is actual music making (notably, the chamber concert at the left), but more to the point, there is a surfeit of potential music, though the available sonorities encompass only music of high caste. There is the potential for considerable sonoric variety, but only for one kind of music.

Whether the inventory existed as one collection does not much matter, given the allegory of the image. In any event, only the richest and most musically interested court could have afforded all the instruments represented, and to my knowledge no inventory survives for the archducal court at Brussels. Despite the painting's allegorical charge, however, the musical instruments demand to be taken literally; they are painted with such precision, for example, that Brueghel must have worked from actual instruments; someone, in other words, had to own them. This fact is one of many that insist on the contemporaneous reality of this paradisaical scene.

Arguably, it is the object centeredness of the inventory that ultimately elicits the viewer's response, far more than the lip service paid to timeless myths in the paintings-within-the-painting and the striking female nude. Whoever owns these objects (in reality or by implication) enjoys wealth and power, both of which are masked and rendered aesthetic by the rich workings of the instruments' manufacture and also by their sonoric implication—the ethereal sounds of art music. Just who the owners are is established by the view through the triple archway of a Flemish landscape containing the Château of Mariemont, the favorite residence of the archdukes.[22]

Whoever commands the spaces delineated in the image controls a world of sound—not natural sounds, but the sounds of culture—for even the birds Brueghel painted are ones that can be "trained" to "speak." Nevertheless, the potential sound here includes more than music. There is the possibility of noise as well, for the image inventories hunting horns and birdcalls (lower right foreground), devices that have nothing to do with music. The sounds of these objects are authorized, however; they fit perfectly into the continuum of valorized sound that is envisioned. Ideologically, they produce sounds every bit as prestigious as those made on the legitimate musical instruments Brueghel painted. The birdcalls in a sense replace the natural sounds of animals, functioning, together with the hunting horns, as devices of the kill, the sign of men's control over and reordering of nature. These cultural objects simultaneously remind the viewer that only certain individuals *may* hunt (severe punishment was administered for poaching). The license to kill, in other words, is a sign and source of power (life and death in ubiquitous ironic linkage), all the more important in a society devastated by warfare, where agricultural production in some regions had dropped precipitously. The lowly birdcalls and the hunting horns are thus agents of prestige, fulfilling this role in close proximity to objects of profound sonoric and socio-historical difference, namely, military instruments, notably the guns and infantry drums (set beneath the harpsichord at the extreme left), whose sounds had echoed across the countryside, warning the Flemish peasantry of mercenary armies who viewed them and their possessions, especially their food stores, as ripe harvest. Brueghel makes no apology for these horrific reminders of the recent past. Indeed, they are treated as fully appropriate, even "natural," to the sonoric world defined here.

I want to digress briefly to two other paintings by this artist, the first his enormous *Allegory of Touch, Hearing, and Taste* (Fig. 19), which repeats the representation of the archducal château in the background. Here not musical instruments but foods are inventoried: the array on the table includes oysters, a lobster,

FIG. 19   Jan Brueghel the Elder, in collaboration with Peter Paul Rubens and Frans Snyders, *Allegory of Touch, Hearing, and Taste* (c. 1617/18), oil on canvas, 176 × 264 cm. Photo copyright Museo del Prado, Madrid.

and a terrine of peacock with the head, neck, and tail decoratively reassembled; and in the lower right foreground pastry, fruit, and, especially, dead game are heaped. It is as if some private Eden exists for this audience alone—the proceedings sanctioned by the ironic inclusion of the wedding feast at Cana as a painting-within-the-painting—and this in a land where all wild game had for several decades been the prey of soldiers, brigands, and the impoverished citizenry alike. The second painting, which represents the sense of smell (Fig. 20),[23] depicts a paradisaical garden where a nude Flora (?) sits at ease, unaware of our glance and comfortable in her total safety. This is a private, walled world where nothing foreign intrudes, a world of silence and sweet scent. The scent itself exists in such abundance that its excess is harvested—at the left in the background there is a vignette of perfume manufacture. (Flemish practicality thus combines ironically with the desire to create another variety of scent beyond that of flowers alone, a more magical, ethereal one, perhaps: a scent that, being a human product, is also a culture, just as the flowers themselves, while seeming natural, are the result of intense horticulture.) And as we know, perfume was a means by which the European aristocracy valorized the sense of smell. By dousing themselves with perfume,

FIG. 20   Jan Brueghel the Elder, *Smell* (c. 1617/18), oil on wood panel, 65 × 109 cm. Photo copyright Museo del Prado, Madrid.

they established their olfactory difference, for in an age when bathing was thought unhealthy, undoubtedly all people smelled much the same without the benefit of perfume.[24]

The smells in Brueghel's gardens were not those of the actual countryside, for in several regions of Flanders the rich pungency of ploughed earth and mowed hay had been replaced by the stench of death so recently that memory must still have been sharp. Only the skunk at Flora's feet marks antithesis, yet it is completely domesticated, a pet whose musky scent is never sprayed. Once again, the scene is not wholly fictional or imaginative. Indeed, it confirms that Brueghel entered the most privileged physical spaces, for his position as court painter gave him access to the botanical and zoological gardens of the archducal palace to study plants and animals[25] (just as the painting's possessor had privileged access to the sight of Flora's nudity—and, by analogy, to her sensual odor, given the valorization of desirable smells around which the painting is organized).

In *Hearing* (Fig. 18) Brueghel does not inventory all musical instruments of the time and place, as I have indicated, but only those instruments (and other sound-making devices) appropriate to the Spanish aristocracy. There may be a plethora of birdcalls and hunting horns, but not a single instrument represented was played by the Flemish peasantry, except the lute, used by all social classes.

There is no bagpipe, though the sounds of both the bagpipe and the hurdy-gurdy, an instrument of beggars, were nothing less than ubiquitous across the Flemish landscape. Few people heard harpsichords; fewer still heard double-manual (transposing) instruments like the one Brueghel represented (at the extreme left). Sonoric ubiquity was no guarantee of admittance to this painting's visual field; it was in fact a guarantee of exclusion.

Many different horns and birdcalls, fiddles and viols, and so forth are displayed in various sizes and shapes. Despite the excess and redundancy we see (and are invited to hear in memory), these are the sounds of an exclusive minority, yet they seem in their implied abundance to have colonized all musical sound. How could anyone looking at the painting even recall that the bagpipe exists? In fact, a non-privileged viewer-hearer would necessarily have had to stand in awe at the visual claims to sonority the painting asserts. These are sounds whose exclusivity of audience was a prime marker of difference. The painting would not have let a non-privileged viewer (were there one) in on the secret; rather, it would have informed him or her that a secret exists.

In this painting seven partbooks are open on as many music stands, referring to a complex bit of polyphonic art music. On the partbook nearest us is a dedication to Albert and Isabella of six-voice madrigals by the English Catholic composer Peter Philips, who was long active in the Spanish Netherlands.[26] The secular pleasures of the madrigals are effectively underwritten and sanctioned by the visual cantus firmus on a sheet of music in the center foreground under the lira da braccio (in Flemish art often the stringed instrument put into the hands of Apollo himself, as in Fig. 21). It is a canon whose incipit reads, "Beati qui audent verbum Dei" (Blessed are those who hear the word of God).[27] The musical sonorities and the order they encode affirm the "pacification" of the Spanish Netherlands under the protectorate of Albert and Isabella.[28] These sonorities, even in their silence, are here *seen* to drown out war and revolution and the cries of the dying. All the noise that led to this sonoric order and its visual inventory is transformed into the secular-sacred political concatenation "Beati qui audent verbum Dei," the tune to be played on the lira da braccio of Apollo, the god of the rational and the civilized—two mythic code words often, unfortunately, equivalent (with no pun intended) to what critical theory names instrumental reason.[29]

One more detail in Brueghel's painting must be accounted for: the numerous clocks and armillary spheres whose tickings, chimings, and turnings signal both change (time), and the field over which change occurs (space). Time in this painting may not suggest much to us, but general conceptions of time in Europe were not linear until the nineteenth-century Industrial Revolution, and timepieces were little more than objects of curiosity in the *cabinets de curiosité* of the rich.[30] In Brueghel's painting, there is a fetishization of time—different from that of the

FIG. 21   Hendrik de Clerck, *Apollo and Marsyas in a Mountainous Landscape,* oil on copper,
43 × 62 cm. Amsterdam, Rijksmuseum. Photo copyright A.C.L., Brussels.

vanitas paintings of the Dutch seventeenth century, where a clock or, more commonly, a simple hourglass supposedly served as a reminder of the ubiquity of decay
and death. Here, because of the historical circumstances, time is not, as in vanitas
paintings, a parameter of universal human experience but a dimension of individual power and control. The consciousness of time is the ultimate mark of prestige in a society generally unaware that time operates, not in circular fashion, but
in a straight line, and that in linear time the world may be explained by its sounds,
all of which are to be increasingly controlled and only a few of which are to constitute the markers of those whose actions in turn control time.

   Historically, the nude woman near the painting's center has been identified as
both Venus and Euterpe, with Venus the favorite, in part on account of the Cupid-
like boy beside her.[31] I would suggest, however, that her identity is ultimately
ambiguous. Logically, we would expect Euterpe, given the musical theme of the
painting and Euterpe's appropriateness to the general subject of hearing. Ideologically, however, Venus may be better. If I am right that the painting is not so
much about hearing as about what we *ought* to hear, then both Venus and Euterpe
encode something worthwhile. In looking back at us looking at her, the woman

constitutes herself as a sight in a painting otherwise ostensibly about sound. And the sight is one intended to give pleasure, for though she actually plays the lute (or so we assume), the instrument and her actual playing are hidden from view. What matters more is the pleasure and drama afforded by her white skin, all the more striking in a setting of dark objects—notably the framing device of the Turkish carpet surrounding her and setting her off from everything else.

To the degree that her identity is ambiguous in a painting where virtually every other object can be pinned down and properly identified, she offers compensation for the reification of culture that is inscribed in the positivism of piles of instruments that make no sounds but nevertheless signify a hierarchy of sound. She offers such a compensation at the cost of her own reification. In a sense she becomes nature, the woman analogue to the stag beside her, an animal, here encoding hearing, that presumably listens not for pleasure but for survival, though we are invited to think that this is not the case. Given the realities of the hunt, the stag who senses (hears) danger constitutes nature fleeing culture. It seems to me that the nude woman is also constituted as nature or, perhaps better, as an intermediary between nature and culture: an Eve, but one holding a lute. In the seventeenth century the lute was a common attribute of procuresses and prostitutes, who carried the instrument with them into public houses as a mark of their profession.[32] Venus or Euterpe or whoever she might be is, in other words, if not explicitly a whore, at least a promise of male pleasure, itself regulated within this perfect order of sound. Both sides of the street are being walked here; the signifier floats. In the end, Brueghel's allegory of hearing fails to map this human sense as something universal, hence natural, or simply biological. Instead, hearing is rendered cultural, and radically historical, whatever the painter's intentions. For only certain sounds are available to be heard, and they are the sounds of a world organized and valorized for the benefit and honor of the few.

Femininity itself is already the effect of the whip. The liberation of nature would be to abolish its self-fabrication. Glorification of the feminine character implies the humiliation of all who bear it.

Theodor W. Adorno,
Minima Moralia

4

SOCIAL ORDER AND THE DOMESTIC CONSUMPTION OF MUSIC

(The Politics of Sound in the Policing of Gender Construction)

THIS CHAPTER TURNS to a new issue, musical consumption, in a different place and time, England in the eighteenth century. Indeed, the remainer of the book chiefly concerns English musical culture, starting in the eighteenth century and ending at the turn of the twentieth.

What is it one "consumes" when one "consumes" music? What is the relationship of this consuming to the construction of personhood, that is, to identity established on the basis of nation, class, and gender? What is the function of consumption, for the performer or auditor, of privatized, domestic music? How should the consumption of this music be philosophically theorized and morally evaluated in comparison with that of public music? What are the social and cultural consequences of maintaining or blurring the boundaries between private and public, domestic and worldly, amateur and professional, native and foreign, female and male musical production and consumption? These questions, of considerable interest to the English upper classes in the eighteenth century, were addressed by numerous writers of philosophy, aesthetics, sermons and moral tracts, educational treatises, and courtesy and conduct literature; they even crop up in novels and verse.[1] The stakes involved the very possibility of Englishness, defined by and for an elite, in light of a cultural practice about which enormous anxiety existed. The appetite for music in England was great; the fear of satisfying that appetite was perhaps still greater. The issue hinged, one way or the other, on properly theorizing what was available for consumption and the conditions under which consumption might take place.

The consumption of music has to be understood in light of the several definitions of music itself—interlocking and mutually mediating but inevitably dialectical and different. First, and most obvious, music comprises certain phenomena experienced as sound via the sense of hearing. Second, in Western high culture music refers to notated "instructions" for producing such sounds. Third, and here the story becomes more complex, music is a sight, a richly semantic visual phenomenon. It is a sight in performance, thus an embodied and interactive, hence social, practice (except when performed for the self, out of the hearing of others). It is an activity subject to the gaze, not least because music, both as social practice and sonority, was thought to possess sensual power. It was understood to act with dangerous immediacy on the sensate body. The "musical" gaze was supercharged with sexuality, producing an "interest" simultaneously encoded with pleasure and anxiety. Music as a sight and a sound together, united in performance prior to the advent of recording technology, cannot be fully understood except in this conjunction.

According to a fourth definition, closely related to the third, music is a potential but *un*realized practice, specifically and only a sight, but one nonetheless semantically rich: musical furniture as an accoutrement of domestic, private space, without regard to whether it was actually played or, if played, how often and how well. Fifth, and last, music was conceived as an abstract subject of the philosophical and mathematical discourse—hence part of formal and informal education—that attempted to sort out the nature of all nature. Discussions ranged from attempts to articulate music's proper place in society, citing sources ancient to modern and often turning on the question of ethics, to pseudo-scientific accounts of Western musical authority based on detailed measurements of intervals and such, with acknowledged debts to ancient Greek music theory, that fetishized number.[2] Here I begin my effort to sort out the question of musical consumption, starting with the abstract and moving toward concrete practice. I lay out the bare bones of these complicated issues only for the English upper classes, since the story was theorized quite differently for the lower social orders.

MUSIC AS SCIENCE: THE VALORIZATION OF SILENCE AND THE FEAR OF SOUND

How men and women approached music and its part in forming their character and identity were strikingly different, and the subjects of endlessly reiterated discussion. Men were provided scant encouragement to study music as a performed practice; instead they were invited to approach it cognitively as a "science" concatenating philosophy and mathematics.[3] Music's value for men was theoretical:

Music is a *science* established on the most sublime parts of mathematical truths; its *theory* founded on the doctrine of *Proportion;* on the most *wonderful,* though the most *simple* and *few Principles;* the knowledge of which, fills the enquiring mind with the most transcendent pleasure, and admiration of the wisdom of the Creator, who *"hath filled all things with good."* [4]

Music in this typical account was valued as pure abstraction, the absence of the very sound for which music might be thought to exist. John Aubrey noted that "statics, music, fencing, architecture and bits of bridges are all reducible to the laws of geometry." [5] To connect a mathematics of music to the geometries of civil engineering and fighting, as Aubrey and many other writers among his contemporaries do, is to connect a nonsonoric "scientific" music to the exclusive male domain of state power and its politics. Through this connection music justifies its existence as a masculine and mental practice even as it makes claims to a radical utilitarianism. Music is valued, not for aesthetic reasons or for its inherent mathematical logic, but as a means to an end: it is a tool for domination (a subject to which I shall return in the following chapter with respect to connections between mathematics, Enlightenment music theory, and colonialism). To operate most effectively, it must be silent. Indeed, music's sound is a threat to the instrumentalized variety of reason, to power, and to men. Put differently, in the texts to which I refer, musical practice—the actual making of music, the sonorities produced in performance—is consistently gendered: as Woman, as Other, and quite often as enemy.

Ambivalences about music became especially serious once it was actually performed. Frequently the target of concern was music's relation to the body and, by implication, the mind and soul. Music's impact on the body was characterized as a moral question, which in truth operated as a smoke screen for anxieties about identities grounded in nation, class, and gender insofar as these might be construed as qualities of the body. This is a far more important matter than a theorization of a "science" of music in the absence of musical sound. To most people with musical interests, music on paper, so to speak, is not really music at all and is, in any but small doses, profoundly boring. Musical "science"—acoustics, scale systems, harmonic relations, and so forth—is not music. So although writers may have urged upper-class men to consume music in an abstract contemplative, nonperformative, and silent act, there is little evidence to suggest that many did so, despite the enormous body of literature devoted to the topic. [6] The ideal of a wholly "intellectual" music was fundamentally unrealized, whereas, as one would expect, actual music was produced and consumed. But here I must emphasize again the extraordinary attention to performed music and its performers, one that revolved around music's necessarily embodied state. To regulate the relation of music to the body profoundly concerned both men and women, though for different reasons. The danger of music lay in its putative power to destabilize virtually every social relation, notably including relations between men and women, one social class and another, England and the Continent, Europeans and racial Others, and so on.[7]

Music as a discursive practice was entirely meaningful. The difficulty ensued from the inability to stabilize and predict its meanings with certainty, though not for want of trying. Sacred music was more approved than secular, yet even sacred music might be papist in its appeal, depending on its sounds and associations. Secular music might be very English and masculine (Squire Western in *Tom Jones* liked his Handel, small irony, but especially his English pop tunes[8]), always to the good, but native English music might also be feminine (feminizing) and textually immoral.

One always needed to keep a sharp ear for foreign music, commonly theorized as the sonoric agent of sedition and, if French or Italian, seduction (of men as well as women). This at least was the lament of xenophobes as different in period and concern as John Dennis and Lord Chesterfield,[9] neither of whom could apparently conceive of Italian music or musicians separately from foppishness and sodomy and the degenerating effects of both on anyone who came within sound and sight of the practitioners, whether on the English stage (Dennis) or on the Grand Tour (Chesterfield).

Yet for many writers, so long as music was consumed passively and in public, the only substantive issue was the quality of the music itself. Everything turned on the distinction between public and private, on the one hand, and between passive listening and active performance, on the other. Debate most commonly ensued once music entered the home's private space, where a first distinction must be made between the professional musician and the amateur upper-class "homeowner."

Music professionals entered the home as performers or, more commonly, as music teachers hired to teach daughters. The practice of music teaching produced an immensely complicated and conflicted discourse centering largely on threats to a daughter's virtue, and hence her father's authority, by a social inferior who commonly was also a foreigner.[10] Professionals who entered the home as performers were generally hired for the occasion, an unproblematic transaction so long as a barrier was maintained between performers and those who hired them. Propriety, in other words, was maintained when the structured difference between production and consumption was mirrored by the structured difference between the social classes of the patron and those he hired. The moment a personal relationship was formed, as sometimes occurred (Dr. Charles Burney being an especially famous example),[11] all bets were off. Because the professional musician was a laborer, fraternizing with him carried social risk. Quite apart from the myriad difficulties of the music in question, whether sacred or secular, English or foreign, and so on, there was, then, the matter of who was making the sounds.

Yet the issue is not settled once professionals are kept out of domestic surroundings. The question of amateur performers demanded theorization. If the performer was a woman, amateur public performance was extraordinarily difficult in that public "display" directly challenged the very category "woman": it was public, not domestic, and active, not passive; it deflected attention from her father or husband; it opened up the question who was managing the domestic economy while she performed, and so on.[12]

Musical education for women, generally accepted as a requisite of class position, typically began during childhood. But whereas an ideal musical education for men was theoretical, that for women was largely practical, aimed at producing performance abilities on keyboard instruments, in particular. Thus John Essex, writing in 1722 from a typical male point of view, produced a list of instruments appropriate to women, beginning with keyboard instruments, together with a list of those that were not (instruments with phallic associations were viewed as contaminating):

> The *Harpsichord, Spinet, Lute* and *Base* [*sic*] *Violin,* are Instruments most agreeable to the Ladies: There are some others that really are unbecoming the Fair Sex; as the *Flute, Violin* and *Hautboy;* the last of which is too Manlike, and would look indecent in a Woman's Mouth; and the *Flute* is very improper, as taking away too much of the Juices, which are otherwise more necessarily employ'd, to promote the Appetite, and assist Digestion.[13]

The connection between music and female domesticity is repeatedly made in this literature, as in an anonymous pamphlet, circa 1778, that urges musical training even for girls showing little propensity for it, not so they can become performers per se, but rather so they can "amuse their *own family,* and for that domestic *comfort, they* were by Providence designed to promote."[14] The Reverend John Bennett encouraged musical training for women, defining its benefits as increasing happiness, inspiring tranquillity, and harmonizing the mind and spirits, during those "*ruffled* or *lonely* hours, which in almost every situation, will be your lot."[15] Bennett's comment refers obliquely to the limitations of women's roles in upperclass society. As Robert Burton put it in *The Anatomy of Melancholy* in 1621, "Vertuous women should keepe house"; this precept was echoed 160 years later by

Henry Home, Lord Kames: "It is the chief duty of a woman, to make a good wife."[16]

Yet the very thing a woman was expected to learn, namely how to perform, was the subject of intense anxiety, involving the question of privacy but much more besides. A woman invariably performed among family and friends; she was cautioned to treat her performance "Carelessly like a Diversion, and not with Study and Solemnity, as if it was a Business, or yourself overmuch Affected with it."[17] Ironically—and impossibly—the common social ideal demanded that she perform with the utmost passivity. To be sure, the anxiety immanent in injunctions of this sort suggests that women by no means universally agreed to the limits defined for them, but not for lack of awareness about what was expected. Erasmus Darwin, among many others, thus unambiguously recommended that a woman restrict the development of her talents so as not, in effect, to compete with her husband in the public eye:

> It is perhaps more desirable, that young ladies should play, sing, and dance, only so well as to amuse themselves and their friends, than to practice those arts in so eminent a degree as to astonish the public; because a great apparent attention to trivial accomplishments is liable to give suspicion, that more valuable acquisitions have been neglected.[18]

By contrast, if the performer was a man, his identity was at risk precisely as regards that component most central to himself and all the men who might view him, his sexuality. Indeed, the discussions about male upper-class music making are legion, and virtually none offer unambiguous encouragement. Most writers judge the practice as a waste of time; the few who grudgingly allow music, and the fewer still who defend it, invariably authorize it only as a leisure exercise, a passing fancy to which no great importance should be attached.[19]

The delight and gratification of making music depend absolutely on the difference of sonority from its opposite, silence, and the signification of silence. Yet music's pleasures are more than the experience of sound as such. When we consume music, we also consume a sight—embodied, active, and situated, all qualities that mediate musical meanings. The result is the consumption and simultaneous production of identity. Writers of the period commonly urged the man who would be a musician to practice his art "at his private recreation"—a tacit acknowledgment of shame. The sight of men making music was consistently disparaged. As Chesterfield put it: piping or fiddling (his words) "puts a gentleman in a very frivolous, contemptible light."[20]

The domestic production, hence consumption, of music—specifically, if problematically, sanctioned for upper-class girls and women—was among the "accomplishments" that made females fit for the marriage market and thereafter fit reflectors of their husbands' station. The principal function of the accomplishments in the domestic economy was containment. Erasmus Darwin, one of many writers on the subject, captured this idea succinctly. The accomplishments serve "the purpose of relieving each other; and of producing by such means an uninterrupted cheerfulness of mind; which is the principal charm, that fits us for society, and the great source of earthly happiness."[21] That is, the accomplishments, by their number and variety, keep women content, allowing them to turn from one to another so as to avoid boredom. The tacit corollary is that women ought engage nothing sufficiently important to make them a danger to men either by interfering in men's affairs or by exercising their sexuality outside tightly prescribed limits. Indeed, one of the great fears about music as regards women was its impact on their sexuality. Many writers worried that musical education encouraged females to overstep the bounds of modesty and deference.[22] Indeed, the potential effects of music were considered profound:

> Our Music has become so totally changed. It is not now sought as a repose for the mind after its fatigues, but to support its *Tumults*,—not to impress the *Delights* of *calm reason,* or prevail on us to *listen* to the *charmer;* but she must leave the purity of her *own Nature,* and by diverting herself of *Simplicity,* force us to *admire,* not *feel,* and yield to *astonishment* and *absurdity,* instead of *chaste Beauty* and delight.

The passage both inscribes and sanctions a split between mind and body, reason and emotion, men and women. The fear of music is a fear of feminine eruption, of a musical "she" who ceases to charm us, who in effect denaturalizes "herself," losing "her" simplicity, becoming complex, astonishing, and more like a man. The argument depends on a preconceived musical ideal. Since music and women are conflated in eighteenth-century English culture—since art, that is, is fundamentally feminized—it follows that music, like women, should be simple ("natural"). Music is understood to be of the body—feelings—not of the mind, though in its simplicity it might appeal to the mind for just this (throwaway) quality. The writer continues: "Let our daughters . . . [not] ever attempt any thing but *select pieces* of *familiar, easy, simple* construction, such as may delight the *ear* of their friends, and contribute to improve their own *Hearts* by directing its influence to the proper object."[23]

Leisured women had time on their hands, and men must see to it that it was spent appropriately. For men time was developmental, lived socially; for women time was nondevelopmental, lived familially. Activities viewed as nondevelopmental and expressive of stationary time, such as music, were peripheral to men's lives and fundamentally improper for them. But for females such activities were

considered *by men* appropriate and important, as delineators both of gender difference and of gender hierarchy. Music helped produce an ideologically correct species of woman and, in men's eyes, contributed to social stability by keeping women
in the place men had assigned them.

A well-bred woman who took music seriously constituted a threat to social
boundaries. Accordingly, most courtesy and conduct literature charged women to
view music as but a trivial pursuit, like virtually everything else they did apart
from bearing and raising children. The trivialization of women's activities, to men
and women alike, was essential to maintaining a status quo based on gender hierarchy. It can be argued that music nonetheless created a compensatory space for
women, one in which to engage in a private action for their own pleasure and thus
to assert their own agency, however circumscribed. But under these circumstances
music was a compensation whose negative dialectics were constantly reasserted.
There was no escaping the functional reality of a woman's music making: it demonstrated her accomplishment as a positive reflection, not on her, but on her husband, and it required her to restrain any acknowledgment of musical devotion (her
attachment to music for her own sake) and also to hide—or limit the development
of—her talents, almost as if they were family secrets. (I will return to this issue at
the end of the chapter.)

DOUBLE INSCRIPTION: PAINTING MUSIC FOR DOMESTIC WALLS

I have argued for an understanding of music in relation to its sound and sight
taken together, mediated by the contemporaneous "philosophies" about music
then enjoying currency. The only effective way to link sound and sight as they
were experienced and understood in past society is by reference to music as a
subject in visual art, painting in particular, though we so do at the ironic expense
of musical sonority as such. I stress painting because of all the visual discursive
media of the eighteenth century it was easily the most important. It had much
greater prestige than drawings or prints—the sums of money spent on commis-
sions were relatively large, especially when weighed against the earnings of ordinary workers (though to be sure there was no unified and uniformly paid working
class prior to the Industrial Revolution). The discursive stakes of painting were
recognized and noncontroversial as such, one sign of which was the high degree of
conventionality established as the sanctioned mode of expression. (Conventions,
the grammar and syntax of any practice, work as devices of cultural stabilization
and internalized self-discipline. Indeed, when they are violated, the destabilizing
effects of the gesture have been loudly debated, whatever the discursive practice.)

The musical images that interest me were displayed in the home. Accordingly, they replicated in paint the very setting of which they were a part. Thus the painted musical subject formed a double inscription; it was a two-dimensional sign, enjoying spatial privilege on domestic walls, of a three-dimensional sign (the musical instrument) that likely resided in the same spatial enclosure and of the practices that may or may not have occurred within and on that sign (musical performance). The intentionality inherent in choosing musical props for paintings should not be downplayed; it necessarily results from a recognition of music's importance as a signifier of identity.

The signifying function of domestic music consumption in visual representation can be examined in a variety of topoi, especially single and group portraits. But I want to begin with pictorial ephemera, namely, the fashion plate (Fig. 22). Artist-illustrators like Robert Dighton produced these images, intended for reproduction, as sources of information on current seasonal fashions for wealthy women. The pictorial emphasis, as one would expect, is on the dresses, but the semantic valorization of the gowns themselves is inevitably established not only by the surroundings of the model wearing the gown but also by the narrative these surroundings imply. Fashion plates are *about* consumption: they are to be visually consumed in an act producing desire, which precedes another, more material, act of consumption, buying. And in many such plates, music is the sign that identifies and valorizes the (consuming) woman, a composite of feminization established both visually and, by implication, sonorically.

The correspondence is profound between Robert Dighton's fashion plate and Johan Zoffany's elaborately decorative portrait of the Armstrong sisters (Fig. 23), though several decades separate the two images. The state of excess in the latter is especially striking, for the aging sisters are overdressed, as though immobilized by drapery that virtually renders their bodies irrelevant, their plain faces an unfortunate distraction from their finery. Their music making provides the visual excuse—and apology—for their immobility. Music aestheticizes the social condition it simultaneously masks. In fact, the two women do not make music, nor do they even promise to do so. Instead music is an impossible and silent icon, here of consumption, all the more excessive by its literal absence: musically speaking, what are the women doing? The English guitarist appears to play, but the sister with a book in her lap—apparently a singer—shows no hint of breaking into song. Nor does she accompany her sister on the two-manual harpsichord. Instead, she sits as if helping her sister to tune but surely does not do so, given the high octave string she engages. Nor do the women address each other, as would be necessary for an ensemble to occur.

The situation is even more interesting because Zoffany himself was not only a music lover but a musician. He knew how to paint musicians. Yet this image has nothing to do with literal music, though everything to do with what underwrites

FIG. 22   Robert Dighton, fashion plate for February (from the series *The Twelve Months*), mezzotint, gouache, and watercolor, 38.7 × 28.6 cm. Minneapolis, The Minneapolis Institute of Arts, The Minnich Collection.

FIG. 23   Johan Zoffany, *The Armstrong Sisters, Mary and Priscilla* (late 1760s), oil on canvas, 78.7 × 91.4 cm. Private collection. Photo courtesy of Leger Galleries Ltd, London.

musical consumption in English domestic life. The picture is a lie masquerading as truth; dialectically, however, it is a picture in which, ironically, the lie *is* the truth of music's relation to women and gender construction. Music's present absence in musical props anchors the Armstrong sisters' identities, in a time when the role of music in women's lives marks their inferiority. Music plays an important role, but its sonorities only accompany the nonsonoric structures the music helps ensure: music, the sonoric medium, in English private life serves as a tool that, by its consumption, silences.

One sort of family group picture that enjoyed considerable currency in eighteenth-century England, the so-called conversation piece, often incorporated music in pictorially notable ways, either in indoor settings (as in Figs. 23–24) or, less commonly, outdoors (see Fig. 25), but always in elaborate surroundings that establish the expenditure of considerable sums on finery and furnishings. At this juncture I only want to make a few points about Figures 24 and 25, by no means exhausting what is interesting and significant about them. The first, attributed to the painter Henry Pickering, is characteristic for the incorporation of a large two-manual harpsichord as the principal piece of domestic furniture at which, also

FIG. 24   Attributed to Henry Pickering, *A Family Gathered around a Harpsichord,* oil on canvas, 101.6 × 127 cm. Private collection. Photo courtesy of Leger Galleries Ltd, London.

characteristic, a young woman sits to play, though judging from her hand position on the keyboard—extremely relaxed—one has doubts as to the musical event. What needs to be asked is, Why this instrument?

To answer this question requires first that something be said about the politics of consumption in mid-century England in relation to the conversation picture. These images were commissioned by families economically located in the upper classes. Despite their typically modest size (this one measures 50 by 40 inches) conversation pictures were ordered up by parvenus to represent their newfound status in idealizations that seemed to support a belief in established pedigree. But members of the landed and secure aristocracy commissioned them as well.[24] It is not easy to detect stylistic differences in the representations intended for one group or the other. Nonetheless, the size of these images made them especially suitable for the modest-sized (not to say small) houses of the newly wealthy. For this group such musical props as double-manual harpsichords, like the large elaborately framed paintings-within-the-painting (much larger than the conversation pictures in which they were included), were signs of wealth, refined taste, and accomplishment.

The importance of the large double-manual harpsichords, which occupy considerable compositional space, looms in the closed world of the picture frame in ways that do not necessarily translate into reality. That is, the instruments may have little to do with familial musical tastes and practices as such. In any event, we seldom know enough about the sitters to be certain. What we do know about the harpsichord represented in Pickering's painting, however, is that its presence plays off pictorial and textual conventions from Plato onward that associate music, or certain kinds of music, with a nonmusical metaphoric harmony that is at once cultural, social, familial, wealth based, and prestigious. This *signifiance* is encoded without regard to whether any music was ever made on the instrument here used as prop—as I have shown elsewhere, once musically trained and even accomplished girls became women and married, they commonly closed up their harpsichords more or less for good.[25]

One other detail requires comment: the sitters' hand gestures. The iconic value of the image centers around the women and their *purported* musicality. The painting's three women are literally framed by men, the father on the right and a son, perhaps, on the left, both of whom gesture elaborately, and unnaturally, toward the women so as to draw our attention to them. Such gesturing reduces the women's status as people and hence diminishes the women themselves in relation to the men—the gesture is arguably almost rude—at the same time that it increases the women's status as signs reflecting on the men. The women are decorative in every possible way: as musicians (the mother holds a music book in her lap so as to allow her other daughter to look on and sing to the harpsichord's accompaniment); as elaborately, fashionably dressed consumers of familial wealth; and as doers of nothing. It is not accidental—indeed, convention virtually demands—that the painter place in the seated daughter's lap a bouquet of flowers and a comb. Her role is her beauty. She is decorative, like the flowers in vases on the wall. And is it any wonder that none of the sitters appears to get any pleasure from this gathering—the faces are typical for the genre—their seriousness, to put the best light on it, confirming the stakes of the representation? Conversation pieces are rarely celebrations; they are fundamentally aestheticized, domesticated polemics, which, ideally, the visual consumer of the image will internalize.

ARTICULATED SILENCE

A Frenchified conversation picture by Joseph Nollekens (Fig. 25), typical of a number he produced,[26] repeats everything contained in the image attributed to

FIG. 25   Joseph Francis Nollekens, *Conversation Piece* (1740), oil on canvas, 127 × 101.5 cm.
New Haven, Yale Center for British Art, Paul Mellon Collection.

Pickering, though with a fundamental difference. In this instance architecture and the Continental landscape take over, with music incorporated via the small harpsichord as well as the classical musical scene in relief on the large urn. The very decorativeness, falseness, and even preposterousness of the image articulate a more aristocratic lineage. The painting seems to record real people, but in a setting that cannot make up its mind between Arcadia and the Roman Forum. Its unabashed French flavor likewise suggests a family certain about its position—in politics, nonetheless, more likely Whig than Tory!—for to valorize the Continental carried the risk of censure for lack of patriotism; only the well established could be expected to buck this dynamic. But what of the music?

As a literal event it makes no sense; people did not characteristically tote harpsichords outdoors; it would disturb the tuning, the sound would be diminished by the setting, and in any case, what would be the point of it? Indeed, Nollekens produced a conceit sufficiently compelling to master the apparent disadvantage of an "event" that makes no sense. But senselessness may be just the point, one that deeply informs certain kinds of consumption, including music. The act of moving the music outdoors tacitly argues for the inconsequentiality of music and hence its value. It is a nothingness—nonmaterial, nonproductive—and thereby a sign of status. The production-consumption of nothing argues better than anything else for the wealth, status, and power of this family.

Once again it is no accident that even with this group of highly privileged sitters, there is no joy, no pleasure registered. As I suggested earlier, this is not to say that music is an anti-emotional, rationalized exercise; rather it is a sign of grim-faced harmony. The scene as a whole, including the allusion to Apollonian classicism in the lyre on the urn, is Plato's utopia calmly realized. Nonetheless, the social harmony thus enacted, under whose "protection" the arts flourish, demands that one's guard never be let down. The paterfamilias may gesture toward his fake garden—its design borrowed from Versailles—thereby making sure we notice, but the gesture itself argues that the visual feast we are invited to consume, including whatever musical echoes it may incorporate, is not entirely secure.

The wind blows hard, so the Boucher-like tree at the center informs us, though its full force is blocked by the fortress portico of the great house. The sky, quite English, is at once sunny and storm threatened. There is much to be kept at bay. What, then, is the man's gesture? In fact, he does not precisely ask us to look at the scene behind him, as I first suggested; if he did, we might expect to see a hand gesturing, palm upward, as in Pickering's image. Oddly, Nollekens's sitter makes a gesture that seems to ask for silence; but if this is so, who or what is silenced? Is it the wind, the ancient sign of change? Is it control over nature itself that his incongruous move articulates? (The gesture is characteristic of those de-

scribed in contemporaneous manuals on body carriage and taught by dancing masters; it was designed to establish visually and publicly one's social position—to
articulate, via grace, its radical opposite: power.[27]) Whether he or his daughter's
music—she a reflection of his power—can still the metaphorical winds, as Orpheus charmed the animals, remains an open question.

But clearly his gesture incorporates our own consumption of the painting's
look, just as every person in the painting is defined by the sonoric harmonies the
harpsichord purports to deliver. The viewer's consumption of the image, like the
consumption of the metaphoric sonorities by the painting's sitters, overdetermines
human identities for the simple but essential reason that identities—theirs and
ours—determine the social order. Musical consumption in eighteenth-century
England—from which we can generalize well beyond both place and time—was
a feminine and feminized practice that served as the visual metaphor for the tranquillity and nurture possible in a culture that constructed the feminine, and the
women confined by that construction, as Other—enemy and threat—as well as
beloved. In this light there can be little wonder at the irony that the most perfect
music was neither heard nor practiced but painted or that the women in paintings
consistently fulfill roles not in their own interest but in that of their men, in whose
image they are, ideally at least, created. I have no way of knowing whether the
women in Nollekens's or Zoffany's paintings were as severe as they are represented;
I do have some idea why they were painted that way, whose interests it served, and
whose anxieties it might have assuaged. There is very little to suggest that English
attitudes toward music were very different from English attitudes toward women,
especially since the two were so conflated; this conflation determines why the consumption of the proper look of both, in a culture of the gaze, was fundamentally
important.

REFUSAL

I hesitate to end on this grim note; indeed, were I to do so, I would have neglected
to acknowledge the existence of another sort of visual representation that mediates the account so far provided. I want to turn briefly to drawing, with its
social "rules" and visual codes governing representation that differ from those of
painting. Drawing allows representation of what in painting is unrepresentable.
The issue hinges on the important distinction between the private and the
(semi)public.

A painting, even when hanging in a house, was never a totally private image,
though in the terms I have discussed it served familial interests first and foremost.

The homes of the elite were invariably visited by many people, notably people sharing the approximate status of the residents. Paintings were important for what they projected to these viewers about their owners—their aesthetic tastes, their wealth, what they held dear. But drawings were different. Some members of the upper classes collected them; a few even produced them. (By no means all drawings, in other words, were preliminary studies for paintings and hence intended principally for artists' eyes—the nineteenth-century taste for watercolors is a dramatic example, though watercolors were a less important phenomenon for the eighteenth century and for the subject matter I am considering.) For protection and efficient storage, drawings were kept in drawers or cartons, from which they could be taken at will to be looked at, shared, passed around. Compared with paintings they not only carried a lesser burden of prestige but also remained less bound to the demands and expectations for outwardly projected ideological correctness. In other words, the representational gap between ideology and practice (not wide, so far as I can determine), and between ideology and desire (often very wide indeed) could be narrowed, if not closed, in this medium.

What can be represented more readily in drawings than in paintings is a music for "purposeless" pleasure (Fig. 26),[28] performed by a woman for herself, so

FIG. 26   Lady Dorothy Savile, Countess of Burlington, *Woman at Harpsichord, with a Dog and a Cat,* pen and brown wash over pencil, 19.8 × 26 cm. Chatsworth, Kent, Devonshire Collection. Reproduced by permission of the Chatsworth Settlement Trustees. Photo: Courtauld Institute of Art, London.

that producer and consumer become one. Only the natural antipathy between a cat and a dog, rendered charming, intrudes on this momentarily pleasured space. If we realize that the image is by Lady Burlington, possibly sketching herself, the issue I am driving at becomes clearer. The drawing represents a woman's projection of her own musical activity. As such, it refuses to acknowledge male-prescribed functions of music for women, except one it cannot avoid: the advantage to men of music as a devourer of women's leisure time, a device for keeping women out of men's affairs. This aside, it cannot be denied that in this drawing a woman's pleasure is her own, and it is a pleasure imbued with symbolic agency. The sign Lady Burlington employs is the dog, which, despite the provocation about to be delivered by the cat, sits up to listen to the tune, perhaps to dance. In the history of Western visual representation, dogs are male (they are invariably so in seventeenth-century marriage portraits, where, as I noted in Chapter 1, they are metaphors of *fides,* fidelity) whereas, by contrast, cats are commonly gendered female (the supposed guarantee of their libidinous temperament). Lady Burlington, in other words, through her music exercises power over a male stand-in for her husband; she calls the tune. (That she might want to do so is hardly surprising given the well-known preference of her husband, Richard Boyle, 3rd Earl of Burlington, for the company of men, notably including George Frideric Handel.)

Lady Burlington's sketch of these two animals is visually striking and quite out of keeping with conventional representation. The dog, for centuries imbued with the familial symbolism of male control, here appears ineffectual and even silly, transfixed and immobilized by music, whereas the crouching cat, like the musician "facing" the dog, as if the lady's ally, prepares to take on a physically larger opponent. If this makes sense, then I must amend my comment about Lady Burlington's musician's pleasure: her playing is not wholly purposeless but expresses her desire to live her own life.

Drawings make clear, as paintings seldom do, that women's pleasure could be mutual, hence social. It might even occur outdoors and thus be subject to others' view (Fig. 27). More unusual, drawing allows the representation of the same sociability among men (Fig. 28), but in closed-in settings that emphasize the absence of observers and almost invariably hint of the comic, as though even in a drawing guilt and implicit shame about their musical proclivities required that musicians acknowledge—or pretend to acknowledge—the limitations of their seriousness. Samuel Pepys (d. 1703), who could appropriately stand in for practically any eighteenth-century male amateur in this respect, admitted to "being fearful of being too much taken with musique."[29]

Among the most affecting images of this sort are the few drawings that both preserve and valorize music in family groups, where affection and sociability intermingle in both the practice of music and the metaphoric harmony represented

FIG. 27   Paul Sandby, *Two Women at Music Seated under a Tree,* pen and watercolor, 22.7 × 16 cm. Windsor Castle, Royal Library. Photo copyright 1992, Her Majesty Queen Elizabeth II.

FIG. 28   John Hoppner, *Quartet,* pencil and gray wash, 24.8 × 33.2 cm. Whereabouts unknown.

(Figs. 29–30). In Figure 29 a mother cradles her child and the father looks closely on, while in the center foreground two young children play at tea and on the left two older daughters sing and play harpsichord, watched by a brother. At the rear by the hearth another man looks on, as witness or even intruder; perhaps he is an acquaintance, perhaps the eldest son, already living on his own. In the second drawing, the situation is much the same except that the ages are advanced; the parents are now grandparents and old. The warmth and affection in the two drawings is extraordinarily rare in contemporaneous paintings, whose purpose largely disallowed representation of affectional relations as such and whose conventions required tight control over practices like music that might exceed appropriate ideological boundaries.

The social danger such drawings articulate is triply contained, by the limited prestige accorded to drawings (and these are hardly by major artists), by their inaccessibility to viewing, and finally by their size. The drawings I have discussed are tiny, the largest being 11 by 17 inches, the smallest less than 9 by 7. Size matters; size means. The paintings discussed earlier are many times larger than these drawings. Their size is discursively emphatic, a rhetorical quality only in-

FIG. 29   Gavin Hamilton, *Family Scene*, pen and brown ink with gray wash, 21.6 × 27.9 cm. Whereabouts unknown.

FIG. 30   Samuel Collins, *Musical Party*, drawing, 28.9 × 43.2 cm. Whereabouts unknown.

FIG. 31   Sir Nathaniel Dance-Holland, *Musical Party,* pen and brown ink, 14 × 20.3 cm. Kensington, U.K., Sabin Galleries.

creased by the medium of oil paint itself—its ability to manifest color, texture, quality of light, and so forth. If paintings shout, drawings whisper. The practices and tastes these drawings represent, whether of affection or music, are unofficial—as any ideal and intended viewer from the period would unquestionably have understood. The values projected *cannot* be "stated" publicly, insofar as they valorize a radically oppositional formula for the identity and subjectivity that sustain both nation and class. Specifically, they organize intersubjectivity on a model marked by the culture as feminine, hence degraded.

The drawings I have considered exist in the company of a still more radical sort: images of nonfamilial groups, adult women and men together in private quarters for the purpose of making music (Figs. 31–32).[30] These minuscule images (each roughly 6 by 7 inches) are, however, quite different from each other. The first example is perhaps about what we might expect; a man sits at a keyboard, perhaps accompanying a singing woman, to whom others look and listen. One visual element is striking. The music acts as a gravitational pull on everyone present. The left side of the drawing is heavy with dark, fast pen strokes delineating the musician(s) and immediate audience. The right side, distinctly lighter in tone and pen stroke, shows two women in very different stance. The one nearer the center stands farther from the picture plane than those at the left, but she seems drawn toward them and unquestionably gives the music her attention. The other woman, farthest right, is slightly ghostly, still further removed. But her profile shows her attentiveness. More to the point, both women are visually pulled toward the music, their lightly sketched bodies overwhelmed by the concentration of much darker lines to the left. As viewers, our eyes complete the task they themselves cannot accomplish, frozen as they are in time: our eyes make the shift from them toward the source of sonority. Something is happening here compositionally that seldom occurs in paintings: the experiential power of music is visually activated; its action on the body is both acknowledged and celebrated.

This happens even more emphatically in the second drawing, thought to be the work of the musicianly Zoffany (Fig. 32). This drawing loses something of the reality of musical practice (the woman's standing position at the keyboard and her hand position on the keys are both preposterous) to gain something else: the celebration of a musical pleasure that momentarily suspends sanctioned gender rela-

FIG. 32   Johan Zoffany, *Musical Party* (c. 1765), pen and ink, 13.5 × 16.5 cm. Oxford, Ashmolean Museum.

tions. Here men and women come together in a setting where a woman literally stands up to men, equalizing the normal relation of lead part to accompaniment. The male flutist sits, though he has the tune; his partner who "merely" fills in at the keyboard stands—and in a pose that is strikingly, purposefully unnatural. She is an icon of difference. Little wonder that her female friend at her side smiles as she prepares to turn the page or that the standing men opposite her seem uncertain how to react. Four men are included. Two of them help form a circle with the women; both may be musicians, but the sketch is unclear. Their pleasure is evident from the concentration they give to their practice. The other two men are compositionally outside this closed circle; they stand apart even from each other. But both stare and frown a bit—I am uncertain that their look is one of concentration; it appears not to be one of pleasure. Whatever else they do, they pass judgment and, I think, acknowledge the real trouble that this ensemble must cause. Here is production and consumption that not only admits its own practice but also acknowledges the ideological and practical implications of its difference: an altered relation of men to women and women to men—not one where women overtake men, become men, so to speak, but something far more dangerous—one in which women are men's joyful equals. The terms of the rampant misogyny of the English in the eighteenth century held that women's *usurpation* of men's position was impossible, risible. It was the possibility of *equality* that defined misogyny's project. Domination by women was never at issue; the sharing of turf was.[31]

Such music both as practice and sonority momentarily enacts unity of mind and body, man and woman; its consumption is simultaneously a production of utopian desire for wholeness. But this is a dangerous valorization, one that must be rejected at the same moment it is embraced. The rage for and against music never fails to preserve this ironic dialectic as insurance for the depth of reaction music prompts. This is the price of its pleasure. The solace music genuinely provides at once protests and condemns the disharmonious relations its sonorities momentarily displace. When Zoffany's musicians and listeners leave off, just as when we depart the concert hall and head for the parking lot, they reclaim the truth they sought to dispel in music. But the music itself does not lie; music by its very nature cannot help encoding the distinction between its own sonorities and the other sounds in life that we seek to drown out with music. Music *is* the utopian promise, though culture has consistently sought not merely to control it but to marginalize its practice, because that utopian promise can never be fully and effectively marshaled against music itself. Nonetheless, music is commonly asked to play the role of liar, to make us find in it—and hence be satisfied with—what we cannot have in excess of music's nothingness. Still, music plays its role of liar poorly, for no matter what it might "say" to our minds, it cannot disguise what it says to our bodies: that most exist in some state of unwilling bondage, which music reminds us of by inviting us to move.

PLEASURE AND THE PERSONAL

I want to say something more about pleasure, to suggest that the appeal of music to men and women alike in eighteenth-century England was sometimes sufficiently strong to overcome the most stringent restrictions, if not outright prohibitions, relating to its production and consumption. It must be kept in mind that music's pleasure was, and is, in part accounted for by its semantic slipperiness. That is, music remains a discourse that can manifest its compliance with the social order in the very act of disclaiming that compliance and making it ironic. Music's "ability" to deny what it claims—which could be theorized as a lack and articulated disingenuously as music's triviality—was already very well understood in the eighteenth century. Music's perniciousness, as it were, was located in its semantic excesses—paradoxically centered on its literal quality of nothingness, which confirmed its immeasurability. Thus in a world soon to be made subject to classificatory scientisms, where what counted was what could be quantified, it is not surprising that one group would seek to account for music as nonmysterious and measurable by its numbers and ratios, or that another group, proto-romantics, would valorize music precisely because such measurements were so utterly meaningless to music's experiential power.[32]

I opened with the question, What is it one "consumes" when one "consumes" music? The answer—or the part of it that interests me here—might be something like the following. One consumes pleasure, with pleasure defined as a category of human experience that is at once disinterested and interested. By *disinterested* I mean that music's pleasure is produced in part by aural stimulations, which in turn elicit physiological and emotional responses that result in some sense, inevitably temporary, of well-being. This pleasure is embodied; it may be simultaneously of body and mind and as such the sonoric simulacrum of an organic totality absent from an otherwise fractured reality. Nonetheless, music's organicism can only be imagined to the extent that it is lost as soon as it is gained, inevitably lost the moment sound ceases. By *interested* I mean that music's pleasures, just described, are never totally innocent, never produced or experienced solely as autonomous reactions (which are disinterested). This says no more than that any discursive practice must give meaning to and gain meaning from not only its own practice and result (in this case, sonority proper) but also the larger system of discursive and semantic practices of which it is never more than a part.

Pleasure by its very nature comes with strings attached. In a culture of scarcity, even among those for whom scarcity is not more than a theoretical possibility, pleasure by definition is understood to be an unstable and exceptional category of human experience. This is because pleasure is not solely dependent on material excess—financial means do not guarantee access to pleasure. It is an uncommodified commodity. Its materiality is only metaphoric; like music it is immaterial. Further, the consumption of pleasure incorporates loss at the moment of gain. This partly accounts for the desire that pleasure produces, to the extent that we understand by *desire* that which we have not (even in the moment of having). Pleasure in our culture is always on loan, and repayment is invariably demanded.

Even when semantically drained, as in the abstract projection "pleasure for pleasure's sake"—an ideology but not a lived reality—pleasure remains semantically rich. It is experiential; it involves consciousness and intentionality. Even when, as is often the case, it locates itself outside the mind by conceiving of its escape from the bounds of rationalization, pleasure's contingency is not only a matter of physical-emotional sensing but also the mental awareness of the difference it allows, momentarily, from the mental (or, better, the rationalized). The desire for pleasure of whatever kind is embodied. But the embodiment I refer to is possible only by conceiving embodiment as a (wished-for) totality of body and mind.

Music is a repeatedly inscribing marker. Its "repetitions," the result of music as an embodied sound and sight, serve as sensory overdeterminations of every semantic value it produces. Indeed, therein lies much of music's power and pleasure: whatever it might mean, it means repeatedly—whether it be a piece of music replayed or the internal repetitions in all music that are especially obvious in formal procedures like dance forms or theme and variations. Repetition inscribes reassurance and predictability; it is the sonoric-visual simulacrum of contentment, the *promesse de bonheur* Stendhal described as art, which was taken up by the Frankfurt School in their account of the utopian moment in culture.[33] What I mean is that music, like dance, with which it is closely associated, both visually and sonorically enacts a stylized and aestheticized order that human beings valorize highly, especially in light of its abundant opposite, chaos or disorder: noise.

Among contemporaneous eighteenth-century discursive practices only theater works somewhat similarly to music to the extent that it acts in time and produces its effects through both sight and sound. But theater works differently, if not necessarily less effectively. This is so because theater never escapes words or the demands that words make on the mind in theoretical absence of the body—even pantomime narrates via language, through the very absence of language and its retranslation into gesture sufficiently exaggerated to re-create the grammar and syntax of the story told. With music—even, perhaps especially, texted music—words' effects are by contrast degraded by acoustic transliteration. Expressing the same thought conversely, all that music adds to words is in effect taken *from* words. Whether in song, cantata, opera, or oratorio, text depends utterly on sonority at the same time that sonority robs text of its word-driven sign value. (This is not to deny the highly self-conscious attempts by some composers—Debussy, for example—to subvert the text-music relation I am describing.) To be sure, words still mean when paired with music, but music takes nearly full charge of them. Paradoxically, texted music acts in discursive excess of words by inscribing the effects of words and music on the mind and body together, but in a hierarchy opposite to that culturally sanctioned: the body excels. Music betrays the very paucity of the words it sets, or rather it makes emphatic the severe limitations of a reason that valorizes a rationality divorced from embodiment. Reason's poverty is unmasked. And it can be no accident that wordless music rises in importance in Western history—apart from the special and important exception of dance, which by definition privileges the body's relation to music over that of the mind by itself—at the precise moment in early modernity that language itself is systematically institutionalized as the bureaucratic tool of would-be corporate and state power, beginning with the slow rise of the literate classes from the ranks of the monastic clergy and ending in the modern boardroom. This says no less than that music's ultimate pleasure lies in its greatest threat, at least to a society defined by the goals of instrumentalized rationalism. Music's pleasure is the temporary "re-alignment" of body with mind, though in prevailing accounts of that pleasure, extant well before the eighteenth century but still largely current in the 1700s, its action was theorized less as a realignment than a usurpation. That is to say that what music offered—a momentary peace between body and mind—was not a gift particularly appreciated.

Thus Philip Stubbes, the English pamphleteer born about 1555, wrote in *The Anatomie of Abuses* (1583) a virulent attack on the manners, customs, and amusements of the period (though there is little original in his diatribe):

> I Say of Musicke as Plato, Aristotle, Galen, and many others have said of it; that it is very il for yung heds, for a certeine kind of nice, smoothe sweetnes in alluring the auditorie to niceness, effeminancie, pusillanimitie, & lothsomnes of life, so as it may not improperly be compared to a sweet electuarie of honie, or rather to honie it-self; for as honie and such like sweet things, received into the stomack, dooth delight at the first, but afterward they make the stomack so quasie, nice and weake, that is not able to admit meat of hard digesture: So sweet Musick at the first delighteth the eares, but afterward corrupteth and depraveth the minde. . . .

> But being used in publique assemblies and private conventicles, as directories to filthie dauncing, thorow the sweet harmonie & smoothe melodie therof, it estraungeth the mind, stireth up filthie lust, womannisheth the minde, ravisheth the hart, enflameth concupisence, and bringeth in uncleannes.[34]

It should not be lost on us that Stubbes's metaphor of music's action is literally one of consumption, involving food (honey) that acts as a poison on the body (stomach). But his concern is with music's attack, once it has entered through the ears, on the mind ("yung heds," "corrupteth and depraveth the minde"), which is overwhelmed and degraded by the awakening of sexuality and the concurrent loss of gender identity marked by difference (music makes the man womanish). The words inscribe pollution ("bringeth in uncleannes," "ravisheth the hart"). Music is pleasure at a high price. What is most interesting is Stubbes's sense that music, when consumed, consumes in turn. Its danger lies in its being internalized: it infects us; it eats us out from within.

Jeremy Collier's account of music in his 1697 conduct book argued for a music "rightly order'd" that exalts the mind, calms the passions, and affords pleasure; the pleasure he acknowledges is explicitly anticorporeal (indeed, he had in mind a simple devotional music). Yet he feared music of all kinds because of its power to affect the listener. It

> Raises, and Falls, and Counterchanges the Passions at an unaccountable Rate. It Charms and Transports, Ruffles and Becalms, and Governs with an almost arbitrary Authority. There is scarcely any Constitution so heavy, or any Reason so well fortified, as to be absolutely proof against it.

In the end Collier lumped secular and devotional music together and implied that it might be best to do without both:

> Yet to have our Passions lye at the Mercy of a little Minstrelsy; to be Fiddled out of our Reason and Sobriety; to have our Courage depend upon a *Drum,* or our Devotions on an *Organ,* is a Sign we are not so great as we might be. If we were proof against the charming of Sounds; or could we have the Satisfaction without the Danger; or raise our Minds to what pitch we pleas'd by the Strength of *Thinking,* it would be a nobler instance of Power and Perfection. But such an Independency is not to be expected in this World, therefore we must manage wisely and be contented.[35]

Thus music is "danger" articulated as antithought; it activates the enemy within: the corporeal passions that destroy reason. It is not accidental that Collier's metaphors locate music's dangers very close to the body via sexuality or that he thinks of music as a feminine entity ("charming" in English culture is invariably a female characteristic) whose mission is to unman men ("strength" in English culture is invariably male). Music at its highest degree of abstraction (like that sometimes associated—quite mistakenly—with Beethoven's late string quartets) never exceeds the body by its appeal to the mind. Music is inevitably of the body, though whether as guest or virus is not easily decided as a general principle in the culture under consideration.[36]

Culture is supposed to assume concern for the individual's claim to happiness. But the social antagonisms at the root of culture let it admit this claim only in an internalized and rationalized form.

Herbert Marcuse,
"The Affirmative Character of Culture"

MUSIC, DOMESTICITY, AND CULTURAL IMPERIALISM

T{HE GREAT ENDEAVOUR} of all commercial states, is to draw the productions of other countries to its own center," wrote Alexander Dalrymple in 1711 in *Observations on the Present State of the East India Company; and on the Measures to Be Pursued for Ensuring its Permanency, and Augmenting its Commerce* (p. 6). The East India Company, chartered by Elizabeth I in 1600, held by the reign of Charles II rights to "acquire territory, coin money, command fortresses and troops, form alliances, make war and peace, and exercise both civil and criminal jurisdiction." In 1689 its directors resolved in writing that "the Increase of our revenue is the subject of our care . . . 'tis that must make us a nation in India." Indeed, the company profited. And the British government shared in the benefits of this great trade organization in ways directly tied to its own political affairs; the company made loans to the British government, including one in 1742 for £1 million to help finance war with France. Over time the development of trade in India was secured and increased by the acquisition of territory, sufficiently vast by 1757 that the British government began its own direct involvement in the country, gradually pushing aside the East India Company, a process finally completed in 1858.[1]

The intrusion of the British political system—and burgeoning bureaucracy—into India in the 1760s not only coincided with but also was a direct cause of the racial estrangement that climaxed in the early nineteenth century in the establishment of rigid distinctions between the two peoples at all levels of interaction. This situation was distinctly different from what had existed before, particularly in the early history of the East India Company and its Anglo-Indian (that is, immigrant British) employees.

Throughout the seventeenth century and well into the eighteenth most East Indiamen (and, later, the British military) were of low class status, though the company's rolls also included some of the high born—usually younger sons or ne'er-do-wells. Many were very young, often still in their teens. (If they survived the climate and tropical diseases—many died within weeks or months of their arrival—they had a good chance of returning to England within a few years substantially richer. Those who were talented and chose to stay with the company might eventually return with a fortune.[2]) The formative years of these young men were shaped by the new culture to which they were daily exposed. Although some maintained in India a life as close to English models as possible, secluding themselves from contact with the local culture, there were also large numbers of East Indiamen who actively involved themselves in Indian life.

One strong inducement to cultural interaction was sex. In the seventeenth century very few British women made the journey to India. English factors, whose residency might last ten years or more before a return to Europe, commonly took Indian women either as consorts or wives. The children from these unions were accepted into the resident European community without question. They were educated in the European tradition, mostly in India; male children frequently entered the service of the company on an equal basis with their English fathers, while female children often married Englishmen in the company's service.[3]

But by the later eighteenth century dramatic changes had occurred. Many of the British now coming to India were adults, fully formed Westerners, already holding positions of social status as politicians, clergy, doctors, attorneys, and sons of landed families. Men no longer came as employees of the East India Company but as civil servants to administer the colonial government or as military men to secure British control. A growing consciousness of race developed as the interest of Anglo-Indians in trade and commerce was gradually channeled toward the demands of imperialism.

All in all, however, the racial estrangement that began in the 1760s did not become inevitable until the governor-generalship of Charles Cornwallis, which began in 1787. Cornwallis excluded all Indians from higher governmental posts in an effort to streamline the bureaucracy and stamp out corruption; in the process he struck a fatal blow—at the highest level—to racial understanding and co-operation.[4] As the colonial administration developed, with growing numbers of Anglo-Indians establishing themselves temporarily or permanently in the country, contacts between the two races and cultures naturally increased, but understanding declined. Increasingly, Indian culture came to be held in contempt as "irrational, superstitious, barbaric and typical of an inferior civilization."[5]

Large numbers of British men who were already married came to India with their wives and children.[6] Across the social spectrum the increased presence of

English women profoundly affected race relations, notably in the steady decrease of racially mixed families. Thus in addition to the immigration of entire families, single women made the journey as well, hoping to marry into the resident British community, thereby reenforcing insular prejudices.[7]

The final contribution to racial estrangement was made by evangelical missionaries, who denounced Hinduism and Islam so vocally as to cast a shadow over Indians as a people.[8] In the end bigotry reigned as the English settled by and large into a way of life made as comfortably English as possible, isolated from a culture they neither understood nor valued:

> In dealing with Orientals, who were reckoned as lacking conscience or soul, to take the most and give the least became axiomatic. [Anglo-Indians] held to the smug and convenient prejudice that Orientals were innately treacherous and depraved. This was countered by Oriental distrust and dislike of Occidentals, provoked by the villainy of early traders and travelers. And strangeness alone bred mistrust. Hence, the average European made no effort to identify with the natives. He lived a virtually segregated existence, communicating with Easterners only in material matters, smugly satisfied that there was little or nothing to learn from "barbarians" save variations of vice.[9]

Racial estrangement, based on an economy of colonialism and an ideology of cultural superiority, was obvious at all levels of society and personal interaction. But I shall consider this matter only with regard to the life of Anglo-Indians in their homes, where the public realities were domesticated and, more important, naturalized. The politics between the races within domestic walls was subtler but no less invidious than that of the government and the military.[10]

MUSICAL RATIO, SCIENCE, AND SOCIAL HARMONY

In about 1784 Johan Zoffany painted a portrait of several members of the Morse and Cator families (Fig. 33), identified by family tradition as Robert Morse (d. 1816) playing the violoncello, his sister Anne Francis (d. 1823, married in 1780 to Nathaniel Middleton, a company servant) playing the harpsichord, her sister Sarah turning the page on the music rack, and Sarah's husband William Cator (d. 1800) standing. The two men were active in India. Robert Morse served as advocate of the Supreme Court and sheriff of Calcutta in 1783–84; William Cator was a factor for the East India Company.[11]

That the portrait was painted in India first attracted my notice, not the image itself. In appearance the painting is fundamentally similar to scores of other examples produced in England during the same period. But the picture's function is

FIG. 33   Johan Zoffany, *The Morse and Cator Families* (c. 1784), oil on canvas, 110 × 99.5 cm.
City of Aberdeen Art Gallery and Museums Collections, Scotland.

changed by its place of origin, all the more because the place of origin is not represented. The absence of India problematizes the relationship between the "objective" image and the "subtextual" meaning transmitted visually by the metaphor of a musical performance in an (implied) domestic setting.

My argument is that this portrait (together with several other similar images) visually establishes a relationship between the arts of music and painting as signifiers and transmitters of cultural values, on the one hand, and as social, political, and economic structures and the necessary supporting ideologies, on the other. Put another way, this oil portrait on a domestic musical subject mediates the political and social reality of British colonialism by reformulating the reality and its claimed benefits—to English and Indian alike—into a visual language eminently attractive, seamless, and unprovocative. In short, the image translates imperial policy and cultural chauvinism into the triumph and reward of Western civilization. It masks the image of realpolitik by erasing all evidence of what has been subdued and how the defeat was accomplished: by trade and labor exploitation, racial separation, bureaucratization, and the brutality of military enforcement. The image, which fundamentally demands to be read as Harmony, Unity, Order, and (by association) Peace, justifies aggression for the aggressor. The question to be answered is, How is this accomplished visually by reference to music?

To begin, the portrait is a typical conversation piece, an informal grouping of sitters, at once casual, self-assured, and homey. Except for the palatial backdrop—the conventional drapery and classically inspired architectural and sculptural detail—the setting represents an "ordinary" musical gathering in domestic surroundings. The sitters resonate against this (unlikely) backdrop with the ease born of the very status the props confirm.

The props are central to channeling the portrait's meaning, so much so that two of them—the harpsichord in the foreground and the classical column at the back—occupy the center of the picture. They serve as standard-bearers of the Western self-image: refinement and high culture (the harpsichord) and strength and historical patrimony, or civilization (the column). Moreover, the two are strongly related, a contemporaneous belief in the principles of a "natural" order making them ideologically perfect reflections of Enlightenment values.[12]

The eighteenth-century English stood in awe of classical or classically inspired architectural styles (they had little taste for the Continental rococo). Historically, one attraction of this architecture was its perceived order and symmetry, which embodied the logical perfection of mathematics through which the proportions of the designs were realized. In this rational perfection it resembled music, and especially music theory. This is the issue I must discuss in some detail to come to terms with the embedded significance of the harpsichord in the picture.[13]

John Keeble in 1784 published *The Theory of Harmonics: Or, an Illustration of*

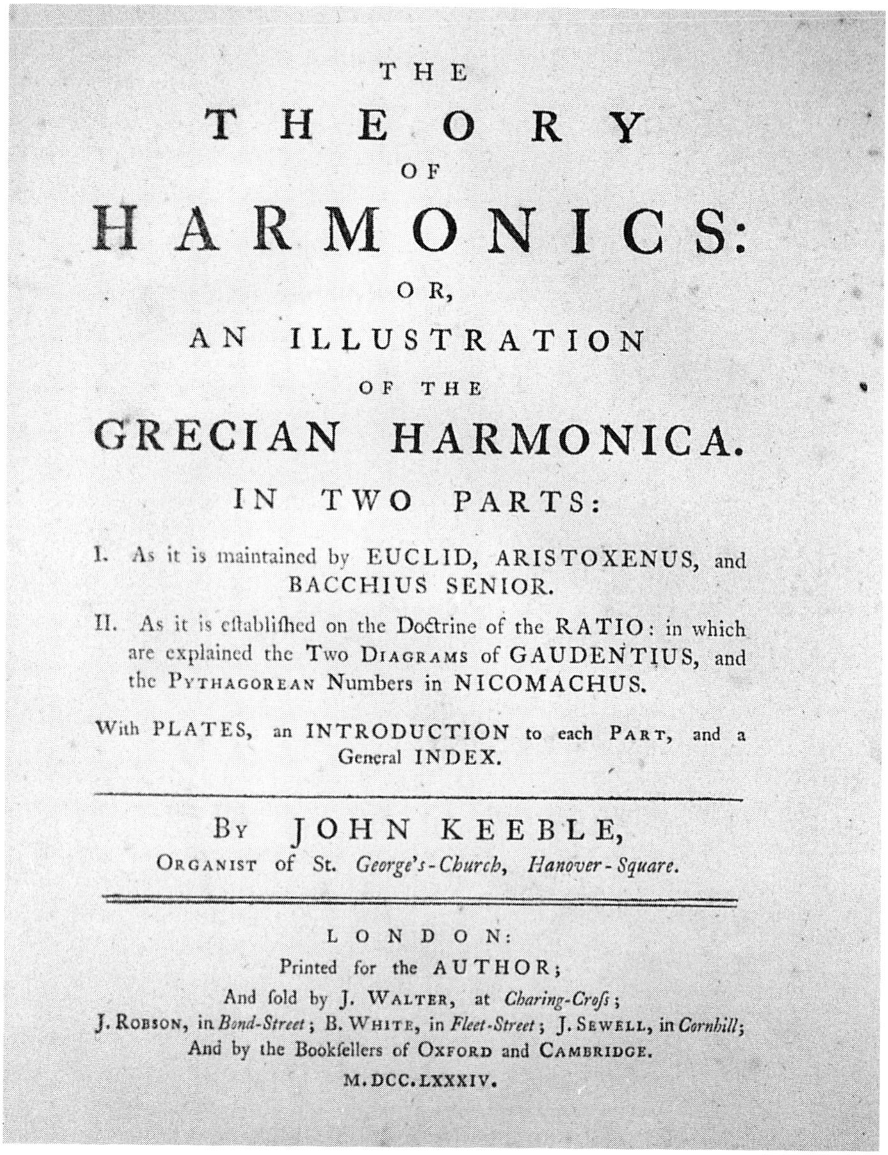

THE
THEORY
OF
HARMONICS:
OR,
AN ILLUSTRATION
OF THE
GRECIAN HARMONICA.

IN TWO PARTS:

I. As it is maintained by EUCLID, ARISTOXENUS, and BACCHIUS SENIOR.

II. As it is established on the Doctrine of the RATIO: in which are explained the Two DIAGRAMS of GAUDENTIUS, and the PYTHAGOREAN Numbers in NICOMACHUS.

With PLATES, an INTRODUCTION to each PART, and a General INDEX.

BY JOHN KEEBLE,

ORGANIST of St. *George's-Church,* *Hanover-Square.*

LONDON:

Printed for the AUTHOR;

And sold by J. WALTER, at *Charing-Cross*;

J. ROBSON, in *Bond-Street*; B. WHITE, in *Fleet-Street*; J. SEWELL, in *Cornhill*;

And by the Booksellers of OXFORD and CAMBRIDGE.

M.DCC.LXXXIV.

FIG. 34   John Keeble, *The Theory of Harmonics: Or, an Illustration of the Grecian Harmonica* (1784). Title page. Minneapolis, O. Meredith Wilson Library, University of Minnesota.

the Grecian Harmonica (Fig. 34), a treatise neither original nor unique to the period, though it attracted considerable attention at the time of its appearance. Keeble was a professional performing musician, but his book's subject was the mathematics of sound. In more than two hundred pages, with the aid of twenty-six engraved plates, he provided a detailed description of the Greek harmonic system, including by means of ratios an account of the scale across several octaves (Figs. 35–37). There is little in the book of value either to musicians or to those seeking to understand music itself. Keeble himself, at the end of his lengthy exercise, seemed to acknowledge this: "The great advantage of discovering the magnitude of all musical intervals by the Ratio cannot but be agreeable to men of science and lovers of truth."[14]

I am interested less in the details of Keeble's examination of Greek theory than in his reasons for undertaking the task in the first place. One of these seems certain: he desired to link what he saw as the germ of future Western music with a culturally and historically specific paradigm of the European Enlightenment. Thus he located music in mathematics, in phenomena that in turn could be "objectively" measured and systematized. The system was legitimated on the claim that it is structured on "natural" principle, and on that basis it became law.

To be sure, Keeble had numerous predecessors in the Middle Ages and the Renaissance who likewise associated music and mathematics. But Keeble added two components to this age-old equation: science and a belief in the evolutionary progress of human affairs. Keeble, like others of his time, believed that numbers were the embodying principle for both truth and progress (a belief opposed to, say, the medieval notion of timelessness):

> Nothing contributes so much to the encouragement of Study, as the knowledge of some governing and leading principle; some visible and faithful guide, that will conduct us through the mazes of Science, and teach us to love and obey her laws. It is this that warms and animates our endeavours in the arduous pursuit, and in the end rewards our labours with success.
>
> This governing principle shews itself in no part of human learning so much as in the various operations of numbers; whose powers, by a kind of magic, have greatly contributed to the many discoveries and improvements that have been made in all arts and sciences; nor can it be otherwise while Truth is the great object to which those powers are directed (pp. 2–3).

Science is anthropomorphized, even deified, situated above the subjective and experiential (though, to be sure, subjectively produced and mythologized). The apotheosis Keeble implies is engendered by science/reason, as a tool by which men (his gender specificity is not accidental) could not only classify and thus under-

HARMONIC TABLE.
FIRST DIAGRAM.

			1	2	4	8	16	32	64	128	256	512
HARMONICS of ROOT 1	1	B	1	2	4	8	16	32	64	128	256	512
	2	B	2	4	8	16	32	64	128	256	512	1024
	3	E	3	6	12	24	48	96	192	384	768	1536
	4	B	4	8	16	32	64	128	256	512	1024	2048
	5	G	5	10	20	40	80	160	320	640	1280	2560
	6	E	6	12	24	48	96	192	384	768	1536	3072
	8	B	8	16	32	64	128	256	512	1024	2048	4096
ROOT 3	1	E	3	6	12	24	48	96	192	384	768	1536
	2	E	6	12	24	48	96	192	384	768	1536	3072
	3	A	9	18	36	72	144	288	576	1152	2304	4608
	4	E	12	24	48	96	192	384	768	1536	3072	6144
	5	C	15	30	60	120	240	480	960	1920	3840	7680
	6	A	18	36	72	144	288	576	1152	2304	4608	9216
	8	E	24	48	96	192	384	768	1536	3072	6144	12288
ROOT 9	1	A	9	18	36	72	144	288	576	1152	2304	4608
	2	A	18	36	72	144	288	576	1152	2304	4608	9216
	3	D	27	54	108	216	432	864	1728	3456	6912	13824
	4	A	36	72	144	288	576	1152	2304	4608	9216	18432
	5	F	45	90	180	360	720	1440	2880	5760	11520	23040
	6	D	54	108	216	432	864	1728	3456	6912	13824	27648
	8	A	72	144	288	576	1152	2304	4608	9216	18432	36864
ROOT 27	1	D	27	54	108	216	432	864	1728	3456	6912	13824
	2	D	54	108	216	432	864	1728	3456	6912	13824	27648
	3	G	81	162	324	648	1296	2592	5184	10368	20736	41472
	4	D	108	216	432	864	1728	3456	6912	13824	27648	55296
	5	Bb	135	270	540	1080	2160	4320	8640	17280	34560	69120
	6	G	162	324	648	1296	2592	5184	10368	20736	41472	82944
	8	D	216	432	864	1728	3456	6912	13824	27648	55296	110592

HARMONIC TABLE.
FIRST DIAGRAM. *continued*

			81	162	324	648	1296	2592	5184
HARMONICS of ROOT 81	1	G	81	162	324	648	1296	2592	5184
	2	G	162	324	648	1296	2592	5184	10368
	3	C	243	486	972	1944	3888	7776	15552
	4	G	324	648	1296	2592	5184	10368	20736
	5	Eb	405	810	1620	3240	6480	12960	25920
	6	C	486	972	1944	3888	7776	15552	31104
	8	G	648	1296	2592	5184	10368	20736	41472
ROOT 243	1	C	243	486	972	1944	3888	7776	15552
	2	C	486	972	1944	3888	7776	15552	31104
	3	F	729	1458	2916	5832	11664	23328	46656
	4	C	972	1944	3888	7776	15552	31104	62208
	5	Ab	1215	2430	4860	9720	19440	38880	77760
	6	F	1458	2916	5832	11664	23328	46656	93312
	8	C	1944	3888	7776	15552	31104	62208	124416
ROOT 729	1	F	729	1458	2916	5832	11664	23328	46656
	2	F	1458	2916	5832	11664	23328	46656	93312
	3	Bb	2187	4374	8748	17496	34992	69984	139968
	4	F	2916	5832	11664	23328	46656	93312	186624
	5	Db	3645	7290	14580	29160	58320	116640	233280
	6	Bb	4374	8748	17496	34992	69984	139968	279936
	8	F	5832	11664	23328	46656	93312	186624	373248
ROOT 2187	1	Bb	2187	4374	8748	17496	34992	69984	139968
	2	Bb	4374	8748	17496	34992	69984	139968	279936
	3	Eb	6561	13122	26244	52488	104976	209952	419904
	4	Bb	8748	17496	34992	69984	139968	279936	559872
	5	Gb	10935	21870	43740	87480	174960	349920	699860
	6	Eb	13122	26244	52488	104976	209952	419904	839808
	8	Bb	17496	34992	69984	139968	279936	559872	1119744

continued

First Diagram Harmonic Table *continued*

HARMONICS of ROOT 6561	1	Eb	6561
	2	Eb	13122
	3	Ab	19683
	4	Eb	26244
	5	Cb	32805
	6	Ab	39366
	8	Eb	52488
ROOT 19683	1	Ab	19683
	2	Ab	39366
	3	Db	59049
	4	Ab	78732
	5	Eb	98415
	6	Db	118098
	8	Ab	157464
ROOT 59049	1	Db	59049
	2	Db	118098
	3	Gb	177147
	4	Db	236196
	5	Bbb	295245
	6	Gb	354294
	8	Db	472392
ROOT 177147	1	Gb	177147
	2	Gb	354294
	3	Cb	531441
	4	Gb	708588
	5	Ebb	885735
	6	Cb	1062882
	8	Gb	1417176

FIGS. 35–37   John Keeble, *The Theory of Harmonics.* Plate 14, harmonic table, first diagram.

stand what was but also, more important, *order* what could be. He sees his intellectual pursuit in developmental terms ("rewards our labours with success") congruent with the "progressive" goals of colonialism. Keeble ironically displays the
deep psychological base of his argument precisely when discussing the attraction
of objective powers. When he admits to "a kind of magic," the supposed objective
foundation for his belief in rationalism slips away in an apparent ecstasy of subjectivity and superstition. He betrays in the process the ultimate magnetism of what
he understands by "governing principle," namely, governing power.

The scientific truth he sets out to discover has no apparent use beyond the fact
of its existence, since it cannot "influence" music. But musical use is not the question. The real use value resides at the cultural level. He is out to prove the musical
complement of Western cultural hegemony: "Among the theories which have appeared at different periods, those of the Greeks seem to have all the advantages
that can be wished to lead us to the true knowledge of Harmonics; for as their
principles are in nature, they must be fixed and immutable" (p. 5). Put differently,
Keeble's argument does not need music to be proved. Indeed, music is irrelevant
and even interruptive to the discussion, for it is intensely subjective at the experiential level. Only when it remains on paper, so to speak, can it be dealt with in
pure form—ideally in numbers—and thus totally contained in a logical system
otherwise divorced from the world.

Keeble obliquely asserts a universal validity to his measurements when, in a
comment on the human voice, he argues that it "is tuned by this scale or gender,
which is universally the same, at all times, in all countries; for as this is the scale
of nature, there is sufficient reason to believe, that the principles of harmony, the
number and quality of consonances and dissonances, are fixed and determined by
certain laws" (p. 8). He compares these laws with universals, the circulation of the
blood and the law of gravity. At the close of his treatise he states his position
directly: "Could all this be by Chance? rather, is there not an absolute necessity,
that All shall comply with principles found in Nature? to whose laws we must be
obedient, whether they are thoroughly understood or not" (pp. 203–04).

Keeble's argument, embodied in mathematics, is that the Western system
developing from the Greeks is natural and must be obeyed. It is an argument
built, not on "pure" reason, but on a subjectively constituted reason at whose base
lies the attraction of power and the firm conviction, held a priori to the entire
discussion, that the Western system is the only one able to claim universal validity.
I am suggesting, not that we get to colonialism from music theory, but rather that
the musical order (theoretical systems and the values attached to them) defined by
Keeble is constituted by, and hence reinforces, an identical ideological base of
Western self-legitimation.[15]

The history of a "scientific" theory of music owes its greatest debt to Keeble's Continental predecessor, Jean-Philippe Rameau (1683–1764). Though Keeble's debt is not to Rameau but rather to Rameau's teacher Pepusch, striking ideological similarities underlie the work of both. Given the status—contemporaneous and later—of Rameau's musical-theoretical writings, it is worthwhile to outline their salient features before returning to a discussion of Zoffany's painting.

In his *Traité de l'harmonie* (Paris, 1722; first published in an incomplete English translation in 1737) Rameau laid out the principles of the system he developed further in later writings.[16] For my purposes the central issue is exposed in Rameau's opening comments in his preface:

> However much progress music may have made until our time, it appears that the more sensitive the ear has become to the marvelous effects of this art, the less inquisitive the mind has been about its true principles. One might say that reason has lost its rights, while experience has acquired a certain authority.
>
> The surviving writings of the Ancients show us clearly that reason alone enabled them to discover most of the properties of music. Although experience still obliges us to accept the greater part of their rules, we neglect today all the advantages to be derived from the use of reason in favor of purely practical experience.[17]

Rameau's theory develops from a position that "all music is founded on harmony, which arises from natural principles derived from the mathematical and physical bases of a vibrating body (*corps sonore*)."[18] Rameau's method is Cartesian in its dependence on mathematical precision; it is equally Cartesian in its effects (he cites Descartes throughout the text). Notably, in his preface, Rameau drives a wedge between experience (the body or, more specifically, the ears) and reason (the mind). He tells us that experience provides no real understanding or—by implication—justification for the form modern music takes. At the same time, he canonizes rationality via the ancients (from whom come the "true principles").

What he means to assert about reason and the ancients is revealed in the full title of the treatise: *Traité de l'harmonie réduite à ses principes naturels.* That is, he claims to have discovered, like Keeble after him, a system (a rational order) that is also *natural,* that highly charged word for the eighteenth century, equivalent of the *good* and carrying explicit moral qualifications in its application. The importance of this assertion is evident in combination with Rameau's central principle, namely, that harmony (and not melody) serves as the underlying basis of all music.

That is, Rameau conceived of harmony as the ultimate determinant in music, governed by chord relations he defined variously as hierarchical ordering and rationalized movement (from one chord to another), and he distinguished between dissonance and consonance—in effect, between conflict and resolution. His is a musical system congruent with eighteenth- and nineteenth-century theories of political economy—from the social contract to production studies (Adam Smith)—to the extent that his theory sought to rationalize and order musical phenomena according to principles of greater and lesser (the primary versus the secondary chords), restated in political terms as a hierarchy of power relations.

It is here, I think, that the importance of the visual metaphors of architecture and, especially, music become evident in Zoffany's painting, where music and architecture stand in for political harmony. At the level of the rational-scientific, these images complement the philosophical-political categories of Order, Reason, the Natural, and, by implication, Right. (The domestic connection, equally important and closely related, has yet to be explained.)

Progress in the Enlightenment was a fundamental concept by which to judge history and set off the present and future from the past. Near the beginning of the preface Rameau touches on this issue:

> But if through the exposition of an evident principle, from which we then draw just and certain conclusions, we can show that our music has attained the last degree of perfection and that the Ancients were far from this perfection [i.e., in their music if not their theory], . . . we shall know where we stand. . . . Persons of taste and outstanding ability in this field will no longer lack of the knowledge necessary for success. In short, the light of reason, dispelling the doubts into which experience can plunge us at any moment, will be the most certain guarantee of success that we can expect in this art (pp. xxxiii–iv).

It is through Rameau's version of the Cartesian *cogito* ("evident principle, from which we then draw just and certain conclusions") that we can be certain of progress: that is, knowledge comes from the mind, not from (embodied) experience. Put another way, external reality can be understood only through a rationalization based on (mathematical) principles *antecedent* to that reality:

> Music is a science which should have definite rules; these rules should be drawn from an evident principle; and this principle cannot really be known to us without the aid of mathematics. Notwithstanding all the experience I may have acquired in music from being associated with it for so long, I must confess that only with the aid of mathematics did my ideas become clear and did light replace a certain obscurity of which I was unaware before.[19]

The mathematics of Rameau and Keeble are thus heavily marked by historical situation, cultural specificity, and valorization. To the Westerner, mathematics became a primary sign of the idealized self, as well as a useful indicator of cultural difference. Thus with regard to India—in a time closer to our own—Evelyn Baring, Lord Cromer, British agent and consul-general in Egypt between 1882 and 1907, noted in his book *Modern Egypt* (1908): "Sir Alfred Lyall once said to me: 'Accuracy is abhorrent to the Oriental mind. Every Anglo-Indian should always remember that maxim.' Want of accuracy, which easily degenerates into untruthfulness, is in fact the main characteristic of the Oriental mind."[20]

Zoffany's painting embeds far more than the taste and cultivation manifested by the large harpsichord, attendant musicians, and audience. The instrument is a signifier for an order based on rational and "natural" principles that define and motivate progress and hence good. The English sitters are by implication devoted to these principles and this order. Indeed, the way they encircle the harpsichord (the painting's compositional anchor) establishes their relationship to the cultural values for which it stands. The image Zoffany paints functions as the visual equivalent of what Barthes describes as political writing, whose function "is to maintain a clear conscience," and whose mission is "fraudulently to identify the original fact with its remotest subsequent transformation," a shift Barthes sees as "typical of all authoritarian regimes; it is what might be called police-state writing: we know, for example, that the content of the word 'Order' always indicates repression."[21]

In Zoffany two orders, one of sound (music), the other of stone (architecture), directly or by implication bear on fundamental issues of morality and civil rights, for they supply an inherent justification for political policies later—and in another country—called Manifest Destiny. The realities of imperialism *experienced* by Anglo-Indians are explained and justified, not on the basis of this experience, but instead by abstract principles of reason—expressed by signs of high culture—that may in fact conflict with what the experience itself suggests. As Rameau recognized, "experience can plunge us at any moment" into doubt; only reason (i.e., rationalization) can save us.[22]

SITTING PRETTY

The sitters in the portrait are full complements to the harpsichord (and violoncello) and the architectural backdrop. They are actors: casual, informal, and forming a tableau—striking an *attitude,* to borrow from eighteenth-century usage. In effect they are on stage, highly aware of the audience for whom they strike their poses.[23]

In the foreground at the right, closest to the viewer, stands William Cator, who, as a factor in the East India Company, represents business, the true end of English colonialism in the eighteenth century. He is absolutely relaxed, with one hand on his hip, the other on the harpsichord, his legs crossed. His pose is confident. His costume, like those of the others, together with his full belly, marks status and success.

Yet the commerce in which he engages finds no reference here, except indirectly, in the class status and economic situation it provides. Such masking is not conventional in eighteenth-century English portraiture. For example, in a portrait (Fig. 38) by Arthur Devis of Colonel James Clitherow and his wife on the grounds of their estate, Boston House, Brentford, Middlesex, James proudly holds a spade-like digging tool known as a "spud," a sign of his pride in agriculture, one source of his wealth. The success of his enterprise is manifested by the well-tended park in which he stands. Clitherow's control over his land is signaled in part by the dammed river Brent directly behind him.[24] One might argue that wealth achieved through agriculture was culturally acceptable in eighteenth-century England

FIG. 38   Arthur Devis, *Colonel James Clitherow and His Wife, Anne, at Boston House, Brentford, Middlesex* (1789), oil on canvas, 91.4 × 109.2 cm. Private collection, London.

whereas that gained from business was not (the parvenu problem). But this is not necessarily the case. For example, a portrait of the Putnam family (Fig. 39) represents the patriarch at the extreme right with his hand on a globe and a ship at his back firing a salute: his wealth presumably results from foreign trade, doubly and openly acknowledged—without apology—by the ship and the globe.[25]

Cator, closest to the picture plane (Fig. 33), half turns to the other sitters, as if pointing them out to us (they are in a recessed plane, framed by him and the open lid of the harpsichord on the right, and the curtain fold at the upper left). In essence, Morse on the cello and the two women at the harpsichord represent a culture whose values are being affirmed, not only for their own sake but also (if unconsciously) as justification for the harsh realities lying beneath the surface, the semiotic "present absence." Any reference to the real reason these people are in India—business and the police system to keep it in place—is avoided. The musical "harmony" of Morse's violoncello, like that produced by the harpsichord, is thus problematized: it stands in tension with what it masks, namely, Morse's real

FIG. 39   Unknown British artist, *The Putnam Family,* oil on canvas, 84.5 × 105.4 cm. Whereabouts unknown.

occupation as sheriff of Calcutta and advocate of the Supreme Court, the way he really spent his time.

Precisely in this way the conventional drapery at the back paradoxically takes on the metaphorical as well as the literal function of a curtain. As it reveals, by being pulled back to allow us to see the tableau, it also hides. It provides a limited view. By this I mean that portraits in delineating success and other attendant qualities show them *only* as products (arrivals) and rarely as processes. In the Morse-Cator portrait process is literally curtained off, hidden. We are not allowed to see the foundation of exploitation and suffering on which this cultured scene depends. Marcuse's comment in the epigraph to this chapter is relevant here.

I want to say more about the harpsichord, its connection to the women, the relation of both to domesticity, and, finally, the bond between each of them and cultural hegemony. The use of the harpsichord—like the fortepiano later—first and foremost in the home is reflected in the large number of instruments in British newspaper advertisements for household sales throughout the century as well as in surviving catalogues for such auctions. References to domestic keyboard instruments are legion in diaries and memoirs, as well as in stage plays on domestic situations and in countless novels. Modest households typically had a small spinet (an instrument of modest cost and limited musical means) or, toward the end of the century, a small square piano. The wealthy bought single- and double-manual harpsichords and, later, large fortepianos.[26] In England vast quantities of music were published for amateur musicians and made available either through outright purchase or through privately operated lending libraries.

These instruments, played predominantly by girls and women, were in fact both signifiers and insurers of females' domestic role.[27] Zoffany's musical women at first glance may appear to play merely decorative parts, like those played— seemingly if not always in actuality—by English women in eighteenth-century portraiture. But they are in fact essential here, for they complete the sense of peace, harmony, and order in this scene by making the event not merely musical but familial. They assure continuance of this scene and the culture it represents by their gender function: they are the producers of the race.[28] Their music is domestic, a signifier of the very tranquillity that makes reproduction possible. It is noteworthy that both women in this painting had borne children in the months before this portrait was painted.[29]

Finally, it must be said that the absence of any reference to Indian culture cannot be attributed to Zoffany's rigid adherence to European portrait conventions. I believe that he was instead reacting to the preference of his sitters, for he himself was genuinely interested in Indian subjects. Beyond painting portraits of rich Indian nawabs, he produced drawings of Indian life and country landscapes, and he "joined the newly founded Asiatic Society, whose researches into all branches of oriental studies were to form one of the most distinguished European contributions to oriental scholarship."[30]

A portrait strikingly similar to Zoffany's was painted in India in 1789 by Francesco Renaldi (British-born but of Italian parentage) of Charles Cockerell and his wife, Maria Tryphena, with her younger sister, Charlotte Blunt (Fig. 40).[31] Cockerell was paymaster general. His wife was the daughter of Sir Charles Blunt, another East India Company servant. She plays a large two-manual harpsichord, apart from house organs the costliest musical instrument of the period. Her sister turns a page of music.[32] In Renaldi's portrait, as in Zoffany's, nothing Indian is reproduced. It is unabashedly English: an entirely tranquil conversation piece, probably celebrating the marriage, which had occurred the same year, a distorting mirror of personal, economic, and social triumph achieved in India, formulated once again on a musical metaphor.

FIG. 40   Francesco Renaldi, *Charles Cockerell and His Wife, Maria Tryphena, with Her Sister, Charlotte Blunt* (1789), oil on canvas, 74.9 × 91.4 cm. Private collection. Photo courtesy of Christie's, London.

Oil paintings provided patrons with self-flattering signs of status and cultivation that naturally increased with the importance of the painter—Zoffany himself was highly regarded and much sought after in England and India. Such paintings produced in India proclaimed a European cultural hegemony by the very impracticality of the medium. India's tropical heat was detrimental to the canvas on which these portraits were executed—though for many Englishmen that was not an insurmountable problem, since the usual intention was to remove oneself from India, together with an acquired fortune, as soon as possible (selling the furniture to someone who had recently arrived or was in any event staying on).[33]

FAMILY ENCLOSURE: PACIFICATION AND EXCLUSION

Two watercolors drawn at Patna in 1824 by Sir Charles D'Oyly of his bungalow's spacious drawing room in summer (Fig. 41) and winter (Fig. 42) bear on this discussion.[34] In both images the Anglo-Indian sitters are de-emphasized by their relative isolation from one another (and half of the D'Oyly family members are posed in profile or from the back). It is their possessions that command the viewer's gaze—furniture, paintings, books, musical instruments, crystal chandeliers, sculptural (or painted) friezes, carpet, and the like.

The two musical instruments, a grand fortepiano and a pedal harp, appear in both drawings. Each enjoyed unassailable status among the European upper classes, the harp having come into its own among women in the late eighteenth century, the piano having simply supplanted the harpsichord. The extra-musical status garnered by their bulk interests me in particular here. These large instruments (the piano comparatively heavy, even before the development of the iron frame) are also oddly shaped and hence difficult and expensive to pack and ship.[35] Like most musical instruments they are also delicate, hence easily damaged, and highly sensitive to climatic change. India's particularly inhospitable climate made them difficult to maintain. In short, these instruments are highly impractical to the setting.

It is precisely this impracticality that increases their ideological use value. In India their significance has as much to do with a totemic function as a musical one. Inessential, like most of the other furnishings, to the economic and political success of colonialism, they are nonetheless important as cultural fetishes and markers of racial difference. Moreover, their delicacy parallels the delicacy men perceived in the women who played them. In sum, neither English women nor British high art and its trappings could appear in India until the way for them had been made safe. The presence of both represents political triumph at the same time that it masks the means by which the triumph was accomplished, as with

FIG. 41 Sir Charles D'Oyly, *The Summer Room in the Artist's House at Patna* (11 September 1824), watercolor, 18 × 34.4 cm. New Haven, Yale Center for British Art, Paul Mellon Collection.

FIG. 42   Sir Charles D'Oyly, *The Winter Room in the Artist's House at Patna* (11 September 1824), watercolor, 19.6 × 34.2 cm. New Haven, Yale Center for British Art, Paul Mellon Collection.

the Morse-Cator portrait discussed earlier. Colonialism is not an arrival but a process. In this context Anglo-Indian women are essential not only for the maintenance of racial purity but also for the transmission of cultural values, especially those that could be embodied in art. For it was in art that Europeans chose to see the clearest signs of mythologized self-justification.

This issue becomes clear if we look again at the winter room and the vignette of Lady D'Oyly playing her harp.[36] Lady D'Oyly does not play for her own enjoyment, or even for the pleasure of her husband. She is an unwitting participant in a more important agenda, the very one I have been discussing. She is the model for the making of an image-within-the-image. Charles D'Oyly sits with his back to us and thereby draws our attention to his sketching of his wife at music. Thus it is the *image* of her at music, not the musical event itself, that matters. D'Oyly's watercolor presents an act of fetishizing in progress, the drawing reconstituting in a specific vignette the general activity the artist engaged in while producing the two watercolors. But the interior image of image making—a woman at music—claims hierarchical supremacy in a scene filled with detail.

In the winter room, in the background, D'Oyly also illustrates a hearth scene, though not apparently because the day is cold, since the doorway at the right provides a view of open French doors leading onto a garden. This vignette can also claim significance as a culturally embedded activity relevant to the general argument I am pursuing. The association between hearth and home was central to English culture, as Derek Jarrett has pointed out: "The social unit was not the individual but the family of the household, a fact that gave great importance to the actual houses in which these units were contained. The possession of a hearth, traditionally the centre and focus not only of the house but also of the people who lived in it, was the thing that defined a man's position and gave him a place in society."[37]

The pairing of hearth with wife is common in contemporaneous British portraiture, as in Richard Cosway's painting of Marianne Dorothy Harland (Fig. 43). The association between the two is so ubiquitous, in fact, that it even occurs in ephemeral imagery like fashion plates (see Fig. 22). A constant in these scenes is the inherent protectiveness provided by men who are often not present but implied. Characteristically the women are doubly cocooned, in fashionable overdress and domestic overfurnishing. Marianne Harland and her anonymous fashion-plate counterpart are perfect models of femininity to the males in whose image they are made. They lead lives of comfortable boredom, metaphorically tending the fire—that is, maintaining domestic order—and, like the little dog at Ms. Harland's feet, waiting, *semper fidelis*. Transplanted to India, as in the D'Oyly watercolors, the wifely motherhood and domesticity imprinted on this imagery accrue cultural significance as confirmations of male triumph, not simply over females

FIG. 43   Richard Cosway, *Marianne Dorothy Harland* (*later Mrs. Dalrymple*), oil on canvas,
71.1 × 93 cm. New York, The Metropolitan Museum of Art, gift of Mrs. William M. Haupt, from
the Collection of Mrs. James B. Haggin, 1969.

who have been domesticated, but over an alien culture rendered harmless, hence
allowing the introduction of women and their domestic trappings.

Most of what D'Oyly draws is resolutely Western; even the architectural enclosure is transplanted. Thus in the winter room, apart from the ubiquitous
hookah,[38] the only reference to India is a picture-within-a-picture at the upper
left depicting an Indian elephant (kneeling, subservient) and some Indian people,
most of whom stand behind a man in British military garb. There are other signs
of India's defeat, notably in the summer room where an adult and child Indian
servant, physically excluded, wait to be summoned, barely visible through the
doorway at the right. In the foreground of the same drawing a tiger's skin adorns
the floor: an archetypal symbol of ferocity and exoticness, now conquered, is tread
upon, made ornamental. D'Oyly himself reiterates this defeat of nature in the
drawing he holds showing a British infantryman, presumably on the march. The
myriad trappings of Western culture in the room as well as the women making

music, reading, and drawing all legitimate the reality of early nineteenth-century India. Ironically, theirs is an ostentation considered in good taste, in contrast to the luxury of Indian nawabs, whose wealth the Anglo-Indians mocked as well as coveted.

Arthur William Devis's portrait of Emily and George Mason (c. 1794–95; Fig. 44), children of Bryant Mason of the East India Civil Service,[39] is composed so as to reinforce, and even proclaim, cultural difference and racial estrangement. Only bits and pieces are visible—part of a room, part of a chair and a harpsichord, a hint of landscape. But we see enough. Anglo-Indian children are in the foreground, adult Indian servants in the back. A visual tension is created between them, despite the physical relaxation of all the actors, because here children take precedence over adults, a visually composed triumph virtually never found in contemporaneous English portraits,[40] a difference that English viewers would have recognized immediately.

In Calcutta at the close of the eighteenth century many English immigrants lived in considerable domestic splendor—made possible in part through the cheapness of labor and made public by the number of laborers involved. An unmarried Anglo-Indian might command a twenty-room mansion and require the attention of several score of servants; married couples sometimes maintained a staff of a hundred or more. The jobs assigned to individuals could be ridiculously specific and confining. Thus some only waited table, and as many as a dozen served their master only when he rose or retired. Those who held the umbrella or carried the palanquin (litter) did nothing else. (Servants' liveries were distinctive and specific to each household, testifying both to the employers' greatness and the wearers' inferiority.[41])

By definition servants mark the status of their employers. Indian servants marked as well the racial and cultural superiority Anglo-Indians perceived in themselves: in England servants were never assigned tasks as profoundly inconsequential or demeaning as the ones I have just described. In domestic settings the races interacted, but only in ways that showed the gulf between them. The home, which served as the perfect microcosm of imperial order, also confirmed the moral appropriateness of empire: it provided a training ground for subsequent generations of colonial bureaucrats, police, and military.

The English Mason children represent the future of colonialism. Little Emily holds a tambourine and executes a gesture of dance, metaphorically celebrating the triumphant imperialism given form by the toy infantry drum and gun held by little George (wearing the standard toddler dress of the period that makes him appear androgynous). The signifiers of the new culture in India—Western, classically inspired architecture and music—once again transform political reality into a highly palatable visual abstraction.

FIG. 44 Arthur William Devis, *Emily and George Mason* (c. 1794–95), oil on canvas,
108 × 99 cm. New Haven, Yale Center for British Art, Paul Mellon Collection.

FIG. 45   Johan Zoffany, *Colonel Blair with His Family and an Ayah* (1786?), oil on canvas,
97 × 136 cm. Private collection. Photo courtesy of Leger Galleries Ltd, London.

Zoffany's portrait of Colonel Blair (1729–1814) with his wife and two daughters (1786? Fig. 45) differs from the other images I have been discussing. Unlike the Morse-Cator and Cockerell-Blunt portraits, where the figures are placed in nonspecific interiors, or the D'Oyly drawings, where the specific interior has taken on the semantic aspect of a European museum, the Blair family is settled in a modest room of their house in Cawnpore.[42] The trappings of Europe are evident in the furniture, not much of which is actually visible since it is covered by the figures (and thus functions more *as* furniture, less as a proclamation of British culture). The most obvious piece is the square piano,[43] yet as an instrument of the middle class it carried little of the status of the large harpsichords (or grand fortepianos) seen in the Morse-Cator or Cockerell-Blunt paintings. The mixture of furniture styles strikes me as more haphazard than purposefully eclectic—from the straight lines of the piano and the table in the right background (the latter is a purely utilitarian piece) to the curvilinear lines of the French rococo chairs and the mirror on the back wall. Colonel Blair seems to have been ill-served by the limitations of the import market! All in all, the house and its furnishings appear to respond more to the demands of physical necessity than self-acknowledgment, at least by comparison with D'Oyly's surroundings.

Particularly interesting in the Blair portrait are the three paintings-within-the-painting depicting Indian life, though the precise subject matter is unclear. (One scholar suggests that the three pictures represent paintings Blair commissioned from Zoffany during a visit to Lucknow and that this portrait commemorates the installation of the paintings in Blair's house, their having been brought down to Cawnpore by the artist himself.[44]) The images grant status to Indian culture by their prominent size and compositional placement as well as by their apparent subject matter. They are also notable for the absence of Europeans, so far as I can make out. To be sure, their existence is due to Colonel Blair, whom they implicitly honor. But they are fundamentally different from D'Oyly's tiger skin (Fig. 41) or the Mason children's servants (Fig. 44), either as geographical markers or as signifiers of European hegemony.

The ease and genuineness of the Blairs' relationship to India is affirmed by the sitters themselves. Zoffany not only depicts them in the conventional informal poses demanded by the genre but also gives them an unusual warmth. The father and mother accord their daughter status by listening to her play (the music book's cover inscription seems to read "Handel"); the devotion they feel for her is echoed in what they feel for each other. Mrs. Blair looks intently at her daughter, as Colonel Blair looks at his wife. They hold hands. These gestures of marital affection (especially a husband looking at his wife instead of the viewer and the physical touching) are highly unusual in contemporaneous English portraits. Unlike the adult sitters in the Morse-Cator (Fig. 33) and Cockerell-Blunt (Fig. 40) portraits, the Blairs are oblivious to the viewer. The painting thus becomes more a personal memento and less a semipublic assertion of one's self and one's values.

A final, implicit (but not unproblematic), homage to India is paid by the figures at the right: Blair's younger daughter who pets a cat held by an ayah (a female servant). The two girls, about the same age, form an unusual image, for Zoffany treats them virtually as equals, though of course they are not. The Indian girl, like her English companion, meets our glance head-on. Both girls stand relaxed, comfortable together. In short, they appear to be friends. The family dog stands next to the ayah, as if she were a family member, and not beside the paterfamilias, as is typically the case in English portraits. All in all this is a striking painting that in a small way mediates the visual norm in cultural relations between the Anglo-Indian and Indian peoples. Although the painting confirms the order of colonialism and reiterates the hierarchy, it does not acknowledge as legitimate the racial estrangement evident in the other images I have discussed.

Nonetheless, the ayah, by her very position, represents submission to the colonizer. In precisely this sense she then becomes, to the European, the "good" native. As such she is represented sympathetically.[45]

As Fuseli expressed it, for the British, "portrait . . . is everything. Their taste and feelings all go to realities." But the English portrait, as Pevsner points out, "keeps long silences, and when it speaks, speaks in a low voice. . . . Or, to put it differently, the English portrait conceals more than it reveals, and what it reveals it reveals with studied understatement."[46] What it tells, nevertheless, is the story of a culture and its values, which art itself helps establish and transmit.

The same can be said of music. Music, that is, has always been a contending force in society, not only as it reflects and reacts to social forces but also as it helps shape a society and its culture. But the role of music in the images I have considered here is limited to that of affirming political and economic policies with epic implications for both England and India, policies of imperialist aggrandizement and the suppression of human rights. I do not suggest that music and musicians (professional or amateur), or visual artists for that matter, were responsible for the British Empire and the East India Company, but that the role assigned to music in the culture was to affirm the status quo or at least not challenge it. In these images, in other words, music and art provide evidence of the very power their presence serves to mask.[47] In the process music and art are marginalized from participation in shaping values alternative to those of the dominant ideology. Instead, they aid the hegemonic drive of imperialistic politics.

Many years ago Walter Benjamin pointed out that history belongs to the victors and that the spoils of victory are what we have come to call cultural treasures. Benjamin suggested that our cultural treasures, which he himself held in esteem, nonetheless have origins to be contemplated with horror: "They owe their existence not only to the efforts of the great minds and talents who have created them, but also to the anonymous toil of their contemporaries. There is no document of civilization which is not at the same time a document of barbarism."[48]

This barbarism is embodied in cultural chauvinism. Perhaps no one expressed that chauvinism more forthrightly, though apparently unknowingly, than Thomas Babington Macaulay in his lengthy speech to the House of Commons (10 July 1833) on the subject of a draft penal code for India. "I see," he said, "the morality, the philosophy, the taste of Europe, beginning to produce a salutary effect on the hearts and understandings of our [Indian] subjects." And a little later: "Consider, too, Sir, how rapidly the public mind of India is advancing, how much attention is already paid by the higher classes of the natives to those intellectual pursuits on the cultivation of which the superiority of the European race to the rest of mankind principally depends." Macaulay concluded his speech by redrawing the connection between Western cultural superiority (defined as art and morality) and the suppression of India by British political power (defined as law); his remarks represent nothing less than the apotheosis of unrepentant nationalism, his well-established liberalism notwithstanding: "There is an empire exempt from all natural causes of decay. [Its] triumphs are the pacific triumphs of reason over barbarism; that empire is the imperishable empire of our arts and our morals, our literature and our laws."[49] In the House of Commons Macaulay thus drew attention to the relationships I have developed here: that political empire is mirrored by the empire of culture: *our* arts, *our* morals, *our* literature, *our* laws. By direct implication, moreover, these cultural markers provided for him the rationalization—hence, justification—for imperialism.

In my room we got to talking about the "piano"
as a piece of furniture that functions in the
petit-bourgeois interior as the true dynamic center
of all the dominant miseries and catastrophes of
the household. Asja was electrified by the idea; she
wanted to write an article on it with me which Reich
would then turn into a dramatic sketch.

Walter Benjamin,
Moscow Diary

Woman has been made the caretaker of all things
beautiful. . . . What remained of the fans, songs, and
dances of Roman slave girls was finally whittled down
in Birmingham to the pianoforte, needlework, and
similar attainments, until the last vestiges of female
wantonness had been clarified down to an emblem of
patriarchal civilization.

Max Horkheimer and Theodor W. Adorno,
Dialectic of Enlightenment

6

SEXUAL IDENTITY, DEATH, AND THE FAMILY PIANO IN THE NINETEENTH CENTURY

THE RELATIONS BETWEEN the piano and the history of the family that are the subject of Walter Benjamin's and his friends' musings are located by Horkheimer and Adorno in the gender politics of the English middle-class household during the Industrial Revolution and centered on the Woman Question.[1] Connections between women and the piano were multiple and complex during the nineteenth century. This chapter sorts out one responsible agent: the gaze.[2] I shall explore how the piano served as an object to be looked at besides being heard or played—and how the looking was insistently gendered, driven by the instrument's extra-musical function within the home as the visual-sonoric simulacrum of family, wife, and mother. But first I want to establish that domestic keyboard instruments generally—the virginals, harpsichords, and fortepianos that precede the Victorian piano[3]—were, from their earliest histories, subject to the gaze, richly discursive "texts" to be *read*. Two issues pertain: that the discourse these instruments embodied changed radically and that with the rise of the middle class the discourse became rigidly gendered.

The virginals and harpsichords made in Antwerp in the sixteenth and seventeenth centuries by the Ruckers family are noted for the literary mottoes printed on paper and glued onto their cases (see Fig. 46). The instruments are thus textual, hence discursive, in literal, direct ways. As we would expect, the mottoes often comment on music, sometimes in the imperative voice. Yet even in their linguistic starkness—I refer to both their visual "plainness" and their brevity—they aestheticize, and for a purpose. Aestheticization is the product not only of the texts themselves but also of the visual frame within which the texts are enclosed. Moreover, the mottoes do not inscribe the everyday, the mundane, and the prosaic but the extraordinary, the obscure, and the poetic. Their language is Latin: less Catholic than classical, hence out of space and time. In essence the mottoes voice a privileged, if not precisely private, language that by being readable admits the reader-viewer not only to meaning but also to belonging. The Latin motto marks identities constructed on the basis of education, class, status, and privilege. Further, it transfers its semantics onto the musical sonorities produced by the instrument to which it is attached: a privileged, ethically elevated discourse defined by the difference of these sonorities from those available to common, public, and hence comparatively degraded audition—the audition, for example, of the tavern music ubiquitous in the Low Countries.[4]

The mottoes are framed—set off—by printed paper borders that operate visually in complementary ways. The border decorates, to be sure; but like the frame of a painting, or like a fence, it also articulates a space. It informs us that what is contained within the borders matters and what is outside them does not. It includes by excluding. The frame is the geometry of possession, and possession is a terrain for meaning. Within the decorative frame knowledge resides, visually and semantically aestheticized and made exclusive.[5] It should be kept in mind, first, that the meanings attached to the instrument itself, to the music suited for it in its almost invariably domestic setting, and to the player are all of sufficient importance that language must intrude as an overdeterminant to sound, as if needing to *say:* "These sonorities mean thus." Second, this need to say something identifies the issue of "assertion," musical or verbal, as important.[6] Third, the intrusion of language on a musical terrain otherwise emptied of words, even perhaps marking an escape from words, tacitly admits, not that musical sonority is otherwise meaningless, but that its meanings are not guaranteed, that they are unstable. The writing on these instruments is the sign of anxiety about unanchored meaning in a culture given, even in early modernity, to spasms of increasing classification and the felt need to control every semiotic parameter, including the sonoric.[7]

Between 1650 and 1660 the Flemish painter Gonzales Coques produced a portrait presumed to be of the van Coudenberg family (Fig. 46). It represents a gathering at music and table, its musical ensemble provided by a woman playing a Ruckers harpsichord who accompanies two other women in song. Other instruments rest unused in the left foreground: a cittern, two lutes, and a viola da gamba. Two couples at the center eat and drink. Over their heads hang two landscape paintings and a storm-tossed seascape, in conventional allusion to the stages between tranquillity and its opposite, a kind of aesthetic transliteration of life's instabilities. But there is more to the story. The image is bifurcated: music on the left, all of it female, with an Arcadian landscape as backdrop; on the right, the

FIG. 46   Gonzales Coques, *Van Coudenberg Family* (?) (c. 1650/60), oil on canvas, 100 × 135 cm. Brussels, S. Bergmans Collection. Photo copyright A.C.L., Brussels.

side with the stormy seascape, violence in the ritual form of a hunting trophy. The vignette of the young man with gun and hare has a long pictorial pedigree in the art of the period; the implied narrative unfolds conventionally. Thus the hunter holds his gun vertically so that it parallels his body and thereby draws our attention. The hare, by contrast, is held by its hind legs, its head near the floor. It is vanquished. Between gun and hare is the young man himself, in effect serving as the verb-agent to this subject-and-object text. The point of the hunt is clarified by the conventional presentation of its results (dead game) to a woman who accepts the trophy. Between the extremes of music and the kill, a meal is consumed by two couples.

The painting addresses a certain understanding about the nature of life. The setting is middle-class and elegant—typical of new wealth, uneasy wealth.[8] The scene is one of achievement, not delight. Everyone does something, but no one does anything for the pleasure of it. Smiles are banished; achievement, a process never completed, inevitably remains unstable—life's barometer rises so that it may fall. Two kinds of food are represented. The product of violent death carried by the hunter coming in at the right, like an intruder, wearing outdoor garb and accompanied by his hounds, will eventually be brought to table to sustain life. One couple at table turn toward this entrance. The other couple, now eating their dessert—the woman prominently holding a piece of fruit—turn to the musicians and get another kind of fill. But the painting draws a logical narrative circle: the music itself depends on the hunter. The outside provides for the domestic inside. The connection of one to the other makes for a painful thought, in the seventeenth century as today. That pain can be dulled by the wine in the cooler in the center foreground, always a sign of the good life in Low Countries paintings, indeed its very product, but also its temporary antidote (cf. the discussion of Fig. 17).

The harpsichord at left carries an inscription found on two surviving Ruckers virginals:[9] "Audi vide et tace / Si vis vivere in pace" (Listen, watch, and be silent if you wish to live in peace). This is an extraordinary imperative. It urges attention to music in the metaphoric language of peace and war—something especially pertinent given the history of the Eighty Years' War of recent memory in the region. Music is theorized as a sound and a sight and a herald: Attend to it; keep your ears and eyes open. The motto is directed at the women around the harpsichord, able to read its injunction, and at us, the painting's viewers. Its message is gendered, and its discursive form is more than slightly shaded by threat—made visible in the binary structure of the painting (tranquillity versus violence) and the transliteration of warfare into the ritual form of killing game. Thus there appears a problematic association of music with death, as well as a valorization of nature's ritual transformation into culture: death brings art. This calls to mind another harpsichord motto: "Arbor eram vilis quondam sed viva tacebam / Nunc bene si tangor mortua dulce sono" (I was once an ordinary tree, although living I was silent; now, though dead, if I am well played, I sound sweetly).[10]

The violence implicit in both mottoes is, in the second, domesticated and gendered, since "sweetly" carries a feminine mark. A few mottoes trace these connections more boldly, locating gender difference in a male lament about marriage relations: "Ducere uxorem est vendere liberatem"[11] (To take a wife is to sell one's freedom). This age-old cliché is inscribed on the one piece of household furniture that commonly came as a gift to a wife from her husband. It argues that her music is the sonoric analogue to his imprisonment, music/Woman as captivation. This abusive judgment is connected to another motto, this time in Italian and on an

Italian instrument: "Io da le piaghe mie forma ricevo" (I receive form from the blows [I receive]).[12] In this instance the virginal, anthropomorphized as Woman, is made woman by the violence imposed on her. Music is posited as harmony, but harmony is produced by a beating. Aestheticized as music, Woman's very being is articulated as a deferential masochism in the face of sadistic revenge.

MUSIC AND THE AESTHETICIZATION OF VIOLENCE

Paintings commonly decorated the cases of virginals and harpsichords from the sixteenth century through the eighteenth.[13] The most striking subjects, painted more commonly than one might expect, involve violence. I shall start with hunting scenes, my example being a clavichord by Barthold Fritz of Brunswick from 1751 (Figs. 47–48).[14] The hunt is a subject about social class and privilege, especially an organized hunt like that represented on the clavichord's lid. It was in fact a highly ritualized exercise of the nobility in which a musical instrument, the valveless horn, served as the sonoric device for directing every action of both men and trained hounds.[15] (The signals, which changed little over the centuries, were a sonoric pedigree of the timeless class privilege the hunt itself underwrote.) The mounted hunters, often separated but staying within earshot of one another, produced a discourse via their horns, whose purpose was to coordinate actions leading to the animal's death. The calls were as precise as those of the cavalry trumpet, kettledrums, and infantry side drums in battle. The hunt was an important subject in Western European painting up to the end of the ancien régime. Thereafter, with the ascendancy of the bourgeoisie, male power was reconceived and visualized in different terms. But during the seventeenth and eighteenth centuries hunting scenes and still-life hunting "trophies" are legion (Fig. 49).[16]

Given that the delicate clavichord, with its small sound, is quintessentially a domestic instrument, how might one account for—and make sense of—the hunt scene that decorates it (and this is not the only example of the kind[17])? Apart from the subject itself, which may seem odd to us today, the lid of Barthold Fritz's clavichord is especially unusual on account of its color, or rather its lack of color; it is painted in blue monochrome. What might this mean, weighed against the convention it violates? Forswearing color, besides drawing attention to its absence, privileges drawing. The subject of the picture—in fact, a narrative—is accentuated. According to art theory articulated in the seventeenth century by the French Academy of Painting and Sculpture, drawing appealed to reason, whereas color appealed to emotion. Not accidentally, these qualities were gendered, the former male, the latter female. That the image overdetermines the charge of its distinctly

FIG. 47   Clavichord (1751, Brunswick), by Barthold Fritz. London, Victoria and Albert Museum. Photo courtesy of Board of Trustees, Victoria and Albert Museum.

FIG. 48   Clavichord by Barthold Fritz; detail of painted lid: *Hunting Scene.* Photo courtesy of Board of Trustees, Victoria and Albert Museum.

FIG. 49   Pieter Boel, *Hunting Still Life,* oil on canvas, 135 × 107 cm. Rotterdam, Museum Boymans–van Beuningen.

masculine narrative by "avoiding" color was unlikely to be missed by the instrument's viewer-player, normally a woman.

The textuality of the clavichord lid painting is doubly indicated, first, because of its relative colorlessness (an un-painting, so to speak) and, second, because of its narrative character, which, like the written word, "reads" from left to right. That is, the painting not only represents the spatial dimension but the temporal or sequential dimension as well. The viewer's eyes move as when reading words on a page, enacting the sensation of movement that encodes the logic of the activity represented and thereby naturalizing it. The montage: at the left, a mounted hunter signals to his compatriots and the hounds; his horn's sonorities organize their movements, providing direction. In the center there is a spatial gap through which the hounds charge, a space to be closed. At the right, that closure is achieved. The dogs reach their prey; the stag's neck is about to be torn open—after which *exeunt omnes* via the gap in the scenery, very noticeable, at the extreme right. A drama is enacted, a story told.

In the picture, as in music, there is antecedent and consequent, theme and development, sequence and closure—an internal, narrative logic, an inevitability, as though no other outcome were possible or appropriate. But what is the relation of the painting to music? Why is this story painted on the lid of a clavichord? It seems to me that the relation is governed not by music as such but by a set of cultural parameters within which music is intended to function. The clavichord's hunting scene provides a frame of reference and a frame of limitation—an inclusion (and a clarification) but also an exclusion.

The hunting scene becomes visible the moment the instrument's cover is raised. One cannot make music without confronting it; nor can one visually escape it by setting a musical score on the rack. For what remains ever visible, next to the score, is that portion of the image wherein the stag takes its last breath in terrified flight. This part of the image connects music to death, a link I want to pursue, but later. For the moment I am after something related but different. In practice the hunt was an almost exclusively male activity. It was authorized as a private right on one's own lands. It demonstrated, in the most dramatic and exaggerated manner, the fullest degree of ownership: the right to kill. To place a hunting scene on a clavichord effectively linked this power over life to the activity of music, the apparent radical opposite to the hunting scene.

In the hunt the horn sounds are preeminently practical (instrumental, in the critical-theoretical sense of the word). They direct an action of consequence. By contrast, the sounds produced by the clavichord are preeminently impractical. They have no consequence; they achieve no "ends"—indeed, one cannot so much as dance to the instrument's sounds, for the noise of the body's physical movements would make the music virtually inaudible. Thus among all other instruments the clavichord is radically private. Yet even in the privacy of the playing, its discursive boundaries must be preestablished. Sounds without consequence are suspect sounds, in that "free-floating" sonorities may transcend established boundaries. These boundaries differ for men and women. If a man plays the clavichord, and some did, the visual field before him serves as a reminder of his higher duties, his identity grounded not in music but in violence and the pleasures of killing; as such, the scene is an argument against music.[18] (That this issue, involving gender identity, might hinge on the cultural contradiction between blood sport and the clavichord can hardly be surprising in a society that continues to rest easier when boys play football and leave off piano lessons.) If, however, the player is a woman, the text reads differently, but as a complement. What she sees before her are at least two accounts on which her own identity and situation depend. She sees that she is the weaker vessel, that next to the activities of her husband hers are trivial; she sees that all she is, all that the culture demands she be—"accomplished," refined, and nurturing—depends on the distinctly opposite behavior of her mate.[19] Musical aesthetics, marked female, serve as the peaceful product of violence.

The eighteenth-century English painter Arthur Devis produced a marriage portrait specifying these relations with dramatic emphasis. Above the head of the seated husband hangs a painting-within-the-painting of a hunt in progress, while above the head of his wife hangs a caged bird.[20] Put differently, the imagery that claims the prerogatives of male power also specifies a price.

The putative distance between art music and the art of war is collapsed in a double-manual harpsichord, dated 1612, built by Hans Ruckers the Elder and rebuilt in 1774 by Pascal Taskin, with case paintings by the Dutch artist Adam Frans van der Meulen, something of a specialist in battle pictures (Figs. 50–53).[21] The main scene, on the inside of the harpsichord's lid (Fig. 51), shows a mounted entourage with Louis XIV riding at the head. A walled town appears in the background. On the instrument's sides (Figs. 52–53) similar scenes show views of distant fortified towns with mounted riders in the foreground. Every pictorial convention employed in the composition recalls the battle picture (Fig. 54). Thus whereas no actual battle is in progress, the effect of one is nonetheless created,[22] especially by the repeated inclusion of galloping horses, their tails stretched out behind to indicate their speed and the insistence with which they move—like a text, from left to right and out of the frame, following a path paralleling the front picture plane. In the side scenes (Figs. 52–53) the viewpoint is raised somewhat, approximating the bird's-eye level typical of siege pictures and providing an opportunity to show the king surveying the field over which he reigns.

These images argue that for music to flourish, political pacification must be

FIG. 50   Double-manual harpsichord (1612, Antwerp), by Hans Ruckers the Elder; rebuilt by
Pascal Taskin (1774). Brussels, Conservatoire Royal de Musique, Musée Instrumental. Photo
copyright A.C.L., Brussels.

pursued militarily. In this extraordinary visual conceit, force and imputed violence
become the agents of art. A panorama of unremitting maleness, these scenes together literally frame and direct the sonorities produced by the harpsichord. Violence and art music are linked, visually and sonorically, answering the cause of
mutual justification. It needs to be mentioned at this juncture that the aesthetics
of violence continues in history beyond the ancien régime, as for example in the

FIG. 51 Double-manual harpsichord by Hans Ruckers the Elder; detail of painted lid by Adam Frans van der Meulen: *Landscape with Louis XIV and Mounted Entourage.* Photo copyright A.C.L., Brussels.

FIG. 52   Double-manual harpsichord by Hans Ruckers the Elder; detail of case painting by Adam
Frans van der Meulen: *Military Scene before a Fortified Town.* Photo copyright A.C.L., Brussels.

FIG. 53   Double-manual harpsichord by Hans Ruckers the Elder; detail of case painting by Adam
Frans van der Meulen: *Military Scene before a Fortified Town.* Photo copyright A.C.L., Brussels.

FIG. 54 Peeter Snayers, *Battle at Höchst* (c. 1622), oil on canvas, 196 × 266 cm. Brussels, Musées Royaux des Beaux-Arts de Belgique. Photo copyright A.C.L., Brussels.

theoretical fantasies of the Futurists. Thus the poet F. T. Marinetti, in an orgasmic ecstasy of words piled atop one another, taking pleasure in the nonpunctuated rhythms of bloody anarchy scripted by a First World War general staff: "What a joy to hear to smell completely *taratatata* of the machine guns screaming a breathlessness under the stings slaps *traak-traak* whips *pic-pac-pum-tumb* weirdness leaps 200 meters range Far far in back of the orchestra pools muddying hyffing goaded oxen wagons"—all this nonsense apparently trying to be music, eliciting the following promotion from Luigi Russolo: "We want to give pitches to these diverse noises, regulating them harmonically and rhythmically."[23]

The opposite of the violence promised in the harpsichord case representing Louis XIV (Fig. 51) is the scene of Orpheus charming the animals (Figs. 55–56) painted on an English virginal, dated 1641, built by Gabriell Townsend.[24] Like battle scenes, the Orpheus story was popular among painters in the seventeenth century (the example here is technically unaccomplished, to say the least).[25] It is an especially interesting subject for inclusion on a virginal and functions in precise conjunction with my account of the stag hunt. As I suggested in Chapter 2, the point of the story, drawn from Ovid's *Metamorphoses* (10:86–105), is male power

FIG. 55   Virginal (1641, English), by Gabriell Townsend. Brussels, Conservatoire Royal du Musique, Musée Instrumental. Photo copyright A.C.L., Brussels.

FIG. 56   Virginal by Gabriell Townsend; detail of painted lid: *Orpheus Charming the Animals*. Photo copyright A.C.L., Brussels.

over nature. Orpheus sings and the wildest animals lie down at his feet; even inanimate nature—trees and rocks—bends toward him. (It is no accident that early Christian artists conflated the story with the coming of Christ.[26]) Orpheus's power comes from knowledge, musical knowledge. In this instance external and violent power does not make possible the harmony of art; rather, art and power are one and the same. In other words, the distance is collapsed between art, typically theorized as a spiritual and spiritualizing realm of human experience, and a man's power to shape the physical world.

The Orpheus story told on the virginal, interesting on its own terms, includes a trope in the form of witnesses to Orpheus's accomplishment, a woman and man in the right foreground (there is also a third figure, less clear, still further to the right and mounted on horseback). Attention focuses on the woman, who in fact all but blocks the man's body from view. She looks over her shoulder, drawn not to the man embracing her but to Orpheus, whose music compels her—but not, apparently, her lover, who pays Orpheus no heed. When the virginal is played, music leaned against the lid, the figure of Orpheus is covered over. He is replaced by audible sonority. The figure of the woman, by contrast, remains visible—like the stag, incapable of escaping, as if caught up by the sound, looking toward the score, the textual authority. She watches and listens, yet for the most part she exercises her surveillance on her own sex, in that throughout the history of domestic keyboard instruments the vast majority of players are known to have been women.[27]

This tale can be told in a different, if complementary, way. When music is set against the lid, eliminating Orpheus from view, the woman witness might be said, in effect, to look back toward the musical text that replaces Orpheus. This text, Orpheus's script as it were, provides a tacit reminder that artistic creativity is a male prerogative—this even though artistic endeavors fundamentally placed a man's identity in doubt, feminizing him in the eyes of others of his sex.[28] The thoroughness of male dominion is such that the arts themselves are fully incorporated; the woman virginalist is left to perform what men have written out for her. Unless she improvises, her own performance is always already scripted.[29] Thus the early history of musical notation, closely tied to the political desire to codify, to establish "universal" norms in the medieval church, must be understood in light of the darker histories the practice embeds.[30] The relation between musical notation and surveillance is closer than the history of aesthetics has preferred to consider. To express this matter still more scandalously, musical notation was developed to give people orders to follow. That indisputably great music is tied to the long history of notation does not lessen the social price of this accomplishment, which is not inconsiderable. Thus the inability of many classically trained musicians of our own day to improvise is hardly accidental; indeed, it is planned as a "natural" outgrowth of the felt need to transmit the *fully texted* traditions of canonic practices. The disgust shown in music schools toward nonschool musicians, especially performers of popular music who cannot *read* music, is coin from the same mint.

DOMESTICITY, ORPHEUS, AND CREATIVITY

Let me recite three well-known facts about the piano in the nineteenth century: first, that it became the ubiquitous and unrivaled instrument of the bourgeois home; second, that it located itself almost exclusively among amateurs as a female instrument, completing a historical trend reaching back into the seventeenth century (this despite the many men of the period who played it); third, that the piano underwent numerous changes of internal and external design. These facts are closely related. The connection that might seem least obvious is that between the first two together and the third—that is, the connection between piano design, on the one hand, and the piano as the quintessential domestic middle-class instrument, played mostly by women, on the other.

The history of internal design changes to the piano is well researched,[31] as is much of the instrument's history of manufacture and marketing;[32] I have nothing to add to that history. Case design and decoration, by contrast, remains unexplored, mostly now the subject of amazed amusement at some of the truly bizarre results that survive. Yet it is unquestionable that manufacturers, however much they experimented with internal and external piano design, consciously attempted both to mediate and to tap a market driven by public taste. The often odd-looking results were anything but idle fancies; they were instead products of a rapidly developing market for domestic pianos.[33] Their design was conscious, in effect learned. All this is obvious. The question remains: What understandings of "public" taste drove the history of piano manufacture?[34] This is a larger issue than I can adequately sort out here, but I will suggest some ways to begin thinking about it.

Consider two upright instruments, the first a clavicytherium, perhaps of German manufacture, from the mid-eighteenth century (Figs. 57–58), the second an English piano made in London in 1801 (Figs. 59–60). The design of both instruments implicitly addresses the problem of space in relation to musical practice. That is, the "grand"-size harpsichords and, later, pianos, quite apart from their musical advantages over smaller instruments in the same family, possessed greater prestige not only because of their higher price but also because of their relatively

FIG. 57 Clavicytherium (mid-18th century, German?). New York, The Metropolitan Museum of Art, gift of Helen C. Lanier, 1981.

FIG. 58 Clavicytherium, with doors opened. New York, The Metropolitan Museum of Art, gift of Helen C. Lanier, 1981.

more commanding look and more impressive "musical capacity." But this prestige factor carried a price tag; these large instruments, "good" only for music, took up a lot of floor space. In the course of the eighteenth century even the European aristocracy downsized their living quarters, a practice adopted at least for a time by the bourgeoisie after them. Musical instruments were at a disadvantage in this emerging ideology of practicality and self-imposed "restraint." Moreover, with the ascendancy of the middle class the place of music, ever more feminized and as such valued less by amateurs, became increasingly precarious.[35]

These two instruments both address the demands of practicality, but the clavicytherium goes only half the distance. Like later space-saving pianos, it is designed to be set up against a wall. Yet when it is played, four doors must be opened up—of solid wood, they would unduly muffle the sound if left closed—and this turns the instrument into something of a spectacle, especially with the raked doors covering the soundboard (Fig. 58). When played, therefore, the instrument appears eminently *im*practical, the preposterousness of its shape mirroring aristocratic privilege, its impracticality a mark of class distinction, an excess that proclaims the owner's freedom from the realm of necessity.

The English piano comes nearer the realm of bourgeois practicality (Figs. 59–60). Its twin doors normally remain closed, for they are merely of cloth surrounded by a wood frame and hence have little acoustic effect. They are rectilinear, hiding the wing shape of the grand piano behind them, thus giving the instrument the look of a cupboard and mitigating its problematic status as "merely" a musical instrument. When the doors are opened, the instrument's utilitarian double function as a music storage cabinet is evident (Fig. 60).[36] The cupboard design marks the piano as middle class—prestigious as a grand yet modest, even a bit severe. It also marks the piano as feminine: the objects it might properly hold, apart from printed music or smaller instruments, are bric-a-brac.[37] The move toward practicality and the feminization of the domestic piano quickly concatenated in the eyes of manufacturers. Thus small pianos early in the nineteenth century were made to double as sewing tables (Fig. 61). The open lid reveals a shallow compartmentalized sewing box set above the soundboard and strings. The lid itself incorporates a mirror, supporting an additional potential function for such instruments in the boudoir, where in fact they were commonly placed.[38] In post–Civil War America the same retail outlets sold both keyboard instruments and sewing machines. One manufacturer in Connecticut even produced a combined sewing machine and melodeon shaped like a parlor sideboard: triply feminine, triply utilitarian.[39]

It is now time to return to Orpheus via an upright piano (*Lyraflügel*) made in Berlin during the second quarter of the nineteenth century (Fig. 62). The strings and soundboard of this instrument (7 feet 3 inches high) are disguised by a gigantic stylized lyre set in front of a silk panel, a form repeated in the lyre shape defining the pedal board. The charmed animals, presumably, are recalled by the claw feet in which the piano's legs terminate and by the twin griffin heads surmounting the lyre's arms. Vaguely classical arabesques and flutings on the gilded lyre contrast sharply with the black case atop which it rests. The lyre motif occurs

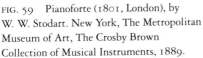

FIG. 59   Pianoforte (1801, London), by
W. W. Stodart. New York, The Metropolitan
Museum of Art, The Crosby Brown
Collection of Musical Instruments, 1889.

FIG. 60   Pianoforte by W. W. Stodart, with doors open. New
York, The Metropolitan Museum of Art, The Crosby Brown
Collection of Musical Instruments, 1889.

repeatedly in pianos of this period, for example in another by the same maker
(Fig. 63) with a medallion bust of Beethoven. The visual effect of this piano resonates from its likeness to an altar or shrine. The design of both cases privileges
men as the source of musical art on instruments principally played by women: the
first via a mythic musician, Orpheus, and the second via a mythologized real musician, Beethoven. What is more, the visual code that privileges men is so preposterously overstated that it does nothing so much as plead a case.[40]

FIG. 61   Square piano in the form of a sewing table (early 19th century, German or Austrian). New Haven, Yale University Collection of Musical Instruments.

FIG. 62   *Below, left:* Upright pianoforte (*Lyraflügel;* 2nd quarter 19th century, Berlin), by Johan Christian Schleip. New York, The Metropolitan Museum of Art, Gift of Theodore R. Sayers, 1968.

FIG. 63   Upright pianoforte (*Lyraflügel;* 1820–44, Berlin), by Johan Christian Schleip. New York, The Metropolitan Museum of Art, The Crosby Brown Collection of Musical Instruments, 1889.

WOMAN AND DEATH

In Victorian culture the piano functioned in sound and sight alike as an analogical referent to social harmony and domestic order. Its sonorities, whether potential or realized, served as the aesthetic metaphor simultaneously connecting and justifying the connection between public and private life—between the outside world of the Industrial Revolution and the protected inner sanctum of the Victorian bourgeois home, between men and women in their social relations, and (in some ways most important) between bourgeois desire and erotic capacity, on the one hand, and their sublimation (a tense and contradictory process), on the other. The analogical function of music in the socio-cultural construction of an idealized, harmonious Victorian life was so well entrenched as to account for the production of innumerable conventionalized musical images, among which three examples will serve my purpose. The subject of each is the reverie or daydream. All three date from near the end of the nineteenth century, so they reflect the deep-seated ideologies of both late-Victorian gender construction and gender-specific appropriations of musical expression.

In the first picture (Fig. 64), the woman at the piano turns her back toward us, making us intruders. Yet given the watercolor's title—*A Reverie*—our intrusive gaze fixes on an ambiguous space, at once physical and psychic. The image invites a sexual response, encoded by the subject's flowing hair, a conventional Victorian sign of sexuality and sexual availability.[41] Her physical immobility is the complement to her marmoreal white skin, which seems drained of blood apart from the slight glow to her cheek. This absence of color gives our gaze a clinical as well as a psychological tinge; it invites association with pathology and the corpse—no surprise in that nineteenth-century medicine (informed by dissection) was obsessed with female anatomy and its psychiatric sexual implications.[42] Indeed, the image's deathly effect is reenforced by the unlighted candles flanking the woman and by the decorative frieze running across the piano's front, a classically inspired procession of women and their children in poses conventionally associated with mourning.

The book on the music rack is a textless "text"; that is, its notation is missing. What of this lack? It seems to me that in this visual fantasy—an explicitly male fantasy—we are at a conclusion, an ending: again, a death. Edward Harper, the watercolorist, arranged the woman's right hand so that we can easily see which two keys she is depressing. They are the notes G and C, outlining the dominant-tonic movement in C major,[43] the fundamental relationship on which the major-minor tonal system depends: sonorically a metaphor for the culture and an indication of finality, closure.[44] We are meant to focus on her hand. Harper draws our attention to it by violating anatomical reality, making it slightly freakish: he distorts the

FIG. 64 Edward Samuel Harper, *A Reverie*, watercolor, 20 × 34.5 cm. Private collection. Photo courtesy of Sotheby's, London.

physical relations of wrist, hand, and fingers. The impossible hand position—one that would be physically painful to replicate—articulates not only the importance of this detail but also a meaning.

Harper's *Reverie* conflates musical ensemble with family, leaving little doubt about the other performers: the husband-father's violoncello (familial and musical foundation/base)[45] leans against the piano at the left, and two violins, one pointing toward the father's instrument and the other away from it (boy and girl), sit atop the piano.[46] But the family is absent, and the many women (on the piano's painted front) mourn. The musical text is likewise absent, leaving the player with no direction, with nothing left but to conclude. She looks off to the right, away from the page on which there is nothing to read, pulling our eyes in the direction of her one musically engaged hand and also suggesting that she looks toward a doorway. We must believe that she waits; there is little to suggest she will do anything else. Meanwhile, the title informs us that someone dreams. We are not told the dreamer's identity, though it seems appropriate to assume that it is she. Yet I think that the viewer is invited to become a dreamer about her—a sexual dreamer who can make her "complete," for she is unquestionably represented principally as the embodiment of lack. Music confirms her desire to be made complete, as well as her own lack of agency to achieve her desire. Seated at the piano, presumably improvising and not singing, she is reduced to a cipher of textless sound, reduced to making musical gestures that confirm her loss of speech. She is Sleeping Beauty, needing to be "awakened." It is not quite appropriate to stop here, however. For in fact she does possess agency, though it is represented as a force that acts on behalf of another's interests: the coded allure of her musical body is intended to produce in men the desire that only she can satisfy, even as she is constructed by a man in the interests of men who would consume her in their gaze.

Henry Stock's *Musician's Reverie* (Fig. 65) could hardly be more different. The male sitter's position is frontal, and his dream is public, hence shared. The musician's intensity is demonic; his dreams are dark, swirling, and conflicted. The woman's musico-familial dream, we are asked to believe, is unalterably domestic, if nonetheless complex. The man's seems richer, more frightening, and less predictable: in a word, more exciting. Yet this is not everyman, nor is his a bourgeois daydream; it is that of the (anti-bourgeois) artist. In my judgment, however, we are not to find comfort in the artist-musician's articulating his existential identity via music. The real issue is the artist's isolation; he conjures a masturbatory fantasy of Watteauesque nudes and Goyaesque demons in an experience that brings on night. Here the concern is not domestic completeness but the yearning for unremitting solitary passion. Woman and devil float together in the dreamer's psyche, pushing reason aside (the man uses books as a footrest). This is not merely an

FIG. 65   Henry J. Stock, *A Musician's Reverie* (1888), watercolor and gouache, 50.8 × 34.9 cm.
Harrow (Greater London), Harrow School Collection. Copyright The Governors of Harrow School.
Photo: Courtauld Institute of Art, London.

image about music as such, however; it is about improvisatory music; notated music lies abandoned on the floor, in the lowest space available in the image. The dreamer's art is a false art, produced by abandoning the text; his music moves into *unscripted,* hence socially dangerous, space. The price of liberation, sexually charged, is the loss of reason—marked in the watercolor's murky background by a bastardized recollection of Goya's famous etching *The Sleep of Reason Produces Monsters,* which opens the series *Los Caprichos.*

On the one hand, the absolutes of gender difference are obvious. The man's playing is interactive with his instrument, impassioned, deeply soulful, as his furled brow encodes. It is hot, threatening, stimulating, and it is ultimately contemporary, not classical; thus it preserves the Victorian male prerogatives over time and history, as opposed to the oddly classicized image of the woman at her piano in Harper's watercolor. On the other hand, the singularity of the subject removes it from the more measurable reality of contemporaneous imagery. Its singularity is embedded principally in the openly acknowledged connection between male desire and music. Yet the sexual desire is nonetheless unrealized; it fails. As a fantasy—a dream and not a "reality"—it marks its own inadequacy in precisely the domain where successful performance codifies masculine identity. The image transfers lack, though a dynamic lack, to a man. Physical sexuality is transformed into musical improvisation. By this means, the putative social dangers immanent in the dreamer's abandonment of the musical text (his refusal to follow the notation, the social script) are rendered harmful to him alone, and not to other men. Still, it is not that simple; the message is mixed. The improvising musician in effect "refuses" to read a musical text that both social convention and cultural practice mark as feminine. By his refusal to read, his determination to improvise, he lays claim to his masculinity at another level. Yet in the very act of performing he reestablishes the link between music and feminine identity that he sought to break. He acknowledges that music is the displacement of his true object of desire: music is woman; woman is evil; both are captivating, castrating. The pleasures afforded by both ironically conflate with evil and terror. Take your pleasure; pay the price.

What does this suggest about music? In this male reverie, music operates on two levels. Visually it is a bit of a sideshow, like modern-day amusement rides that simultaneously promise the thrill of a lifetime and an utterly predictable, completely safe sixty-second experience, a kind of assembly-line excitement: we have it; we walk away from it. Music operates as the analogical manifestation of the thrill (and not coincidentally the climax), extraordinary yet peripheral and inevitably momentary. The socio-erotics of music established by these private-public dichotomies, wherein the visual inscription of music serves as a substitute for both emotion and sensuality, operates also as a momentary compensation and consolation for the social fracturing within the increasingly competitive, class- and gender-separated world of nineteenth-century capitalist industrialism. (To say this does no more than acknowledge the ideological component of most nineteenth-century aesthetics.) Imagery preserves the sedimented memory of what has been lost in the process, even as memory is continually mediated by the fast-changing present.

Sir Frank Dicksee, a major Victorian painter, produced in 1895 *A Reverie* (Fig. 66), involving another night scene (the painting is very dark), where a husband sits off to one side, contemplative and limp—note his prominently displayed left arm—while his wife at the piano sings to him. The only difficulty is that she is dead, her ghostly spirit hovering at the far left, dressed in a bed gown. When the image was first exhibited at the Royal Academy, Dicksee included in the catalogue the following verse:

> In the years fled,
> Lips that are dead
> Sang me that song.[47]

There is something curious about Dicksee's emphasis in his text on the word *lips*. However strained the metaphorical association of lips and song may be, it privileges something consistent in my discussion: it associates the music with words. I suggest that his reverie, an impotent fantasy on the lost body of his wife, is driven simultaneously by a transfixing necrophilia focused on "lips that are dead" and by the text they pronounce. These texts, literally the Victorian song literature of the day, were commonly, though by no means always, written by men, who thus availed themselves of the opportunity to define the nature of love and of relations between lovers. The widower, in other words, finds self-pitying comfort in the fantasy that even from the grave his wife speaks/sings the patriarchal art laid down for her, by which he seeks to preserve his own sense of identity.[48] Nor should it be forgotten that Dicksee, by providing the exhibition catalogue doggerel, sought to produce semiotic closure on alternate readings of the image. In the man's dream, song itself is silenced. The phenomenon of music—its very materiality, so to speak—is absented and, I think, made less dangerous, more a philosophical notion than an embodied practice, paralleling the memory of the decreased spouse whose body no longer exists. "In dreams, the sense of hearing is never solicited. The dream is strictly a visual phenomenon, and it is by the sense of sight that what is addressed to the ear will be perceived: a matter, one might say, of acoustic images."[49]

FIG. 66   Sir Frank Dicksee, *A Reverie* (1895), oil on canvas, 102.9 × 137.2 cm. National
Museums and Galleries on Merseyside (Walker Art Gallery, Liverpool).

DEATH AND THE PIANO

Two pianos remain to be considered. The first (Fig. 67) is a very small upright
("pianino") built by the London firm of Priestly circa 1860. Unquestionably a
domestic instrument, it is significant for its case decoration, executed by Sir Edward Burne-Jones, the instrument's original owner, who received it as a marriage
gift from his aunt; the instrument was regularly played by his young wife.[50] At
the far right side of the open lid, hence always in sight even when music sits on
the rack, Burne-Jones produced a scene of a woman personifying Love playing a
small organ, whose bellows are worked by an angel.[51] Stretching entirely across
the instrument's lower front is a bizarre scene of young women—two musicians

FIG. 67   Upright pianoforte (c. 1860, London), by Priestly. London, Victoria and Albert Museum. Photo courtesy of Board of Trustees, Victoria and Albert Museum.

FIG. 68   Upright pianoforte by Priestly; detail of panel painted by Sir Edward Burne-Jones: *Death and the Maidens.* Photo courtesy of Board of Trustees, Victoria and Albert Museum.

and their auditors—in a garden enclosure where Death seeks entrance (Fig. 68).[52] Odd as it might seem at first glance, the two images are related. One is quite small, the other large and imposing. The darkness of the second image, set in the dark recess of the instrument's lower half, is exacerbated by the predominant browns and golds of its palette, in sharp contrast to the white costumes worn by the two upper figures, who form a surprisingly bright spot on a cabinet made from American walnut. Burne-Jones connects the two images by the visually jarring color binary, light-dark, the degree of difference between the two poles attracting notice.

The issue of difference, the ground to which this binary is anchored, in turn depends on an additional binary, well established in Western theology and philosophy: life/body/lower against afterlife/soul/higher. But the body in question is gendered; it is only the female body that is subject to the evaluating, devalorizing gaze. Further, whereas the painting is in effect philosophical in its discourse— abstract, as it were—its metaphorical content is transferred visually to functional reality by the actual woman who sits before it, namely, the painter's bride. In some weird way music itself transports her from her base condition as a woman—whose role is to cower in her garden among other women and wait for Death (patriarchal, crowned as a king)—to disembodied and sexless status as a white-gowned, virginal female.[53] The montage signifies rather in the manner of a slash film with a musical soundtrack, wherein the narrative describes the good bride as a dead one—the scythe carried by Death is enormous, and Burne-Jones highlights the blade's edge; it is profoundly threatening.[54]

The lower and upper images relate to one another precisely because of their physical separation and differences of size and color. Obviously, their subjects are related. Each involves an aspect of the sequence life-death-afterlife. Unquestionably, the two vignettes taken together replicate the tension in cultural—notably medico-sexual—paradigms concerning the nature of woman.[55] Finally, both scenes are "about" music itself, especially because the piano constitutes the ground on which they are painted and also frames them. There can be no question about the cultural associations between music and the feminine in Victorian culture; it is no accident that pianos like this one were seen as appropriate wedding gifts or that the music to be played on them signified domestic happiness. What is unusual is that Burne-Jones's "decoration" makes problematic this otherwise common significatory regime, though to be sure it does so by transporting the subject into a time and space different from the "lived" terrain the piano and its player occupy.

The "problem," then, is woman *and* the "problem" is music. Music is a problem precisely because the culture genders it as feminine; it is simultaneously a source of bliss to men and a threat to them. The presumed narrative of the lower panel does not take up its story in medias res so much as it rushes us toward a conclusion, as though we already knew what preceded this highly dramatic event. Blood is about to flow. But is it inevitable; is it just deserts? Whatever the answer, other questions are raised only so as *not* to be answered: does woman/music cause the visit of Death? or is Death's visit, inevitable, temporarily held off by music/woman? The answers are not within reach. The scythe cuts flesh; its promised horror fixes our (pleasured) gaze on its shining metal, rendered perhaps more transfixing because the man who wields it will enter the women's space by knocking at their gate, as it were under false pretense, like a neighbor gone mad—and ironically repeating the identical gesture of Christ in William Holman Hunt's already famous picture *The Light of the World,* painted only a few years earlier.[56] The end result is the transportation of the women and their music to the celestial sphere above. This is a better place; presumably this is a better woman (we know that from the iconographical tradition of St. Cecilia). And this is a better music. The trouble is that this "better" woman is disembodied, and the (safer) celestial music she makes cannot be heard.

We do not know how this image affected Burne-Jones's wife, the actual pianist, or her understanding of music. When she played the instrument, its threatening lower panel was hidden from view. Whether its narrative was thereby erased from her memory is a separate question, one I am inclined to answer in the negative, not least because there remained in her sight the painted angelic vignette next to the music rack, inviting remembrance of the other image to which it was the foil.

A concert grand built by Alexandre Charpentier in 1902, its case painted by the art nouveau artist Albert Besnard (Fig. 69), constitutes a lurid visual summary of the arguments I have advanced in this chapter. By virtue of its size this is not a domestic instrument but rather one for the public stage. Yet its decoration, notably the inside of the lid, makes it an instrument to be kept from the sight of—at the least—children: it is explicitly private. Thus the instrument stands isolated, not only between two musical traditions (classical and popular; sacred and profane) but also between the amateur, female, domestic, and private, on the one hand, and the professional, male, and public, on the other. The piano provides a visual discourse on music best fitted for a men's club. Yet its visual discourse is at once apparently contradictory and paradoxically logical.

The instrument's lid is like a Victorian photographic album of erotica, properly kept closed when not in use. To open it is to engage in a sexual-musical, implicitly forbidden, pleasure. The woman's body is swept over by a golden-edged water-music that at once engages her sexually—erotically washing between her legs, drawing attention to the swelling form of her pubic area—and threatens her with drowning. Her raised arms gesture ambiguously, to be sure, but certainly

FIG. 69   Concert grand pianoforte (1902), by Alexandre Charpentier; case paintings by Albert Besnard. Nice, Musée des Beaux-Arts Jules Chéret.

incorporate the body rhetoric of fending off an attack. Her outspread fingers are an old pictorial convention used to represent women's horror of impending rape.[57] But ambivalence is suggested by the painter's handling of her legs, for the left one is raised so as to encourage the movement of the wave between her thighs, a metaphoric penetration. Moreover, her body is composed like that of a Venus or an odalisque reclining on a bed, sexually available and willing. Thus her upper body resists; her lower body admits. Madonna and whore.

The sides of the case provide a striking contrast, a linear narrative that clarifies and amplifies the primary text, the lid. Unlike the flowing and relatively fuzzy upper image, the subsidiary scenes are painted with exacting precision. Like footnotes, they gloss and anchor what otherwise might remain obscure; they purport to provide closure. Their subject matter, contextualizing the lid painting, involves marriage, adultery, and murder. Sex concatenates with death; the infamy of the faithless woman is joined to music—that is, the grand piano itself. At the right extreme on the piano's side appears the iteration of male resolve, the battle scene, wherein masculine authority is emphasized in the form of the pawing stallion: angry men at war, faithless women punished, the warrior hero responding to the antagonisms of desire—woman and music. All these vignettes recall the Siren song from the *Iliad*, subjected to a brilliant—and scandalous—reading by Horkheimer and Adorno, according to whom Odysseus, the proto-bourgeois, despising the weakness his desire unleashes, avoids the erotic dangers promised by the Sirens' music. He has his men tie him to the mast so that he can hear the enticing melody but cannot act on it; he then commands his men to row close to shore. To prevent the boat's loss on the coastal shoals, he orders his sailors to place wax in their ears; thus they cannot be enticed by the Sirens' song.[58]

The visual-sonoric pleasure enacted on the piano's lid will be paid for by the death of the one who provides the pleasure. She is Woman; she is Music. But, ironically, the death of the woman ends the auditor-gazer's pleasure. Once the lid is closed, like that of a coffin before burial, the sight of her body and the waves of sound washing over her are sealed off, so that the loss is ours. As with Odysseus, pleasure comes—perversely—from desire's unrealized aspirations. Self-denial, built on a foundation of domination, holds sway.

The piano, as the predominant musical instrument of its time among the hegemonic classes, reflected and produced associations, both sonoric and visual, between pleasure, sexual desire, hatred, murder, and women. One cannot understand the histories of nineteenth-century music—its production and reception, in the salon or the concert hall—without taking account of these associations. Music is the lover; the lover is despised. In the ancient history of textual and visual representation in the West, music is commonly personified as a beautiful young woman; the culmination of this representational history comes together in 1905 as both a sight and a sound in Richard Strauss's *Salome*, providing an epitaph for the musical-sexual history of the nineteenth century and an epigraph for that of the twentieth: "Man töte dieses Weib!"[59] The opera ends with the end of music (I will explain) *and* the death of Salome; the two are linked. Following her musically provocative and sensually charged final scene, the music of which produces a simulacrum of sexual fervor unlike almost any other in the history of opera apart from *Tristan und Isolde*, Herod has a final *word*. I give emphasis here because I want to suggest that at the opera's close two things happen that touch my concerns. Salome's murder, unlike the offstage beheading of Jokanaan, is seen and meant to be savored. It is accomplished by a sonoric closure, *more noise than music*, that defeats our pleasure in the extraordinarily embodied music Salome has just performed over and on the severed male head. This closure is achieved by recourse to the traditional sonoric inscription of male authority, the military sounds of brass and percussion,[60] rhythmically punctuated at the loudest possible volume.

This militaristic gesture emphasizes the reinstatement of the Word into the opera. There is a double irony here. Salome's final music takes words out of discourse, if by discourse we mean something like "rational address," and uses them solely for their ability to increase the erotics of the accompanying music. We do not much care about the text she sings, or if we care it is because we have been made to invest in the forbidden pleasures the text invites, specifically on account of the music. Salome in effect uses words against the Word, which it is Jokanaan's role to enforce. Herod in effect takes up Jokanaan's part in the end. He reasserts order, in the "ideal" cultural form of Strauss's lived time: the Imperative, the non-dialogic. Herod's final command returns privilege to text. Though this phrase is very short and moves quickly, it is hardly surprising that two words, *töte* and *Weib,* receive accentual and durational emphasis; and though the phrase is scored to be sung, the speed and ambitus of the six notes, spanning an octave and a minor third, are such that singers commonly shout it, essentially preserving the proper effect. As this occurs, the final rhythmic accents choreographing Salome's death and coinciding with her final heartbeats are all that remains of music. Melody is gone; so is woman. Order is restored. Nonetheless, I suggest that Herod, like Odysseus, knew the price he himself would have to pay in his pleasured anguish once he abandoned song in favor of speech. Salome's death for Herod means the death alike of desire and its agency. The end of music follows the death of desire in an implicit paradigm whereby men surrender music in the interest of retaining domination, with the ironic result that domination dominates them in the bargain.

Noise is a weapon and music, primordially, is the formation, domestication, and ritualization of that weapon as a simulacrum of ritual murder.

Jacques Attali,
Noise: The Political Economy of Music

[Sex] is that aspect of [the bourgeoisie] which troubled and preoccupied it more than any other, begged and obtained its attention, and which it cultivated with a mixture of fear, curiosity, delight, and excitement. The bourgeoisie made this element identical with its body.

Michel Foucault,
The History of Sexuality

THE PIANO, MISOGYNY,
AND "THE KREUTZER SONATA"

IN VICTORIAN MIDDLE-CLASS CULTURE, as elsewhere and earlier, the social functions of music operated always in conjunction with music's value as a sign. What seems changed in nineteenth-century practice, however, was the semiotics of music, which became radically unstable, especially when music was employed to establish and legitimate several crucial binaries on which the society largely framed itself: man/woman, public/private, good/evil, center/periphery, self/other. The trouble was that in binaries such as these, inevitably marked positive and negative, music's place could not be guaranteed.

To the Victorian bourgeoisie the domestic pianoforte was as essential as the dining room table—in an ideological sense perhaps more important; respectability demanded its purchase as a marker of family position and accomplishment. Indeed, the history of piano design, manufacture, and distribution in the nineteenth century serves not only as a perfect metaphor of capitalist economic principles in operation but also as an agent of capitalism's political, economic, and ideological success, to the extent that these categories of success may be understood as part and parcel of domesticity. Yet the socio-cultural organization of Victorian life was so new, conflicted, self-contradictory, and self-conscious that the preferred "reading" of the sign "piano"—like that of the sign "music"—was unstable despite the centrality of its cultural semiotics. The piano seems to have been something of a floating signifier, a semantic pendulum that swung in an extreme arc.

Set up in the principal room of the semipublic portions of the home where guests as well as family members would gather, the piano bridged the gap between the public world and the private. It did this by means of its aesthetic correlatives, which together, in essence, overdetermined its ideological worth. First, the piano

FIG. 70   Grand pianoforte (c. 1840, London), by Erard; marquetry case designed and executed by George Henry Blake. New York, The Metropolitan Museum of Art, Gift of Mrs. Henry McSweeney, 1959.

FIG. 71   Grand pianoforte by Erard; detail of marquetry on lid. New York, The Metropolitan Museum of Art, Gift of Mrs. Henry McSweeney, 1959.

was an object of beauty, often overdecorated; it was intended to be looked *at*—to be visually consumed (Figs. 70–71). Second, it was to be heard. As with all music, as I have suggested elsewhere in this volume, its aesthetic worth, ideologically driven, derived in part from the radical departure of musical sonority itself from the world of material objects. In other words, the domestic piano bespoke a principal contradiction of bourgeois society. Its physical presence commonly fetishized materiality, a materiality that had nothing to do with musical sonority and in some instances might well have detracted from it; at the same time, the music to be played on the instrument was valorized precisely because of its immateriality, to the nineteenth century the sine qua non of music's supposedly socially transcendent autonomy. In parallel fashion, oil paintings, bought by the tens of thousands by Europe's wealthy bourgeoisie, at once claimed prestige on purely aesthetic grounds and celebrated mundane luxury, like the piano viewed as furniture. Paintings also helped decorate and articulate the space of increasingly large domestic interiors.

The frequent representation of music in domestic visual art, both family portraits and genre scenes, is closely related to the "decorative" character of music itself and, more important, to the need to define, establish, and thus *use* music's cultural meanings, particularly as these related to the ideology of domesticity and the meaning of woman, on which hinged the identity and meaning of men.[1] Put differently, the visual fascination with the piano connects to the scopophilic fascination with women's bodies in art. The compulsion to sort out and stabilize the sign "woman," an obsession with Victorian men, is tied not only to the demands of identity, sexual difference, and power but also to the equally troublesome categories "desire" and "pleasure."

Bourgeois patriarchy, which defined women by principles governing domesticity, constructed two contradictory categories of woman: the privatized angel of the house, not subject to the pleasured gaze, and her radical public opposite, the prostitute. In the terminology of painting, woman was either Madonna or Venus. General suspicion that she was both fed both fear and loathing and was also the fantasy and the guarantee of her transfixing look. Whatever constituted the feminine hung in the balance. Music provided the visual means for discoursing on the subject in art because in Europe, at least since the eighteenth century, music and femininity were viewed interchangeably.[2]

MUSIC AND THE (UN)DISCIPLINED BODY

The semiotics of musical imagery develop not only from instruments employed as props but also from the representation of gestures and other expressive qualities of the human body as these relate to musical activity. The function of music in the

FIG. 72   Frederick Daniel Hardy, *Music at the Parsonage*, oil on canvas, 74.9 × 107.3 cm. Private collection. Photo courtesy of Christie's, London.

lives of Victorians, especially its relation to desire, eroticism, and sexuality, was attended to with extraordinary self-consciousness. At one extreme was the effort to confine severely the representation of female sensuality, replacing it with a stiff purity, as for example in *Music at the Parsonage* (Fig. 72), where the setting itself seems to overdetermine female piety. (I shall later examine a radically opposite representation.) Such seriousness pervades the scene as to circumscribe any sensual associations the music itself might otherwise produce. Indeed, the image valorizes the sitters' concentration on music making, envisioned as a discipline imposed on the body, that is, as work. Under these circumstances, music gains respectability: Foucault points out that the bourgeoisie first imposed their work-ethic severities on themselves, to define their identity apart from an aristocracy they viewed as degenerate; later, to consolidate their newly established hegemony, they tried to inculcate their behavior and supporting ideologies in the working class.[3]

In *Music at the Parsonage* both the discrepancy between interior/inside and exterior/outside and the distinction according to people's ages are noteworthy. Outside is physical play and childhood, inside, work and adulthood. Outside there is freedom from responsibility, enacted and articulated by the body in action, but confined to youth; inside there is wisdom, thought, order, and age. There is a visual link between the two in the prominent hand gesture at the left: the mother seated with her back to us (thus we do not focus on her face) raises her hand, alerting the children seen through the open doorway to be silent. The reproving look on the mother's face, which we cannot see, is registered by her daughter, who is responsible for the younger boys at the swing. (The painter's use of light draws our attention to the gesture of the raised hand and pointed finger.) As for the musicians, the physicality of their activity is erased, as though it were shameful. This is especially evident in the players' hands, none of which appear to exert any effort in depressing keys, bowing, or stopping strings. Nothing is tensed except their faces, which exhibit concentration, the only kind of "work" appropriate to the class. Music activates nothing, presumably, except their minds. The joy of music is in the thinking about it.

I need to suggest what I am getting at by means of a very different image (Fig. 73) by a roughly contemporaneous Italian painter. Here an adolescent girl plays the violin, immediately setting up a tension in that the instrument was still

FIG. 73   Paolo Bedini, *Girl Playing the Violin*, oil on canvas. Private collection. Photo courtesy of Christie's, London.

principally a male prerogative—throughout most of the eighteenth century it was uncommon, and usually judged improper, for a female to play the violin.[4] She violates a taboo, though by the late nineteenth century its potency was fading. Nonetheless, that taboo is directly acknowledged by both the eroticism invested in her body and the slight coquettishness of her face. In other words, she is made *different,* different from decent women, as it were. The painting's subject *is* the girl's sexuality. Music serves as the sign and agent of that sexuality and of its illicit nature.

What renders this young woman explicitly sexual is her bodily movement, quite at odds with homely decorum. She bends her torso inward toward her instrument in a way very unlike the man playing with his back to us in *Music at the Parsonage* (Fig. 72); her physical involvement with the violin is made an issue. That by itself, however, is insufficient to produce the effect I am claiming. More is accomplished by the handling of her drapery. Specifically, her dress seems to move as it splays out from the chair. This movement is created not only by a sharp diagonal but also by the vivid contrast between light and shade, between her gown and the wall behind her. Another detail that underlines a sense of movement entirely absent from the other painting is the scattering of flowers and flower petals on the floor, recalling conjunctions of nature, dance (petals scattering from bodies in motion; her hair also looks windblown), and sensuality. Indeed, dancing nymphs in flower-bedecked bowers, commonly pursued by satyrs, were a favorite subject in contemporaneous French painting. These associations violate the proprieties of domesticity, as does the painter's eroticizing of the young woman's body. Finally, the sensual charge immanent in this picture comes from a primary absence, that of the father. It is unquestionably a man's chair drawn up to the table covered with books in disarray—the very disorder marks his absence. The seat is one of judgment that silently allows us to condemn her actions while taking our pleasure. I will come back to this issue later.

A portrait of Mrs. John Pettie (Fig. 74), the wife of the Royal Academy artist, dutifully encodes via the piano virtually every value of Victorian domesticity. The instrument itself, with its burled cabinet, is a sign of the good life but also of the life of moderation expected of a successful middle-class artist (but not of an industrialist; see Fig. 70), for it is an upright, not a grand. Mrs. Pettie, dressed in black, is situated in a simply decorated drawing room. The good wife, she is somber and musically serious. Patient, dependable, undemanding—there is nothing about her to suggest a capacity for responding to or producing surprise.

The qualities that characterize her also describe the two women in a Danish painting (Fig. 75) of a duet; both are middle-aged, a conventional sign of spinsterhood or perhaps widowhood (the woman at the piano wears a wedding band). Both sitters are desensualized in at least two ways. The pianist is hunched over

FIG. 74   Sir William Quiller Orchardson, *Mrs. John Pettie* (1865), oil on canvas, 99.9 × 79.5 cm. Photo copyright City Art Galleries, Manchester.

FIG. 75   Johan Frederik Nicolai Vermehren, *The Duet* (1898), oil on canvas. Private collection. Photo courtesy of Sotheby's, London.

FIG. 76   Sir Frank Dicksee, *Harmony* (1877), oil on canvas, 157.5 × 94 cm. London, Tate Gallery.

slightly, in rapt concentration, the severity of her face complementing that of her costume. She creates an atmosphere of study. The singer, by contrast, seems more relaxed, an impression supported by her gown with its elaborate ribbon. Yet whatever she may gain by her body language and dress is lost by the painter's having put spectacles in her hand, a hand she might otherwise have used for the expressive gesturing common in contemporaneous paintings of women in recital. Her spectacles mark lost youth and also study, but not passion. The duet genre in paintings normally evokes the harmony of lovers (Fig. 76); but the absence of the male partner and the substituted presence of a woman render the music and its performers virtually frigid. The aesthetic "creativity" of performance here is circumscribed and indeed diminished by male absence—ironically, despite both the categorization (indeed, stigmatization) of music itself as feminine, and the giving over of domestic music principally to women. In other words, male "presence" served ideologically to define and substantiate the signs "music" and "woman." A duet involving two women invests in, and depends for its meaning on, a sense of loss; loss identifies itself through the intertextual relation of the woman-woman duet to the man-woman lovers' duet it references.

The harmony of lovers in many images was sacramental, with the woman playing the role of St. Cecilia, as is the case in Figure 76. But by no means all the representations encapsulate this reading. Indeed, the duet of lovers provided the opportunity for salacious scopophilia. Painters took up this theme in the music lesson, a duet genre that presumed the inequality of the partners, an older male teacher and a younger female student, whose relation mirrors perfectly the domestic rank of husband to wife, and father to daughter.

MUSIC AND FORBIDDEN LESSONS

The music lesson is represented as early as the seventeenth century in Western European art; it became especially popular in England in the eighteenth century, notably as a source of comedy, in literature and drama as well as visual art. By contrast, in courtesy and conduct literature and in tracts on education, both invariably serious in tone, it was looked on with moral alarm. The music lesson provided an opportunity for the seduction of a virgin who was nonetheless commonly presented as sexually curious (Fig. 77).[5] As a visual subject in the nineteenth century, the lesson became less comic, more voyeuristic. When it was portrayed as a chaperoned event (Fig. 78), its strict "purity" was preserved. More common, however, were representations in which the music lesson was a pretext for depicting seething passions: a young man might stare intently at his considerably younger pupil while she plays demurely, here (Fig. 79) a tune called "Love's Young Dream" that stands in metaphorically for passion and is simultaneously its occasion and catalyst. Given the age of the pianist, her teacher's attentions are improper, if not strictly abusive. Accordingly, in this instance music is not the analogue to domestic harmony but the agent of forbidden desire. The image evokes a sexual, extra-domestic harmony that, though perhaps out of reach, is infinitely more exciting than the vignette of domestic propriety and control represented by the chaperone doing her needlework behind the would-be lovers. The point is that music's place is contradictory; it is both the sign of domesticity—this *is* the family piano—and the sign of what domesticity displaces. The music lesson confirms what the Victorians at once valorized and regretted: sexuality in domesticity was licit but also repressed and repressive. The sexualization of the young pianist is precisely mirrored in the desexualization of the old woman the girl is destined to become.

The music lesson inscribed Victorian domesticity and maternity when the

FIG. 77 Thomas Rowlandson, *Mathew Bramble's Trip to Bath: Private Practice Previous to the Ball,* watercolor, pen and ink, 12.1 × 18.8 cm. New Haven, Yale Center for British Art, Paul Mellon Collection.

FIG. 78 George Goodwin Kilburne, *The Music Lesson,* watercolor, 34.3 × 45.7 cm. Private collection. Photo courtesy of Christie's, Glasgow.

FIG. 79   George Goodwin Kilburne, *Love's Young Dream*, watercolor heightened with white, 30.5 × 22.9 cm. Private collection. Photo courtesy of Christie's, London.

FIG. 80   George Dunlop Leslie, *Home, Sweet Home,* oil on canvas. Private collection. Photo courtesy of Sotheby's, London.

teacher was the mother and the student her offspring. The "pure" handling of the subject could be uncompromisingly educative, as in Figure 80, where a governess (a mother stand-in) instructs an entire brood, all female, in the library–music room of the home, which might otherwise pass for a schoolhouse—all hard surfaces (no carpets or drapes) and all business (the hourglass at the rear center seemingly marks out the time given to this exercise—titled by the artist, with no apparent irony, *Home, Sweet Home.* The painting substantiates the middle class by means of its favorite denominator, recreation as work, the painting's cool colors an accurate reflection of an accompanying emotional barrenness, where music is less a pleasure than a task. Alternatively, the maternally directed music lesson could be handled with unremitting sentimentality (in Fig. 81 the pupil is a boy, though his features are strikingly feminine), with the sitters' soft faces almost unbearably saccharine. Music lessons offered by mothers, especially to their daughters, strove principally to inscribe domestic sensibilities: in Figure 82 three "generations" of women—mother, child, doll—learn the steps, child and doll alike wearing small aprons as certificates of their graduation.

What might be desensualized in one instance, however, could be given a peculiar erotic charge in another. The specific, sometimes lurid, eroticization of the

FIG. 81   Charles West Cope, *The Music Lesson* (1863), oil on canvas, 61 × 72.4 cm. Private collection. Photo courtesy of Christie's, New York.

FIG. 82   George Goodwin Kilburne, *Learning the Steps* (1869), watercolor heightened with white, 46 × 36 cm. Whereabouts unknown.

domestic music lesson constitutes one of the most striking developments in the Victorian imagery of music. It can come as no great surprise that the visual-musical metaphor for a desensualized female (the "good" mother) was the most tantalizing subject by which simultaneously to violate this ideological paradigm (the return of the repressed) and, for the presumed male viewer, to preserve it. In some instances the instructor remains female, but the student, instead of a child, is a pet dog (Fig. 83). Here a protective historical and geographical distancing inoculates the image from the present, so that the woman, with her more than slightly kinky sexuality, is identifiable, not as the archetypal Victorian wife and mother, but as a creature from another age and place. Thus the instrument she plays could be either a harpsichord or a piano, but its neoclassical case marks it as early nineteenth century at the latest, though the painting was executed in 1896, and the stool on which she sits is French in style, not English, while the screen behind her is vaguely Asian.

Kinky sexuality is particularly evident if one focuses on the carefully delineated difference between the woman at the keyboard in the foreground and the woman in the portrait-within-the-portrait on the back wall, very proper by comparison, in fact copied after Gainsborough's famous 1785 portrait of the actress Mrs. Siddons, a picture whose canonical status is matched by its sitter's virtually aristocratic reserve. The two "sitters" in *An Attentive Pet* are actually screened from

FIG. 83   Jules Adolphe Goupil, *An Attentive Pet* (1896), oil on canvas. Private collection. Photo courtesy of Sotheby's, London.

each other's view as though to separate a dissolute present from a morally superior past. This issue hinges on the pose of the woman at the piano, a musically impossible one. Her chair is so far from the instrument that she must lean forward to play, placing her in a physically uncomfortable position that nonetheless gives pleasure to the viewer: it defines her as sexually "available" to the gaze via the exaggerated profile of her hips. The pose is masochistic. Its eroticism is reenforced by her full and fiery red lips and by her highly light-reflective and voluminous blue-black gown, anything but a costume appropriate to the Victorian mother.

Sander Gilman has shown how obsessed Victorians were with women's backsides;[6] corseting practices common to middle-class women achieved a tiny waist and accentuated the bulge of the hips.[7] The emphasis placed by the painter on the woman's hips in Figure 83, however, reflects a more rabid Victorian fascination—with women's genitalia, especially of blacks, and Hottentots in particular. Thus one medical authority writing in 1819 claimed that black women's "voluptuousness" was "developed to a degree of lascivity unknown in our climate, for their sexual organs are much more developed than those of whites." The most famous of such women, the so-called Hottentot Venus, was Saartjie Baartman (d. 1815), whose genitalia and protruding buttocks received the transfixed attention of many Europeans—in fact people literally paid to see her, both in life and after death. Her genitalia and buttocks are on display to this day in Paris at the Musée de l'homme, preserved following her death in a gesture that smacks not only of racism but also of a conflation of medical pathology with fantasies of necrophilia. Gilman argues that for the scopophiliac her buttocks—if not in the flesh then in cheap popular prints, some of which he reproduces—substitute for the genitalia, and he cites medical treatises, literary narratives, and a body of visual representations to establish the primacy of this phenomenon.

In Jules Adolphe Goupil's picture (Fig. 83) a similar substitution occurs. The woman's hips directly parallel the hind quarters of her dog, whose position, equally awkward, mirrors hers. It takes no great imagination to recognize the sodomy fixation involved here. Like the black females discussed by Gilman, Goupil's "attentive pet"—so named by the artist—as *female* is represented at once as a pathology, as Other, and as the desired. The ironic ambiguity of the painting's title, the uncertainty of the referent, is intentional; it is indeed a textual confirmation of the source of pleasure. But herein lies the problem. For the woman in question is set in a domestic enclosure, a home with a familial genealogy, as the interior portrait both references, via Mrs. Siddons's decorum, and denies, in that Mrs. Siddons was an actress, thus contradicting Victorian expectations of homely propriety. The attentive pet is the contradiction rising above the tranquil surface of domestic piety.

TOLSTOY'S MUSICIAN AND HOMOSOCIAL DESIRE

The Victorian theorization of female sexuality as pathology is nowhere more strikingly apparent than in the novella by Tolstoy named after Beethoven's Opus 47 sonata for violin and piano, "The Kreutzer."[8] For my interests it is a crucial text in that it incorporates both music and male sexuality into the equation I have been developing, using a domestic performance of Beethoven's sonata as the inspiration and catalyst for a husband's brutal murder of his wife. Tolstoy had a great deal of trouble writing the story; indeed it seems to have haunted him. The idea was born in a fragment called "The Wife-Murderer" from the late 1860s, involving a situation that was on his mind at least as early as the beginning of his own troubled marriage in 1862.[9] He returned to the tale in 1887 and over the next two years put the text through nine drafts. (Tolstoy's original conception was a dramatic monologue to be recited in conjunction with a painting on the same title that he wanted his artist friend Ilya Repin to paint; this project came to nothing.) His final plan for the story was developed in the spring of 1888 following a performance in his home of Beethoven's sonata—his son, a pianist, like Tolstoy himself, accompanied the violinist.[10]

The story is introduced by two scriptural citations concerning human sexuality (Matthew 5:28, 19:10–12), the second of which advocates the ideal of abstinence. This passage supports Tolstoy's increasingly troubled thoughts on the subject, especially as regards men, that led him to espouse an ideal of "absolute chastity" in marriage.[11] The first citation ("Whosoever looketh on a woman to lust after her hath committed adultery with her already in his heart") supports Tolstoy's predilection, characteristic of his age, to see women as the occasion for sin and male degradation.

The tale unfolds as a story-within-a-story, involving a first-person speaker who repeats what was related to him on a railroad journey by a man named Pozdnyshev who, we eventually learn, murdered his wife. For long stretches of the text Pozdnyshev tells his own story, but from time to time the original narrator intrudes, thereby insulating us from the immediacy of the events that fascinate and simultaneously horrify him, in his role as stand-in for Tolstoy himself: the embedded narration provides a putative cover of dissociation.

The story begins with a young man's sexual innocence but leads immediately to his transformation through sexual experience until, at age thirty, the debauched antihero meets his future wife and falls in love, or so he briefly thinks. The engagement is short; the honeymoon, in effect, still shorter. Jealousy pursues him incessantly; in endless spirals of mistrust and passion, the couple quarrel and make up. All the while Pozdnyshev sees himself living a life of perpetual rut: "That's the sort of pig's existence I led," he says, referring solely to faithful marital relations (p. 63). Years pass; several children are born. Hostilities increase. (Ironically, but not accidentally, in the course of the novella, he never divulges his wife's name.[12] In Tolstoy's imagination she cannot be identified as one woman, insofar as she is a stand-in for every woman.)

Halfway through the story music is introduced: "She took up the piano again with enthusiasm—previously she had let it go completely. That was how it all started" (p. 79). It is from this moment that Pozdnyshev tracks his wife's supposed infidelities: "Yes, and then this man appeared. . . . Yes, he was a musician, a violinist; not a professional musician, but part professional, part man of the world." Raised in Paris and tutored at the Conservatoire, "he turned up in Russia, and turned up, what's more, in my own home."

It is Tolstoy's physical description of the musician (named Trukhachevsky) that interests me:

> He had moist eyes, like almonds, smiling red lips, and a little moustache that was smeared with fixative; his hair was styled in the latest fashion; his face was handsome in a vulgar sort of way, and he was what women call "not bad-looking." He was of slight physique, but not in any way malformed, and he had a particularly well-developed posterior, as women have, or as Hottentots are said to have. I believe they're also said to be musical. . . .
> He and his music were the real cause of it all (pp. 79–80).

The concatenations here are remarkable. Trukhachevsky, in the eyes of Pozdnyshev, is a man-woman ("moist eyes"; "smiling red lips"; moustache *smeared with fixative*," like makeup), an exotic (eyes "like almonds") in the recurring orientalist imagery of the time. The crucial passage equates the musician with the African female, in effect the slave, and, in the common culture of the period, the European whore—at which point Pozdnyshev makes the connection between female sexuality and music ("they're also said to be musical").[13] Tolstoy has difficulty with this passage; the image of the musician both compels and repulses him. He twice acknowledges that the man is attractive. "His face was handsome," he says but adds, self-protectively, "in a vulgar sort of way," disguising his own libidinal investment in his body. In the same sentence, he repeats the judgment, as though he cannot leave it alone, though he feels obliged to locate that assessment outside himself, in women ("he was *what women call* 'not bad-looking'").

Tolstoy's Pozdnyshev fixes his gaze on the musician's buttocks,[14] which are "*particularly* well-developed" and "as women have." The passage is extraordinary, for in it Tolstoy invokes the Hottentot Venus. His alter-ego wife murderer teeters back and forth between man-woman desire, in rising anger and frustration. At the end, he deflects this hatred, this confused sexuality, onto music itself,[15] which he directly equates with the man-woman of his obsession. As the narrator later confesses, following the musician's admittance into his home: "I didn't like the look of him from the very outset. But it was a strange thing: some peculiar, fatal energy led me not to repulse him, get rid of him, but, on the contrary, to bring him closer" (p. 85).[16] Immediately thereafter he describes a conversation with the violinist in which it develops that Pozdnyshev himself was a musician, but had given up music. Thus music binds all three together. It is not that the husband is musically ignorant; quite the opposite, he is musically literate, like Tolstoy himself. He has insider knowledge; he acknowledges music's effects:

> I introduced him to my wife. The conversation immediately turned to music, and he offered to play duos with her. My wife was . . . very elegant and alluring, disturbingly beautiful. It was obvious that she *did* like the look of him from the very outset. What was more, she was delighted at the prospect of having someone to play the violin with her—so fond of playing duos was she that she used to hire the services of a violinist from the local theatre orchestra—and her joy was written all over her face (p. 86).

Once again Pozdnyshev focuses on the musician's looks and his wife's response to them. More to the point, the duet is marked as a metaphoric stand-in for sexual intercourse. Pozdnyshev having given up music, his wife hires a duet partner to answer her desires. That is, she is the agent to her own needs; she takes the initiative in response to her desires—and the fact that she hires a stranger to perform with her tacitly introduces the subject of prostitution. This constitutes a reversal in the hierarchy of power governing marriage, all the more because Pozdnyshev equates the duet with adultery. His response to his wife's musical-cum-sexual proclivities is governed by a common anxiety in the nineteenth century about the kinetic power of female sexuality, a force that, if awakened, might know no bounds. Thus the *Westminster Review* (1850) in a classic example of acknowledgment by denial:

> In men, in general, the sexual desire is inherent and spontaneous, and belongs to the condition of puberty. In the other sex, the desire is dormant, if non-existent, till excited; always till excited by intercourse. . . . If the passions of women were ready, strong and spontaneous, in a degree even approaching the form they assume in the coarser sex, there can be little doubt that sexual irregularities would reach a height, of which, at present, we have happily no conception.[17]

In Tolstoy's narrative, musical and sexual stimulation meld; the result is the man's moral deterioration, which will culminate in murder, and the deterioration of the family itself—"perceived as the foundation of social stability and progress"[18]— all because of the woman's transgression, her awakened desire. In the medical-psychological science of the time "awakened" female sexuality was commonly understood to be the root cause of female hysteria, the psychological analogue to social anarchy.[19] Moreover, the agency of the wife's sexuality is also the agency of music: Pozdnyshev later refers to music as "the most refined form of sensual lust" (p. 100).

Having noted the "electric current" (p. 86) passing between the pair, Pozdnyshev invites the musician to return with his violin to play duets with his wife. The wife looks shocked, for in essence the husband is pimping for her. The psychosexual import of his gesture is as obvious to her as to the reader. The husband then fixates on the musician's neck, "its white flesh with the black hairs standing out against it," and in the same breath adds, "I'm not exaggerating when I tell you that the man's presence used to drive me out of my mind" (p. 87).

The description of the first musical evening, occurring the same day the invitation is issued, preserves the sexual metaphor. Indeed, the event begins with a foreplay unnecessary to the narrative if taken literally ("It took them quite a while to get their playing organized"). Pozdnyshev continues in the role of procurer, adjusting the musician's music stand and turning pages. The wife and guest make the music and Pozdnyshev "took an interest," in aural analogy to voyeurism. Afterward, Pozdnyshev courts his wife's would-be seducer, as he sees him, with compliments and expensive wine at dinner. "It's strange, the effect that man's presence had on me" (p. 89), he confesses.

THE "KREUTZER" SONATA (PRESTO) AS WOMAN

Soon thereafter another dinner, followed by a musical entertainment, is arranged involving other guests, for whom the wife and violinist perform the "Kreutzer" Sonata. Tolstoy's account of the performance is too extended to quote at length; a few passages will have to suffice (from pp. 96–98).

> "Do you know its first movement, the presto? You know it?" he burst out. "Ah! It's a fearful thing, that sonata. Especially that movement. And music in general's a fearful thing. What is it? I don't know. What is music? What does it do to us? And why does it do to us what it does?"

His queries resonate with the Woman Question in nineteenth-century ideology, not simply because of the hysteria pervading that discourse and the passage in question but because of Tolstoy's choice of the word *fearful*. Fear is not an ordinary descriptor for the category "music," but it makes sense for Tolstoy to employ it in this context precisely because he has so clearly cemented music to women and to women's sexuality, the fears of which were both common and deep-seated. Indeed, as Pozdnyshev labors to account for music's effects, he moves toward the metaphor of orgasm:

> How can I put it? Music makes me forget myself, my true condition, it carries me off into another state of being, one that isn't my own: under the influence of music I have the illusion of feeling things I don't really feel, of understanding things I don't understand, being able to do things I'm not able to do.

And he continues the analogy in a passage describing his union with the composer: "Music carries me instantly and directly into the state of consciousness that was experienced by the composer. My soul merges with his, and together with him I'm transported from one state of consciousness into another."

Finally, he turns back to Beethoven's sonata, whose power over him and, he imagines, over others is so great that its performance should be limited to special, controlled, circumstances: "On me, at any rate, that piece had the most shattering effect; I had the illusion I was discovering entirely new emotions, new possibilities I'd known nothing of before then. . . . [M]y awareness of this new state of consciousness filled me with joy." But also with hate, for the performance producing these reactions involves what the narrator recognizes as an illicit sexual union between his wife and a man to whom he himself is powerfully attracted. In other words the sonata's effect on him is produced in part by what he *sees*—the lovers, who in fact are not lovers; his wife and the musician are innocent—as well as by the music he *hears*.

The murder occurs soon after the sonata's performance. It silences not only the wife but the music as well. Indeed, it is the narrator's desire, in essence, to murder sound that is critical. Pozdnyshev's rage is given both form and ultimate agency through Beethoven's violin sonata. His—and Tolstoy's—anger, however, is directed against sexuality itself in general and his own desires in particular. "From his youth to his old age, Tolstoy was body-haunted, obsessed equally by sexual desire and the guilt of sexual satisfaction. In the diary of his youth he claims that 'I'm dissatisfied with only one thing: I cannot overcome my sensuality, especially because it is a passion which has now become a habit with me.'"[20] What I have earlier noted as Pozdnyshev's homoerotic fixation on the musician's body might now be placed in a larger and more interesting context related specifically to music. Arguably, Pozdnyshev (and Tolstoy) see in the musician their own repressed selves, but not simply because of repressed same-sex desire, though body and sexuality are very much involved. For Pozdnyshev the body *as such*—his own, the musician's, and his wife's—is the enemy, or, perhaps better, it is an alien Other from which he cannot free himself. He is attracted to bodies; he takes pleasure in the very attraction he simultaneously abhors. Tolstoy wrote often and at length about the division between body and what he hypostatized as mind, arguing that the latter should command and control the former. (His radical hatred of the body, however extreme, is nonetheless a manifestation of paradigmatic Western dualism.[21]) The body Pozdnyshev simultaneously desires and loathes can be kept at bay, if imperfectly, until Pozdnyshev physically confronts in the male musician a feminine Other that was part of himself until "I'd let my playing go" (p. 86). The same holds for his wife (the ideal wife for Tolstoy was very much the "angel in the house"): it is her supposed sexual response to the musician that enrages him. It confirms not only that she is not what he wants her to be but also that her awakened sexuality is the mirror image of what he seeks to stifle in himself. The agent for these awakenings is the body, the body of a musician.

The effect of the musician's embodied agency is felt when he makes music, especially when he plays the first movement of Beethoven's Opus 47. The sight and sound of the music remind Pozdnyshev simultaneously of what he wants and what he wants to repress: music, woman, himself. Tolstoy thus replicates the Western principle that music is fundamentally feminine and the corollary that as such it constitutes the enemy. Nor does it matter that Tolstoy's story was much attacked in print by his contemporaries the moment it appeared—not for its views on music, incidentally, but for its convoluted, if obvious, misogyny. The extreme nature of his formulation was and is undeniable; but what his critics failed to see, or at least failed to admit, was that Tolstoy's position enjoyed a long historical pedigree, one by no means generally masked from open view.[22]

Tolstoy's lengthy postface to his novella gives us more to go on.[23] It articulates a philosophy of radical celibacy in marriage based on Christian theology. Tolstoy himself recognizes, as he must, the uncommonness of marital abstinence as a practice and the consequence of its general adoption: the end of the species. For him, abstinence nonetheless remains the ideal to which humans should aspire. To the extent that his story concatenates sexuality, women, and music—actually, instrumental or "absolute" art music—his sad narrator speaks for the twin deaths of women and sonority. (This is a subject of some complexity, one that I can do no more now than identify; I take it up again in Chapter 9.)

I must add to my earlier comments on embedded narration. Were the story to stand by itself, without its postface, we might initially acknowledge an ambiguity between Tolstoy's own position and that of Pozdnyshev, since the first-person narrator who opens the tale is not the husband-murderer. Yet even without the postface it is clear that the fundamental position the husband articulates finds a sympathetic listener—the story, whose telling the narrator continually encourages, goes on for a very long time. In the end, both men express sorrow for the wife and horror over her murder. Nonetheless, the crucial account of the intertextuality of

music, woman, and sex is never challenged; indeed, it enjoys a position of philosophical privilege as the dramatic, if confused, insight, agent, and climax of the
story.

It is impossible to know Tolstoy's precise thoughts on the presto movement,
though he differentiates it from other music mentioned (including a "Mozart sonata"), all of which he dismisses as "trite," "weak," or merely "pleasant.") I feel
obliged to suggest, however tentatively, something about the presto's character
that might have fit his purpose—and might in turn indicate something about the
broader fears haunting Pozdnyshev. What I think he fears in Beethoven, and what
he cannot, or will not, name as its effect is the erotic—the best he can manage is
to call it an "irritant," a designator he repeats. In trying to account for the special
character of the presto movement, he compares it to other musics, each of which
has a distinct, clear, and unambiguous function. Thus he says that if a march is
played, he marches; if a dance is played, he dances; and if a Mass is sung, he takes
communion. Beethoven's presto also acts on the body, to be sure, but its function
involves a confused and sublimated sexuality. The other sorts of music named
provoke physical action (marching, dancing); the Opus 47 presto provokes desire.

In *What Is Art?*[24]—written during the same period as "The Kreutzer Sonata"—Tolstoy's conservative, if nonetheless culturally authorized, views on music come to light in three related topics of concern to me: body-mind dualism, sex,
and Beethoven. Complaining about the low general quality of the arts, he notes:

> The substitution of effect for aesthetic feeling is particularly noticeable in musical
> art—that art which by its nature has an immediate physiological action on the nerves.
> Instead of transmitting by means of a melody the feelings he has experienced, a com-
> poser of the new school accumulates and complicates sounds, and by now strength-
> ening, now weakening them, he produces on the audience a physiological effect of a
> kind that can be measured by an apparatus invented for that purpose. [He has in mind
> an actual machine.] And the public mistake this physiological effect for the effect of
> art (p. 188).

On the one hand, he tacitly acknowledges that this "new" art moves its auditors,
as if involuntarily: body supplants mind. Music acts like a virus whose effects can
be measured medically. The metaphor is one of sickness; medicine (and psychology) at the century's end were fixated on the sexuality of women.[25] Neither his
aesthetics nor the relation he establishes between music and (illicit) sexuality is
new or original to this point:

> It is art [he means to include music] in our time that serves as the chief cause of the
> perversion of people in the most important question of social life—in their social

relations. . . . All art real and counterfeit, with very few exceptions, is devoted to describing, depicting, and inflaming, sexual love in every shape and form (p. 260).

What is unusual is his musical example of degradation: Beethoven, though he includes other composers as well, notably Wagner. The passage in question concerns the Piano Sonata No. 28 in A, Opus 101 (1817); Tolstoy's attack is fixed on the late works. (He generally speaks better of the earlier compositions; Tolstoy begins this discussion by pointing out to his imagined critics that he knows Beethoven's late works.) What he objects to in the Opus 101 is exactly what infuriates Pozdnyshev as regards the Opus 47 first movement: its "shapeless improvisations," in opposition to "those pleasant, clear, and strong, musical impressions which are transmitted, for instance by . . . Beethoven himself in his earlier period." What inheres in the later Beethoven is "the obscure, almost unhealthy, excitement." At the start of the discussion Tolstoy makes a confession about the music he is about to condemn: "For a long time I used to attune myself to delight in those shapeless improvisations."[26]

This helps explain Tolstoy's precision: it is the "Kruetzer" Sonata's first movement that affected his alter-ego Pozdnyshev, inspiring him to commit murder.[27] The second movement, a theme and variations, and the third, a presto tarantella, are more conventional, especially by comparison with the initial movement. Their formal structures and compositional procedures contain few of the first movement's surprises. It is the presto that incorporates the effects described by the composition's original title: "scritta in uno stilo molto concertante quasi come d'un Concerto"—rendering it unlike Beethoven's earlier violin sonatas. Although its date is early (1803), what Tolstoy correctly hears in the opening movement is what he claimed to despise in the later works.

The Sonata opens with an eighteen bar *adagio sostenuto*. The first four bars for solo violin, very difficult to play, hold the tonic in abeyance. There follows a four-bar solo piano response that establishes the tonic only to abandon it immediately by moving to a minor subdominant on d. The ambiguity and contingency of this gesture set the paradigm for the long presto sonata movement that follows. The adagio is motivic, not thematic; more than anything it is a series of harmonic moves designed to disguise direction and to make us desire direction the more. The adagio, as it were, refuses to show its hand until the moment it is transformed into the presto. Suddenly there is clarity, in the form of an assertive, aggressive, rhythmically punctuated theme. Yet no sooner is the theme stated, in nine bars, than it is interrupted by a fermata, thereafter to gain ascendancy again in its abbreviated consequent phrase. So the music proceeds, by advances and retreats. Often in the movement the second theme seems to serve as little more than an interruption, a brake on the frenetic action of the primary theme. There are virtuosic display passages, but they are procedurally complex, almost convoluted, and, like the entire movement, passionate in the extreme. They are also dialogic, both voices, violin and piano, in a duet—often in identical rhythm, a musical coupling, intense, heated—sometimes contested. Indeed, it is Beethoven's use of broken phrases, interruptions, and rapid and extreme tempo shifts, presto to adagio and back, which together must have produced Tolstoy's and Pozdnyshev's reactions. In essence the movement does not conform. Its intensities and shifts render it formally ambiguous to the ear, improvisational, and perhaps incoherent as sonata procedure, the classical mold against which it strains. Its energies, waxing and waning, are never negligible. The presto for Pozdnyshev is sexual ("Can one really allow it to be played in a drawing-room full of women in low-cut dresses?" [p. 97]). It is everything the subsequent movements are not. It plays the musical prostitute to the other movements' "good wives." What Pozdnyshev despises is what he hears as (sexual) anarchy (it "doesn't lead anywhere" [p. 97]), something that is beyond his control yet part of him, something that in rejecting he wants all the more—all these feelings are displaced onto the bodies of his wife and the musician. The music takes him onto terrain he fears. The distinct formal structure of the theme-and-variations movement, as with the tarantella finale, are by contrast procedurally certain, as it were choreographed. Their putative content is servant to a recognizable form *that is followed.* Yet what is striking, in a way, is that these movements in essence hardly interest either Tolstoy or Pozdnyshev: "After the presto they played the attractive but unoriginal andante with its rather trite variations, and then the finale, which is really weak" (p. 98).[28]

There may be something else at work to provoke his rage. The presto, notably different from the sonata's subsequent movements, is not salon music; it is not music of and for women. It is as fundamentally masculine, even phallic, in character as Beethoven's music can be. By comparison with the other music played that evening, which Pozdnyshev dismisses as inconsequential, this movement provokes conflict on account of a profound contradiction.[29] Pozdnyshev maintains the effeminacy of music and musicians in general. He eroticizes the musician Trukhachevsky's body as female and both desires and simultaneously claims superiority to it on that account. Yet once Trukhachevsky and Pozdnyshev's wife begin the sonata, all bets are off, precisely because the music itself does not conform to this map. The feminine is erased from the score. Pozdnyshev's wife and her partner both take on the sonoric roles of men, a violation scripted by Beethoven that Pozdnyshev cannot tolerate. The sonoric code of the presto movement enters Pozdnyshev's brain as a challenge to his identity: he *will* be made whole again—by killing his wife, by killing music.

One final point: when Tolstoy describes Pozdnyshev's knife attack on his wife, while she and the violinist are at music, he cannot resist disposing of the musician by resort to a self-protective cliché. The violinist to this moment has represented a profound threat on account of his physical sensuality and his music. He represents not only the phallic alien destroying Pozdnyshev's home and life but also what Pozdnyshev desires, his own feminine self, otherwise rigidly denied and suppressed. In the moment of truth, near the end, Pozdnyshev makes his first and only phallic gesture in the story, with a dagger. The musician, seeing the impending attack on the woman, momentarily seizes Pozdnyshev's arm ("something I'd never expected he'd do"). But when Pozdnyshev pulls free and lunges at him, the musician "turned as white as a sheet [read: "just like a woman"], even his lips turned pale; his eyes started to glitter in a peculiar way, and then suddenly—this was something else I hadn't been expecting—he *ducked under the piano and was out of the room in a flash*" (emphasis added; pp. 111–12). Having the musician turn tail and run, by crawling under the piano to make good his escape, is gratuitous, even logically absurd, but for Tolstoy is both psychically and ideologically necessary. The musician in the end is flaccid in the face of Pozdnyshev's metaphorical potency. Tolstoy thus confirms *by physical means* that the musician himself, like music, is woman, hence contemptible. That which Pozdnyshev and Tolstoy so convincingly desired—in spite of themselves—is written off by means of a cheap shot whose transparency announces the failure of the gesture.

ANACHRONISM AND THE VALORIZATION OF EFFEMINACY

I would like to return briefly to the duet, to amplify my earlier point about its connection to male-female eroticism, an eroticism repressed in the female-female duet (Fig. 75) looked at previously. The image that interests me, by Arturo Ricci (Fig. 84), is both a duet and a singing lesson. The teacher and pupil are the same age; to judge by costume, the man is the class equal of the woman. Two things are jarring. First, given the painting's late-nineteenth-century date, the setting is dramatically anachronistic—resolutely ancien régime, down to the Boucher-like Venus and nymphs on the painted panel at the back (typical of Ricci's work in this regard). The image is nostalgic, without the slightest hint of irony. Second, the faces match each other in their femininity. The man is at least as pretty as his lover; indeed he distinctly resembles her, not only in visage but also in posture and hand gestures. How can this image square with ideals of the Victorian middle class, even in a transliterated Italian version? To be sure, Italy was not England. But this painting is contemporaneous with Verdi, and there is nothing in his music or his dramatic situations that would support this representation—indeed, quite the opposite. The same effects are produced by an American painter, Edward Percy Moran, in *The Recital* (Fig. 85), except that a male soloist entertains a quar-

FIG. 84   Arturo Ricci, *The Singing Lesson,* oil on canvas, 41.2 × 29.2 cm. Private collection. Photo courtesy of Christie's, London.

FIG. 85   Edward Percy Moran, *The Recital,* oil on canvas, 73.7 × 99 cm. Private collection. Photo courtesy of Christie's, New York.

tet of young, pretty women who are obviously stimulated by his performance. The image replicates both Ricci's historically anachronistic setting and the effeminacy of its male character. Presuming, as I think we must, that neither picture is intentionally comic or ironic, what is their function?

Both pictures provide visual pleasure by articulating, and indeed valorizing, a normally repressed eroticism operating within what Eve Kosofsky Sedgwick has termed male homosocial desire (which she distinguishes from homosexual desire while recognizing that the former exists in relation to the repressed form of the latter). She outlines a continuum between the two, "whose visibility, for men, in our society is radically disrupted."[30] Nevertheless, the feminization of the male is not unproblematically celebrated by these paintings. It is there for our pleasure, for our fantasy, but it is also presented so as to be condemned. Condemnation is encouraged, by a class distinction, not a tabooed sexuality. The setting is not bourgeois but aristocratic. As is now well established, the bourgeoisie constructed its class identity in large part on their moral distinctness from a dissolute nobility, one whose dissoluteness was particularly suspect on sexual grounds.[31]

Both paintings, one by an Italian and the other by an American, seek to arouse us sexually through an erotic fantasy involving men *not* acting like men.[32] Not only are their gestures and postures feminine, but their costumes are also those of the fop; seen in color, they are at least as elaborate and eye-catching as the women's and, in the instance of the duet picture, far more anachronistic than the female partner's outfit. These are men who have refused what one scholar has termed, with regard to the fashion habits of the male middle class, the Great Masculine Renunciation—now epitomized, in unbroken lineage from the late-eighteenth-century bourgeoisie, by the three-piece business suit.[33] In short, both men dress like women, gesture like women, are set in elaborate domestic surroundings, and in effect (very important) *do* nothing—for such was the characteristic opinion of middle-class males concerning fine arts "activities." Thus music constitutes the putative agent in the feminization of men, simultaneously held at bay and made the subject of scopophilic desire: in both images the erotic charge is produced by the males insofar as they are constituted as aberrant, whereas the females by comparison are treated conventionally. (I should add that pictures like Ricci's and Moran's are by no means unusual; similar examples exist in large numbers, though almost all are very small—thus semiprivate—and many are done in watercolor, rather than oil, which privatizes them the more, in that such images might be stored in folders and looked at out of sight of others.)

HARD WOMEN, SOFT MEN, AND THE REVENGE ON MEDUSA

The dialectic evident in these two pictures invites return to the Woman Question, though the feminization of men will remain part of the discussion. How is one to make sense of the contrast between, say, the portrait image of Mrs. Pettie at her piano (Fig. 74) and the female model in the rather cheaply teasing picture by William Breakspeare entitled *The Reluctant Pianist* (Fig. 86)? That the two paintings are profoundly different is evident at first glance in their colors, which I can only describe, not show. Whereas the portrait of Mrs. Pettie is dominated by browns, and the lady herself is dressed in black, Breakspeare's palette is consistently pastel. Its brightness is tempered, however, by a clinical quality, in particular from the picture's harsh lighting, which in fact possesses discursive agency. The cold lighting makes the carpetless and highly reflective floor appear hard; its reflective surface attracts our glance, and the piano case replicates the effect. The harshness of the image's "atmosphere" helps overdetermine the emotional coldness

FIG. 86   William A. Breakspeare, *The Reluctant Pianist*, oil on canvas, 61 × 102 cm. Private collection. Photo courtesy of Sotheby's, London.

of the domestic scene, otherwise evident in the strained relations between the man and the woman.

Nonetheless, an opposing softness is incorporated, principally—and dialectically—in the archly coquettish body of the central figure: a teasing softness, a tantalizing mauve-begowned white-skinned woman whose demeanor utterly violates the principles of domesticity.[34] If she is a wife, as the scene would suggest, she is altogether too sexual: by contrast, ideally structured Victorian marriages did not so much control female sexuality as confirm its putative nonexistence.[35] She displays her sexual being in the (for the time) unseemly and exceedingly immodest profiled pose that accentuates the outline of her legs and hips. The husband or lover sitting forlornly, *explicitly effeminately,* in the adjoining room laments the lack of music, here an unambiguous cipher for sex, which does not happen because she is unwilling.

The richly entwined hair piled up on her head recalls the Medusa figure, another male Victorian pictorial obsession.[36] The impact of this detail may be made more obvious by comparison with a portrait of unassailable wifeliness (Fig. 87) where female eroticism is entirely supplanted by a steadfast, virtually religious, motherhood, replete with the rather heavy-handed incorporation of two Raphael Madonna and Child prints on the wall, in addition to one of Leonardo's *Last Supper.*[37] The Medusa figure, hated and desired, offered pleasure via her purportedly limitless and aggressive sexuality. Entwined snakes, supplanting her hair, overdetermine her visually confronting phallic powers. For this rampant transgression of gender hierarchy she *must* be punished. Her beheading by Perseus is her castration and also the restoration of sexual normalcy, the return of the phallus. The ultimate pleasure of Medusa, in other words, is beating her at her own game. The viewer of *The Reluctant Pianist* may take pleasure in the woman's sexuality and, indeed, in the fantasy, as it were, of forcing her to "play" (to comply), unlike the man in the picture who will offer no substantive competition to the image's would-be aggressor-spectator. Nonetheless, the viewer's fantasy victory is empty in that the fantasy on which the pleasure of viewing her depends confirms the lack that looking is intended to supplant—and the viewer knows it. It is that hate-pleasure, victory-loss combination that in part accounts for fear of women. It is what allows Victorian medical "science" and moral ideology alike to theorize that due to the wife's inability to satisfy her husband's sexual needs, due to the very terms imposed on her that organize their relationship, he might appropriately take his sexual pleasure elsewhere—for the good of the family, the society, and the nation!

Musical harmony by analogy stands in here, and in many other domestic narrative and portrait paintings, for domestic harmony: but with a price to pay. The piano served as a sign by which men defined and empowered themselves; it was a code for "woman," by which was really meant "not man." The piano as a sign of

FIG. 87   Sir John Everett Millais, *Mrs. James Wyatt, Junior, and Her Daughter* (c. 1850), oil on wood panel, 35.6 × 45.1 cm. London, Tate Gallery.

woman was also a cipher for the domestic erotic economy, such as it was, and therein lay the problem. In the case of the reluctant pianist, the erotic economy of Victorian life could operate successfully only if the supply might be tapped whenever needed, whenever demand existed. Woman, as wife, should contain within her the passive sexuality that can be taken as raw material and molded into the pleasure of its owner, without her enjoying it (that was crucial). What this picture violates is the expectation of passivity. The ability to imagine taming the woman's sexual agency drives the pleasure to be derived from looking at her. In short, the image's putative subject is invitation to rape, otherwise more politely known as the taming of the shrew. In a sense this is very much in the tradition of the music lesson topos, except that the reluctant pianist is in desperate need of a proper male "teacher" who better understands how to operate in accord with dominant

FIG. 88   Frank Huddlestone Potter, *Girl Resting at a Piano,* oil on canvas, 51.4 × 71.4 cm. London, Tate Gallery.

ideological principles. That ideal is captured in another image of this general sort (Fig. 88) in the languid slouch of a young woman possessing barely the energy to fan herself as she waits beside her piano (again it is useful to compare her pose with that of Mrs. Pettie in Fig. 74).

The issue I am addressing can perhaps be highlighted by comparing *The Reluctant Pianist* with a painting executed at least a century and a quarter earlier by the well-known portrait painter Arthur Devis (Fig. 89). On the surface there is considerable similarity between this 1749 portrait and the later image. In both pictures the female sitters are elaborately and fashionably costumed. Both are set into physical spaces marking the domain of an established upper middle class. In both images the view through a window conventionally registers land as the basis for an economy of power and wealth. Beyond these concordances, however, the pictures sharply diverge. In Devis's portrait social position and class status are as well grounded as the heavy classical architecture of the estate house: they are a given, and seemingly permanent. The marriage on which the scene depends is settled, not open to question. The bodies of the women mark this difference. Devis's sitter is formally posed, even somewhat stiff, as is nearly always the case with his sitters, but this is a positive quality since it establishes the certainty of her social standing. Eroticism plays no part in the visual economy—it is a portrait, after all, whose cultural norms eschew any hint of sensuality. What replaces the sensual is a lack of contingency, the absence of risk; in the later image the absence of certainty effects excitement. We know exactly what sort of music Devis's sitter will play; one cannot go so far in the case of the other. Nonetheless, contingency remains the enemy, notably where sexuality is concerned. The risk produces excitement only so long as the proper outcome can be imagined.

If erotic agency is controlled from more than one side of the male-female equation, the system breaks down; in the end, the pianist is not supposed to refuse to perform. It is the woman who is blamed: Breakspeare painted his reluctant pianist as a refusing tease, a tart, not the domesticated wife but in effect the whore. Her refusal can be responded to, of course, by the man's departure, which in turn ruptures the domestic bond, as in another painting by the same artist called *The Tiff,* a subject of considerable popularity among Victorians (Fig. 90).[38] The sym-

FIG. 89   Arthur Devis, *Lady at the Harpsichord* (1749), oil on canvas, 54 × 39 cm. Private collection. Photo courtesy of Sotheby's, London.

FIG. 90   William A. Breakspeare, *The Tiff,* oil on canvas, 69.2 × 51.5 cm. Private collection. Photo courtesy of Christie's, London.

bolic doorway through which the disgruntled man is about to pass replicates perfectly, and with obvious intention, the medieval iconography of the maw of Hell,
eventually transformed, with little apparent effort, into the imagery of the vagina
dentata. Yet the hell into which the man will pass, baton-phallus prominently in
hand, promises reciprocal punishment for the woman. His sometime lover in essence is made to bear responsibility for his moral downfall. Beyond the archway
through which he is about to pass is a view to the outside. In true Victorian
character, the woman, front and center, has the momentary opportunity to "save"
her man, to support him morally, as he pauses at the door, if only she can rise to
the occasion. In the mythology—if not necessarily the history—of Victorian sexuality, a man leaving his wife and home following a domestic dispute conventionally headed for the streets, where he might hire one of the many thousands of
available urban prostitutes.

What is it about the function of music in the lives of this class that rendered
it a metaphorically appropriate prop to activate this narrative? To the Victorian
bourgeoisie the home served as sanctuary, a place to which a man could retire for
a recompense principally invested in his woman. She in turn was imagined not
only as physical and spiritual but also as sonoric. In essence, the man's world was
silent and the woman's sonorically fecund; her ideal essence, in sonoric terms, was
harmony. Yet musical harmony conflated with woman was simultaneously despir-
itualized, hence de-aestheticized, by its association with female sexuality, at once
abhorred and desired. The connections between music, woman, and sexuality, inevitably masked by the conditions of Victorian domesticity, were acted out explicitly on the contemporaneous operatic stage and were likewise hinted at in music
journalism, where references to passionate emotion abound. We would do well to
refocus our attention on these relationships as we continue our relatively recent
revival of interest in nineteenth-century music and its connections to socio-
cultural formations. In my judgment these relations account to no small degree
for the unstable locus of music in Victorian society, an instability of which professional musicians themselves were keenly aware. Desire was acted out largely, in its
licit manifestations, within domestic surroundings. That a specifically domestic
music served as the sonoric cipher for these operative ideologies in no way separates them from the public (and often greater) music with which we are much
more familiar. In fact, in addition to all the song literature and piano music produced principally for the home market,[39] much of the music people played and
sang in their drawing rooms consisted of arrangements of precisely the music Victorians otherwise heard professionals play in public. The semantic and ideological
congruence between the two was necessarily apparent; to function successfully in
the culture, it had to be. Finally, I would suggest that the pronounced "masculinity" evident in the aggressiveness, assertiveness, and insistence in so much nine-

teenth-century instrumental music, from piano sonatas to symphonies, in part constitutes an impassioned outburst by male artists entreating for the centrality of their artistic exercise not only as a protest over their own marginalization but also as the sonoric denial of the effeminization the culture attached to them as artists. At the same time, however, these expressions of sonoric protest serve to reenact and thereby sanction the ideology of male hegemony on which artists' own marginalization depends.[40]

You cannot paint or sing yourselves into being good men; you must be good men before you can either paint or sing, and then the colour and sound will complete in you all that is best.

John Ruskin,
"The Relation of Art to Morals"

8

MALE AGONY:
AWAKENING CONSCIENCE

A MAN AND A WOMAN, alone in a gaudy Victorian room, have been at music
(Fig. 91),[1] just now seemingly interrupted as the woman rises awkwardly from
her seated position. The picture is richly narrative; its story is governed by music.
Yet its musical situation is demonstrably "wrong." What might this mean? How,
for example, can the man play the piano from a tilt-backed easy chair whose seat
is too low for him properly to reach the keys? How can he play the instrument
while a woman sits in his lap? His mouth is open, and he gestures as if expressing
a song's words. We might reasonably think she is singing as well; her lips are
parted, and her hands are held together as if in recital pose. Yet there is no audience
for her performance except the unseen viewer; thus her formality is gratuitous.
Perhaps she is wringing her hands (people wring their hands in opera, in the
theater, and in paintings as a conventionalized indication of grief).[2] She stands
bent forward at the waist, not a singer's stance. Nor do singers perform while
dressed in nightgowns like hers,[3] except in operas, and then only when they have
committed a crime (Lucia) or are about to die for a (supposed) crime (Desdemona).
Operatic transgressions of this sort are invariably linked both to desire and
sexuality.

Is she singing, or is she crying out in horror—at what he sings? The music
on the piano rack begins, "Oft, in the stilly night." It is a song about love, loss,
and memory; it is not a proper love song. Why is he singing to her a tale to evoke
sadness and, in this instance, the moral revulsion attested to by the painting's
title? The song cannot address his interests. She is, after all, his illicit lover. The
song is only going to cause him problems; indeed, it already has. Although the

189

FIG. 91　William Holman Hunt, *The Awakening Conscience* (1853), oil on canvas with arched top, 76.2 × 55.9 cm. London, Tate Gallery.

painting concatenates sex with music and music with a woman, the representation is contradictory as regards both music and woman.

In opera a scene like this would occur at night, the "time" for sex, and sometimes death. Not so here. The sun shines brightly in the garden at the back, and the room is bathed in light, accentuating the garish colors of the carpet. In the light of day things are clearer. Objectivity triumphs like an ancillary to science. Light vanquishes darkness and puts on display, almost clinically, the dark urges of the flesh. In Victorian culture sexuality was the urgent concern of medicine, psychiatry, law, and public morals, invariably focused on the illegalities of the night involving the bodies of prostitutes,[4] among whom painters commonly found their female models, including this one.[5] William Holman Hunt "discovered" her when she was fifteen.

> Child prostitution was a booming industry; virgins were particularly prized by gentlemen as "green fruit," and some parents, made heartless by desperation, sold their daughters' maidenheads for as little as five pounds or as much as twenty pounds—more money than some working-class people made in a year. (To salve everyone's conscience, the child was sometimes given chloroform during the defloration.)[6]

Hunt's interest in his model, whose name was Annie Miller,[7] was more than professional. He wanted her for his wife, provided he could get her made over into a proper bourgeois.[8] At age twenty-six he was himself a virgin, unlike his artist friend(s) who became her lover(s) after Hunt's temporary departure, following the completion of this very painting, for (where else?) the Holy Land to paint biblical scenes. Hunt's image of her "proper" self proved of little interest to Annie Miller.[9] In the end, Hunt married someone else and eventually had his literary revenge; in his end-of-life thousand-page autobiography he suppressed Annie Miller's name entirely, though her memory continued to haunt him. In *The Awakening Conscience* he also completely obliterated her face with repainting; it is not Annie Miller whom we now see. The original, incorporating the look of a woman fully realizing her sexual sin—as Hunt had imagined it—was called *The Awakened Conscience,* and it proved too much to bear for the man who had bought the picture.

Had she not risen from the man's lap, a second tune, just out of its wrapper and lying on the floor, might have been sung. Its too-blue cover opens to reveal the title page of Edward Lear's setting of Tennyson's 1847 verse "Tears, Idle Tears." (This was a bit of artist-to-artist commercial solidarity: Lear was Hunt's friend, whose tune had just been published.) Why did the man bring her this song (his hat is on the table; he is the visitor and gift-bearer)?

Tears, idle tears, I know not what they mean,
Tears from the depth of some divine despair
Rise in the heart, and gather to the eyes,
In looking on the happy autumn-fields,
And thinking of the days that are no more.

What on earth could Hunt be thinking? This tune is even sadder than the other one. The painted pair are lovers; we know that. She is his mistress, his whore. He is a young man about town, a seducer, and a man of money. He has fine clothes. The apartment is hers, but he pays for it. It is at Woodbine Villa, No. 7, St. John's Wood, the suburb fashionable in those days for apartment-based assignations; Hunt rented the space and posed his model there, presumably so he could get it all just so—he did not know about these things firsthand.[10] A contemporary observed sarcastically that "if Hunt had wanted to paint Everton toffee, he would have felt obliged to take a studio in Everton."[11] There is more. "On the same principle that induced Hunt to boil a horse to produce a skeleton on which to base an accurate portrayal of its outward appearance, he invariably painted his models in the nude before adding their clothes."[12] All this—just to get it "right"? Surely there was another reason as well, one Hunt did not acknowledge in his memoirs. Hunt the virgin, obsessed with his beautiful model, about whose beauty everyone agreed, drew her again and again: as Lady Godiva and as the Lady of Shalott with flowing hair, or lying in bed, or, small irony, kneeling by the bed for *Morning Prayer*.[13] He painted his model as the icon of piety, but naked and sexually ravishing and stationed by furniture whose use, as conventionalized in painting, was not for sleeping but for sex. Yet if Hunt was only aiming to get his paintings' details "right," might we not ask, What kept woman, and what man who keeps a woman, would decorate the site of their pleasures with a print, the one over the piano, of *Christ and the Woman Taken in Adultery?* We have two songs, neither likely to elicit a mood conducive to lovemaking, and an interior image warning of the moral consequences of the act, all in a painting nonetheless virtually overwhelmed by "correct" detail appropriate to the residence of a kept woman. We have here an infusion of allegory into a painting of modern life.

She "grants" him her favors; it beats starvation. He is like the cat, under the table at the left, toying with the little songbird (did it fly in through the open window?). The cat is sneaky, crouched down, eyes glaring satanically. The man's glove, soiled, lies at her feet on the floor. Is it a sign of his passionate carelessness; or is it a gauntlet thrown down, a device for slapping, for waking someone to a new reality; or does it forewarn of her own fate, to be cast off; or is it none of these? Why is the glove, so prominently without its companion and half turned inside out—turned back so as to show that it was once clean but is now filthy? Why does the man wear the other glove, and on the hand with which he touches the piano's keys? What is the connection: naked/clothed, bright/dark, unclean/clean? Or has Hunt framed, instead of a binary, a conjunction: music and prostitution?

MONEY AND THE BODY

Is there not too much to look at? Is not the reality overwhelming, vulgar, too much of a visual feast? The painting is governed by excess. Surely Hunt knew that. Is the man's effort to secure regulated, steady sex with a whore-made-mistress not an *economic* scandal as well as an ethical one? Are the two not related, money and women's bodies?[14] Access to a woman's body cost money; in Victorian culture such an expenditure was conventionally regarded as waste, a condition that produced moral panic in men.[15] Indeed, men commonly spoke of both women and music in the discourse of contagion. By the close of the seventeenth century music in English culture was held a waste of time and money, an enervation of a young man's substance.[16] Sex, like music, is a momentary pleasure that vanishes but leaves its trace: physical and moral disease and weakness—the signs of women and the signs of death.

The painted conscience in the state of awakening takes no account of the material body, as if her found morality exists outside the realm of the physical and, closely related, the economic. Moreover, whereas men's sexual misadventures were readily forgiven and forgotten, no reciprocal pardon and amnesty were available to women. I speak here of the bourgeoisie, those who defined the official rules. Her refusal of his advance, money for sex, now promises the future life of her soul, but it will come at the expense (money again) of her body. How will she eat? No matter; she is saved. The "real" Annie Miller managed better than most; Hunt's phantasmagoria about saving her soul, like that of nearly every other Victorian painter of the very popular fallen-woman theme, was not hers. She had her own image of what she was after.

What gives the picture its moral charge? Is it the man's scandalous sexual spending or the scandalous spending of his money, as on garish furniture, for his mistress? The anonymous Victorian author of *My Secret Life* wrote in his voluminous sexual-accounts journal that he liked the "mercantile business" of buying the prostitute. (Until the laws and the police began to regulate "the trade," prostitution was commonly part-time work—hardly a "profession"—for poor women, who were typically married and had hungry children to feed.[17]) As he tells the tale, on two occasions he made his women's vaginas the literal bank to receive his presex shillings.[18] Nevertheless, the vaginal receptacle for both the flow of cash and, later, semen produces *his* loss, specifically of embodied energy. In the economy of power, his domination of his whore, a sign and self-confirmation of his strength, is maddeningly also the sign and confirmation of precisely the opposite. This confounding produces desire but also rage. A man giving in to sex showed a weakness of body over mind and—not coincidentally—resembled a man giving in to music: "I heard one of [two gentlemen] exclaim,—'I hate to see a *man* at the Harpsichord!' I had never before annexed the idea of effeminacy to that instrument; but from that moment, I began to be of that gentleman's opinion."[19] The sex act itself for men, so the medical authorities had it, exhausted the "vital force," life itself—Foucault has shown that this reading was already authorized by the ancient Greeks[20]—thus the obsessive Victorian fear of masturbation and thus the fear of prostitution, made worse by the threat of bacterial infection.

John Ruskin, Hunt's apologist for *The Awakening Conscience,* on art: "A maiden may sing of her lost love, but a miser cannot sing of his lost money. And with absolute precision, from highest to lowest, *the fineness of the possible art is an index of the moral purity and majesty of the emotion it expresses*" (Ruskin's emphasis).[21] Ruskin implies that the relation of song, love, money, art, and morals stakes out the difference between good and evil. The woman who can sing of love is she who has not embodied it in sex (else she could not remain a "maiden"). She who has embodied sex is like the miser whose money is spent and cannot be recovered. Proper art, like *The Awakening Conscience,* is an index of proper purity. Proper art is an economy of hoarding.

Is the vulgarity of too much carpet and too much rosewood and gilt—all of it, in its *newness,* purposely and appropriately shocking to the picture's original apologist, John Ruskin[22]—an easy out, a condemnation of the new bourgeoisie whose monied circumstances the painter did not share but among whom he wanted nonetheless to be (after all, he had to eat)? None of the decor is appropriate to the family parlor; this is furniture from Rent-a-Room. No wife and children will ever gather at this flat's imagined hearth. This unsettling picture is the dark reverse image of the cult of domesticity. The room and its furnishings mark the scandalous misuse of money for illicit sexual pleasures, an abhorrent waste the Victorian bourgeoisie preferred to associate with the aristocracy, their class enemy, and not with themselves, though they were in fact quite as guilty.[23] The painting's moral tale depends on articulating a prophylactic difference: the seducer is not middle class. Hunt's friend Fred Stephens, who advised Hunt on how to exact revenge for Annie Miller's blackmail (involving love letters and drawings, presumably nudes) following their breakup, interpreted the picture in describing the seducer's gesture: "One of his *patrician* arms surrounds the victim of his passions" (emphasis added).[24] Stephens condemns the sexual sin of an aristocrat. This is the irony: prostitution was all the rage among the urban bourgeoisie. Indeed, solicitation of prostitutes was medically explained, even justified, as the safety valve of the middle-class man, who had to confront the supposed sexual purity (read: frigidity) of the good bourgeois woman, deemed—by men—uninterested in sex. This painting is about a woman and her soul, but the device that governs everything is music—a piano and two songs, though only one is performed. It is about harmony, duet, and coming together but also about music and decay, death, and damnation. It is about pleasure and pain: our pleasure at her pain; our pleasure at his comeuppance, his softness, his smooth skin and perfect hands. Not like us, he is more of a dandy. He has no right to look as he does; his looks are altogether too much like those of a women. Small wonder that it is, unquestionably, he who sings.

TIME AND DETAIL

Music is time that draws attention to itself. On top of the piano rests a clock, encased in a bell jar: gilded time attended to by small classically garbed figures who lean over the clock face—over time—and embrace it, watch it, fetishize it. Does such a clock keep time or remind us of it? Does it keep time with the music, or the reverse? Music is time; time is life; here both are mechanical. Time is a machine that keeps watch on the young woman's life. Time keeps her date with her "lover," on whom she waits and depends: he feeds her. Time sits lavishly on top of the piano, and time acts itself out in the musical order of the song. This is the age of industry ("Be on time"), recently, for the first time, regulated by Greenwich mean time, and also the age of music regulated by the metronome ("Keep in time"). Time as we now know it, as though our time were somehow "natural," was defined in the nineteenth century on account of the same money force that underwrote the psychologies of timely pleasure in Hunt's picture. Our "time" was invented for the railroad *schedule*—so that raw materials could be gotten to the factories, to keep them running, ostinato fashion, and get goods to the towns, cities, and ports for consumption.[25] Music in Hunt's painting, like time, is order, *an* order; it is imposed. It is a harmony that makes demands, and in this instance does so "Oft, in the Stilly Night." To regulate time in Victorian factories was to regulate the one weak link in the production process, the human bodies that operated the machinery. The worker's body came to be defined by time. Annie Miller is a worker; in Hunt's painting, wherein music and time are concatenated, time regulates, defines, and organizes her body for sex; music aestheticizes the oppression and offers some compensation for her pain.

That this picture has too many details,[26] that everything seems to be shown, precisely drawn and brightly lit, is not accidental. "For the English painters of the middle of the century, moral truth and material fact, relentlessly pursued down to the last stitch in the last antimacassar, seem to be absolutely equated."[27] But can we "see" the antimacassar for the stitches? Can or will Hunt? This is a modern painting, or rather a modern discourse. It comes to us rich in data, clinically lighted, its contents seemingly inventoried. Ruskin claimed that the objects force themselves on us with a "ghastly and unendurable distinctness, as if they would compel the sufferer to count, or measure, or learn them by heart." [28] The non-modernist element, by contrast, is the intentionality of the allegory, a bit old-fashioned, like Hunt himself. The image is a paradise of consumption; it is very much "about" goods. Ruskin claimed horror at the room's vulgarity, to him an appropriate moral commentary on the illicit relationship Hunt depicted, though his charge rings a bit false. Part of the painting's "problem" is that it provides too much to consume. As in vanitas paintings of yore, its putative moral competes with an "extra," possibly contradictory, discourse about the pleasures of posses-sion. In the process, the sin governing Hunt's vision is at once lost sight of and otherwise made to *appear* quite attractive, even bourgeois. After all, to the Victo-rian bourgeoisie material goods spelled success, and success itself was a sign of grace. On this score, Hunt seems to have confused his first viewers: "The effect was to generate demand for more and more doses of the scopic." [29] Ruskin explic-itly sought to clear up the confusion: "People gaze at it in a blank wonder, and leave it hopelessly." [30] The *Athenaeum* reviewer reported that "innocent and unen-lightened spectators suppose it to represent a quarrel between a brother and sis-ter," [31] confirming that the picture was not so different from scenes of proper family life. All these distractions notwithstanding, our eyes are eventually led back to her face projecting outward from the picture plane. It is the painting's focal point, despite the intrusive commentary of object data.

HER FACE

"The author of 'The Bridge of Sighs' could not have conceived a more painful-looking face." [32] The investment is too much to bear; it pricks the conscience. It was not pretty: "an ugly woman in the incipient stage of a hysterical attack." [33] The buyer lived with her face only briefly. In 1856 he returned the picture to Hunt and paid him to do it over; Hunt obliged. What survives of the original exists only in written text. Thus Lady Trevelyan wrote in her diary (13 May 1854), having seen the picture on exhibition: "The half insane horror in her eyes is mar-velous." [34] Hunt, ill with fever, was dissatisfied with his repainting, but he soon sent the work back to the owner for an exhibition, where the title was changed. What that change admits is a progression, the passage of time. The frozen image is momentarily unfrozen, the film set in reverse a few frames—ironically, in this new age of progress, forward motion is halted, too much to bear. Now the con-science is not awakened but awaken*ing*.

In 1857 the picture was again back in Hunt's studio. This time he thought he had improved it: "Lately, I have had the 'Awakening Conscience' on my easel for a week, in the spring I had worked on the head of the girl before sending it to

Birmingham, when I was suffering from fever, which defeated my attempt to improve it. I think that I have materially bettered it now."[35] Annie Miller's face passes back and forth between two men somehow obsessed by it; one of them refashions it to the other's better pleasure. Artist as pimp? In the end, Annie Miller's face is gone, cut off, replaced by the hand of male creative authority, a new face sutured in, beautiful but Frankenstein's monster nonetheless, object of the paintbrush/scalpel.[36] The fussed-over face is the product of Victorian phrenology: "The very reading of Victorian faces itself was fostered by the restraints of Victorian social life and obsession with propriety. The constriction of behavior necessitated acute attention to emotional signs."[37]

John Ruskin, Hunt's champion, "read" her original face in a letter about the painting printed in the *Times* (25 May 1854):

> I suppose that no one possessing the slightest knowledge of expression could remain untouched by the countenance of the lost girl, rent from its beauty into sudden horror; the lips half open, indistinct in their purple quivering, the teeth set hard, the eyes filled with the fearful light of futurity and with tears of ancient days.[38]

One change we can be sure of: her teeth are no longer set hard. Her jaw is relaxed. Her parted lips, no longer "purple" or "quivering," might even be given over to song. No horror remains. But what is her recital? What is the "tune" Hunt has given her to sing, he who attempted to script her life, who saw her as a once-dirtied tabula rasa on whose soul's surface he desired to write his own response to the Woman Question?

THOMAS FAIRBAIRN

The man who bought *The Awakening Conscience* was Thomas Fairbairn from Manchester,[39] an established art patron and an industrialist—his father was the "founding father of mechanical engineering"[40]—whose family firm first had a hand in supplying machinery to textile mills but expanded into making steam engines, boilers, patent riveting machines, and iron steamboats.[41] Why did Fairbairn buy the picture? What did he see in it? How might it have functioned for him? The beginnings of an explanation can be located in his role in industrial worker relations, his perception of the family, and the connection between the two.

Carolyn Arscott has sorted out these issues very well.[42] She tells us that Fairbairn was a leader among Manchester industrialists, just as he was a leader in the formation of the city's cultural life. He established his position in the community in 1852–53 by helping put down, via a four-month lockout, a major labor strike by workers against local engineering firms. Under the name Amicus, Fairbairn published a series of letters in the *Times* that stated the position of the employers and attempted to discredit the union organizers by exaggerating the workers' demands; the effectiveness of his writings was acknowledged by people on both sides of the issue. These letters urged workers to abandon the strike so as to preserve home and family from undue suffering, the family being projected as the foundation for social morality. The ideology of domesticity, which Fairbairn in effect urged on the workers, was the basis on which he hoped to secure his own financial position.

The woman in *The Awakening Conscience,* purchased just one year after these events, occupies a middle ground between wife/mother and worker/whore. As a kept woman she is positioned above the streetwalker, but because she is hired for sex just the same, she is a prostitute.[43] In Hunt's painting, however, she literally rises from her position, via music, toward the goal (for her, unrealizable) of wife/mother. Her physical rising governs the entire image and probably governs as well Thomas Fairbairn's response, his desire to have the painting, to look at it/her at will. Her rising projects a dynamism that might be located in the mutually supporting economy of morality and the profit motive of capitalism; it is ideologically charged and culturally affirmative. She is the reformed worker who internalizes the cult of domesticity as the promise of her salvation. She is music to Fairbairn's ears.

Hunt's painting is about the possibility of improvement and accumulation, in which all sorts of things might be converted into "capital" and in which space itself is treated as distinctly developmental, not static. The moral charge and the charge of pleasure encoded in *The Awakening Conscience* are registered in Annie Miller's body—and not by the face, not hers, that rises so abruptly, like the line on the growth chart of the annual report. It is her *movement* that excites the viewer, Thomas Fairbairn, because that movement is an investment in both power (the power to make her over, in his own image, "better") and sex (a fantasy that he can enjoy while remaining morally insulated from it). But one small detail failed to work its charm on Thomas Fairbairn: Annie Miller's face had to go; its horror worked as the equivalent of an unannounced visit from the auditors. The face is *of* the body; it registers the sensation of pain. The "replacement" face is conventional, interchangeable with those from countless other Victorian moral narratives. Thomas Fairbairn is not hurt by looking at it. This one "fits" him better; his purchase is now satisfying. Thus the painting is like other consumer goods; if unsatisfactory, it may be exchanged. The buyer trades in Annie Miller for another woman—a simulacrum of prostitution. Did Hunt hire a different model off the streets to provide the "new" face? His autobiography is silent on this score.

The Awakening Conscience should be seen in conjunction with a later picture Hunt painted for Thomas Fairbairn, an 1865 portrait of Fairbairn's wife and five youngest children known as *The Children's Holiday* (Fig. 92)—the title, ironically,

FIG. 92   William Holman Hunt, *The Children's Holiday* (1864), oil on canvas, 213 × 146 cm.
Torquay, Torre Abbey.

was suggested to Hunt by Lewis Carroll.[44] The two paintings were in fact exhibited together in 1865.[45] Although the setting is outdoors, the image serves as a repository of domestic virtue and harmonious domestic life. In effect, the tranquillity and fundamental moral goodness of the scene both explain and justify the social order imposed by the industrialist in his public life. I want to describe and compare two details with their counterparts in *The Awakening Conscience.* The first is the shawl worn by Allison Fairbairn. In *The Children's Holiday* the adult woman wears it around her shoulders and indeed pulls it modestly together at the waist as she pours tea for her children on the lawn. In the earlier image, a similar shawl has been removed from the woman's shoulders and is tied around her hips, emphasizing their curvature; here the painting repeats the primary effect seen in *An Attentive Pet* (Fig. 83). In dressing her Hunt discloses what the garments hide. This single object in the two paintings, both overburdened with iconic signs, registers a difference in two ways: by color (Allison Fairbairn's shawl is cream and brownish gold) and by the position of the bodies. The "good" woman's shawl is in place; the "other" woman's emphasizes her sexuality. The large knot securing the shawl around Annie Miller's hips, together with the shawl's deep red color, which is set off by the neutral nightgown, attracts our gaze; in the painterly vocabulary of the time, the effect is orientalist, suggesting the odalisque, the harem. The second detail involves rings. Mrs. Fairbairn wears a wedding band on the hand that clutches her shawl. Annie Miller wears many rings, the overdetermined sign of her many "husbands."[46]

FRAME AND TEXT, AUTHORITY AND PAIN

The Awakening Conscience is surrounded by a frame designed by Hunt. He painted chiming bells and marigolds, emblems of warning and sorrow,[47] and a single star, perhaps a reference to Christ or truth.[48] (The reproduction here shows the picture removed from its frame; the writing visible in the upper corners, normally hidden by the frame's arched top, is Hunt's and indicates details about his retouchings of 1864 and 1886.) The frame also carries an inscription from Proverbs: "As he that taketh away a garment in cold weather, / so is he that singeth songs to a heavy heart"; by Hunt's own account these words provided guidance for the development of the picture.[49] The 1854 Royal Academy exhibition catalogue entry cited scriptural verses from Isaiah (Bishop Lowth's translation) and Ecclesiastes (14 : 18), the former giving courage to the timid ("Strengthen ye the feeble hands, and confirm ye the tottering knees; say ye to the faint hearted: Be ye strong; fear ye not; behold your God"), the latter developing a metaphor for moral rise or decline ("As of the green leaves on a thick tree, some fall and some grow, so is the generation of flesh and blood").[50]

Proverbs: to sing songs to someone with a heavy heart effects the reverse of what we might expect; it offers not comfort but *cold* cruelty, intentional meanness. Hunt in his autobiography offers this reading:

> These words, expressing the unintended stirring up of the deeps [*sic*] of a pure affection by the idle sing-song of an empty mind, led me to see how the companion of the girl's fall might himself be the unconscious utterer of a divine message. In scribbles I arranged the two figures to present the woman recalling the memory of her childish home, and breaking away from her gilded cage with a startled holy resolve, while her shallow companion still sings on, ignorantly intensifying her repentant purpose.[51]

Music and sin; sin as voice of salvation: the ambiguity is striking. The piano,[52] what Edmond de Goncourt called the "lady's hashish,"[53] foremost fetish of domesticity, marriage, the good wife, is in a house of ill repute, but *not* a home, so Ruskin informs us—that "fatal newness" again: "Nothing [is] there that has the old thoughts of home upon it, or that is ever to become a part of home." The piano's case, so precisely inscribed, "painted even to the last vein of the rosewood," given a "terrible lustre,"[54] is the visual source of Ruskin's horror. It is the is-not of domestic purity, of bourgeois identity. Yet it *is* that which it is not. In its "terrible lustre," it serves metaphorically as a terrible swift sword, for the tunes emanating from it strike to the depths of her soul, to her heart, and she is purified. Reborn, she leaps up, and remains forever rising, as if in resurrection from death, decay, contagion. What horrors might ensue were she to sit back down?[55] There is a catch. Is it the tune (music) or the text that reaches her conscience? Hunt tries to separate the two; he speaks of "words" yet he acknowledges that what stirs things up is not simply text but sonority. In a sense he attempts to transpose song into melodrama that operates, as Peter Brooks has shown us,[56] by displacing word: music at war with language.

Music functions within the image as the pretext for passion. To explain, I must digress briefly to consider *Music Hath Charms* (Fig. 93), painted four years after *The Awakening Conscience.* In the later work it is spring; the early flowers are blooming, and the willow (variety: weeping, never an accident in "love" pictures) is leafing out. A young man sits on the banks of a brook and sings, and a young woman hears him and comes—furtively? Or do the two of them play a game, act out a ritual? His sidelong glance will catch her at the earliest moment. He knows she is there.

But something is not right; there is a mistake. The young man is following a script; he reads his song from a sheet of music, a text. Worse: he beats time with his right hand. He conducts, like a leader or maybe a pied piper. Perhaps she, like the rats in the fairy tale, cannot resist his tune. The "victims" of this springtime story are several but among them count spontaneity. The young man may have all

FIG. 93   George Adolphus Storey, *Music Hath Charms* (1857), oil on canvas, 75 × 62.2 cm. Private collection. Photo courtesy of Christie's, London.

the right moves as a would-be lover, but he is leaving nothing to chance. The sheet in his hands, an abbreviated sonoric love manual, recommends: make it musical, get all the notes, keep in time, inflect properly; then you'll get the girl. The scene projects music as a calculation. One buys it, for surely he did not write it out himself, and puts it to use. Music, indeed, hath charms but things have gotten a bit clinical, and loving has become a bit of a bore. I use *clinical* advisedly, so as to invoke a related trope:

> The dangerous affective power of music was a current commonplace in medical literature. Thomas Laycock, in *A Treatise on the Nervous Diseases of Women* (1840) quoted a Dr. J. J. Johnson's comment that "the stimulus of music is of a very subtle and diffusible nature, and the excitement which it produces in the nervous system is of a peculiar character, by no means generally understood" (p. 141).[57]

Hunt intended to pair *The Awakening Conscience* with *The Light of the World* (1851), destined to become the most famous religious painting of the Victorian age (Hunt painted three versions of the picture, and it was engraved in 1858 and again in 1865).[58] The paintings were exhibited together at the Royal Academy in 1854. Hunt addressed the question of the pairing as an intertextuality: "It occurred to me that my spiritual subject called for a material counterpart in a picture representing in actual life the manner in which the appeal of the spirit of heavenly love calls a soul to abandon a lower life."[59] The two images employ light differently. Unlike the stark brightness of the *maison* in St. John's Wood, *The Light of the World* is an outdoor night scene. It shows Christ in flowing robes carrying a lantern and knocking at a cottage door. Embedded in the putative sanctity of this subject is a curious fact: the two original models Hunt used for the Christ figure were both women. Did he first paint them in the nude, as was his ordinary practice with female models? Was Christ first sexed female?[60]

As Annie Miller's conscience awakens, she rises from her lover's lap, in moral transformation.[61] But her physical movement is itself transformed into something between a gesture and a tableau. The improbability of her pose translates her into a text about discipline. The pose required of Annie Miller to affect this rising would produce backache, leg strain, and general fatigue. It marks the visual-physical punishment for the transgression of being poor, a woman, and sexual. Discipline-punishment pays off; discipline *produces*—what? Marriage to the aspiring Hunt. But *only* if she can be "preached" to. She must listen—the ears again, music to his ears, apparently, but not to hers. Is it accidental that Hunt began speaking to Annie Miller about marriage at the same moment he undertook the picture?[62] He wanted to make her a lady; send her to school; correct thereby her "wretched false pride" and her "fatal indolence,"[63] as he put it.

Hunt framed Annie Miller in text, but she likewise framed him—and not only by blackmail. Hunt's obsession was not confined to paint. He excised her name from his writings, offering nothing about their stormy relationship, though in his autobiography he discussed the picture itself in some detail.[64] The excision notwithstanding, he spoke obsessively of her in the company of others in the summer of 1880, more than two decades after their breaking up, avoiding, it seems, all mention of her name:

> A very simple story, but recited in so vivid a minuteness as to hold the hearers spellbound; the reciter's wonderful memory supplying the actual conversations between the artist and his model. . . . It began in the afternoon, it went through dinner to bedtime, it was finished the next morning.[65]

The witness recounts Hunt's obsession, flowing through time, seemingly stopping time. Hunt's story about the unnamed Annie Miller is like music—in time, but taking his auditors beyond time in its pleasure.

BOOKS

On the table at the left are three books, together with a man's top hat, which rests against two of them. Ruskin remarked on their presence: "Those embossed books, vain and useless—they also new [i.e., like the furniture]—marked with no happy wearing of beloved leaves"[66] (thus the antithesis of domesticity). One book's title is sufficiently clear to permit identification; it is Henry Noel Humphries's *Origin and Progress of the Art of Writing* (1853), a text that traces "the forms of hands from hieroglyphics to modern scripts."[67] How might one account for Hunt's choice of this book, Ruskin's tacit "explanation" aside? We know of the artist's infatuation with Annie Miller and of his concern to make her sufficiently respectable to be his wife. To this end and at his own expense he placed her in the care of a governess charged with softening her rough edges. At one level, I think *The Art of Writing* references Hunt's personal obsession with both his own and Annie Miller's identity as would-be bourgeois. Hunt, however, need not have included any books in the picture; having decided to include some, he need not have rendered any of their titles identifiable. What was it about *this* book that moved him to draw it to our attention, especially given the obscurity of its subject, which includes the study of both hieroglyphics and paleography?

Humphries's book is fundamentally "about" the *visuality* of textuality: script. Hunt draws attention to writing but also to its connection both to privilege and to men. I take this to be the import of the man's top hat set against the books. The world is *written* in script, and writing, in the sense I am after, is and always has been an act of men. I am reminded of the medieval, chiefly monastic, scriptorium, wherein sanctioned discourse was given permanence and authoritative status as (true) knowledge. In this context writing is "about" power. In Hunt's world it is also about money, about which he was self-conscious, for his own resources at the time were limited, and money was the sine qua non of his own desire for bourgeois status and respectability. Humphries himself on the first page of his book unambiguously connects writing to money and the merchant class.

> Indeed, carelessly viewed, [the study of the art of writing] would merely seem to consist in the minute examination of the inscribed entries in the ledger of some London merchant, and accurately noting their superiority in flowing freedom and general neatness over those in the account-books of his ancestor, written a century ago.[68]

Annie Miller is the text Hunt himself at the time was attempting to "write," or get rewritten. In a bitter comment about his failure, he wrote: "If she cannot be preached to from the texts of her own bitter experience, then she cannot be awakened at all."[69] Thus he invoked his own painting (by the word *awakened*), conflating its model and subject with Annie Miller; he likewise invoked the authority of the scriptorium ("preached") and Annie Miller herself *as* writing ("the texts of her own bitter experience," a striking image). Hunt's comments present a difficulty, for they lead to his own conflation with the seducer who plays the piano.

I want to pursue the conjunction between writing and money to incorporate women and, specifically, prostitution, via Giuseppe Verdi's opera *La Traviata*, which premiered in 1853, the date of Hunt's *Awakening Conscience*. It is also about the working girl, though not a working-class girl, as in Hunt's painting. Like Mimi nearly a half century later (*La Bohème*, 1896), Violetta spends the opera's final act interrupting her own speech to cough blood, her mouth now an oracular wound, and thereby to trigger in her lover that delicious agony of regret.

Shortly after the opening of the last act, Violetta takes from her bosom a letter from her lover's father. In a striking gesture, she reads—rather than sings—it aloud, in the opera's only moment of true melodrama. It is nothing like a love letter, or even like a letter from a friend; indeed, it reads like a newspaper account or, perhaps, a telegram. It is mostly just facts. It is a businessman's text, the writing of the "perfect" bourgeois:

> Teneste la promessa—la disfida
> Ebbe luogo! Il barone fu ferito,
> Però migliora. Alfredo
> È in stranio suolo; il vostro sacrifizio
> lo stesso gli ho svelato;
> Egli a voi tornerà pel suo perdono;

lo pur verrò. Curatevi—mertate
Un auvenir migliore.

(You kept your promise. The duel has taken place! The Baron was wounded, but is recovering. Alfredo has gone abroad; I myself revealed your sacrifice to him; he will return to ask your pardon; I too shall come. Take care of yourself. You deserve a happier future.[70])

Verdi gives these words special status *as* words; he makes Violetta break character as an *operatic* heroine to speak a man's words, acknowledging in the process that this text controls her very reason for being. The words' power momentarily drives music from her lips and, indeed, off the stage. The music that survives, however, in the orchestral accompaniment to her reading, preserves the trace of textuality, in that it reprises the initial love melody sung to Violetta by Alfredo in his act 1 aria ("Di quell'amor ch'è palpito"). Violetta's world is overdetermined by two unseen men: one whose writing she *sees* and reads aloud and another whose once-sung sonorities she *hears* in the orchestra. The sight and sound overwhelm her; she puts the letter down and asks God's forgiveness.

CODE AND CODA. TWO TUNES

It is time to reconnect sight to sound. To us as viewers "everything" within the image is within sight, none of it left to chance, given the painting's intense lighting and precise detail. Inside the picture, however, glances do not meet: we know of the woman's awakening (we have Hunt's title to confirm it); but her "keeper" knows nothing, because he cannot see what is visible to us. He is blind, without insight. He sees instead something else, a script, "Oft, in the Stilly Night." He plays it for her to sing; maybe he sings along, or maybe he sings it to her. She has insight; she sees beneath and beyond that text. But what is it that she sees beyond, for the lyrics are suitably innocent, perfectly respectful of bourgeois domestic ideals?

Music functioned variously in Victorian society; today we may be inclined to think of it principally as art, but the parlor song, like those incorporated in Hunt's painting, did not enjoy the status of art. Indeed, far from transcending the mundane world of capital, as required of true Art under the terms of contemporaneous aesthetics,

the bourgeois "popular song" was the first product which showed how music might be profitably incorporated into a system of capitalist enterprise. It is in the production, promotion, and marketing of the sheet music to these songs (and the pianos to accompany them) that we witness the birth of the modern music industry.[71]

Thus while the songs themselves are "innocent," they reference commerce, and not incidentally the commerce of the body. As I have been at pains to establish throughout this volume, music under the conditions of modernity was concatenated with woman (especially with her dangerous sexuality) and sometimes with the body of the prostitute, the woman for sale, on the market, like music—for prostitution was also a major industry in Victorian England in ways never previously actualized, involving the attention, concern, and profit of medical, psychiatric, judicial, and law enforcement institutions, paralleling the rapid and complex development of the music industry and its legal regulation.[72]

From the start popular music was a product, a sign, and a material-immaterial test case for an emerging consumer culture. In buying music, one bought "nothing," for thus had music in general been widely theorized in England by men for nearly two centuries.[73] The enterprise of profitably selling mere "sound" could hardly be a greater testimony to the heady implications of capitalism. Indeed, it seems to me that the bond being forged between music and money accounts in part for the implicit social antagonism in the ideological foundation of much nineteenth-century aesthetics—the protest of artists against an emergent condition they not only recognized but increasingly depended on for their economic well-being.

Nonetheless, one must acknowledge that the musical text itself may exceed its function to produce profit. To produce a song by itself does not respond to the demands of capitalism; the song must ultimately be consumed (sold) to produce profit. To be consumed, the music must in some sense "speak" to its auditor-performer. It seems safe to assume that the man in Hunt's painting bought the songs so as to engineer a sex act or, afterward, to serve as balm to the conscience and hence the pretext for the sex act next time. (The songs *must* drive the picture's primary narrative; otherwise there is no reason to incorporate a musical theme and to give it primary place in the composition. Hunt's own words on the matter establish as much, as I have already shown.) Accordingly, there is something in the tunes that she is supposed to hear, yet that sound must act against the texts, to the extent that they tell a story quite different from the one I am outlining; textually, the songs are far from sexual turn-ons. Is Hunt's patrician seducer thus a fool when it comes to buying music for his mistress? Is the tunes' textual propriety intended to serve both man and woman as a veneer of romantic love, a disguise for the truth of their relation?

Here is the song that brings him grief and her salvation:

> Oft, in the stilly night,
>   Ere Slumber's chain has bound me,
> Fond Memory brings the light
>   Of other days around me;

> The smiles, the tears,
>   Of boyhood's years,
> The words of love then spoken;
>   The eyes that shone,
>   Now dimm'd and gone,
>   The Cheerful hearts now broken!
> Thus, in the stilly night,
>   Ere Slumber's chain has bound me,
> Sad Memory brings the light
>   Of other days around me.
>
> When I remember all
>   The friends, so link'd together,
> I've seen around me fall,
>   Like leaves in wintry weather;
>   I feel like one,
>   Who treads alone
>   Some banquet-hall deserted,
>   Whose lights are fled,
>   Whose garlands dead,
>   And all but he departed!
> Thus, in the stilly night,
>   Ere Slumber's chain has bound me,
> Sad Memory brings the light
>   Of other days around me.[74]

And here is the song on the floor, still partly in its wrapper—the backup, so to speak:

>   Tears, idle tears, I know not what they mean,
> Tears from the depth of some divine despair
> Rise in the heart, and gather to the eyes,
> In looking on the happy autumn-fields,
> And thinking of the days that are no more.
>
>   Fresh as the first beam glittering on a sail,
> That brings our friends up from the underworld,
> Sad as the last which reddens over one
> That sinks with all we love below the verge;
> So sad, so fresh, the days that are no more.
>
>   Ah, sad and strange as in dark summer dawns
> The earliest pipe of half-awaken'd birds

To dying ears, when unto dying eyes
The casement slowly grows a glimmering square;
So sad, so strange, the days that are no more.

Dear as remember'd kisses after death,
And sweet as those by hopeless fancy feign'd
On lips that are for others; deep as love,
Deep as first love, and wild with all regret;
O Death in Life, the days that are no more![75]

Hunt chose his tunes carefully, and not only to help his composer friend Lear peddle the second song. There are connections between the two texts that I can evoke with a list of words encountered in other chapters of this volume: sleep, dreams, love, death, memory, silence, sorrow; and in the first, winter, in the second, autumn. The texts inscribe the reverie of loss, the pleasure of bankruptcy, the self-loathings over missed opportunities—even a self-loathing of self-loathing: *idle* tears, not productive ones.

In his autobiography a half century later, Hunt, an old man who even then could not forget Annie Miller, though pretending to, engaged in a bit of spin control:

> I spoke freely of this intended subject, but, while cogitating upon the broad intention, I reflected that the instinctive eluding of pursuit by the erring one [Annie Miller] would not coincide with the willing conversion and instantaneous resolve for a higher life which it was necessary to emphasize.[76]

Contaminated, she is incapable of self-redemption; yet the mouth and hands of her seducer, twin agents of an "empty mind," produce the music that supplies her salvation. Are we thus to understand that the man's own performance is little more than a pathetic self-remonstrance over his own dissolute life, a nostalgic ecstasy of self-directed abuse and sentimental sing-song idling? Both tunes narrate devolution, in the imputed story of the man who sings them, stupidly, with a grin on his soft, effeminate face and the so-soft hands (Hunt is careful to represent this detail), one still gloved. Nonetheless, the ballad he sings about bygone boyhood years reforms the erring woman—not its lyrics but the *sonorities;* were mere words sufficient to Hunt's purpose, he might have gone with a poetry reading—certainly the Tennyson verse, still in its wrapper on the floor, might have done nicely.

If it is the tune that awakens her conscience, what does Hunt think she hears? Tom Moore's *Irish Melodies* setting of "Oft, in the Stilly Night," piano arrangement by the church musician Sir John Stevenson, is (pseudo-) folklike, its C-Major melody, spanning no more than a major seventh, structured in uniform 4-bar phrases: $AA_1BB_1AA_1/AA_1BB_1AA_1$; its scale is entirely diatonic, without chromatic inflection; it is rhythmically square, except for an occasional syncopation; the harmonies are sweetly consonant but for the mildest occasional spice provided by a suspension—the chords employed never exceed tonic, subdominant, and dominant seventh; its dynamics range between piano and pianissimo—to be sung "With Melancholy Expression." In short, the tune is devoid of musical surprise. It is the music of parlor domesticity, more so in light of the text, to the extent that the words narrate boyhood memories and the innocence of first love, in conjunction with an implied maternal protection. The song's sonoric "purity"—ironic, given the occasion—evokes the angel in the house. That is, the male voice, recalling childhood, "reverts" to the rhetorically feminine so as to recall loss: the music is Oedipal; as such it must be cast off. The musical text, briefly taken up, is feminine and, in effect, castrating. It may save her—thus what Annie Miller is made to hear is Hunt's self-described sing-song vision of the wife—but in the same moment it condemns him. Little wonder that Hunt exaggerated the seducer's corporeal softness—and in his own words belittled the tune.

Had Hunt given the seducer "Tears, Idle Tears" to sing, a difficulty would have ensued, not on account of the text, which would do nicely, but because of the musical setting. While strophic, Lear's tune is considerably more complex, musically more interesting, sonorically and rhetorically more slippery and uncertain than "Oft, in the Stilly Night." With a melody far less repetitive than the other song, midway through it modulates from D Major to G Major and remains there. This shift is likewise reflected in the song's other musical parameters. Thus the accompaniment changes from struck to arpeggiated chords; and its tempo moves from larghetto to allegretto. In effect, the tune musically turns its back on the past, via the shift in key, accompaniment, and tempo, never to look back, even while textually invoking the past. Chromaticism, with its shifts and momentary uncertainties, plays a significant, if already clichéd, role throughout the song; moreover, the general harmonic vocabulary is richer, just as the ambitus is wider, spanning nearly two octaves. By comparison with the tune on the piano, this one seems almost dangerously passionate, for it plays off generic male self-pity more than male constructions of feminine self-control and nurture.

In Hunt's painting there are two open mouths, his and hers. He is singing, that much seems certain, but what of her? She no longer has a look of horror, and her lips are no longer quite so purple, but Hunt still invests in her mouth. Why is it open? What leads him to this repainting? She does not scream—no mouth from Munch here by a long shot—but perhaps, instead, merely half smiles, or shows something of open-mouthed shock. But it *could* as well be that her mouth opens to sing. To replicate the shape of her mouth, the upper lip must be pulled upward so as to expose the teeth as she does. This mouth shape is characteristic not of speech, not really of smiling, but of song. Once song is evoked, so also is the body. Hear Roland Barthes:

> The singing voice, that very specific space in which a tongue encounters a voice and permits those who know how to listen to it to hear what we can call its "grain"—the singing voice is not the breath but indeed that materiality of the body emerging from the throat, a site where the phonic metal hardens and takes shape.[77]

And Kaja Silverman:

> The voice is the site of perhaps the most radical of all subjective divisions—the division between meaning and materiality.[78]

At some level both the painting's actors engage speech. The quotation from Proverbs on the picture frame characterizes the man's; hers remains ambivalent. All speech, or would-be speech, in the painting asks the Woman Question, to a necessarily musical accompaniment. Hunt responds to the question in a chain of contradictions involving hatred and love, loathing (also self-loathing) and desire, and painful embodied pleasure. My interest in the sight of sound—in this (still our) age of visuality, when every human phenomenon is invested in by being looked at—hinges on the link between music's sounds and the human bodies that produce them, and in the perfect reciprocity by which each defines the other. Hunt's own attempt to locate the terms of this reciprocity failed in both art and life because Annie Miller refused; she chose her own song: Annie Miller took to "composing" her own self. It is hardly accidental or surprising that Hunt's chosen tunes are male products, literally and discursively. That Annie Miller's recital of men's songs was short-lived offers primary hope for what awakening is all about, though this is nothing like the wakefulness Hunt imagined, and it is quite different from the effect of men's speech on the fate of Verdi's Violetta. The social-musical future, measured from the real, not obliterated, Annie Miller, is very much up for grabs, though it has been hopefully suggested that the utopia she advanced in rejecting Hunt's tune is already in the making and recognizable as such. Notwithstanding the pleasure of contemplating such a prospect, I ask indulgence for a last word, to confront not the sight of sound, but the sight of silence.

Music, therefore, has an effect utterly different from sight; it can effect orgasm.

Roland Barthes,
S/Z: An Essay

The goal here is to capture the law of desire that makes music, that produces writing.

Julia Kristeva,
Desire in Language

9

ASPIRING TO THE
CONDITION OF SILENCE
(The Iconicity of Music)

Mendelssohn's "Lieder ohne Worte," composed between 1829 and 1845, are solo piano pieces "about" night, dreams, memory, regret, lost happiness, leaving, returning, spring, spinning, and death (besides a few that are called boat songs). Nearly all their "subjects" are associated with subjectivities used contemporaneously to characterize bourgeois women.[1] Like songs, these compositions are organized mostly as principal melody with accompaniment (as it were, two-part), thus evoking the "duet," a name given to one of the forty-eight pieces, no. 18, though in fact the duet partner, implicitly male, is invariably missing. The "Lieder ohne Worte" were marketed to women: "Probably no piano music was performed more often, or more painfully, in the drawing-rooms of Victorian England than these charming and slight, but by no means insignificant, miniatures."[2]

It does not matter that Mendelssohn himself supplied names or designators to very few of these pieces. In fact, for the point I am after, it makes better sense that he did not. Mendelssohn named only the "Duet," the "Folksong," and the three boat songs.[3] All the other titles came from elsewhere—presumably, almost necessarily, from music publishers, who themselves in effect "read" the pieces purposely, and smartly, in terms of their potential audience. Publishers, themselves bourgeois, understood women's social roles; accordingly, they knew, or at least thought they knew, women's subjectivities: the desires, anxieties, and investments underwriting their identities. The supplied titles preread for these performers the compositions' musical semantics. In keeping with the prevailing terms of gender construction, the naming insists on the priority of love, articulated implicitly as deferential, dependent, and unstable.

The titles in effect attempt to undercut Mendelssohn's own renunciation of words,[4] as if to render objective, and objectively visible, what he was determined to leave unspoken. It is arguable, of course, that Mendelssohn's lack of interest in supplying titles generally for these pieces was political in effect, if not necessarily by intention, insofar as the resulting semantic openness produced what Roland Barthes aptly termed the "writerly" text, which the reader in effect "re-writes" out of her own interests and experiences, unlike the closed, "readerly" text, which, comparatively, disempowers her: "the readerly is controlled by the principle of non-contradiction."[5]

In response to a question about meaning in the "Lieder ohne Worte" Mendelssohn remarked:

> People usually complain that music is so ambiguous; that they are doubtful as to what they should think when they hear it, whereas everyone understands words. For me, it is just the reverse. And that is so not only for whole speeches, but for single words also: they too seem to me so ambiguous, so indefinite, so open to misunderstanding in comparison with real music which fills one's soul with a thousand things better than words. To me, the music I love does not express thoughts too indefinite to be put into words, but too definite. If you ask me what I thought, I must say: the song itself as it stands.[6]

Most pertinent to my concerns in this remarkable and oft-cited comment is Mendelssohn's inscription of the following relation: language is to mind as music is to mind-body. Language is ambiguous precisely because it is radically abstract, and because it operates, as it were, divorced from the body. Music, which for most philosopher-aestheticians is peculiarly, totally abstract, is for Mendelssohn concrete ("definite") and *hence* unspeakable because its impact is sensual / emotional, embodied and physical—but *not* separate from cognition. Music is an excess that seemingly judges the abstraction of language, and its divorce from the body, lamentable at best. "Songs without Words": the appellation announces a text-subject but refuses to state it, not because the composer cannot do so but because that subject is of the mind-body—deeply personal, *felt,* and thus personally specific. Naming is redundant, for the subject is always already "known" (one scholar aptly refers to the "Songs without Words" as a "diary form which might well seem the most private of all forms of music"[7]).

Mendelssohn may be getting at something expressed well by Barthes in an interview about music and his own status as an amateur pianist: "Despite lagging tempi and false notes, I still manage to attain the materiality of the musical text [in his bad playing], because it passes into my fingers. The sensuality of music is not purely auditory, it is also muscular."[8] Barthes's metaphor alludes to union, envelopment, and pleasure; music is *jouissance*. Music's auditory impact is insufficient to produce these effects, which come about through self-performance, *listening-doing*, the activity of music *making* and not the passive act of "mere" listening. Thus music's performance is *in and of* the body, but a *whole* body, an *interpreting* body.[9] To make music is a cognitive-physical act, in which the separation of mind from body momentarily disappears. If Barthes is right, the radical political act of making music for oneself—in Victorian culture, this meant especially women—involves the temporary reinscription of human "totality" (mind *with* body *at* art) in the lived experience of "humanity's" second sex. This reinscription marks a refusal to abide by the terms of Cartesian dualism, the very foundation of the politics of gender, class, and racial difference—according to which certain men think and all women merely feel. Moreover, granting Mendelssohn's and Barthes's complementary insights, the scandal of female musical performance, the binding of the physical to the cognitive, produces pleasure, toward which Victorians were pointedly antagonistic precisely because it implicitly privileged the otherwise devalorized body and because it was immanently shameless—erotic.

Barthes understood the erotics of music as an embrace. As such music is more than meaning. It beats like the heart; it throbs, quivers, tenses, relaxes. Its pleasures occur again and again, a repeatable, not single, ecstasy. If this kind of music making is semantically and experientially akin to the orgasmic—profoundly physical but also exceeding the physical—at a time when music itself as a practice is culturally marked as female, then music's scandal is still more serious than I have suggested. The musical functions of the Victorian drawing room, as both the locus of domesticity and its metaphorical defining principle, may arguably have violated precisely what they were to inscribe and authorize: parlor music, principally a women's genre,[10] did not always remain enclosed in the semantic boundaries assigned to the bourgeois woman. Barthes's insight is that making music, unlike "mere" listening, necessarily brings the sensual body "back" into the equation. In Victorian culture the body—assuredly female—was profoundly feared. Thus Nina Auerbach: the "lovable woman [was] a silent and self-disinherited mutilate, the fullness of whose extraordinary and dangerous being might at any moment return through violence. The taboos that encased the Victorian woman contained buried tributes to her disruptive power."[11] Barthes recognized, and took pleasure in, the embodied and disruptive power of music, whose sensual potential he associated with orgasm—precisely the physical response in women officially abhorred in male Victorian society, as theorized in both medicine and psychiatry. Women's pleasure marked the awesome

FIG. 94 Frederic, Lord Leighton, *Lieder ohne Worte* (1861), oil on canvas, 101.6 × 62.9 cm. London, Tate Gallery.

possibility of a general reconfiguration of society based on the utopian rebridging of mind and body.

WOMEN WITHOUT WORDS

Frederic, Lord Leighton effectively addressed the conflicted relation between music and the economy of desire in two paintings, one of them aptly titled *Lieder ohne Worte* (Fig. 94). Leighton's subject invokes, not love anxieties and domesticity, but the female body, erotic desire, and sexuality. If Mendelssohn's refusal to name his pieces leaves the semantic door ajar, Leighton's painting closes it abruptly. His *Lieder ohne Worte*—that is, woman herself—is made wordless; the speech act of the painting's title renders her speechless, and without the need of speech. The title, together with her visual representation, makes her "legible." Leighton transforms her into Song, hence into the category "music."

But this explanation is insufficient. The title encodes a music of sonoric particularity and specific social function. The German title *Lieder ohne Worte* (for an English painting) and its explicit reference to Mendelssohn's then-popular piano pieces characterize her, oddly, as domestic and familiar but also as Other, the Teutonic "not us"; as Art writ large; and as Feminine (uppercase, as though implying that she exceeds the very category she defines). Her femininity is not in question, but I mean more than a biological sexual coding. Leighton's Ur-referent, Mendelssohn's piano compositions, leads us not merely to the general world of art music but also to the specific world of small-piece amateur domestic music aimed at bourgeois home consumption. The sonoric locus of this image, in other words, is the space allotted to the hausfrau. The association, however, produces contradiction.

The problem occurs in the dramatic gap between the painting's title and the domesticity it encapsulates, on the one hand, and what we actually see, on the other. Leighton's model hardly has much in common with Mrs. Pettie at her piano (Fig. 74). If Mrs. Pettie was playing Mendelssohn,[12] as many of her counterparts did, and if Leighton's understanding of the musical code thus realized by Mrs. Pettie is the *Lied ohne Worte* of his painted imagings, then we have some major trouble on our hands. The culprit, as always, is female deviousness—in metaphoric terms, woman's instability as sign: angel in the house or whore of Babylon. The culprit is also music.

The painting's title recalls the social function of the wife at the piano: to produce domestic respectability. Going no further than the title, the musical referent transliterates frightful female sexuality into aesthetics and social harmony.

However, the reassuring authority of the title *Lieder ohne Worte fails* in the sight of the woman's body.[13] The physical datum of her figure is alarming. It is not contained, perhaps cannot be contained, by the sonorities of art music heard as the simulacrum of domesticity. But if this is so, music itself, this sort of music, is equally suspect for the dangers it enshrines. The rage over the "Kruetzer" Sonata returns, sans the paranoia of Tolstoy but with his in-spite-of-himself insight intact: the feminine and social "truth" of music is sufficient to make a man (want to) kill.

The gap, or excess, between title and painterly realization does not slip by Leighton's consciousness, as though he were somehow incapable of theorizing or recognizing what he was doing. I suggest instead an intentionality both in his recognizing this gap and choosing to represent it. I would suggest further that Leighton explicitly valorizes the gap and that in so doing he acts in full accord and solidarity with the homosocial world he inhabits.[14] The dominant ideology defining the cults of woman and family depended on the simultaneous desexualization of women (Madonna) and hyper-sexualization of woman (whore). For these ideologies to have paradigmatic social utility in Victorian culture, maintenance of the polar opposition between women and woman was necessary. Furthermore, the category "woman"—*not* the category "man"—served, perversely and ironically, as the center of social organization. The preferred definitions and realizations of social reality, as controlled by men, depended on deflecting an examination of one category, "man," onto the other, "woman." On woman were heaped the antagonisms and contradictions of masculinity. It was woman whose goodness (wife/mother, private world) harbored its radical opposite (whore, public world). It was man's duty to order—to contain but preserve and render useful—the dialectic of woman within real women, so as to articulate men's own identities and responsibilities within putative ethical boundaries.

Leighton understood this dialectic, not least because as an artist he functioned within a dialectic complementary to that of women, one defined by his own marginality to the male public sphere—doubly so on account of his own emotional-sexual investments. Leighton never married; he spent much time in the company of men, young male models prominent among them. He took repeated solitary, extended trips to Greece and North Africa, as well as to the Continent. But he also had strong attachments, demonstrably nonphysical, to some women, notably his favorite model, Dorothy Dene. And he had an interest in girls; he compared notes on his young female models with Lewis Carroll.[15] Because he was an artist, Leighton's sexuality was automatically suspect;[16] suspicion was only increased by his not having married, given the increasingly rampant homophobia in late-Victorian culture. He could not have been ignorant about the risks of his own sexual ambivalence, even if he never acted physically on any of his desires. Yet whether Leighton was homosexual or bisexual, for him as for any man in Victorian culture, the problem remained Woman. His lack of desire for women defined him as social pariah. Woman remained the problem, the common denominator against which men anxiously, sometimes angrily, measured themselves.

Leighton's contradictory position—a man but an artist, a man whose sexuality exceeded socially sanctioned parameters—shares something of the stigmatized position of women. It cannot be surprising that he was an acute observer of sexuality and difference; no one can look long at his pictures and remain insensitive to that. Arguably, he was both an observer and a participant in the gender politics of "femininity," someone simultaneously on the margins and in the thick of things, and self-reflexively *interested:* he located himself close to the contradiction of women/Woman. His painting *Lieder ohne Worte* exposes the radical gap between the two "categories," that is, between wife and whore, between loved and hated, and between wanted and feared. But at the same time that it implicitly critiques the gap by naming it, it valorizes the gap by taking pleasure in its complex "look." Although Leighton's status as an artist and as a bi- or homosexual provided him with a socially constructed sense of marginality, he remained a man, hence also constructed so as at least to recognize the investment demanded by hegemonic "masculinity." More important, his doubly articulated ambiguous locus allowed him to recognize that, however unstable and contradictory female gender construction may have been, its very instability was the source of its dynamics, which defined and ran the social economy. The instability produced the charge, the electric spark, the arc between the two poles. If this is so, the gap must be maintained at all costs; the contradictions were the foundation of the social and economic order.

I have suggested in this study that the suspicious relation between the categories "woman" and "music" are fundamental to the social construction of both women and music, but also to the category "man." By far the most consistent suspicion, in fact fear, about music in the West, going back to Plato (*The Republic*) and continuing to this moment in the anxieties of Allan Bloom (*The Closing of the American Mind*), revolves around music's connection to the body, notably its sexual parts, and the closely related paranoia that the sexuality awakened by music and becoming addictive (Bloom's word) will weaken men, make them womanish.

Thus Plato:

> Then when any man lets music flute his soul away, and pour flooding into his mind through his ears, as though through a funnel, those sweet and soft and mournful melodies which we have described, till he spends his whole life piping and cloying

himself with sound, that man at first tempers the spirited element in him, as steel is tempered, and makes it useful instead of useless and hard; but if he continues without ceasing to beguile that element, after a time he begins to dissolve and melt it away, till he pour out his spirit in a stream, cuts as it were the sinews of his soul, and makes it "a feeble warrior."[17]

The text that speaks of an excess of soft music as self-seduction, onanism, and finally self-castration also provides an uncanny metaphoric description of the female body in Leighton's *Lieder ohne Worte*. In this context, the feminization of men by music deprives them of the very determinant of their sex: the power of speech, the ability to name, the *logos*.

And Bloom:

> But rock music has one appeal only, a barbaric appeal, to sexual desire—not love, not *eros*, but sexual desire undeveloped and untutored. . . . Rock gives children, on a silver platter, with all the public authority of the entertainment industry, everything their parents always used to tell them they had to wait for until they grew up and would understand later.
>
> Young people know that rock has the beat of sexual intercourse.[18]

Bloom's problem is that he "hears" sexuality nowadays only in rock and roll or, to be more accurate, in Mick Jagger and not in the classical repertory he allows himself as a connoisseur. (He does acknowledge noticing it, like his imagined teenagers, in *Bolero;* I take that to mean he has seen the movie *10* and really believes the vapid movie heroine's claim that Ravel's score works wonders in the bedroom.) Beyond Jagger, Bloom adds the names of Michael Jackson, Prince, and Boy George, all three "gutter" phenomena of "our weak exhausted Western civilization"[19]—that is, the contagion of the feminine in its most scandalous form, as he would have it, in lightly veiled homophobic panic. (Without the slightest hesitation or apparent irony, Bloom in the next breath valorizes Lessing's aesthetic pantings on Greek male statuary, the bit about beautiful men making beautiful statues, where we are supposed to believe that the marked attraction involves more the soul and less an eye for pectorals.)

Thus music is feminine, and like the sexuality of women (except Victorian wives), its sexuality is limitless. As such it functions on men as a sewer for their vital fluids. Music/music and Woman/women, both binaries in their entirety, in other words, *are* sex, and sex is death. In *The Republic* as in *The Closing of the American Mind* the addressee in the lengthy section on music requires only the masculine pronoun. Bloom's fictive case study is a "thirteen-year-old boy," a "pubescent child whose body throbs with orgasmic rhythms . . . whose ambition is to win fame and wealth in imitating the drag-queen [on MTV] who makes the music."[20] It is no accident that Bloom models his diatribe on Plato and cites him with near scriptural authority on the general subject of his book.

SLEEP AND SILENCE

The woman in Leighton's *Lieder ohne Worte* is languid, anorectic, heavy lidded, an adult's lower torso with an adolescent's head. And she is silent. It is as though she cannot utter a sound, the energy to do so having evaporated.[21] She approaches sleep, loss of consciousness, escape from reality (Art), entry to reverie: "Sleep is the closest parallel to death in living beings, and in literature of all ages sleep has been employed as a synonym for death."[22] In this imagery, while women nod off, men watch them, not merely taking pleasure in their silent vulnerability, but also keeping watch lest they wake;[23] men in Victorian paintings seldom sleep. She *is* music, and, to be sure, she is sexual. Her sexuality, and accordingly the music she signifies, is an exotic spectacle. Her music is to be looked at, a sight without sound. She is a goddess and a harem girl, a pre-Raphaelite angel, and indeed as much a boy as a girl, in an architectural setting whose weirdness removes her from history, from the here and now. She is the promise of an omnisexuality that refuses nothing, that answers demand, a signifier awaiting *signifiance*. In essence, her sexuality is defined as a lack, especially against contemporaneous imagery like that considered in earlier chapters. That is, we have moved a great distance from *The Reluctant Pianist* (Fig. 86) or even *The Awakening Conscience* (Fig. 91), where active sexuality is either explicit or implied. Here sexuality exists only in the elegiac memory of the viewer, who sees conventional passivity exaggerated to a degree of torpor on the border between the fantasies of sleep and necrophilia.

Lord Leighton's *Lieder ohne Worte* marks the *visual* point from which we might measure the crisis in music that Mahler and Schoenberg confronted, one that continues to confront music in its divides across cultural lines, gender lines, and the lines separating high art from popular and mass culture—a crisis not only of music's meaning but also of its social functions.[24] Walter Pater's famous claim that "all art constantly aspires to the condition of music" addressed the need for the distinction between matter and form to collapse;[25] with this collapse the autonomous practice of painting would define the art act and the art work. Autonomy for Pater displaced meaning, and the displacement of meaning rendered painting true art, and as such *like music*. What Pater valorized in this gesture is semantic silence in the face of sonoric plenty, sound without signification, in essence the loss of history.[26] Nothing. Music might thus achieve the status Schopenhauer assigned it, that of the "universal language,"[27] but the difficulty therein is that it is a language of void. If, as the romantics intended, music provided the paradigm of escape from the reification of art's relation to capital, that escape came by means of annihilation. Thus Pater:

> In its primary aspect, a great picture has no more definite message for us than an accidental play of sunlight and shadow for a few moments on the wall or floor: is itself, in truth, a space of such fallen light, caught as the colours are in an Eastern carpet, but refined upon, and dealt with more subtly and exquisitely than by nature itself.[28]

The relation of this remark to the musical aesthetics of Eduard Hanslick are sufficiently obvious to demand no elaboration, though not everyone in the nineteenth century agreed with either Pater's or Hanslick's position. To Pater's insight into Victorian social theory, masquerading as aesthetics, I would add a corollary: music itself aspires to the condition of silence. In the West the tacit hatred of music, in the presence, ironically, of music's sonoric ubiquity—always most noticeably unauthorized musics—is the sonoric analogue and (sometimes) agent of the hatred of women. The goal of these hatreds is *metaphorically* to silence both: if literal silencing were ever achieved, after all, its necessary result would be Armageddon. Going quietly into that night is not, however, on everyone's agenda, as is clear from the actions of both women and men, of people who by race or class are excluded from or marginalized by the operative paradigms of this dialectic of enlightenment. Equally important, the musics of such "excluded" people serve as agents against the silence being imposed on them. Music's force against the silencing of its own "speech," even *ohne Worte,* is critical to our survival.[29]

Near the end of his long essay on Giorgione, which early on features a discussion of the painter's famous *Concert* picture in the Pitti Palace, Pater returns to this picture. He judges it an example of art achieving the stated goal of the condition of music. But his perfect exemplar directly signifies, narrativizes, and *represents* the condition that is putatively *un*representable—which to *be,* supposedly just *is.* In other words, art that achieves the condition of music—the success story is Giorgione's painting of a musical subject—attains immateriality by means of its own verifiability as visual *data.* We can *see* what we cannot hear; and seeing is believing. Science takes over from art, as clinical proof. If that one painting were not proof enough, Pater, aesthetician-empiricist in spite of himself, catalogues Giorgione's other musical images: "men fainting at music; music at the pool-side while people fish, or mingled with the sound of the pitcher in the well, or heard across running water, or among the flocks; the tuning of instruments; people with intent faces, as if listening, [etc.]."[30]

Despite these concretizations, which would appear to belie the very thing Pater seeks to advance, he recognizes that something escapes, "lie[s] beyond, and must supplement, the narrower range of the strictly ascertained facts."[31] He sees something more in the data of the pictures he describes, which he names happiness and play, and he acknowledges the general loss of both. This "something" he names the *vraie vérité* of Giorgione. What Pater ultimately sees—hears—in Giorgione is loss:

> In these then, the favourite incidents of Giorgione's school, music or the musical intervals in our existence, *life itself is conceived as a sort of listening*—listening to music, to the reading of Bandello's novels, to the sound of water, to time as it flies. Often such moments are really our moments of play, and we are surprised at the unexpected blessedness of what may seem our least important part of time; not merely because play is in many instances that to which people really apply their own best powers, but also because at such times, the stress of our servile, everyday attentiveness being relaxed, the happier powers in things without are permitted free passage, and have their way with us [emphasis added].[32]

This passage recalls Schopenhauer on the question of musical affect:

> The inexpressible inner essence of all music, by virtue of which it flows past us so utterly comprehensible and yet so inexplicable, like a familiar but eternally distant paradise, is rooted in the fact that it reproduces all the movements of our innermost being but quite divorced from phenomenal life *and remote from its misery* [emphasis added].[33]

Pater and Schopenhauer thus acknowledge that the "condition" of music is less an aspiration of art than a desire for an embodied happiness that does not exist in material life but resides in the imagination. In the ahistorical aesthetics of autonomy, in other words, the social breaks in by the back door, its presence denied yet named.

MUSIC AND THE CRISIS OF THE PHALLUS

The problematics under discussion reach their conflicted apogee in Lord Leighton's painting *Music* (c. 1865; Fig. 95), a large canvas whose standing figure is life-size. The painting's dimensions establish its importance as a statement; that it is an image insistent on being seen is evident also in the oddly surreal conjoining of quasi-classical, grisaille-like architectural-sculptural base; static medieval gold ground (the light background in the black-and-white illustration reproduced here); stylized funereal Italian cypresses in pots; and the extraordinary quasi-male

FIG. 95   Frederic, Lord Leighton, *Music* (c. 1865), oil on canvas, 267 × 154 cm. Private collection. Photo courtesy of Sotheby's, London.

figure of Music in the center, the figure itself bracketed by the almost grotesquely excessive red drapery hanging around his body, enveloping him in the conventional color of passion, blood, bleeding: Woman.

To understate the issue, this is an image deeply troubled by history. That is, it both claims and denies history, in a sense all of Western history, even the present, which finds no visual referent except indirectly, in a representation of conflicted Victorian desire. It is a world turned upside down, where the fragmentation (honestly pre-postmodern) incorporated into its every aspect is openly acknowledged by the overturned Ionic capital reduced to visual bricolage. The past is askew, damaged, misshapen like the cypress trees, and spatially flat. The confident fedundity of deep space that characterizes Western painting from the Renaissance to the late nineteenth century is gone. This is a world of scarcity.

The fertility of the human holds little promise, either. The solidity of the hegemonic male world is held open to question. The man is at once absurdly phallic and fundamentally feminized. Precisely where the rule of the phallus should be visible—at his crotch—it is erased, replaced by a mandolin whose neck has been altered, increased ridiculously, and pathetically, in length, as a substitute for the lack within his tights, which is carefully denoted, anything but an "oversight." This striking visual gesture cannot overcome the consistent feminization of his body, his pose, his gesture, and his expression. Indeed, the mandolin's function is not to compensate for lack but to confirm it.

What then does Lord Leighton's *Music* have to do with music history—that is, with musical practices, always meaningful, in Victorian bourgeois culture? The painting, I think, lays out in explicitly visual terms music's relation to society via its connection to human sexuality and the construction of woman. It posits music, by analogy, as an erotic entity or, if you like, as a "higher" substitute for or expression of sexuality. It is simultaneously desired and untouchable: desired visually in the provocative ambiguity of male-female, untouchable in the ahistorical, or omnihistorical, setting that effectively places it outside time and in all time. It is the passion of the enveloping blood red drapery that seemingly warms a torso of bloodless marble. It is the body of dark mystery, accessing the clichéd sensuality of the sunny south, painted in and for the clammy north. It is what we want but cannot have: the phallus conducts no fluid just as the stringless instrument, phallus substitute, produces no sound. The musician/Music focuses our look on his lack. His outstretched arm can stop no strings. The gesture is empty, masturbatory. His castration, music's silence, is doubly articulated by Leighton's hiding from view the arm and hand that would pluck the strings, had they not been broken or removed. Thus nothing will happen. Music becomes that which we can no longer hear. Music's silence becomes music's pleasure; and silence, like the cold hearth, equals Death—in its perverse form of *Liebestod*.[34]

All art constantly aspires to the condition of music (how ironically perfect the name, Pater/Father, to attach to this utterance). A lot of Victorian artists took Pater's account directly to heart, as their pictures' titles inform us. Invariably the art that aspires to music, by representing music, is feminine (Leighton's male Music is exceptional).[35] If music's geographical locus is represented as terrestrial, we might see/hear *The Prelude* (Fig. 96). In the background sits an older woman, loosely gowned, fully covered, spinning—the wifely sign. But the focus is on her opposite, the woman in the foreground. The *prelude* is musical and embodied as sexual. She is visual *foreplay*—shoulder bare, her orientalist shift tightly wound around her hips, emphasizing their shape—as she engages in self-serenade. By

FIG. 96   William Wardlaw Laing, *The Prelude* (1892), oil on canvas. Private collection. Photo courtesy of Sotheby's, London.

FIG. 97   John Melhuish Strudwick, *A Symphony,* oil. Private collection. Photo courtesy of Sotheby's, London.

contrast, if the locus is nonterrestrial, we might see/hear *A Symphony* (Fig. 97), a celestial Harmony, borrowed heavily and somewhat clumsily from more talented pre-Raphaelites. These "women"—one can hardly do without quotation marks in identifying them—are slightly Byzantine and thoroughly iconic, like marble, though they are nonetheless notably sexual. Their music is from the ensemble of St. Cecilia. But again, what matters is what is constant: music = Woman. That constancy is *labeled,* named in language, texted: to be read as absolute confirmation. And never in the history of painting did so many artists supply their own titles to the images they produced.[36] The visual *Lied* was seldom *ohne Worte.*

The music defined in these pictures is one removed from society: it has no place in the world. It is perfectly mental, ethereal, disembodied, ahistorical, or of another place—or all of these at once. Yet the music depends for it effects on physical desire, usually perverse and illicit. It is the mind-body split activated to the level of art. Were we to look solely on the androgynous face of Leighton's personified Music, we might incorporate sentimentality into the equation, but in truth it does not fit. The image is unwilling to give us that. In an age when music increasingly was theorized, as art, as the aesthetic and transcendent, Leighton correctly understood what was lost and gained,[37] namely, embodiment in the human figure itself and all that implies about social and cultural alienation: ultimately, forgetting is preferable to alienation.[38] The archetypal musicians in nineteenth-century mythology were the virtuosi—Paganini, Liszt; virtual factories of sound, they were embodiments of the superman and the supersexed (Ken Russell got that much "right" in his outrageous filmic "account" of Liszt, *Lisztomania* [1975], with Roger Daltrey of The Who, fittingly enough, in the title role). Such performers realized a socially impossible unity of the public with the private, of power with desire, but only as men who were bracketed from quotidian life by their status as entertainers and artistic freaks.

DIFFERENCE: SONORIC PLENITUDE

The musical culture of Victorian society I have outlined was profoundly different from what had preceded it, despite the historical trajectory that began in the first recorded moments of Western history. For a moment I would like to move back to the eighteenth century (Figs. 98–99), to two paintings of professional musicians, both undoubtedly resident in Munich at the court of Karl-Albert (r. 1727–45) and his successor Elector Maximilian III-Joseph, his son (r. 1745–77), where the painter, Pieter Jacob Horemans, served. There is a sharp stylistic divergence between Leighton's *Music* and these pictures; one would expect that. The difference, however, entails more than the usual tale of "evolving" painterly practice.

FIG. 98   Pieter Jacob Horemans, *Portrait of a Court Musician* (1762), oil on canvas, 65 × 80 cm. Munich, Bayerische Staatsgemäldesammlungen.

FIG. 99   Pieter Jacob Horemans, *Portrait of the Violinist Johann Georg Holzbogen* (1774), oil on canvas, 90.1 × 76.5 cm. Munich, Bayerische Staatsgemäldesammlungen.

What interests me specifically involves the handling of the instruments, which are treated as objects of worth, as a collection, like Brueghel's still-earlier musical inventories (Figs. 18–19). The drawing is very precise, but the jumble of instruments suggests more than "mere" inventory—more than instruments recorded as verifiable data. The jumble triggers the memory of music's *sociability,* rather than of musical sonority, precisely on account of the privileged position given the musician. (The social privilege organizing Horeman's two pictures is undeniable but not especially interesting or pertinent to this discussion.) These pictures recall the "musical conversations" of the Englishman Marcellus Laroon the Younger (Fig. 100) with which I began this study, where the represented comings and goings of people in a social context take their meaning from music involving players of both sexes. Neither Laroon nor Horemans titled his picture "Prelude," "Symphony," or even "Music," and for good reason. The naming of paintings by the Victorian artists, far from incorporating music into social function, brackets it therefrom, as if to *say,* this is this, not that, to tighten the discursive noose around music's personified neck. The social-musical culture pictured by Horemans,[39] and earlier by Laroon, is not absolutely different. Music's meanings, like its functions, were there to be "read" in and by the culture, for to be read was to mean, to be able to mean, and music is invariably meaningful. But music's *signifiance,* to borrow Barthes's most useful coinage, enjoys greater semantic liberty in Horemans and Laroon precisely because the meanings ascribed to music were more closely allied to music's noisy social function, with little energy expended, by comparison with the situation at the close of the nineteenth century, on articulating music's semantic silence—ironically amid a growing ubiquity of sonority.[40] In Laroon's painting, which is similar to many others by this artist, music is singled out for our attention, especially in the instrument cases on the floor in the foreground. The silence they encode is overwhelmed by the radical, almost scandalous, amount of sonority being produced: the silence they recommend is, in practice, excessively overcome. Thus to get in on the musical act at the left, a man at the extreme right stands on a chair to reach a lute hanging on the wall: people clamor for music. Music's meanings include the possibility of sociality itself, in which the role of music is not yet problematic; that this is Laroon's own wishful thinking is beside the point, but I have treated that matter elsewhere.[41]

In Victorian times, given the extreme historical, economic, and social changes engendered by the successes of capitalism, the bourgeoisie, and the Industrial

FIG. 100   Marcellus Laroon the Younger, *A Musical Conversation* (c. 1760), oil on canvas, 68.2 × 88.9 cm. Boughton House, Kettering, Northamptonshire, Collection Duke of Buccleuch and Queensberry KT. Photo: Paul Mellon Centre for Studies in British Art Limited, London.

Revolution, the rewriting of history is wrenchingly self-conscious and disingenuous. But for all its fictive and conflicted character, it establishes an explanation of reality that retains currency in our culture, especially in contemporaneous musical life in the extreme split between a highly eroticized, embodied popular culture and a profoundly cerebral elite culture: between, if you like, Madonna or Prince on the one hand and—name your composer among usual suspects—on the other. The Victorian realization of the Cartesian divide is today nowhere more disturbingly evident than in Western musical life, though its consequences continue to be inadequately theorized.

The visual analogies I have traced here are significant, not because sight is linked to hearing, but because sonority is visually defined through social practices that are invariably embodied. Music is a metaphor of self and being in history. And the issue is not simply that what we see is not a very pretty picture but that, for the most part, in viewing Victorian images we are still looking at ourselves. Victorian musical imagery, in its conflicted manifestations, offers one means of understanding how we got this way and thus perhaps one way by which we might begin to figure out how to escape. The concatenous fury enacted against women *and* music is the product of an awareness that both women and music exceed meaning, to the extent that meaning is "given" to both under conditions of patriarchy. The stakes over meaning could hardly be higher. Thus Julia Kristeva:

> Music itself is a derivative. It is simply the sonorous indicator of a break, of a deaf, mute, mortal, and regenerative rhythm. It takes place where the body is gashed by the blows of biology and the shock of sexual, social, and historical contradiction, breaking through to the quick, piercing through the shield of the vocal and symbolic cover.[42]

CONCLUSION

En écoutant du Schumann (Fig. 101): listening but not seeing. The old woman (the mother of the artist, Fernand Khnopff, was the model), her body framed by the fireplace, looks away from the pianist and, as though that were not sufficient to establish the rupture, shades her face from our gaze.[43] The musician's body exists as an intrusion, a penetration into the picture's space, but also as an apology—it is an unfortunate necessity if Schumann is to be listened to. Schumann is thus disembodied, or almost so, and music itself is desocialized—sociability fails when backs are turned. *En écoutant du Schumann* is a turning away from the musical body, as though it were the very enemy of the music it produces. Music is bracketed off as sound. Yet its sonorities are notably valorized and given primacy.

FIG. 101 Fernand Khnopff, *Listening to Schumann* (1883), oil on canvas. Brussels, Musées Royaux des Beaux-Arts de Belgique. Photo copyright A.C.L., Brussels.

The scene is bourgeois and domestic, the site private and privileged. Yet pleasure seems absent, in essence denied. This I think is the key. This is a scene of bodies—or of a body and a body part. The bodies refute each other, turn away, look away, refuse each other, exist in separate spheres, in proximity but isolated. Moreover, the bodies refuse and refute us as well and do so, ironically, by means that the image nonetheless evokes. That is, the painting informs us that its subject is sonority, and it tells us what we should hear while looking—Schumann. But the effects of the music, which we can only look *at,* and not hear, are doubly denied us. If *En écoutant du Schumann* is, as it must be, about looking at music, the image defines the category of looking only to subvert it. The specific connection between seeing music and hearing music, established through the embodied practice of making music with the body, is undercut as well. The performer is made sufficiently present only to remind us of his absence, the irrelevancy of his identity; the listener in the painting herself refuses to acknowledge music's embodiment, preferring a meditative fantasy of music's transcendent, utopian promise. An arm makes music, a mechanics ensues. Another body listens, meditates, but turns away. The musical "conversation" is anticonversational.

What Schumann is evoked? We cannot say, though we might gain insight from Roland Barthes, who loved the music of Schumann and wrote extensively about the body, notably the musical body.

> There are two musics (or so I've always thought): one you listen to, one you play. They are two entirely different arts, each with its own history, sociology, aesthetics, erotics: the same composer can be minor when listened to, enormous when played (even poorly)—take Schumann.[44]

The music one plays, Barthes says, "depends not so much on an auditive as on a manual (hence much more sensuous) "activity"; for him this is a "muscular music" in which "the auditive sense has only a degree of sanction: as if the body was listening, not the 'soul.'" In this instance the body "proposes, leads, coordinates."[45] This insight marks the loss in *En écoutant du Schumann;* Schumann in effect is made minor precisely through the rupture of the listener from *doing,* for the body of the listener is immobilized and functionally reduced to the singular organ of the ears. The vitality of music as an enlivener of the body is surrendered to an act of meditation. What is surrendered in the process is the erotics of doing, for Barthes the sensual, sensate, tactile *effort* to *do.* In this instance, he who does, the man playing Schumann, consists visually of only an arm; he has no ears for us to see him hearing.

Barthes could not leave Schumann alone. He loved Schumann, and he knew why:

> It is because Schumann's music goes much farther than the ear; it goes into the body, into the muscles by the beats of the rhythm, and somehow into the viscera by the voluptuous pleasure of its *melos:* as if on each occasion the piece was written only for one person, the one who plays it; the true Schumannian pianist—*c'est moi.*[46]

Barthes's point is about the body, the erotic, the sensual; the music of Schumann is for him *relational:*

Loving Schumann . . . inevitably leads the subject who does so and says so to posit himself in his time according to the injunctions of his desire and not according to those of his sociality. But that is another story, whose narrative would exceed the limits of music.[47]

For Barthes, to love Schumann is to adopt—to risk—a philosophy of "the Night," a phrase I take to mean not only a philosophy of darkness (Barthes cites Nietzsche and the untimely, perhaps the out-of-time), which we may equate with the escape of reverie, but also, because he embeds his metaphor in the erotic body, the philosophy of lovemaking—a consolation fantasy to be sure, but a specifically embodied one (for the performer). It is a sonoric connection, a transliteration of physical desire. What it is *not* for Barthes is meditation. The averted eyes of the painting's listener register the horror of the body, and a plea for something that cannot—ought not—be: Schumann without loving, Schumann *qua* thought. Perhaps there is a better way to express this. What Barthes recognizes in loving (to play) Schumann is, in the making of the music, a sonoric palimpsest of the body whose traces cannot be "seen" by the averted gaze. In other words, what Barthes hears and sees in music is a sensate and historical materiality, which aesthetics has worked hard to erase. The issue is not that all art aspires to the condition of music, but that the totality music sometimes encodes is an otherwise unrealized aspiration—not in art but in life.

NOTES

1. Lester Bangs, "James Taylor Marked for Death," in *Psychotic Reactions and Carburetor Dung,* ed. Greil Marcus (New York: Knopf, 1987), p. 61.

2. See further Alan Durant, *Conditions of Music* (Albany: State University of New York Press, 1984), pp. 9, 86–88.

3. But see Chapter 1, n. 2, below.

4. There were of course occasions when people who were consciously or "automatically" excluded from seeing musical performances might nonetheless be within range of hearing them (for example, chambermaids in great houses). A different issue arises from musical activity as represented in the visual arts, where a sight of music exists in perpetuity but divorced from music's sound, except as the sight of music evokes the memory of particular actual music (and I am doubtful that this is what typically happens). In my judgment the sight of music in an image serves most directly to signify a musical practice rather than sonority per se, though the two are mutually mediating and mutually defining. I am grateful to my colleague Bruce Lincoln for his suggestions on this issue.

5. See Norman Bryson, *Vision and Painting: The Logic of the Gaze* (New Haven: Yale University Press, 1983); and Richard Leppert, *Music and Image: Domesticity, Ideology, and Socio-Cultural Formation in Eighteenth-Century England* (Cambridge: Cambridge University Press, 1989), pp. 3–8.

6. Donald M. Lowe, *The History of Bourgeois Perception* (Chicago: University of Chicago Press, 1982), especially pp. 2–83. Lowe's account is particularly indebted to Michel Foucault, notably *The Order of Things: An Archaeology of the Human Sciences* (New York: Vintage Books, 1970).

7. In this regard musical memory, and music as an aid to memory, play a special part, as in the "recitation" of epics.

8. Robert Raines, *Marcellus Laroon* (London: Routledge and Kegan Paul, 1966), p. 2.

9. See ibid., pp. 86–87.

10. See, for example, Klaus Theweleit, *Male Fantasies,* vol. 1, *Women, Floods, Bodies, History,* trans. Stephen Conway in collaboration with Erica Carter and Chris Turner (Minneapolis: University of Minnesota Press, 1987); William Manchester, *Goodbye, Darkness: A Memoir of the Pacific War* (New York: Laurel, 1979), pp. 87–91, for a particularly grotesque instance; and Max Horkheimer and Theodor W. Adorno, *Dialectic of Enlightenment,* trans. John Cumming (New York: Continuum, 1972), pp. 81–119.

11. See Michel Foucault, *The History of Sexuality,* vol. 1, *An Introduction,* trans. Robert Hurley (New York: Pantheon Books, 1978).

CHAPTER 1

1. P. J. J. van Thiel, "Marriage Symbolism in a Musical Party by Jan Miense Molenaar," *Simiolus* 2 (1967–68), pp. 90–99. I have previously commented on this painting in my "*Concert in a House:* Musical Iconography and Musical Thought," *Early Music* 7 (1979), pp. 13–14.

2. See further David R. Smith, *Masks of Wedlock: Seventeenth-Century Dutch Marriage Portraiture* (Ann Arbor: UMI Research Press, 1982). Most of Smith's study, however, concerns the pair portrait (pendant pictures of husband and wife), by far the more common type of marriage picture produced by Dutch artists. See also the exhibition catalogue by Eddy de Jongh, *Portretten van echt en trouw: Huwelijk en gezin in de Nederlandse kunst van de zeventiende eeuw* (Zwolle: Uitgeverij Waanders; and Haarlem: Frans Halsmuseum, 1986); on Molenaer's picture see Thomas Kren, "Chi non vuol Baccho: Roeland van Laer's Burlesque Painting about Dutch Artists in Rome," *Simiolus* 11 (1980), pp. 75–78; and David R. Smith, "Courtesy and Its Discontents: Frans Hals's *Portrait of Isaac Massa and Beatrix van der Laen*," *Oud Holland* 100 (1986), pp. 21–22.

3. Van Thiel, "Marriage Symbolism," p. 99. The visual antithesis to the temperance emblem is the servant at the left peering into the jug. He is a *kannekijker,* that is, a tippler; in emblematic literature such a figure commonly signifies gluttony (p. 93). On the uniqueness of the monkey-cat representation see pp. 95–96. The "domestic" enclosure at the right, not likely the representation of a real dwelling, is a symbolic fortress of the marriage vows; it is metaphorically mirrored at the left by the ivy-covered wall topped by two pots of carnations. Van Thiel describes the emblematic associations; the wall alludes to the husband, the ivy to the wife, and the flowers to fidelity; see pp. 98–99. For more on the broad range of symbols conventionally employed in Dutch marriage portraiture, see Smith, *Masks of Wedlock,* pp. 57–89.

4. Quoted from Simon Schama, *The Embarrassment of Riches: An Interpretation of Dutch Culture in the Golden Age* (New York: Knopf, 1987), p. 400.

5. See Simon Schama, "Wives and Wantons: Versions of Womanhood in Seventeenth Century Dutch Art," *Oxford Art Journal* 3 (1980), pp. 5–13:

> Woman, as the incarnation of caprice, vulnerable to the enticements of the world, had to be confined within a system of moral regulation. . . . [W]omen in Dutch art were immediately

encumbered with a massive baggage of secondary associations concerning their duties in the home and towards their husband. . . . These took the form of a comprehensive inventory of symbols and visual allusions. . . . Planted conspicuously in the middle of genre paintings, or portraits, they turned ostensibly anecdotal subject matter into visual disquisitions on human frailty (p. 7).

The essay also includes information on misogynist literature, though much fuller treatment of this topic is provided in Schama, *Embarrassment of Riches,* pp. 445–54.

6. "The home was of supreme importance in determining the moral fate, both of individuals and of Dutch society as a whole. . . . In other words, the home was the irreducible primary cell on which, ultimately, the whole fabric of the commonwealth was grounded" (Schama, *Embarrassment of Riches,* pp. 384, 386). See also Wayne E. J. Franits, *Paragons of Virtue: Women and Domesticity in Seventeenth-Century Dutch Art* (Cambridge: Cambridge University Press, forthcoming).

7. This is not a conventional arrangement, but it is not unique. See for example Rubens's famous *Garden of Love* in the Prado, representing Rubens himself standing with his second wife at the left edge of a strikingly rectilinear painting to witness the allegorical celebration of their marriage that occupies the rest of the canvas. In Molenaer's portrait the man's coat sleeve is slightly cropped by the frame; the painting may have been trimmed slightly, judging from similar slight cropping of the fighting peasant's foot at the far left.

8. The costume that makes her appear pregnant is only a reflection of dress style; moreover, "it was apparently impossible until the late seventeenth century for a woman to have too big a belly" (Anne Hollander, *Seeing through Clothes* [New York: Penguin Books, 1978], p. 98; see further pp. 99, 109).

9. It is not to be assumed, however, that a Dutch wife felt compelled to define herself in the terms set out by her husband. Though prevailing ideologies of gender and domestic relations in Holland did not differ from those in the rest of Western Europe, foreign visitors in the seventeenth century commonly remarked, usually critically, on the freedoms enjoyed by Dutch women. See further, Schama, "Wives and Wantons," and Schama, *Embarrassment of Riches,* pp. 402–04, 420–27.

10. Emblems, commonly published in large collections, consist of an image accompanied by a verbal gloss. Emblem illustrations sans text found their way into the cultural vocabulary of other discursive practices like painting (and, indeed, music). See further John Landwehr, *Emblem and Fable Books Printed in the Low Countries, 1542–1813: A Bibliography* (Utrecht: HES, 1988); Eddy de Jongh, *Zinne- en minnebeelden in de schilderkunst van de zeventiende eeuw* (Antwerp: Openbare Kunstbezit in Vlaanderen, 1967); and Mario Praz, *Studies in Seventeenth-Century Imagery,* 2nd ed. (Rome: Storia, 1964).

11. The vast majority of Dutch marriage portraits (i.e., pendants) are devoid of such an overt sensual charge. See Smith, *Masks of Wedlock,* pp. 28–30.

12. Sexual referents, common in Dutch art of the period, ran the gamut from the obscure and symbolical to the obvious and bawdy. See, for example, a discussion of several paintings by Jan Steen in Schama, *Embarrassment of Riches,* pp. 204–11. According to Schama, "Wives and Wantons," "Money, as well as sex, was something of a Dutch fixation . . . [and it] is represented by the visual equivalent of a wink, a leer or a nudge: the proffering of a single coin, or a glass of wine held at the stem, or a *strategically placed*

foot. The point of this symbolism was not to expose sexual behaviour but to shroud it behind a gauze of allusions and metaphors" (p. 12; italics added).

13. I have written about this in detail in my *Theme of Music in Flemish Paintings of the Seventeenth Century,* 2 vols. (Munich and Salzburg: Musikverlag Emil Katzbichler, 1977), *"Concert in a House,"* and especially *Music and Image: Domesticity, Ideology, and Socio-Cultural Formation in Eighteenth-Century England* (Cambridge: Cambridge University Press, 1989).

14. See Schama, *Embarrassment of Riches,* especially the detailed discussion on pp. 388–480 in the chapter titled "Housewives and Hussies: Homeliness and Worldliness." Dutch prostitutes even carried lutes with them into taverns as a sonoric-visual advertisement of their profession. Numerous Dutch paintings connect the lute to prostitution via the subject of the procuress. See Leppert, *Theme of Music,* vol. 1, p. 185. These representations conflict with emblematic associations of the lute with the virtue of temperance (on which see van Thiel, "Marriage Symbolism," p. 91).

15. See Petrus Johannes Blok, *History of the People of the Netherlands,* vol. 3, *The War with Spain,* trans. Ruth Putnam (New York: Putnam, 1900); Pieter Geyl, *The Revolt of the Netherlands (1555–1609),* 2nd ed. (London: Ernest Benn, 1958), and Geyl, *The Netherlands Divided (1609–1648),* trans. S. T. Bindoff, in collaboration with Pieter Geyl (London: Williams and Norgate, 1936); and Geoffrey Parker, *The Dutch Revolt* (Ithaca: Cornell University Press, 1977).

16. See Schama, *Embarrassment of Riches.* The book contains an up-to-date bibliographic guide to the study of Dutch culture, pp. 655–70.

17. See Leppert, *Music and Image,* for the situation in England and *"Concert in a House"* for that in the Low Countries. Though the concern was Continent-wide, the severity of the complaint varied over time and place, across religious and other divides.

18. The classic study is Ingvar Bergström, *Dutch Still-Life Painting in the Seventeenth Century,* trans. Christina Hedström and Gerald Taylor (New York: T. Voseloff, 1956). Concerning vanitas paintings, see especially pp. 153–56. On representations of musical instruments in this genre, see Albert Pomme de Mirimonde, "Les Natures mortes à instruments de musique de Peter Boel," *Jaarboek, Koninklijk Museum voor Schone Kunsten* (Antwerp, 1964), pp. 107–43; and Peter Fischer, *Music in Paintings of the Low Countries in the Sixteenth and Seventeenth Centuries* (Amsterdam: Swets, 1975), pp. 45–72.

19. Among all instruments employed by Dutch burghers as part of art music practices, only the violin and, occasionally, the lute crossed class boundaries (see n. 14, above). In the Spanish Netherlands, if not in Holland, the lute's use—potential or real—by the lower orders was itself a subject for the mocking enjoyment of the upper classes. See my "David Teniers the Younger and the Image of Music," *Jaarboek, Koninklijk Museum voor Schone Kunsten* (Antwerp, 1978), pp. 77–82, 96–97. On the musical opposition between noise and order see Jacques Attali, *Noise: The Political Economy of Music,* trans. Brian Massumi (Minneapolis: University of Minnesota Press, 1985).

20. For example, despite notable stylistic differences, there is little ideological divergence between Teniers's representations of the lower classes and those of many other Dutch and Flemish painters, such as Cornelis Bega, Pieter de Bloot, Andries Both, Joos van Craesbeck, Egbert van Heemskerck, Frans van Mieris the Elder, Bartholomeus Molenaer, Adriaen van Ostade, Isaac van Ostade, David Ryckaert the Younger, Pieter Verelst, and even

Jan Miense Molenaer. Examples of relevant work by these painters are reproduced in Walther Bernt, *The Netherlandish Painters of the Seventeenth Century,* trans. P. S. Falla, 3 vols., 3rd ed. (London: Phaidon, 1970).

21. See Leppert, "Teniers," pp. 95–98 and figs. 24–25.

22. See further ibid., pp. 141–42.

23. In musical practice the instrument's nasal, reedy sound locates it as Dionysian. See ibid., p. 141 n. 140.

24. "Met een goed gevulde buik wil het zingen beter lukken" (It's better to sing with a well-filled belly [here, the bagpipe's swelled windsack]). The meaning of *sing* is preserved in another proverb: "Voor het zingen de kerk uit" (Before singing, leave the church), a reference to coitus interruptus.

25. The seriousness of sitters in portraits is conventional, for precisely the reasons I am suggesting, whether or not musical activities are included. Such seriousness, however, is antithetical to Dutch Merry Company scenes, including those with musicians like Molenaer's lutenist. Regarding the decorum of sitters in another group picture by Molenaer, see Smith, *Masks of Wedlock,* pp. 29–30.

26. No one has argued this point more effectively than Theodor W. Adorno. See, for example, *Introduction to the Sociology of Music,* trans. E. B. Ashton (New York: Continuum, 1976). See also the famous formulation by Herbert Marcuse, Adorno's sometime colleague at the Frankfurt Institute: "The Affirmative Character of Culture" (1937), in *Negations: Essays in Critical Theory,* trans. Jeremy J. Shapiro (Boston: Beacon, 1968), pp. 88–133; see also Alan Durant, *Conditions of Music* (Albany: State University of New York Press, 1984); Christopher Small, *Music, Society, Education* (New York: Schirmer, 1980), pp. 60–96; and Richard Norton, *The History of Western Tonality: A Critical and Historical Perspective* (University Park: Pennsylvania State University Press, 1984), pp. 138–230.

27. Plato, *The Republic,* trans. A. D. Lindsay (New York: Dutton, 1957), for example, pp. 99–103 (Book III/398–399), 117–19 (Book III/410–412).

28. Allan Bloom, *The Closing of the American Mind: How Higher Education Has Failed Democracy and Impoverished the Souls of Today's Students* (New York: Simon and Schuster, 1987), pp. 68–81.

29. Schama, "Wives and Wantons," p. 13:

> This uncompartmentalised world, fraught with confusion, disguise, ambiguities and stratagems was, by definition, riddled with anxiety (even if Calvin had not added his own brand). In keeping with its undifferentiated components, women were rarely seen as exclusively given to either vice or virtue, to the purified world of the conjugal home, or the soiling world of vanity and lust. It was precisely the daunting suspicion that the two identities—paragon and hussy—might cohabit within the same frame that, literally, *bedeviled* Dutch men. . . . Culture and nature; morality and instinct, were locked in perpetual and unresolvable combat in the Dutch mentality.

Thus the woman with the partbook has the gesture and facial expression conventional to representations of the Madonna, but the lower-body pose of, if not precisely the prostitute, someone of more ambiguous virtue. Her body maps the general terrain of difference and physically locates the defining moral bifurcation.

CHAPTER 2

1. The work of Walter Salmen is perhaps the most distinguished effort to date to address this imbalance. See, for example, *Haus- und Kammermusik: Privates Musizieren im gesellschaftlichen Wandel zwischen 1600 und 1900*, Musikgeschichte in Bildern, vol. IV/3 (Leipzig: Deutscher Verlag für Musik, 1969); and the recent festschrift dedicated to Salmen, *Musica Privata: Die Rolle der Musik im privaten Leben*, ed. Monika Fink, Rainer Gstrein, and Günter Mössmer (Innsbruck: Helbling, 1991).

2. A brief account of some of this work is available in Richard Leppert and Susan McClary, introduction to *Music and Society: The Politics of Composition, Performance, and Reception*, ed. Richard Leppert and Susan McClary (Cambridge: Cambridge University Press, 1987), pp. xi–xix. Among the studies published most recently see especially Lawrence Kramer, *Music as Cultural Practice, 1800–1900* (Berkeley and Los Angeles: University of California Press, 1990); Susan McClary, *Feminine Endings: Music, Gender, and Sexuality* (Minneapolis: University of Minnesota Press, 1991); and Rose Rosengard Subotnik, *Developing Variations: Style and Ideology in Western Music* (Minneapolis: University of Minnesota Press, 1991).

3. Kramer, *Music as Cultural Practice*, pp. 1–20.

4. See for example, Theodor W. Adorno, *Introduction to the Sociology of Music*, trans. E. B. Ashton (New York: Continuum, 1976); on Adorno and deconstruction, see Martin Jay, *Adorno* (Cambridge: Harvard University Press, 1984), pp. 21–22; and Fredric Jameson, *Late Marxism: Adorno, or, the Persistence of the Dialectic* (London: Verso, 1990), pp. 9–10, and p. 254 n. 10, who properly cautions against an unproblematic acceptance of Adorno as a proto-post-structuralist.

5. The best attempt to date—by no means wholly successful—to develop a theory for this history is Jacques Attali, *Noise: The Political Economy of Music*, trans. Brian Massumi (Minneapolis: University of Minnesota Press, 1985).

6. See pp. 246–47 n. 21.

7. See the different, though partly complementary, accounts of what I would call rationalized landscape painting by Ann Bermingham, *Landscape and Ideology: The English Rustic Tradition, 1740–1860* (Berkeley and Los Angeles: University of California Press, 1986); and John Barrell, *The Dark Side of the Landscape: The Rural Poor in English Painting, 1730–1840* (Cambridge: Cambridge University Press, 1980).

8. In the painting a small river separates foreground from background; it marks the division between the two types of human subject represented. But the stream's presence is obscured or disguised at the crucial point where the two groups of people come into closest proximity. Here the division seems momentarily to disappear, as if the river itself disappeared, as if the two groups engaged in free intercourse after all. But this is merely an illusion of oneness. Indeed, the river disappears as a barrier only to have its function taken up by a hedge, and the hedge opens up, like a gate, to lead to the river bank: access is controlled. To cross the barrier one needs a boat, and the only boat in the picture is occupied by aristocratic lovers, who look, not toward the workers, but toward the château, the architectural confirmation of their identity and the guarantee that they will retain their status.

9. Cf. Laura Mulvey, *Visual and Other Pleasures* (Bloomington: Indiana University Press, 1989), p. 167: "The mind/body opposition is characteristic of other oppositions of dominance (black/white, colonised/conqueror, peasant/noble, bourgeoisie/worker) and in each case the oppressed are linked to nature (the body) and the dominant to culture (and the mind)."

10. Antonio Gramsci, *An Antonio Gramsci Reader: Selected Writings, 1916–1935,* ed. David Forgacs (New York: Schocken Books, 1988), pp. 306–07. In a later passage (p. 356), Gramsci acknowledges music in his list of "sources of linguistic conformism" through which the socially dominant articulate their interests and inculcate them in the population at large. He is primarily concerned here with the linguistic means of mass producing consent: the educational system, newspapers, theater, film, radio, and so forth. Music enters in a discussion of relations between "the more educated and less educated strata of the population" via the following lengthy parenthetical insight: "A question which is perhaps not given all the attention it deserves is that of the 'words' in verse learnt by heart in the form of songs, snatches of operas, etc. It should be noted that the people do not bother really to memorize these words, which are often strange, antiquated and ba- roque, but reduce them to kinds of nursery rhymes that are only helpful for remembering the tune." Gramsci does not consider how the music itself performs the role of agent via its own sonorities beyond the semantic quotient of the word text the music accompanies, which is the argument I am advancing, though he implies as much when he points out music's power to overwhelm words.

11. I am borrowing here from Michel Foucault, *Discipline and Punish: The Birth of the Prison,* trans. Alan Sheridan (New York: Vintage Books, 1979).

12. See further Christopher Small, *Music, Society, Education* (New York: Schirmer, 1977), chapter 1, "The Perfect Cadence and the Concert Hall," pp. 7–33.

13. Andreas Capellanus, *The Art of Courtly Love,* trans. John Jay Parray (New York: Norton, 1969).

14. Among the best painted examples are works by David Teniers the Younger, on which see my "David Teniers the Younger and the Image of Music," *Jaarboek, Koninklijk Museum voor Schone Kunsten* (Antwerp, 1978), pp. 63–155 passim.

15. John Berger, "Painting and Time," in *The Sense of Sight,* ed. Lloyd Spencer (New York: Pantheon Books, 1985), p. 207.

16. I have written extensively about this phenomenon in my book *Music and Image: Domesticity, Ideology, and Socio-Cultural Formation in Eighteenth-Century England* (Cambridge: Cambridge University Press, 1989).

17. See Mulvey, "Film, Feminism, and the Avant-Garde," in *Visual and Other Plea- sures,* pp. 111–26.

18. See on this point Donald M. Lowe, *The History of Bourgeois Perception* (Chicago: University of Chicago Press, 1982); and John Shepherd, "Music and Male Hegemony," in *Music and Society: The Politics of Composition, Performance, and Reception,* ed. Richard Leppert and Susan McClary (Cambridge: Cambridge University Press, 1987), pp. 152–58; re- printed in John Shepherd, *Music as Social Text* (Cambridge, U.K.: Polity, 1991), pp. 152–73.

19. Mulvey, *Visual and Other Pleasures,* p. 135.

20. Whether the argument was unvaryingly "accepted" by viewers is hardly the issue. The narrative must be "read," and the reader-viewer in the act of reading can never be fully controlled. The discursive activity of the painting is a plat or map, and a plot—in the double sense of a narrative or story and a scheme. The representation, like any other, makes an argument the viewer may or may not accept, though not freely, for the reading-viewing is invariably constructed in part by the society and culture of which the image is a projection. The ideal viewer, in other words, has partly internalized the image prior to its being painted.

21. I have not located any emblematic connection between the guitar and the parrot, though the striking combination hints at one.

22. See Leppert, "Teniers"; a discussion of this painting occurs on pp. 143–44.

23. According to the Dutch poet Jan van der Veen, "De Vedel of Fiool die wert God betert, meer/ Gebruyckt tot ydelheyt, als tot Godts lof en eer" (The fiddle or violin is alas used more in the service of vanity than in the praise and glory of God). See Ingvar Bergström, *Dutch Still-Life Painting in the Seventeenth Century,* trans. Christina Hedström and Gerald Taylor (New York: T. Voseloff, 1956), p. 156; and Richard Leppert, *The Theme of Music in Flemish Paintings of the Seventeenth Century* (Munich and Salzburg: Musikverlag Emil Katzbichler, 1977), vol. 1, p. 77.

24. See further Richard Leppert, *Arcadia at Versailles: Noble Amateur Musicians and Their Musettes and Hurdy-Gurdies at the French Court (c. 1660–1789); a Visual Study* (Amsterdam: Swets, 1978), pp. 29–31. For another example by Teniers similar in composition and subject see Leppert, "Teniers," fig. 54, pp. 133–34.

25. See Curt Sachs, *World History of the Dance,* trans. Bessie Schönberg (New York: Norton, 1937), p. 280.

26. Mikhail Bakhtin, *Rabelais and His World,* trans. Helene Iswolsky (Bloomington: Indiana University Press, 1984). For a history of the difficulty of maintaining political control over carnival, see Emmanuel Le Roy Ladurie, *Carnival in Romans,* trans. Mary Feeney (New York: Braziller, 1979). Carnival purposely structures the transgression of the law of the dominant; it acts as a safety valve for pressures building from below. But the entire point of carnival is ultimately to contain, to channel, to control by other means. Mockery was not only tolerated but expected and encouraged. It was comic; its purpose was to take charge of the serious: body over mind, peasant over aristocrat, the immoral over the moral, nature over culture, low art over high art. And carnival is contradictory in that the spontaneity is in effect organized; so long as organizing principles hold, it remains a mask that fails to transform the face of surveillance underneath.

27. See the discussion of this phenomenon in Attali, *Noise,* pp. 21–24; the sonoric difference between carnival and Lent is the organizing principle of this book.

28. The concern with the "good" peasant has a long history in Western art, extending into the early romantic period, with its nostalgia for a disappearing agricultural economy. See Barrell, *Dark Side of the Landscape.*

29. See Leppert, *Theme of Music,* vol. 1, pp. 201–23.

30. Teniers's own interests and self-location in this history are evident in his representing in the background the château, known as De Drij Toren, that he himself rented

and eventually bought; it marks his lifelong quest to be granted a title. See Léon Bocquet, *David Teniers* (Paris: Editions Nilsson, 1924), pp. 41–46, 62–75 passim.

31. See the moving, insightful account in Max Horkheimer and Theodor W. Adorno, *Dialectic of Enlightenment,* trans. John Cumming (New York: Continuum, 1972), "Man and Animal," pp. 245–55. See also the excellent account by Mark Johnson, *The Body in the Mind: The Bodily Basis of Meaning, Imagination, and Reason* (Chicago: University of Chicago Press, 1987).

32. The best visual account of the ubiquity of musical sonority in European history, a history very imperfectly known, is by Walter Salmen, *Musikleben im 16. Jahrhundert,* Musikgeschichte in Bildern, vol. III/9 (Leipzig: Deutscher Verlag für Musik, 1976).

CHAPTER 3

1. Here I am borrowing, and diverging somewhat, from Jacques Attali, *Noise: The Political Economy of Music,* trans. Brian Massumi (Minneapolis: University of Minnesota Press, 1985), especially pp. 3–45.

2. Willi Apel, *Gregorian Chant* (Bloomington: Indiana University Press, 1958), p. 79. See also the primary sources quoted in Piero Weiss and Richard Taruskin, eds., *Music in the Western World: A History in Documents* (New York: Schirmer, 1984), pp. 42–45.

3. I do not mean to suggest that class distinction was never marked by musical difference during the Middle Ages; rather, the distinctions were considerably less clear and more fluid than was later the case. See, for example, the various remarks on musical life in Paris circa 1300 in the treatise by Johannes de Grocheo, *Concerning Music (De musica),* trans. Albert Seay, 2nd ed. (Colorado Springs: Colorado College Music Press, 1974). I am grateful to my colleague Susan McClary for drawing my attention to this source.

4. There were of course neo-Platonists at work during the Middle Ages. See, for example, the musical writings of Anicius Manlius Severinus Boethius (c. 480–c. 524), *De institutione musica.* See also Calvin Bower, "Boethius," *The New Grove Dictionary of Music and Musicians,* ed. Stanley Sadie (London: Macmillan, 1980), vol. 2, pp. 844–45. Boethius's theories of music enjoyed general acceptance throughout the Middle Ages and the Renaissance.

5. See Walter Salmen, *Musikleben im 16. Jahrhundert,* Musikgeschichte in Bildern, III/9 (Leipzig: Deutscher Verlag für Musik, 1976).

6. Gioseffo Zarlino's *Istituzioni armoniche* (Venice, 1558) is the most important single example of a mathematically based theory of sound that categorizes consonances and dissonances and deduces the rules of ("good") composition from these categories. A lengthy excerpt is provided in Oliver Strunk, ed., *Source Readings in Music History: The Renaissance* (New York: Norton, 1965), pp. 39–71; book 3 is available in a translation by Guy A. Marco and Claude V. Palisca (New Haven: Yale University Press, 1968). See further Claude V. Palisca, "Zarlino," *New Grove,* vol. 20, pp. 646–49.

7. See further Richard Leppert, *Music and Image: Domesticity, Ideology, and Socio-*

Cultural Formation in Eighteenth-Century England (Cambridge: Cambridge University Press, 1989), especially chapters 2–4.

8. Thus the descendants of the Flemish peasantry still perform their traditional music, now called folk music. It is now self-consciously *performed* so that the very culture (whose sound the music originally articulated) can survive; and if the culture is to survive at all, the music must necessarily express itself in ways that acknowledge both the decline of the culture and the music's own existence as a mere leftover. For a less pessimistic expression of this problematic, see John Blacking, *How Musical Is Man?* (Seattle: University of Washington Press, 1973), especially pp. 37–38.

9. Thus Baldassare Castiglione, *The Book of the Courtier {Il libro del cortegiano (1528)},* trans. Sir Thomas Hoby (London, 1561), distinguishes between the music of "the boisterous laborers in the fields . . . with [their] rude and carterlike singing" and that of the nobility, who by their music "flee the multitude, and especially . . . the ignoble" (Strunk, *Source Readings in Music History,* pp. 93–94). In similar fashion Pierre de Ronsard, in the dedication of his *Livre des mélanges* (Paris, 1560) to François II reiterated that "music has always been the sign and the mark of those who have shown themselves virtuous, magnanimous, and truly born to feel nothing vulgar," by which he implicitly sought to reaffirm the pedigree for one kind of music (Strunk, p. 97). Giovanni de' Bardi, in his "Discourse on Ancient Music and Good Singing" (c. 1580), argued for the reestablishment of a music "true and perfect . . . so highly praised by the ancients" (Strunk, p. 105), a project echoed by Vicenzo Galilei in his *Dialogo della musica antica e della moderna* (Venice, 1581), entirely predicated on a neo-Platonic ideal of a highly theorized art music (see Strunk, pp. 112–32).

10. See further Chapter 5. Scholars like Susan McClary and Rose Rosengard Subotnik, among others, have addressed the connection of compositional procedure to prevailing conceptions of socio-cultural order. See, for example, Susan McClary, "The Blasphemy of Talking Politics during Bach Year"; and Rose Rosengard Subotnik, "On Grounding Chopin," both in *Music and Society: The Politics of Composition, Performance, and Reception,* ed. Richard Leppert and Susan McClary (Cambridge: Cambridge University Press, 1987), pp. 13–62, and 105–31

11. Robert F. Chirico, "Some Reflections on Sound and Silence in the Visual Arts," *Arts Magazine* 56 (April 1982), pp. 101–05, briefly touches on the present absence of sound (especially music) in painting in examining "what it was that produced in painting its soundlessness and, subsequently, why we predominantly perceive the visual arts as silent" (p. 102). The essay raises some interesting points, but its value is limited by its brevity.

12. The various members of the viol family were employed in secular ensemble and solo art music throughout the period, beginning with consort music in the sixteenth century, which at first consisted largely of transcriptions of vocal music, both ecclesiastical and secular. During the baroque period the bass viol and harpsichord conventionally provided continuo accompaniment.

13. Adolf Layer, "Tieffenbrucker," *Die Musik in Geschichte und Gegenwart,* ed. Friedrich Blume, vol. 13 (Kassel and Basel: Bärenreiter, 1966), col. 402. Little is known of

Tieffenbrucker's life. A German by birth, he settled in Lyon in 1553 and acquired French citizenship in 1558. See further Willibald Leo von Lütgendorff, *Die Geigen und Lautenmacher vom Mittelalter bis zur Gegenwart* (Frankfurt am Main: Frankfurter Verlags-Anstalt, 1922), vol. 2, pp. 515–16; Ian Harwood, "Tieffenbrucker," *The New Grove Dictionary of Musical Instruments,* ed. Stanley Sadie (London: Macmillan, 1984), vol. 3, pp. 583–84 (which misstates the date of Tieffenbrucker's arrival in Lyon); and Henry Coutagne, *Gaspard Duiffoproucart et les luthiers lyonnais du XVIe siècle* (Paris: Fischbacher, 1893), especially pp. 25, and 37–43, concerning the instrument. Also on the instrument, see Victor-Charles Mahillon, *Catalogue descriptif et analytique du Musée instrumental (historique et technique) du Conservatoire royal de musique de Bruxelles* (Ghent: Ad. Hoste, 1893–1922; reprint, Brussels: Les Amis de la Musique, 1978), vol. 3, pp. 47–49. The factual information concerning the viola da gamba is from these sources (note that Mahillon mistakenly indicates that the instrument was made for François I). On Henry II see the biography by H. Noel Williams, *Henry II: His Court and His Times* (London: Methuen, 1910).

14. That the decoration may have been added to the instrument some decades after it was made does not affect the issues I am discussing. See Coutagne, *Gaspard Duiffoproucart,* p. 38.

15. See Richard Leppert, *"Concert in a House:* Musical Iconography and Musical Thought," *Early Music* 7 (1979), pp. 3–17.

16. See further Louis Réau, *Iconographie de l'art chrétien,* vol. 2 (Paris: Presses Universitaires de France, 1958), pp. 827–32; and James Hall, *Dictionary of Subjects and Symbols in Art* (New York: Harper and Row, 1974), pp. 128–29, 195–96. According to Coutagne, *Gaspard Duiffoproucart,* pp. 38–39, repeated by Mahillon, *Catalogue descriptif,* vol. 3, pp. 48–49, the representation of St. Luke was inspired by Raphael's small painting *The Vision of Ezekiel* (on wood, 40 × 30 cm.; painted c. 1518; Florence, Galleria Pitti, no. 174), illustrating God the Father and the attributes of the four Evangelists (Ezekiel 1:4–26). In my judgment the relation between the two images is tenuous. Raphael's male figure, God the Father, is shown frontally, not in profile, naked to the waist, with outstretched arms and windblown hair. He is the opposite of the bookish, contemplative man illustrated on the viol. The overall scheme (of male figure on cloud with bull beside him) is the same in both, but Raphael's conception is vastly more complex compositionally. Moreover, the disparate elements are arranged differently in each representation. On the Raphael painting, see Luitpold Dussler, *Raphael: A Critical Catalogue of His Pictures, Wall-Paintings, and Tapestries,* trans. Sebastian Cruft (London: Phaidon, 1971), pp. 44–45; and Roger Jones and Nicholas Penny, *Raphael* (New Haven: Yale University Press, 1983), pp. 89–91 (illustrated in color).

17. See Williams, *Henry II,* pp. 228–29. To my knowledge there is no specific relation between Luke and either the city of Paris or the house of Valois to which Henry II belonged.

18. Coutagne, *Gaspard Duiffoproucart,* p. 9, indicates that the plan nearly replicates a map in the Bibliothèque nationale (Cabinet des estampes, book IV, 2) dated 1564, that is, within about a decade or less of the probable date of the viol itself. And Mahillon, *Catalogue descriptif,* vol. 2, p. 48, indicates that the map is similar to a tapestry that hung

in the Paris Hôtel de Ville until its loss in the fire of 1871. If the map on the viol was executed around the time of the 1564 engraving, that would place it during the reign of Charles IX (1560–74), Henry II's second son, a weak man entirely dominated by his mother, Catherine de Médicis. The violence of his reign, marked by civil wars, the Catholic party against the Huguenot, culminated in 1572 in the St. Bartholomew's Day Massacre (24 August) and its aftermath extending into the fall of that year.

19. See further Albert Pomme de Mirimonde, "Les 'Cabinets de musique,'" *Jaarboek, Koninklijk Museum voor Schone Kunsten* (Antwerp, 1966), pp. 141–78; Richard Leppert, *The Theme of Music in Flemish Paintings of the Seventeenth Century* (Munich and Salzburg: Musikverlag Emil Katzbichler, 1977), vol. 1, pp. 109–14; vol. 2, pp. 24–29, 242–43, plates 24–25. See vol. 2, cat. no. 100, reproduced as plate 24, for a virtually exact replica of the Prado original; Simone Speth-Holteroff, *Les Peintres flamands de cabinets d'amateurs au XVIIe siècle* (Paris and Brussels: Elsevier, 1957); Klaus Ertz, *Jan Brueghel der Ältere (1568–1625): Die Gemälde, mit kritischem Oeuvrekatalog* (Cologne: DuMont, 1979), pp. 328–62, concerning Brueghel's entire series of allegories of the senses paintings, and pp. 329, 350–52, in regard to the paintings on hearing; Fritz Baumgart, *Blumen Brueghel (Jan Brueghel d. Ä.): Leben und Werk* (Cologne, DuMont, 1978), pp. 121–31; and Hans Kauffmann, "Die Fünfsinne in der neiderländischen Malerei des 17. Jahrhunderts," in *Kunstgeschichtliche Studien: Festschrift für Dagobert Frey,* ed. Hans Tintelnot, pp. 133–57 (Breslau: Gauverlag, 1943). On the general subject, see Chu-tsing Li, "The Five Senses in Art: An Analysis of Its Development in Northern Europe," Ph.D. diss., State University of Iowa, 1955.

20. For details, see Ertz, *Jan Brueghel,* pp. 14–16; and Gertraude Winkelmann-Rhein, *The Paintings and Drawings of Jan "Flower" Bruegel,* trans. Leonard Mins (New York: Harry N. Abrams, 1968), p. 28; and Baumgart, *Blumen Brueghel,* p. 11.

21. The Netherlands in the sixteenth century comprised seventeen provinces, ruled from 1519 by the Holy Roman Emperor Charles V from his court at Brussels. In 1556 Charles abdicated, leaving the Netherlands to Philip, his son. Philip II (1527–1598), thoroughly Spanish by both education and lifelong residence (he did not set foot in the Netherlands after 1559), was a fanatical Catholic intent on reestablishing Roman orthodoxy in the Netherlands (increasingly a Calvinist stronghold) at any cost. Within a decade of his ascent to power the region was in open revolt, and warfare was inaugurated that would continue intermittently for nearly a century, until 1648.

In 1566 Catholic iconoclastic riots broke out in Antwerp, then the most Calvinist of Netherlandish cities, and spread in the following weeks to other communities. The eventual response from Philip II was carried out by the infamous duke of Alva ("Iron Duke"), sent directly from Spain, in the company of tens of thousands of troops, mostly mercenaries, who effectively initiated a reign of terror. Their violence led to open revolt that within decades brought about the independence of the Dutch provinces and the formation of Holland, as well as the segregation of religions by geographical boundary that still prevails: Calvinists in the North, Catholics in the South. Alva was stationed in the Netherlands from 1567 to 1573. For excellent accounts in English of the events leading to the revolt of the Spanish Netherlands against Philip II's Spain, the regime of the duke of Alva, and the condition of the region by 1584, see Petrus Johannes Blok, *History of the People of the Netherlands,* vol. 3, *The War with Spain,* trans. Ruth Putnam (New York: Putnam, 1900), pp. 1–78, 181–96; and the more recent—and partially corrective—studies by Pieter Geyl, *The Netherlands Divided (1609–1648),* trans. S. T. Bindoff, in collaboration with Pieter Geyl (London: Williams and Norgate, 1936), and *The Revolt of the Netherlands (1555–1609),* 2nd ed. (London: Ernest Benn, 1958); and Geoffrey Parker, *The Dutch Revolt* (Ithaca: Cornell University Press, 1977). On the bloodiness of Philip II's suppression of Protestantism in the Spanish Netherlands, see Cecil John Cadoux, *Philip of Spain and the Netherlands: An Essay on Moral Judgments in History* (n.p.: Archon Books, 1969), pp. 84–85, 89–100.

The duke of Alva's chief claim to infamy among the region's population was the Council of Troubles, popularly referred to then as the Council of Blood, established in the early fall of 1567, shortly after Alva's arrival in Brussels. At the height of its activity, people were condemned in groups of up to nearly one hundred. Executions were carried out across the countryside—by hanging, decapitating, and burning—and near the end of the terror were sometimes preceded by torture (Cadoux, *Philip of Spain and the Netherlands,* p. 96). The total number of people executed by Alva has been considerably reduced in modern historical accounts (though Alva himself bragged of 18,000). Geoffrey Parker, *The Dutch Revolt,* p. 108, suggests that the Council of Troubles ordered the execution of more than 1,000 of over 12,000 individuals brought before it (nearly 9,000 of whom lost all or part of their property through confiscation). The best record of the council's activities, though it contains some errors, is that by A. L. E. Verheyden, *Le Conseil des Troubles. Liste des condamnés (1567–1573)* (Brussels: Palais des académies, 1961), on which see Parker, *The Dutch Revolt,* p. 293 n. 35. Pieter Geyl summarizes Alva's council: "Never was a nation subjected to a reign of terror with more calculated deliberation or more systematic persistence" (*The Revolt of the Netherlands,* p. 104).

The effects of Alva's actions and the revolt that followed (the years 1578–92 constituted a period of high military activity) were directly experienced by the general population, for no distinctions were made between combatant and noncombatant. Cities declined severely in population—Antwerp lost more than half its inhabitants between 1568 and 1589 (though it more than recovered early in the seventeenth century). Rural areas suffered most, especially between 1567 (beginning with Alva) and 1609, when the Twelve Years' Truce was inaugurated. Peasants were vulnerable to the ravages of mercenaries on or off the battlefield, to soldier mutineers, to the forced billeting of troops without recompense, to forced labor, to acts of *vrijbuiters* (independent adventurers taking advantage of the war for personal gain), to flooding of lands, to the extortion of payment for protection (a *brandscaft,* or fire tax, was paid to enemy troops to prevent the burning or plunder of one's property—payment of which might bring down the wrath of the opposing side and result in the very act the payment was intended to preclude), and so on. The provinces of Flanders and Brabant were hit especially hard by these collective misfortunes, and by 1609 the region had largely been reduced to a wasteland: general depopulation, ruined farms and villages, cultivated lands abandoned, and so forth. For example, in the Courtrai region "only one percent of the rural population remained on the land at the peak of the crisis," and near Ghent only 10 percent of the arable land remained in cultivation. Peasants and villagers fled to the cities, where overcrowding and famine spread disease among a generally weakened populace. The populations of villages throughout Brabant, Flanders, and Hainaut were reduced by 50 to 75 percent of what they had been in the 1560s (Jane Susannah Fishman, *Boerenverdriet: Violence between Peasants and Soldiers in Early Modern Netherlands Art* [Ann Arbor: UMI Research Press, 1982], pp. 1–17; quotation from p. 13).

22. Even if the picture was not painted for Albert and Isabella, it nevertheless privileges them. By 1636 it was inventoried in the Madrid collection of King Philip IV. "Philip IV's avid love of fine painting made it an especially successful vehicle by which loyalty and esteem could be expressed [by courtiers] for their sovereign" (Mary Crawford Volk, "Rubens in Madrid and the Decoration of the King's Summer Apartments," *Burlington Magazine* 123 [1981], p. 525). On the identity of the original commissioner(s)—the archducal couple or the duke of Pfalz-Neuburg—see Ertz, *Jan Brueghel,* pp. 336–37.

23. See further Ertz, *Jan Brueghel,* pp. 355–56.

24. See Alain Corbin, *The Foul and the Fragrant: Odor and the French Social Imagination* (New York: Berg Publishers, 1986), "The New Calculus of Olfactory Pleasure," pp. 71–85, concerning this matter in the eighteenth century and the early ninteenth.

25. Winklemann-Rhein, *Paintings and Drawings,* p. 28.

26. The six-part madrigals of Peter Philips were published at Antwerp in 1596 and 1603 (the latter collection also contains eight-part madrigals) and reprinted in 1604. See further *Peter Philips: Select Italian Madrigals,* transcribed and ed. by John Steele, *Musica Britannica,* no. 29, general ed. Anthony Lewis (London: Stainer and Bell, 1970), p. 29.

27. Mirimonde, "Cabinets," p. 153.

28. On the South under Albert and Isabella, including the style of the court and the politics, authority, and orthodoxy of the regime, see Geyl, *The Netherlands Divided,* pp. 22–26, 30–32.

29. See Max Horkheimer, *Critique of Instrumental Reason,* trans. Matthew J. O'Connell and others (New York: Continuum, 1974).

30. The most insightful, if controversial, account of the object centeredness of northern art is Svetlana Alpers, *The Art of Describing: Dutch Art in the Seventeenth Century* (Chicago: University of Chicago Press, 1983), pp. 119–68, though the school of painting and time frame differ slightly from mine.

31. On her identification see Mirimonde, "Cabinets," p. 149; and Ertz, *Jan Brueghel,* pp. 350–52.

32. See Leppert, *Theme of Music,* vol. 1, pp. 185–86. For more on this subject see the discussion p. 238 n. 14, above.

CHAPTER 4

1. For a detailed discussion of these sources see Richard Leppert, *Music and Image: Domesticity, Ideology, and Socio-Cultural Formation in Eighteenth-Century England* (Cambridge: Cambridge University Press, 1989), chapters 2–3 in particular.

2. See my discussion of the ideological underpinnings and socio-cultural implications

of a treatise on the mathematics of sound by John Keeble, *The Theory of Harmonics: Or, an Illustration of the Grecian Harmonica* (London, 1784), and its relation to Rameau's music theory, in Chapter 5.

3. See, for example, Henry Curson, *The Theory of Sciences Illustrated; or the Grounds and Principles of the Seven Liberal Arts* (London, 1702), pp. 129–31.

4. *Euterpe; or, Remarks on the Use and Abuse of Music, as a Part of Modern Education* (London, c. 1778), p. 15. Cf. the similar views on music, order, and morality expressed by John Dennis, "Advancement and Reformation of Poetry," in *The Critical Works of John Dennis*, ed. Edward Niles Hooker, vol. 1 (Baltimore: Johns Hopkins Press, 1939), p. 336.

5. J. E. Stephens, ed. *Aubrey on Education: A Hitherto Unpublished Manuscript by the Author of "Brief Lives"* (London: Routledge and Kegan Paul, 1972), p. 113.

6. See Jamie Croy Kassler, *The Science of Music in Britain, 1714–1830: A Catalogue of Writings, Lectures, and Inventions,* 2 vols. (New York: Garland, 1979).

7. See Richard Leppert, "Imagery, Musical Confrontation, and Cultural Difference in Early Eighteenth-Century London," *Early Music* 14 (1986), pp. 323–45.

8. Henry Fielding, *Tom Jones* [1750], ed. Sheridan Baker (New York: Norton, 1973), p. 128.

9. See John Dennis, *An Essay on Opera's after the Italian Manner, Which Are About to Be Establish'd on the English Stage: With Some Reflections on the Damage Which They May Bring to the Publick,* in *Critical Works of John Dennis,* vol. 1, pp. 382–93, 520–24; and Leppert, "Imagery, Musical Confrontation, and Cultural Difference," pp. 337–38; see also Philip Dormer Stanhope, *Letters to His Son by the Earl of Chesterfield on the Fine Art of Becoming a Man of the World and a Gentleman,* ed. Oliver H. G. Leigh (London: Navarre Society, 1926), vol. 1, p. 170 (letter 68, dated 19 April O.S. 1749). In another letter (p. 186, no. 73, dated 22 June O.S. 1749) of similar vein he cites the musical proclivities of the Italians as direct proof of the country's decline.

10. See Leppert, *Music and Image,* pp. 56–66, and Leppert, "Music Teachers of Upper-Class Amateur Musicians in Eighteenth-Century England," in *Music in the Classic Period: Essays in Honor of Barry S. Brook,* ed. Allan W. Atlas (New York: Pendragon, 1985), pp. 133–58.

11. See Percy A. Scholes, *The Great Doctor Burney: His Life, His Travels, His Works; His Family and His Friends,* 2 vols. (Oxford: Oxford University Press, 1948).

12. For a famous example of a father's attempting to prevent a public musical performance by his daughter, the case of Ann Ford, see Leppert, *Music and Image,* pp. 40–42.

13. John Essex, *The Young Ladies Conduct: Or, Rules for Education, under Several Heads; with Instructions upon Dress, Both before and after Marriage. And Advice to Young Wives* (London, 1722), pp. 84–85. As the century progressed, harpsichords were generally replaced by fortepianos, lutes by English guitars, violas da gamba ("bass viols") by violoncellos.

14. *Euterpe,* p. 18. On the authorship of this essay see Kassler, *Science of Music,* vol. 2, pp. 1107–09.

15. John Bennett, *Letters to a Young Lady, on a Variety of Useful and Interesting Subjects Calculated to Improve the Heart, to Form the Manners, and Enlighten the Understanding* (Warrington, 1789), vol. 1, p. 234.

16. Robert Burton, *The Anatomy of Melancholy* (1621; reprint, New York: Da Capo,

1971), p. 704; Henry Home, *Loose Hints upon Education, Chiefly Concerning the Culture of the Heart* (Edinburgh and London, 1781), p. 228.

17. *The Whole Duty of a Woman, or a Guide to the Female Sex. From the Age of Sixteen to Sixty,* 3rd ed. (London, 1701), pp. 48–49. The anonymous author was female.

18. Erasmus Darwin, *A Plan for the Conduct of Female Education, in Boarding Schools, Private Families, and Public Seminaries* (Philadelphia, 1798), p. 13. The book appeared in Derby and London editions in 1797. Although the author was male, the work is formatted in a series of letters from a mother to her daughter. For more information on the author and the text, see Kassler, *Science of Music,* vol. 1, pp. 263–64. Cf. *Euterpe,* p. 18; *The Polite Lady; or, a Course of Female Education,* 2nd ed., corrected (London, 1769), p. 24; and Hester Chapone, *Letters on Improvement of the Mind, Addressed to a Young Lady* (Hagerstown, Md., 1818–19), p. 193:

> It is but seldom that a private person has leisure or application enough to gain any high degree of excellence in [music]; and your own partial family are perhaps the only persons who would not much rather be entertained by the performance of a professor than by yours: but, with regard to yourself, it is of great consequence to have the power of filling up agreeably those intervals of time, which too often hang heavily on the hands of a woman, if her lot be cast in a retired situation.

(This book was first published in 1773, with four additional editions in Great Britain by 1783; it was published in American editions as late as 1834.)

19. See Leppert, *Music and Image,* pp. 16–27, 107–46.

20. Stanhope, *Letters to His Son,* vol. 1, p. 170.

21. Darwin, *Plan for the Conduct of Female Education,* p. 125. For a detailed treatment of this general issue see Leppert, *Music and Image,* pp. 29–45.

22. See, for example, William Darrell, *A Gentleman Instructed in the Conduct of a Virtuous and Happy Life* (London, 1704), p. 129.

23. *Euterpe,* pp. 6, 13–15.

24. See on this point Ellen G. D'Oench, *The Conversation Piece: Arthur Devis and His Contemporaries* (New Haven: Yale Center for British Art, 1980), pp. 21–22.

25. See further Leppert, *Music and Image,* pp. 43–45.

26. See ibid., pp. 201–04, for a discussion of a similar painting by Nollekens (fig. 93) and additional information about the artist.

27. See further ibid., pp. 99–105.

28. For other examples, see ibid., pp. 159–61, figs. 63–64, both by the artist Paul Sandby. For another, radically different, drawing by Lady Burlington from the same album see pp. 192–93, fig. 86.

29. Quoted in Alice Anderson Hufstader, "Samuel Pepys, Inquisitive Amateur," *Musical Quarterly* 54 (1968), p. 448.

30. Cf. a well-known drawing of similar sort by Thomas Gainsborough reproduced in John Hayes, *The Drawings of Thomas Gainsborough* (London: Yale University Press, 1971), no. 47; also reproduced in the Tate Gallery exhibition catalogue by John Hayes, *Thomas Gainsborough* (London: Tate Gallery, 1980), no. 26.

31. Little wonder that when Zoffany took up in paint the subject of music and sociability, what he projected in this drawing is present only as the most distant—dangerous—reflection. For example, see Leppert, *Music and Image,* pp. 91–92, fig. 25.

32. Romantic aesthetics attempted to locate art in a "disinterested" autonomous realm separate from a lived and mundane reality, viewed as debased. The ideal music, best able to claim autonomy, was nontexted, nonprogrammatic instrumental music (that is, music at its most abstract), never previously in Western history valorized so highly. Adorno pointed out that the plea for musical autonomy is not only ideological (a word which he used in its narrow sense of "false consciousness") but also unrealizable, in that art is incapable of being removed from lived social reality. But he argued that the ideology of aesthetic autonomy nonetheless incorporated a truth at its deepest core. By demanding to find in art something better than mundane reality, romantic aesthetics implicitly acknowledged the inadequacy of the social reality from which escape was sought through art. See further by Theodor W. Adorno, *Introduction to the Sociology of Music,* trans. E. B. Ashton (New York: Continuum, 1976), and especially *Aesthetic Theory,* ed. Gretel Adorno and Rolf Tiedemann, trans. C. Lenhardt (London: Routledge and Kegan Paul, 1984), though the translation of the latter is notoriously unreliable. For pertinent primary sources, see two excellent anthologies: Peter Le Huray and James Day, eds., *Music and Aesthetics in the Eighteenth and Early-Nineteenth Centuries* (Cambridge: Cambridge University Press, 1981); and Edward A. Lippman, ed., *Musical Aesthetics: A Historical Reader,* 2 vols. (New York: Pendragon, 1986–88).

33. See further Fredric Jameson, *Late Marxism: Adorno, or, the Persistence of the Dialectic* (London: Verso, 1990), pp. 146–47; and Herbert Marcuse, "The Affirmative Character of Culture" (1937), in *Negations: Essays in Critical Theory,* trans. Jeremy J. Shapiro (Boston: Beacon, 1968), p. 115.

34. *Philip Stubbes's Anatomy of Abuses in England in Shakespeare's Youth, A.D. 1583,* ed. Frederick J. Furnivall, vol. 1 (London: New Shakespeare Society, 1877), pp. 169–70.

35. Jeremy Collier, *Essays upon Several Moral Subjects. In Two Parts,* 2nd ed., corrected and enlarged (London, 1697), pp. 21, 24–25.

36. A closely related issue, to which I can only point, is the consumer's ability to produce his or her own meanings for what is consumed. One consumes meanings in consuming music, opening oneself, willingly or not, to the complicated processes of internalization and naturalization by which cultural and social identities are forged and then maintained. Saying this does not establish whether the identities forged are necessarily those dominant in the society and culture, but it does indicate that internalization and naturalization processes always act in relation to the dominant, even if specifically to oppose them. This fact was lost on no one philosophizing on music's relation to society in the eighteenth century. Indeed, every sort of written record I have alluded to acknowledges, implicitly or explicitly, that these are the stakes involved.

Yet when people "consume" meanings, their role is by no means entirely or even primarily passive, because consumption is inevitably always already production as well. Consumption, whether reading a novel or making or listening to music, involves an ongoing process of assessment: "rewriting." In the sense given to this term by post-modern cultural theory, the act of consumption is in part one of the reproduction of meanings, which are never identical to those of the "original." In other words, consumption is a component of human agency. To consume means to decide to consume (more so in history predating mass culture). Nonetheless, no reading is Archimedean; the force of sanctioned or preferred readings, established by the institutions of the socially dominant (state, church, education, and so forth), cannot be eliminated or even easily rendered marginal except over enormous spans of time, if at all, precisely because these readings are internalized into the gestures and practices of every discursive act prior to their ever being challenged.

CHAPTER 5

1. See further *Encyclopaedia Britannica,* 11th ed., s.v. "East India Company." The quotations are from p. 834.

2. J. H. Plumb, *England in the Eighteenth Century,* The Pelican History of England, no. 7 (Harmondsworth: Penguin Books, 1950), p. 174.

3. R. Pearson, *Eastern Interlude: A Social History of the European Community in Calcutta* (Calcutta: Thanker, Spink, 1954), pp. 65–66. See also Thomas G. P. Spear, *The Nabobs: A Study of the Social Life of the English in Eighteenth Century India* (London: H. Milford, 1932), p. 13.

4. Spear, *Nabobs,* p. 137.

5. Ibid., p. 129.

6. Mildred Archer, *India and British Portraiture, 1770–1825* (London: Sotheby Parke Bernet, 1979), p. 50.

7. See Spear, *Nabobs,* pp. 140–41; and Pearson, *Eastern Interlude,* pp. 171–76.

8. Spear, *Nabobs,* pp. 141–42; see also Plumb, *England in the Eighteenth Century,* pp. 177–78.

9. Allen Edwardes, *The Rape of India: A Biography of Robert Clive and a Sexual History of the Conquest of Hindustan* (New York: Julian Press, 1966), p. 15. For more on this subject see Edward Thompson and G. T. Garratt, *Rise and Fulfilment of British Rule in India* (London: Macmillan, 1934), pp. 306–17, covering the first half of the nineteenth century. For a good general study of the violence of British colonialism in India, see Edward Thompson, *The Making of the Indian Princes* (London: Oxford University Press, 1943). See Peter J. Marshall, *Problems of Empire: Britain and India, 1757–1813* (London: Allen and Unwin, 1968), pp. 191–92, for an extract from an 1813 speech by Charles Marsh, former barrister at Madras, "defending Hinduism against the denigration of missionaries and their supporters."

10. In England a man's house was his ultimate possession, the confirmation of his status. Accordingly, vast sums of money (often a family's whole substance) were spent to build, decorate, improve, maintain, and furnish the domestic enclosure. In India, where the class status of British immigrants was assured by Western birth, at least relative to the native population, the house and its furnishings asserted the racial superiority of its owners, thereby contributing to the estrangement of the two peoples.

Anglo-Indians, especially in major settlements like Calcutta, transplanted European building styles to the tropics, with only the slightest accommodation to practical necessity (such as adding venetian blinds to tall windows to keep out the afternoon sun, which made rooms uninhabitable). Thus only toward the end of the eighteenth century did the British acknowledge the advantages of coolness allowed by ground-floor rooms. Only slowly did they take to the practical one-story bungalows with shade-giving verandas in place of porticoed two-story neoclassical structures.

The English transplanted landscaping as well as architecture and design. In India, at great trouble and greater expense, Anglo-Indians often maintained English lawns and gardens, like those used in England to "frame" country houses. Beyond that—whether in elegant neoclassical mansions or in more modestly scaled bungalows—they furnished their houses by and large to mirror the life they had left, all impracticalities and expenses of importation aside (Spear, *Nabobs,* pp. 48–51). For a discussion of changing house designs during the eighteenth century, together with some information on the decoration of interiors and the use of furniture, see Pearson, *Eastern Interlude,* pp. 46–47, 80–82, 140–42. Mildred Archer, *Company Drawings in the India Office Library* (London: Her Majesty's Stationery Office, 1972), reproduces a watercolor drawing of a "classical European-style house with a garden in the foreground," cat. no. 93, plate 42. On the connection between architecture and ideology, albeit for a later period, see Thomas R. Metcalf, "Architecture and the Representation of Empire: India, 1860–1910," *Representations* 6 (1984), pp. 37–65. On the bungalow see especially Anthony King, "The Bungalow," *Architectural Association Quarterly* 5 (1973), pp. 6–25; and Sten Nilsson, *European Architecture in India, 1750–1850,* trans. Agnes George and Eleonore Zettersten (London: Faber, 1968), especially pp. 176–90, on the bungalow and the relation between architectural form and climate.

11. Zoffany, though a German, was active in England for many years. He resided in India between 1783 and 1789. For more information on his career in India, see Archer, *India and British Portraiture,* pp. 130–77; and the exhibition catalogue by Mary Webster, *Johan Zoffany, 1733–1810* (London: National Portrait Gallery, 1977), pp. 74–81, nos. 98–107, and pp. 14–16 of the introduction; William Foster, "British Artists in India, 1760–1820," *Walpole Society* 19 (1930–31), pp. 80–87; Sacheverell Sitwell, *Conversation Pieces: A Survey of English Domestic Portraits and Their Painters* (1936; reprint, London: Batsford, 1969), pp. 31–33; and Victoria Manners and G. C. Williamson, *John Zoffany, R.A., His Life and Works, 1735–1810* (London: John Lane, 1920), pp. 80–113. Manners and Williamson must be used with extreme caution; the book is notoriously unreliable. Unfortunately, it remains the only full-length monograph on the artist.

Zoffany's profits from his Indian sojourn, according to statements in several London newspapers early in 1785, were staggering: "The emigration of artists has received an additional spur by Zoffany's having already remitted home £36,000, accompanied with a letter which states that he intends coming home as soon as he has finished the portraits that are bespoke, which will produce to the amount of £30,000 more" (quoted in William T. Whitley, *Artists and Their Friends in England, 1700–1799* [London: Medici Society, 1928], vol. 2, p. 19). Many years later, in 1811, Zoffany's widow told a Miss Green, niece of the artist George Dance, that in India her husband had "made a considerable fortune by

His paintings & drawings" (quoted in Oliver Millar, *Zoffany and His Tribuna* [London: Routledge and Kegan Paul, 1967], p. 39). See also Foster, "British Artists," pp. 85–86. It seems that most of Zoffany's Indian earnings were realized from English sitters and not his Indian patrons.

The first professional English artist to visit India was Tilly Kettle, who resided there from 1769 to 1776. He returned to England at age forty-one, having already made a considerable fortune. See James D. Milner, "Tilly Kettle," *Walpole Society* 15 (1926–27), pp. 47–103 (with illustrations); pp. 64–74 cover Kettle's period in India; pp. 89–95 catalogue the paintings he executed there. Foster, "British Artists," pp. 56–57, refers briefly to Kettle. This study contains brief biographical summaries of the careers of sixty-one artists. Foster updated it in "Additional Notes to British Artists in India, 1760–1820," *Walpole Society* 21 (1932–33), pp. 108–09; Archer, *India and British Portraiture*, is the standard account on the general subject; its contents are also arranged by artist. The discussion on Kettle occupies pp. 66–97.

The Morse-Cator portrait is discussed in Webster, *Zoffany,* p. 76, cat. no. 101; and Archer, *India and British Portraiture*, pp. 137–38 (illustrated), from which my information on the sitters is drawn.

12. On the range of meanings for the word *nature* in the eighteenth century, see the outline by Arthur O. Lovejoy, "'Nature' as Aesthetic Norm," *Essays in the History of Ideas* (Baltimore: Johns Hopkins Press, 1948), pp. 69–77. I wish to thank Mary Bellhouse for drawing my attention to this article.

13. Robert Morris (c. 1702–1754), in his *Lectures on Architecture. Consisting of Rules Founded upon Harmonick and Arithmetical Proportions in Building* (London, 1734), explicitly connects architecture and music; John Archer, *The Literature of British Domestic Architecture, 1715–1842* (Cambridge: MIT Press, 1985), pp. 581–82, quotes and explains Morris:

> "Nature has taught Mankind in *Musick* certain Rules for Proportion of Sounds, so *Architecture* has its Rules dependant on those Proportions." [Morris] conceived a hierarchy of disciplines, all based on proportion, with architecture at the top: "The Square in *Geometry,* the Union or Circle in *Musick,* and the Cube in *Building,* have all an inseparable Proportion" (p. 74). Extending the musical analogy further, Morris established seven fundamental architectural proportions based on musical intervals, and he illustrated geometric solids based on those proportions in a plate facing page 75. The ratios of height, depth, and width in these solids are as follows: $1:1:1$ (a cube), $1:1:1\frac{1}{2}$ (a cube and a half), $1:1:2$ (a double cube), $1:2:3$, $2:3:4$, $3:4:5$, and $3:4:6$. In the sixth and seventh lectures Morris suggested that these architectural proportions would create a kind of beauty that would lead to perception of the greater harmony of all Nature: "Beauty, in all Objects, spring[s] from the same unerring Law in Nature, which, in *Architecture,* I would call Proportion. The joint Union and Concordance of the Parts, in an exact Symmetry, forms the whole a compleat Harmony, which admits of no Medium. . . . When I consider Proportions, I am led into a Profundity of Thought. . . . If we immerse our Ideas into the infinite Tract of unbounded Space, and with the Imagination paint out the numberless Multitudes of Planets, or little Worlds, regularly revolving round their destin'd Orbs . . . we must feel Emanations of the Harmony of Nature diffus'd in us; and must immediately acknowledge the Necessity of Proportion in the Preservation of the whole Oeconomy of the Universe" (pp. 81, 101–02).

Morris's book was reprinted in 1736 and published in a second edition in 1759. I thank my colleague John Archer for bringing this text to my attention.

14. From p. 200. John Keeble (c. 1711 – 1786) was organist at St. George's Church, Hanover Square, and later organist as well at Ranelagh Gardens. For the variety of critical responses to Keeble's book see Jamie Croy Kassler, *The Science of Music in Britain, 1714 – 1830: A Catalogue of Writings, Lectures, and Inventions* (New York: Garland, 1979), vol. 1, pp. 617 – 19. Kassler lists more than 50 printed texts dealing with music and mathematics, more than 200 dealing with proportions, and about 130 dealing with musical doctrines of antiquity. As one would expect, there is considerable overlap among these categories. Keeble's text, in other words, is representative of a much larger corpus of work generally concerned with this subject. See also John Neubauer, *The Emancipation of Music from Language: Departure from Mimesis in Eighteenth-Century Aesthetics* (New Haven: Yale University Press, 1986).

15. The famous extraordinarily long and detailed histories of music written in late-eighteenth-century England by Hawkins and Burney also devote a great deal of space to ancient Greek music theory. The discussions are as unremittingly tedious to the modern reader as they were apparently fascinating to their authors, whose willingness to cover every aspect of the theory seems limitless, even though the theory could be associated with only a few short musical examples. See Sir John Hawkins, *A General History of the Science and Practice of Music* (1776; reprint, Graz: Akademische Druck und Verlagsanstalt, 1969), vol. 1, pp. 1 – 68; Charles Burney, *A General History of Music, from the Earliest Ages to the Present Period,* 2nd ed. (London, 1789), vol. 1, pp. 1 – 108. For the short pieces reproduced by Burney, see vol. 1, pp. 86–91.

16. See Jean-Philippe Rameau, *Treatise on Harmony,* trans., with introduction and notes, by Philip Gossett (New York: Dover, 1971), pp. vii–xii, for information on publication history (the text is divided into four sections, the first two of which were first translated into English only with Gossett's modern edition; sections 3 and 4 were partially and freely translated in the eighteenth century); Kassler, *Science of Music,* vol. 2, pp. 863 – 71, gives information on eighteenth-century editions and English published reaction to them.

Although Hawkins only mentions Rameau's *Traité,* his overall assessment is complimentary: "As a theorist, the character of Rameau stands very high; and as a testimony to his merit in this particular, it is here mentioned as a fact, that Mr. Handel was ever used to speak of him in terms of great respect" (vol. 2, p. 901). Burney offers a two-paragraph reaction to the *Traité* that is little more than a challenge to its originality: "If any one were to ask me to point out what was the discovery or invention upon which his system was founded, I should find it a difficult task" (vol. 4, p. 612).

17. Rameau, *Treatise on Harmony,* p. xxxiii. Gossett points out in a footnote to the passage that Rameau's reference to the "Ancients" means "all musicians preceding Zarlino" (1517 – 1590) and that "there are few direct references to Greek theory in this treatise, but in his later writings Rameau cites the Greeks more freely."

18. Cuthbert Girdlestone, Albert Cohen, and Mary Cyr, "Jean-Philippe Rameau," *New Grove Dictionary of Music and Musicians,* ed. Stanley Sadie (London: Macmillan, 1980), vol. 15, p. 568. Cf. Rameau's definition in his *Génération harmonique* (Paris, 1737): "La

Musique est une Science Phisico-mathématique, le Son en est l'objet Phisique, & les rapports trouvés entre differéns Sons en sont l'objet Mathématique; sa fin est de plaire, & d'exciter en nous diverses passions." Quoted from Jean-Philippe Rameau, *Complete Theoretical Writings,* vol. 3, *Miscellanea,* ed. Erwin R. Jacobi (n.p.: American Institute of Musicology, 1968), p. 30 of the original, p. 29 of the facsimile reprint. This treatise was the first of his works to contain a dedication—significantly to the Académie Royale des Sciences. According to Jacobi, it represents "a first clear indication of [Rameau's] ambitions for a closer connection with that august body and of his striving through his theoretical works to raise music to the level of a scientific discipline in the spirit of the academy" (p. xix). The publication of this treatise elicited considerable discussion in Parisian periodicals (see pp. xxi–xxix), one writer deploring "the absence of the musician in the writer of *Génération,*" finding in its place "too much of the physicist and geometrician" (p. xxiv).

In his *Démonstration du principe de l'harmonie* (Paris, 1750)—with his text now "Approuvée par Messieurs de l'Académie Royale des Sciences," as proclaimed on the title page—Rameau states in the preface: "C'est dans la Musique que la nature semble nous assigner le principe Phisique de ces premieres notions purement Mathématiques sur lesquelles roulent toutes les Sciences, je veux dire, les proportions, Harmonique, Arithmétique & Géométrique, d'où suivent les progressions de même genre, & qui se manifestent au premier instant que résonne un corps sonore" (pp. vi–vii of the original, pp. 157–58 of the facsimile reprint).

19. Rameau, *Treatise on Harmony,* p. xxxv. Gossett notes the difficulty of following Rameau's "mathematical, pseudo-scientific explanations" which constitute book 1, pointing out that "the instinctive reaction of most readers . . . is simply to skip it" (p. xv). By far the best source for information on this general subject is Kassler, *Science of Music,* a compendium that amply demonstrates the extraordinary level of interest in the "philosophy" and "science" of music during the eighteenth century. See also Neubauer, *Emancipation of Music from Language,* pp. 76–84.

20. Quoted in Edward Said, *Orientalism* (New York: Vintage Books, 1978), p. 38; see also p. 35. Baring served in India prior to his time in Egypt.

21. Roland Barthes, *Writing Degree Zero,* trans. Annette Lavers and Colin Smith (New York: Hill and Wang, 1968), pp. 25–26. See also Said, *Orientalism,* which develops the following thesis, stated in the introduction (p. 3): "Without examining Orientalism as a discourse one cannot possibly understand the enormously systematic discipline by which European culture was able to manage—and even produce—the Orient politically, sociologically, militarily, ideologically, scientifically, and imaginatively during the post-Enlightenment period."

22. East Indiamen at least tolerated Indian music and sometimes appreciated it in the early decades of their occupancy. But "country musick," by the late eighteenth century, "was banished from public functions as it was from the army; instead European musicians multiplied and concerts began to be given." Whereas previously the East India Company itself had regularly made arrangements for Indian bands on great occasions, the "general verdict was [now] summed up by Major Blakiston when he wrote of the Indians: 'in fact they have no music in their souls'" (Spear, *Nabobs,* pp. 33–34).

About 1856 Captain George F. Atkinson produced a satire on the pettiness of British colonials, *"Curry and Rice," on Forty Plates, or, the Ingredients of Social Life at "Our" Station in India,* with an explanatory text provided for each plate. The book was lithographed in London and published without date. An edition also appeared in Calcutta in 1911. No. 6, "Our Magistrate's Wife," belittles a woman (Mrs. Chutney) whose Englishness is sadly affirmed by her meager but loudly proclaimed musical pretensions (much of the account describes the activities of Mrs. Chutney and her rivals in the church choir). For a brief discussion of the performance of European art music in India during the eighteenth century see Raymond Head, "Corelli in Calcutta: Colonial Music-Making in India during the Seventeenth and Eighteenth Centuries," *Early Music* 13 (1985), pp. 548–53. See pp. 551–52 regarding the interest in the music of India on the part of a few Anglo-Indians.

23. The stage effects evident in this portrait are not achieved accidentally. Zoffany was on close terms with David Garrick, whom he painted numerous times (along with other actors) in scenes from contemporaneous plays. Garrick, in fact, was Zoffany's first major English patron. For a discussion of these pictures, see Webster, *Zoffany,* pp. 9–10, and catalogue entries (some illustrated) 10, 15, 18, 23, 29, 33, 34, 47, 48, 50, 57–59, 65, 92, 94, 109, 110.

24. The Clitherow family was a line of London merchants descended from Sir Christopher Clitherow, lord mayor of London in 1635. My information on this painting comes from the exhibition catalogue by Ellen G. D'Oench, *The Conversation Piece: Arthur Devis and His Contemporaries* (New Haven: Yale Center for British Art, 1980), pp. 62–63, no. 37.

25. The shield mounted on the fluted pilaster at center has been in part identified; the right half corresponds to the arms of the Sussex branch of the family. See Sitwell, *Conversation Pieces,* p. 99, no. 55.

26. Two of the most important makers of harpsichords were the Swiss immigrant Burkat Shudi (1702–1773), and the Alsatian immigrant Jacob Kirckman (1710–1792), both of whose firms continued after the death of their founders—Shudi's eventually passed by marriage to Broadwood after the death of Shudi's son. Shudi numbered his instruments consecutively; the highest number known is 1115. Kirckman's instruments were not numbered (about 110 still exist), but about 2,000 are thought to have been made between 1750 and 1800.

As for cost, Shudi charged between 35 and 40 guineas for single-manual instruments, 50 guineas for the single-manual with an added "Venetian swell" device he invented, and 80 guineas for double-manual harpsichords with the swell. See further the entries in *New Grove* by Donald Howard Boalch and Peter Williams, "Kirckman," vol. 10, pp. 76–78, and "Shudi, Burkat," vol. 17, pp. 278–79; and Frank Hubbard, *Three Centuries of Harpsichord Making* (Cambridge: Harvard University Press, 1965), p. 159. On the Venetian swell see pp. 160–61. Keyboard instruments could be bought secondhand through shops—numerous newspaper and advertiser notices make that clear—and could also be rented.

By the 1760s five firms in and around London manufactured fortepianos; by the 1770s there were 15, by the 1780s 27, and by the 1790s at least 38. During the 1790s the

Broadwood firm was probably producing about 400 square and over 100 grand fortepianos a year, far more than competitive firms. See further Derek Adlam and Cyril Ehrlich, "Broadwood," *New Grove*, vol. 3, p. 324; and Derek Adlam and William J. Conner, "Pianoforte, 1,5," *New Grove*, vol. 14, p. 695. My information on piano firms was compiled from the list of makers in London and its environs, 1760–1851, in Rosamond E. M. Harding, *The Piano-forte: Its History Traced to the Great Exhibition of 1851* (1933; reprint, New York: Da Capo, 1973). Harding provides a history of the Shudi workshop and the Broadwood firm. See especially pp. 9–132.

According to Head, "Corelli in Calcutta," p. 550, harpsichords "were shipped to India as early as the 1760s (possibly earlier although no mention of one has been traced)." Regarding the availability of pianos and other instruments during the 1780s, see pp. 550–51.

27. See further Richard Leppert, *Music and Image: Domesticity, Ideology, and Socio-Cultural Formation in Eighteenth-Century England* (Cambridge: Cambridge University Press, 1989), pp. 28–50.

28. Cf. Derek Jarrett, *England in the Age of Hogarth* (Frogmore, St. Albans, Hertfordshire: Paladin, 1976), p. 126: "One problem had not changed with the changing attitude to women and to their intellectual achievements. Whatever form masculine condescension might take . . . it still assumed that marriage and motherhood should be the goals of all feminine endeavour." See further pp. 103–27; and Lawrence Stone, *The Family, Sex, and Marriage in England, 1500–1800,* abridged ed. (New York: Harper and Row, 1979).

29. In Zoffany's painting the violoncello played by Morse strengthens the sense of a blissful union of the two families. Stringed (hence Apollonian) instruments often served in marriage portraits as a sign of fidelity and the *mesure* of a good relationship—enhancing the sense of order and harmony. See the discussion in Chapter 1 and my comments on musical marriage symbolism in a portrait by Zoffany of the Cowper and Gore families (at the Yale Center for British Art) in "Men, Women, and Music at Home: The Influence of Cultural Values on Musical Life in Eighteenth-Century England," *Imago Musicae* 2 (1985), pp. 100–01, fig. 37.

30. Webster, *Zoffany*, p. 15. See pp. 89–91 for reproductions of some of the drawings, and also Archer, *India and British Portraiture*, especially pp. 165–67, figs. 101–06. The Blair portrait discussed later in this chapter (Fig. 45) is a further case in point.

31. For more on Renaldi's career in India, see Archer, *India and British Portraiture*, pp. 280–97 (the Cockerell-Blunt portrait is discussed and illustrated on pp. 288–89, from which comes my information on the sitters); and Foster, "British Artists," p. 65. A small ovular modello, reproducing the two women at the harpsichord, sold at Christie's, London, 17 March 1978, lot 63. Renaldi was active in India from 1786 to 1796.

32. According to Head, "Corelli in Calcutta," p. 550, where this painting is also reproduced, the harpsichord "would appear to be . . . a Kirckman or Shudi." The image is otherwise not discussed.

After returning to England, Charlotte, in 1794, married Charles Imhof, the stepson of Warren Hastings (governor-general of India from 1773 to 1785). As for Cockerell, following his retirement he built "a country mansion at Sezincote in the Cotswolds in which he celebrated his stay in India by incorporating in it motifs drawn from Indian architecture" (Archer, *India and British Portraiture*, p. 288).

33. The importance of oil portraits to Anglo-Indians can be measured by their willingness to pay the substantial British import duties charged against pictures when they were brought home. These levies increased so much that during the nineteenth century the popularity of oil portraits "declined until they came to be commissioned only when presentation pictures were needed for public buildings." (In 1803 the duty for a canvas under 2 feet square was 2 guineas; for a canvas about 8 feet square, 6 guineas. The levy was later increased.) Shipping was also expensive. See further Foster, "British Artists," pp. 1–2; and Mildred Archer and W. G. Archer, *Indian Painting for the British, 1770–1880* (London: Oxford University Press, 1955), p. 10, whence the quotation.

34. A biographical entry on D'Oyly appears in H. L. Mallalieu, *The Dictionary of British Watercolour Artists up to 1920* (n.p.: Antique Collector's Club, 1976), p. 87. The only detailed assessment of his life and work is that by Mildred Archer, "'The Talented Baronet': Sir Charles D'Oyly and His Drawings of India," *Connoisseur* 175 (November 1970), pp. 173–81, from which the bulk of my information about him is drawn.

Charles D'Oyly, 7th baronet, was born in Calcutta in 1781 and educated in England; he entered the service of the East India Company in Bengal in 1798. Between 1821 and 1832 he was stationed in Patna, on the River Ganges in Bihar, over three hundred miles northwest of Calcutta. His first assignment there was as opium agent, though he later served as commercial resident. (In 1838 he retired to Italy, where he died in 1845.)

In addition to his watercolor drawings, D'Oyly produced light verse, most notably a satirical poem, *Tom Raw, the Griffin* (1828), which, among other things, "ridicul(es) the daily life of the British in India" (Archer, "Talented Baronet," p. 175). In 1824 he established an art colony at Patna, intended for Anglo-Indians in the surrounding area. Patna was also the seat of a group of Indian painters attracted there by the British community and British travelers, to whom they sold their work. D'Oyly made contact with these painters and "showed them books of European prints and encouraged them to adjust their indigenous style to British taste. He purchased their work and sent it as gifts to his friends" (p. 177). D'Oyly set up a lithographic press at Patna to publish his portraits, views, and scenes of Indian life as well as caricatures.

In 1819 George Chinnery painted a portrait in Calcutta of Sir Charles and Lady D'Oyly (the head of D'Oyly was soon after engraved). Both sitters are in Vandyck dress, anachronistic, incongruent, and profoundly impractical (but unquestionably European) "presentation" garb. The portrait is reproduced and discussed briefly by Richard Ormond, "George Chinnery and the Keswick Family," *Connoisseur* 175 (December 1970), pp. 250–51, fig. 7; and by Archer, *India and British Portraiture*, p. 372.

For information on the opium trade organized by the East India Company (opium was exported chiefly to China), see Thompson and Garratt, *Rise and Fulfilment*, pp. 263–64.

35. Instruments shipped to India became very expensive. A Broadwood grand sent to Bengal, but ultimately stranded in Canton, in 1801 was sold to "the only Lady in this Settlement" for 130 guineas. In England at the same time, Broadwood was selling grands

to provincial agents (discounted) for about £73, though the price of individual instruments varied widely, depending on the quality and decoration of the case. See David Wainwright, *Broadwood, by Appointment: A History* (London: Quiller, 1982), pp. 99, 101–02, 105. By 1815 a Broadwood grand could be had for £48 with an ornamented cabinet. See Harding, *Piano-forte,* pp. 377–80.

The harp was as expensive as grand fortepianos. The London maker Johann Andreas Stumpff in 1827 charged £105 for a double-action pedal harp (although in the account from which this price is taken he indicates a willingness to offer a £30 discount). See Pamela J. Willetts, "Johann Andreas Stumpff, 1769–1846," *Musical Times* 118 (1977), p. 31.

36. In the summer room Lady D'Oyly is apparently accompanied on the fortepiano by a daughter. Lady D'Oyly played both the harp and the piano; she was judged an adept musician by a Captain Mundy who dined at Patna with the D'Oylys in 1829 ("in the evening we heard some beautiful music"). The D'Oylys' bungalow was a gathering place for English visitors (see Archer, "Talented Baronet," p. 179, whence the quotation).

The piano is shown from the front in the winter room, an angle allowing its identification as a Broadwood. Its shape and decoration appear different in the two drawings, as if to suggest that D'Oyly possessed two such instruments, whether or not this was actually the case. One instrument has a lyre-like pedal board not evident on the other. And one has a plain case, whereas the other is decorated, apparently with a line of inlay, on its circumference. On the identification of the Broadwood, see Helen Rice Hollis, *The Piano: A Pictorial Account of Its Ancestry and Development* (New York: Hippocrene Books, 1975), pp. 64–65; and Wainwright, *Broadwood, by Appointment,* pp. 128–29 (which repeats Hollis). Wainwright, p. 8, illustrates a Broadwood grand from 1810 that bears a marked similarity in its details to both instruments in D'Oyly's drawings. See p. 204, regarding the Broadwood company's care and success in shipping pianos to India.

The status of Broadwoods was sufficiently great to inspire imitation. In 1803 the firm ran advertisements in English-language newspapers in India asserting that in the previous nine years only three authentic Broadwoods had been sent to India (two grands and a "small one"), all others being "very imperfect" copies. From Wainwright, pp. 101–02.

37. Jarrett, *England in the Age of Hogarth,* p. 132.

38. The hookah had become popular among Anglo-Indians by the middle of the eighteenth century. "A hookah was more expensive than a pipe and required a hookahburdar [a servant], and it would therefore naturally come into fashion with increasing wealth and ostentation. To the new arrivals it was a luxury, and so, in spite of all their increasingly English tastes they were devoted to its charms. By 1778 it was 'universal.'" The preference for the hookah among the English in India declined in the early nineteenth century. Spear, *Nabobs,* p. 36. See also pp. 98–100.

39. See further D'Oench, *Conversation Piece,* p. 78, cat. no. 69; Sydney H. Pavière, *The Devis Family of Painters* (Leigh-on-Sea: F. Lewis, 1950), pp. 101–41 and plates 37–48. Pavière's account represents to date the fullest study of this painter, the nineteenth child of Arthur Devis, the famous painter of conversation pieces. In addition to a short biography, Pavière provides a list of 178 works arranged alphabetically by sitter. On Devis's

years in India, see pp. 101–06. The portrait of the Mason children is not included in this list of works. See also Archer, *India and British Portraiture,* pp. 234–69; and Foster, "British Artists," pp. 24–31, for an account of Devis's life and works during the years in India (1784–95).

40. Although Zoffany sometimes arranged Indian servants differently in group portraits of Anglo-Indians, the semiotic effect is identical. For example, in his portrait of the Auriol and Dashwood families (1783/87) five English men and two women in a landscape park are attended by four adult servants. See the color reproductions in Archer, *India and British Portraiture,* plate 5, discussed on pp. 158–60; and in Webster, *Zoffany,* p. 75, cat. no. 100. Similarly, his family group representing Sir Elijah and Lady Impey with their three children includes four servants and six Indian (traveling?) musicians, who accompany one of the Impey children who dances. Here the scene is crowded with native people to such an extent that the English sitters seem packed together, even though they occupy the front picture space and the natives the back. Semiotically the native peoples mark Impey's wealth and power. The inclusion of so many servants is, as far as I know, unprecedented in conversation pieces produced in England. Here, in other words, imperialism encourages the creation of a new convention in portraiture: not the absence of servants but an abundance of them. This painting is reproduced and discussed in Archer, *India and British Portraiture,* p. 136.

41. At the bottom end of the servant class were slave boys; the East India Company traded in slaves until 1764 and prohibited their export by proclamation only in 1789. See Pearson, *Eastern Interlude,* pp. 155–56, 158–59; and Dennis Kincaid, *British Social Life in India, 1608–1937* (London: G. Routledge and Sons, 1938).

42. Colonel Blair entered the Bengal army as a major in 1768. He was made governor of Chumar Fort by about 1780 and was promoted to colonel in 1781. He resigned his commission in 1788. My information on the sitters comes from the sale catalogue, Sotheby's, London, 18 March 1981, p. 64, lot no. 37 (illustrated); and Archer, *India and British Portraiture,* p. 157. See also Manners and Williamson, *John Zoffany,* p. 111, catalogue entry on p. 274.

43. Head, in whose "Corelli in Calcutta," p. 548, this painting is also reproduced, says the fortepiano is "probably" by Johannes Pohlmann or Johannes Zumpe. The image is not otherwise discussed.

44. None of the paintings, however, is known to exist, though Zoffany unquestionably executed scenes of Indian life, as I have already indicated. The smaller painting at left is almost completely undecipherable. Yet its very sketchiness adds credence to the possibility that it recalls an existing painting, since only the barest reminder of the other's form would mark the association. Archer, *India and British Portraiture,* p. 157, states flatly that the three pictures reproduce paintings "obviously by Zoffany himself." See further the Sotheby's catalogue entry referred to in n. 42

45. Leonard Bell, "Artists and Empire: Victorian Representations of Subject People," *Art History* 5 (1982), pp. 82–84, convincingly discusses examples from the mid-nineteenth century of European versions of "good" and "bad" natives. As he points out, the "good" natives (whether represented visually or in literary texts) have in common their

docility and passivity. Whereas non-European facial features are sometimes de-emphasized for "good" natives, they are exaggerated for the "bad," especially so as to make the non-Europeans appear coarse or ugly.

46. Nikolaus Pevsner, *The Englishness of English Art* (Harmondsworth: Penguin Books, 1964), p. 79; Fuseli is quoted on p. 31.

47. The process of discovery I have undertaken in this essay accords with Walter Benjamin's assertion, in *Ursprung des deutschen Trauerspiels* (1927), that truth is to be discovered in the *unintentional*, or as he—so characteristically and obliquely—put it, "Truth is the death of intention." (Adorno adopted this premise in his later formulation of negative dialectics.) See the detailed discussion of "unintentional truth" in Susan Buck-Morss, *The Origin of Negative Dialectics: Theodor W. Adorno, Walter Benjamin, and the Frankfurt Institute* (New York: Free Press, 1977), pp. 76–81, whence the quotation (p. 77).

48. Walter Benjamin, "Theses on the Philosophy of History," in *Illuminations*, ed. Hannah Arendt, trans. Harry Zohn (New York: Schocken Books, 1969), p. 256. Bell, "Artists and Empire," undertakes a complementary examination of several paintings executed in the mid-nineteenth century of native peoples in colonial Africa, Hong Kong, and New Zealand. He remarks (p. 73) that

> what unifies a seemingly bewildering variety of imagery is that most, if not all, of these representations had a common ideological base. They can be seen as attempts to fashion "realities" for the "natives"—"realities" primarily geared to prevailing British beliefs, values and interests—however much the "reality" asserted or implied might be at variance with socio-political, psychological and physical actualities as perceived by the "natives" themselves or by later European historians and critics.

Bell concentrates on European painters' reshaping of the very way native peoples looked, so as to convey their "meaning" to European viewers according to the fundamental tenets of colonial ideology. As he puts it, "British artists were fundamentally creating 'myths' or 'fictions,' that were important and necessary for the dominant culture in so far as they contributed to the 'justification' of its actions" (pp. 73–74).

49. Thomas Babington Macaulay, *The Works of Lord Macaulay* (London, 1898), vol. 11, pp. 567, 571, 586. I thank Derek Longhurst for drawing my attention to Macaulay's speech. See also Bernard S. Cohn, "Representing Authority in Victorian India," in *The Invention of Tradition*, ed. Eric Hobsbawm and Terence Ranger (Cambridge: Cambridge University Press, 1983), pp. 165–209; this essay relates to the 1857 uprising and its aftermath.

CHAPTER 6

1. Benjamin was in Moscow from 6 December 1926 to 1 February 1927. The reference to Asja in the chapter epigraph is to Asja Lacis, whom Benjamin loved; Reich is Bernhard Reich, a director who previously had been with the Deutsches Theater in Berlin, and who later married Asja (see further pp. 5–8; p. 9 nn. 2–3). I am grateful to my colleague Amitava Kumar for drawing my attention to this passage. Benjamin's account is

echoed, if more prosaically, by Max Weber's succinct phrase "a domestic instrument of the bourgeoisie"; quoted in Dieter Hildebrandt, *Pianoforte: A Social History of the Piano,* trans. Harriet Goodman (New York: Braziller, 1988), p. 123.

2. The bibliography on the gaze and woman is enormous, not only in histories of painting but also in film studies. As regards the former the locus classicus is John Berger, *Ways of Seeing* (Harmondsworth: Penguin Books, 1972), to which there is a growing body of critical response, most recently by Marcia Pointon, *Naked Authority: The Body in Western Painting, 1830–1908* (Cambridge: Cambridge University Press, 1990).

3. I will not consider house organs.

4. To the extent that the discourse is elevated, the Latin mottoes atone for the guilt of taking sonoric pleasure in a culture historically none too sure about pleasure in general. That story, however, begins well before the sixteenth and seventeenth centuries. See the account of ancient Greece by Michel Foucault, *The History of Sexuality,* vol. 2, *The Use of Pleasure,* trans. Robert Hurley (New York: Vintage Books, 1990).

5. On the frame see Jacques Derrida, *The Truth in Painting,* trans. Geoff Bennington and Ian McLeod (Chicago: University of Chicago Press, 1987), pp. 60–79.

6. I have discussed the nature of the counterclaim in another essay, "*Concert in a House:* Musical Iconography and Musical Thought," *Early Music* 7 (1979), pp. 3–17.

7. My dependency on Michel Foucault here is obvious; see especially *The Archaeology of Knowledge and the Discourse on Language,* trans. A. M. Sheridan Smith (New York: Pantheon Books, 1972); and *Discipline and Punish: The Birth of the Prison,* trans. Alan Sheridan (New York: Vintage Books, 1977).

8. See Simon Schama, *The Embarrassment of Riches: An Interpretation of Dutch Culture in the Golden Age* (New York: Knopf, 1987).

9. See Thomas McGeary, "Harpsichord Mottoes," *Journal of the American Musical Instrument Society* 7 (1981), p. 20, motto no. 8. This study provides a detailed list of harpsichord mottoes on surviving instruments and those preserved in paintings with musical subjects that include harpsichords. See also McGeary, "Harpsichord Decoration—a Reflection of Renaissance Ideas about Music," *Explorations in Renaissance Culture* 6 (1980), pp. 1–27; and Grant O'Brien, *Ruckers: A Harpsichord and Virginal Building Tradition* (Cambridge: Cambridge University Press, 1990), pp. 165–67.

10. McGeary, "Harpsichord Mottoes," p. 19, motto no. 4. For variants, p. 21, no. 15; and p. 34, no. 73. None of these is a Ruckers instrument.

11. Ibid., p. 21, motto no. 13.

12. Ibid., p. 23, motto no. 27.

13. Painted cases—especially lids—held special value among owners. See Jeannine Lambrechts-Douillez, "Documents Dealing with the Ruckers Family and Antwerp Harpsichord-building," in *Keyboard Instruments: Studies in Keyboard Organology,* ed. Edwin M. Ripin (Edinburgh: Edinburgh University Press, 1971), pp. 37–41. On the subject of French harpsichord decoration, principally bird and flower designs, see Sheridan Germann, "Monsieur Doublet and His *Confrères:* The Harpsichord Decorators of Paris," *Early Music* 8 (1980), pp. 435–53; and 9 (1981), pp. 192–207.

14. Regarding this instrument and its specifications, see Raymond Russell, *Victoria*

and Albert Museum Catalogue of Musical Instruments, vol. 2, *Keyboard Instruments* (London: Her Majesty's Stationery Office, 1968), p. 58, no. 28 (illustrated).

15. See further Richard Leppert, *The Theme of Music in Flemish Paintings of the Seventeenth Century* (Munich and Salzburg: Musikverlag Emil Katzbichler, 1977), vol. 1, pp. 224–34, and Leppert, *Music and Image: Domesticity, Ideology, and Socio-Cultural Formation in Eighteenth-Century England* (Cambridge: Cambridge University Press, 1989), pp. 183–88.

16. See Leppert, *Theme of Music,* vol. 1, pp. 234–36.

17. Other examples include a double virginal by Johannes Ruckers the Elder from 1591 in the collection of musical instruments at Yale University, described and illustrated in William Skinner, comp., *The Belle Skinner Collection of Old Musical Instruments: A Descriptive Catalogue* (privately printed, 1933), pp. 31–34; an Italian pentagonal spinet or virginal by Alexander Bertoloti from 1585 (the hunting scene may postdate the instrument itself), described and illustrated in *The Russell Collection and Other Early Keyboard Instruments in Saint Cecilia's Hall, Edinburgh* (Edinburgh: Edinburgh University Press, 1968), pp. 2–3; and a seventeenth-century Venetian harpsichord, described and illustrated in *Katalog der Sammlung alter Musikinstrumente,* vol. I, *Saitenklaviere* (Vienna: Kunsthistorisches Museum [Neue Burg], 1966), pp. 13–14, no. 10, pl. 4.

18. See Leppert, *Music and Image,* especially pp. 22–25, 107–29, about music and the effeminization of men. On this same topic in the nineteenth century see Craig H. Roell, *The Piano in America, 1890–1940* (Chapel Hill: University of North Carolina Press, 1989), p. 16.

19. The literature on the piano's role in the Victorian cult of domesticity is considerable, but for a succinct, insightful statement on the topic see Roell, *Piano in America,* pp. 3–28, from which I quote the following (p. 5):

> The piano became associated with the virtues attributed to music as medicine for the soul. Music supposedly could rescue the distraught from the trials of life. Its moral restorative qualities could counteract the ill effects of money, anxiety, hatred, intrigue, and enterprise. Since this was also seen as the mission of women in Victorian society, music and women were closely associated even into the twentieth century. As the primary musical instrument, the piano not only became symbolic of the virtues attributed to music, but also of home and family life, respectability, and women's particular place and duty. Indeed, most piano pupils were female, and both music making and music appreciation were distinctly feminized. The glorification of the piano was no mere fad; it was a moral institution. Oppressive and opulent, the piano sat steadfast, massive, and magnificent in the parlors and drawing rooms of middle-class homes, serving as a daily reminder of a sublime way of life.

The situation Roell describes in America parallels that in England. See also Arthur Loesser, *Men, Women, and Pianos: A Social History* (New York: Simon and Schuster, 1954), pp. 267–79; this study also provides much information on the music played in domestic settings in Western Europe and America. For more recent research on piano music produced in England see Nicholas Temperley, "The London Pianoforte School," *Musical Times* 126 (1985), pp. 25–27, which briefly describes the contents of his projected twenty-volume edition of this music, and Temperley, "London and the Piano, 1760–1860,"

Musical Times 129 (1988), pp. 289–93. For a good introduction to Victorian patterns of domestic consumption, and accompanying ideological apparatus, see Asa Briggs, *Victorian Things* (Chicago: University of Chicago Press, 1988), p. 248, on the piano; and Michelle Perrot, ed., *A History of Private Life,* vol. 4, *From the Fires of Revolution to the Great War,* trans. Arthur Goldhammer (Cambridge: Belknap Press of Harvard University Press, 1990).

20. This painting is illustrated and discussed in detail in my *Music and Image,* pp. 183–88.

21. See further Christoph Rueger, *Musical Instruments and Their Decoration: Historical Gems of European Culture,* trans. Peter Underwood (Cincinnati: Seven Hills Books, 1986), p. 58.

22. See F.-C. Legrand, *Les Peintres flamands de genre au XVIIe siècle* (Brussels: Editions Meddens, 1963), pp. 189–226; and Walther Bernt, *The Netherlandish Painters of the Seventeenth Century,* trans. P. S. Falla from 3rd German ed., 3 vols. (New York: Phaidon, 1970).

23. Luigi Russolo, *The Art of Noises,* Monographs in Musicology, no. 6, trans. Barclay Brown (New York: Pendragon, 1986), pp. 26–27.

24. See further Victor-Charles Mahillon, *Catalogue descriptif et analytique du Musée instrumental (historique et technique) du Conservatoire royal de musique de Bruxelles,* vol. 3 (1900; reprint, Brussels: Les Amis de la Musique, 1978), pp. 158–59, no. 1591.

25. See for example Albert Pomme de Mirimonde, *L'Iconographie musicale sous les rois Bourbons: La Musique dans les arts plastiques (XVIIe–XVIIIe siècles),* La vie musicale en France sous les rois Bourbons, no. 22 (Paris: Picard, 1975), pp. 62–65; and for a later period Dorothy M. Kosinski, *Orpheus in Nineteenth-Century Symbolism* (Ann Arbor: UMI Research Press, 1989), especially pp. 5–7, 81–90.

26. James Hall, *Dictionary of Subjects and Symbols in Art* (New York: Harper and Row, 1974), p. 230.

27. See Loesser, *Men, Women, and Pianos;* Leppert, *Music and Image,* pp. 147–75; and, for iconographical evidence, Lucas van Dijck and Ton Koopman, *Het klavecimbel in de Nederlandse kunst tot 1800 (The Harpsichord in Dutch Art before 1800)* (Zutphen: Walburg, 1987), with text in Dutch and English, a collection of 266 reproductions.

28. Male artistic creativity and the sexual identity of the male artist are the subjects of insightful discussion throughout Pointon, *Naked Authority,* as regards the painters Eakins, Delacroix, and Renoir.

29. See Alan Durant, "Improvisation in the Political Economy of Music," in *Music and the Politics of Culture,* ed. Christopher Norris (New York: St. Martin's Press, 1989), pp. 252–81. A second subject popular among seventeenth-century painters that also made its way onto harpsichord lids and restated male dominion over musical art was Apollo in concert with the Muses. In these compositions Apollo's privileged position is articulated via spatial hierarchy, Apollo forming the apex of a compositional triangle whose base is constituted by the Muses. For an example on an Italian harpsichord, circa 1600, see *Russell Collection,* pp. 4–5; for examples among seventeenth-century Flemish paintings see Leppert, *Theme of Music,* vol. 2, cat. nos. 5, 60, 96, 122, 124, 207 (illustrated p. 240), 219, 312, 389, 703 (illustrated p. 239). See also Albert Pomme de Mirimonde, "Les Concerts

des muses chez les maîtres du nord," *Gazette des beaux-arts,* 6th ser., vol. 64 (1964), pp. 253–84, and Mirimonde, *L'Iconographie musicale,* pp. 70–81.

30. See Chapter 3, n. 2, above.

31. See, for example, the historical account and bibliography in Edwin M. Ripin et al., *The New Grove Piano,* The Grove Musical Instrument Series, ed. Stanley Sadie (New York: Norton, 1988).

32. For an economic history see Cyril Ehrlich, *The Piano: A History* (London: Dent, 1976); for social histories see Loesser, *Men, Women, and Pianos;* and Hildebrandt, *Pianoforte: A Social History,* an account that centers on the great performer-composers of piano music rather than on amateurs; on the latter see pp. 121–27; and the important recent study by Andreas Ballstaedt and Tobias Widmaier, *Salonmusik: Zur Geschichte und Funktion einer bürgerlichen Musikpraxis,* Archiv für Musikwissenschaft, vol. 28 (Stuttgart: Steiner, 1989), especially pp. 183–236.

33. Concerning estimates of piano production in Europe, America, and Japan between 1850 and 1970, together with a list of makers since 1851, see Ehrlich, *Piano,* pp. 203–21. On this same topic, see also an essay by Ehrlich published as a monograph, *Social Emulation and Industrial Progress—the Victorian Piano,* New Lecture Series, no. 82 (Belfast: Queen's University, 1975). According to Ehrlich's calculations, "By 1910 there were some two to four million pianos in Britain—say one instrument for every ten to 20 people. Since few households contained more than one piano, even the lowest estimates imply that ownership was not confined to the middle classes" (p. 7). On the merchandising of pianos in the United States see Roell, *Piano in America,* pp. 139–82; and Christine Merrick Ayars, *Contributions to the Art of Music in America by the Music Industries of Boston, 1640 to 1936* (New York: H. W. Wilson, 1937), pp. 99–101; on piano prices to the midnineteenth century, together with a list of English makers around London, see Rosamond E. M. Harding, *The Piano-forte: Its History Traced to the Great Exhibition of 1851* (1933; reprint, New York: Da Capo, 1973), pp. 376–409. David Wainwright's *Broadwood, by Appointment: A History* (London: Quiller, 1982) contains valuable information about that firm's sales history, prices, and merchandising techniques.

34. Pierre Bourdieu, *Distinction: A Social Critique of the Judgement of Taste,* trans. Richard Nice (Cambridge: Harvard University Press, 1984), is the best recent study of the general topic.

35. See Leppert, *Music and Image,* especially pp. 11–70.

36. See C. F. Colt, with Antony Miall, *The Early Piano* (London: Stainer and Bell, 1981), p. 62, illustrating this use of the storage compartment of a Clementi upright grand from 1816.

37. See Norman E. Michel, *Historical Pianos, Harpsichords, and Clavichords* (Pico Rivera, Calif.: N. E. Michel, 1970), p. 164, illustrating such a use. For other examples and variants of this design, see Helen Rice Hollis, *Pianos in the Smithsonian Institution,* Smithsonian Studies in History and Technology, no. 27 (Washington, D.C.: Smithsonian Institution Press, 1973), pp. 25–27 (a Broadwood, c. 1815); and Clemens C. J. von Gleich, *Pianofortes uit de Lage Landen* (The Hague: Haags Gemeentemuseum in conjunction with Knuf, 1980), pp. 22–23, cat. no. 6 (text in Dutch and English).

38. See further Edwin M. Good, *Giraffes, Black Dragons, and Other Pianos: A Technological History from Christofori to the Modern Concert Grand* (Stanford: Stanford University Press, 1982); Nicholas Renouf, *Musical Instruments in the Viennese Tradition: 1750–1850,* exhibition catalogue (New Haven: Yale University Collection of Musical Instruments, 1981), p. 22, no. 16. For a mid-nineteenth-century American example of a small side table doubling as a piano, see Helen Rice Hollis, *The Piano: A Pictorial Account of Its Ancestry and Development* (New York: Hippocrene Books, 1975), p. 83, pl. 75. For additional information on the general topic see Andrew Clements, "Eccentric Pianos," in *The Book of the Piano,* ed. Dominic Gill (Ithaca: Cornell University Press, 1981), pp. 248–57; Harding, *Piano-forte,* pp. 264–66; and Franz Josef Hirt, *Meisterwerke des Klavierbaus: Geschichte der Saitenklaviere von 1440 bis 1880* (Olten: Urs Graf-Verlag, 1955), pp. 377–80.

39. Loesser, *Men, Women, and Pianos,* pp. 560–61; see further pp. 562–64, and p. 245. For an illustration of Wagner's combination writing desk and upright piano, made in 1864 by Bechstein and given to the composer by Ludwig II, see Norman E. Michel, *Old Pianos* (Pico Rivera, Calif.: Privately printed, 1954), p. 167.

40. Few instruments of this visually overwhelming design were included as props in contemporaneous paintings. The piano is a critical and defining object in middle-class family pictures, but it cannot be allowed to dominate the visual field; if it did so, it would mediate the place of music—and hence of women—to the relative disadvantage of the family males.

41. Timothy J. Clark, "Preliminaries to a Possible Treatment of *Olympia* in 1865," *Screen* 21 (1980), p. 36:

> Hair let down is decent, but unequivocal: it is some kind of allowed disorder, inviting, unkempt, a sign of Woman's sexuality—a permissible sign, but quite a strong one. Equally, hairlessness is a hallowed convention of the nude: ladies in paintings do not have hair in indecorous places, and that fact is one guarantee that in the nude sexuality will be displayed but constrained: nakedness in painting is not like nakedness in the world.

Clark points out that in images of hairless women, "pubic hair . . . was indicated by its absence." See also T. J. Edelstein, "'The Yellow-Haired Fiend'—Rossetti and the Sensational Novel," *Library Chronicle* 43 (1979), pp. 180–93; Michael Bartram, *The Pre-Raphaelite Camera: Aspects of Victorian Photography* (Boston: Little, Brown, 1985), pp. 139–41; and Anne Hollander, *Seeing through Clothes* (New York: Penguin Books, 1978), pp. 72–75. Perrot, *A History of Private Life,* vol. 4, p. 533: "Hair down, face illuminated by candles, eyes vacant, the female pianist was depicted [by male novelists] as a prey to male desire." On the specific and conscious Victorian associations between the piano and sexuality, see Roell, *Piano in America,* pp. 26–27.

42. The considerable nineteenth-century interest in female anatomy and its dissection was driven by far more than an interest in science as such. This history is well accounted for by Londa Schiebinger, "Skeletons in the Closet: The First Illustrations of the Female Skeleton in Eighteenth-Century Anatomy," *Representations* 14 (1986), pp. 42–82; as regards the interest in this subject among artists see France Borel, *The Seduction of Venus: Artists and Models* (New York: Skira/Rizzoli, 1990), especially the chapter "In Praise of

Flayed Souls," pp. 166–79; and Pointon, *Naked Authority,* pp. 35–58, concerning two paintings, *The Gross Clinic* and *The Agnew Clinic,* by Thomas Eakins.

43. The woman does not in fact perform a G to C cadence; in a single image that would be impossible since cadencing involves temporal sequence. In other words, in an image only one chord could be represented, not both. I believe Harper nonetheless signals his intent, not through an addition but via subtraction. Dominant to tonic chord movement requires three-note chords, so as to define unambiguously the sonorities involved. Instead, Harper gives us, not three notes, but two, a fourth apart. Although these two pitches may be "read" differently as regards the harmonies they imply, the most obvious suggestion is, I believe, the one offered here, especially given the larger context in which it occurs. Ruth Solie, in a private communication, rightly points out that if we read the notes not as an oblique reference to a cadence but simply as the interval of the perfect fourth, a very different signification is indicated. "The fourth is the most ambiguous of all intervals in tonality, consonant in acoustical theory but dissonant in practice, the one interval that demonstrates the helplessness of rationality in the face of experience."

44. See my comments on Enlightenment music theory in Chapter 5. Not coincidentally, the harmonic relationship, especially manifest in closing formulas, carries a powerful sonoric claim that this musical-social order is defined on the basis of male sexuality. That is to say, the dominant-tonic relationship typically played out in nineteenth-century music may often be read, reasonably though hardly necessarily, as semiotically phallic. The most interesting work on this matter to date is by Susan McClary, *Feminine Endings: Music, Gender, and Sexuality* (Minneapolis: University of Minnesota Press, 1991).

45. The painter draws on the traditional iconographical association between stringed instruments and the lyre of Apollo or Orpheus.

46. Cf. *At the Piano,* by James McNeill Whistler, in the Taft Museum, Cincinnati, reproduced in Hollis, *Piano,* p. 97, pl. 82. In Whistler's image the stringed instruments, a violoncello and violin, are housed in their cases, which lie on the floor beneath a grand piano seen in profile and played by Whistler's half sister.

47. Quoted from Graham Reynolds, *Victorian Painting,* rev. ed. (New York: Harper and Row, 1987), p. 93, cat. no. 59.

48. For more on the place of the dream or reverie in nineteenth-century European culture, see Perrot, *A History of Private Life,* vol. 4, pp. 512–18.

49. Roland Barthes, "Listening," in *The Responsibility of Forms: Critical Essays on Music, Art, and Representation,* trans. Richard Howard (New York: Hill and Wang, 1985), p. 257.

50. Penelope Fitzgerald, *Edward Burne-Jones: A Biography* (London: Hamilton, 1975), p. 71.

51. This vignette foreshadows a painting in the Metropolitan Museum of Art titled *Chant d'Amour* (1868–77) and a small watercolor version (1865) in the Boston Museum of Fine Arts. My information comes from Michael I. Wilson, "The Case of the Victorian Piano," *Victoria and Albert Museum Yearbook,* no. 3 (London: Phaidon, 1972), p. 140. Concerning the instrument's technical specifications, see Russell, *Victoria and Albert,* pp. 65–66, cat. no. 41 (illustrated).

52. A study drawing is held by the National Gallery of Victoria, Melbourne, dated

1860, according to Wilson, "Case of the Victorian Piano," p. 140, reproduced p. 141. Burne-Jones adopted the subject from the fresco *The Triumph of Death*, in Campo Santo, Pisa, which he saw in 1859; from the exhibition catalogue *The Pre-Raphaelites and Their Circle in the National Gallery of Victoria* (Melbourne: National Gallery of Victoria, 1978), no. 11. For more on this piano and its decoration see Fitzgerald, *Edward Burne-Jones*, p. 71. Concerning other instruments, especially Broadwood pianos, decorated by Burne-Jones, see further pp. 140–50; and Wainwright, *Broadwood, by Appointment*, pp. 209–12; and on the general subject of case decoration, David Wainwright, *The Piano Makers* (London: Hutchinson, 1975), pp. 113–18.

53. Burne-Jones himself liked "old Italian Music," notably Carissimi and Stradella; his wife's preferences are unknown. Fitzgerald, *Edward Burne-Jones*, p. 71.

54. As regards biographical details, it may be worth noting that Burne-Jones was fearful of marrying and later developed a strong attachment to another woman. See Jan Marsh, *The Pre-Raphaelite Sisterhood* (New York: St. Martin's Press, 1985), p. 176. About Burne-Jones's wife's musical talents see pp. 149, 151.

55. See, for example, Frank Mort, *Dangerous Sexualities: Medico-Moral Politics in England since 1830* (London: Routledge and Kegan Paul, 1987); Cynthia Eagle Russett, *Sexual Science: The Victorian Construction of Womanhood* (Cambridge: Harvard University Press, 1989); and Jeffrey Weeks, *Sex, Politics, and Society: The Regulation of Sexuality since 1800*, 2nd ed. (London: Longman, 1989).

56. See Chapter 8.

57. See Rudolf Wittkower, *Gian Lorenzo Bernini: The Sculptor of the Roman Baroque*, 2nd ed. (London: Phaidon, 1966), *Pluto and Proserpine*, pl. 12, cat. no. 10, p. 178; cf. *Apollo and Daphne*, pl. 14, cat. no. 18, pp. 183–84; and the painting *The Rape of the Sabines* by Nicolas Poussin in the Metropolitan Museum of Art.

58. See Max Horkheimer and Theodor W. Adorno, *Dialectic of Enlightenment*, trans. John Cumming (New York: Continuum, 1972), pp. 32–37, 43–80. The contradictory impulses defining Victorian male sexuality and the relation to art are traced by Richard Dellamora, *Masculine Desire: The Sexual Politics of Victorian Aestheticism* (Chapel Hill: University of North Carolina Press, 1990). Some of my information about the case decoration of this piano is drawn from Rueger, *Musical Instruments and Their Decoration*, pp. 87–88.

The decoration of instruments with battle scenes foreshadows the writing of so-called battle pieces for the piano (made with various gadgets to imitate appropriate noise) in the early nineteenth century. See Loesser, *Men, Women, and Pianos*, pp. 167–74, 243–44, 252–53, 448–50; and Albert E. Wier, *The Piano: Its History, Makers, Players, and Music* (London: Longmans, Green, 1941), pp. 42–45.

59. The most insightful study of this opera addressing the general subject of my concern is by Lawrence Kramer, "Culture and Musical Hermeneutics: The Salome Complex," *Cambridge Opera Journal* 2 (1990), pp. 269–94. The fascination of Salome as a subject for nineteenth-century painters is briefly addressed here as well, and at greater length by Bram Dijkstra, *Idols of Perversity: Fantasies of Feminine Evil in Fin-de-Siècle Culture* (New York: Oxford University Press, 1986), especially pp. 352–401.

60. See further my *Theme of Music*, vol. 1, pp. 201–13, 220–23.

CHAPTER 7

1. See Deborah Cherry and Griselda Pollock, "Woman as Sign in Pre-Raphaelite Literature: A Study of the Representation of Elizabeth Siddal," *Art History* 7 (1984), pp. 206–27; this essay also appears in Griselda Pollock, *Vision and Difference: Femininity, Feminism, and the Histories of Art* (London: Routledge, 1988), pp. 91–114, and should be read together with the chapter "Woman as Sign: Psychoanalytic Readings," pp. 120–54.

2. This is the subject of much of my book *Music and Image: Domesticity, Ideology, and Socio-Cultural Formation in Eighteenth-Century England* (Cambridge: Cambridge University Press, 1989).

3. Michel Foucault, *The History of Sexuality*, vol. 1, *An Introduction*, trans. Robert Hurley (New York: Pantheon Books, 1978), pp. 120–27.

4. See Leppert, *Music and Image*, pp. 168, 237 n. 2.

5. See ibid., pp. 63–65.

6. Sander L. Gilman, "Black Bodies, White Bodies: Toward an Iconography of Female Sexuality in Late Nineteenth-Century Art, Medicine, and Literature," *Critical Inquiry* 12 (1985), pp. 204–42. Quotation in this paragraph is from pp. 212–13.

7. See Valerie Steele, *Fashion and Eroticism: Ideals of Feminine Beauty from the Victorian Era to the Jazz Age* (New York: Oxford University Press, 1985), especially pp. 85–101, 161–91.

8. Leo Tolstoy, *The Kreutzer Sonata and Other Stories*, trans. David McDuff (Harmondsworth: Penguin Books, 1985), pp. 25–118. The translator's introduction provides valuable background information about the long gestation of the novella; its relation to Tolstoy's own marriage; the critical reaction to the story, which in fact occurred even before publication of the final version because of the wide and fast circulation of unauthorized drafts; and Tolstoy's lengthy attempt to respond to his scandalized critics via a postface (reprinted on pp. 267–82). My information on the writing of the story comes from the translator's introduction. For a relatively recent list of critical studies of the novella, see David R. Egan and Melinda A. Egan, *Leo Tolstoy: An Annotated Bibliography of English-Language Sources to 1978* (Metuchen, N.J.: Scarecrow Press, 1979), pp. 98–101. Most of the sources listed date from near the story's original publication; critical opinion of Tolstoy's extreme views on sexuality, women, and marriage was principally negative.

9. On Tolstoy's wife, Sofya Andreyevna, and her "pathetic infatuation" in the mid-1890s with a concert pianist and family acquaintance that involved indiscretion but no sexual infidelity, see Ruth Crego Benson, *Women in Tolstoy: The Ideal and the Erotic* (Urbana: University of Illinois Press, 1973), p. 113. Concerning Tolstoy's misogyny in both the novella and his marriage see Andrea Dworkin, *Intercourse* (New York: Free Press, 1987), pp. 3–20.

10. See April Fitzlyon, "Tolstoy, Lev Nikolayevich," *The New Grove Dictionary of Music and Musicians*, ed. Stanley Sadie (London: Macmillan, 1980), vol. 19, pp. 31–32.

11. From the postface (p. 268). "Abstinence is possible, and is less dangerous and injurious to the helath than non-abstinence: every man will find around him a hundred proofs of this"; this line of thought is followed by ten pages of argument employing Christ

as the ideal. While Tolstoy was working on the novella, he secured a gynecological manual by an American, Alice Bunker Stockham (whom he met in 1889), part of which dealt with marital chastity and advocated sexual abstinence during pregnancy; Tolstoy incorporated material from the book into his novella. He also obtained American Shaker tracts, which preached total sexual abstinence. This information is from Tolstoy, *Kreutzer Sonata*, p. 14 (introduction). For more about Tolstoy's position on these issues see Benson, *Women in Tolstoy,* especially pp. 1–15 and, on "The Kreutzer Sonata" in particular, pp. 111–38, which also take up two other late stories espousing a radical position on women and sex, "The Devil" and "Father Sergius."

12. Benson, *Women in Tolstoy,* p. 120, goes further: "She is neither personalized nor distinguished from any other woman. Anonymously and archetypally, she is Sexual Woman."

13. See Gilman, "Black Bodies, White Bodies": "One excellent example of the conventions of human diversity captured in the iconography of the nineteenth century is the linkage of two seemingly unrelated female images—the icon of the Hottentot female and the icon of the prostitute" (p. 206).

14. See further Ben Karpman, "*The Kreutzer Sonata:* A Problem in Latent Homosexuality and Castration," *Psychoanalytic Review* 25 (1938), pp. 20–48. But note Karpman's views on the "innocence" of music in its relation to sexuality: "Our man's comments on the playing of the Kreutzer Sonata are striking. So preoccupied is his mind with sexuality that he sees sex and nothing but sex in a beautiful but otherwise wholly innocent piece of music. To him it has only one effect—that of erotic stimulation" (p. 33). See also I. Velikovsky, "Tolstoy's Kreutzer Sonata and Unconscious Homosexuality," *Psychoanalytic Review* 24 (1937), pp. 18–25. Velikovsky (p. 21) draws attention to Tolstoy's fixation on buttocks, whereas Karpman oddly ignores this crucial passage.

15. The same overdose of sexual energy was attributed to several nineteenth-century virtuosos, nearly always violinists and pianists (Paganini, Mendelssohn, Liszt, Rubinstein); see Mary Burgan, "Heroines at the Piano: Women and Music in Nineteenth-Century Fiction," *Victorian Studies* 30 (1986), p. 66.

16. My thanks to Lawrence Kramer for the following insight, conveyed in a private communication, concerning the musician's body: Tolstoy's fixated

> description of Trukhachevsky, with his red lips and bulging bottom, suggests to me that masculine desire, the result of unstinted participation in a libidinal economy, is in and of itself feminizing within the nineteenth-century bourgeois order. The man who becomes the subject of desire finds himself prompted to identify with the object of desire, and thus paradoxically defaces himself as a masculine subject. Worse yet, the character of this identification suggests that (masculine) desire entails the (feminine) desire to be desired, to relate to the object of desire not as a proprietor but, uncertainly and ambivalently, as both property and interlocuter. Hence on the one hand Trukhachevsky's stylishness, his effort to look attractive, and on the other, some facts about Pozdnyshev: his discovery that he wanted to take total possession of his wife's body only to find that she could [do] what she liked with it, his conversation with her on her deathbed, and his actual (latter-day) experience of desire only in the displaced form of her murder, with its penetration through a protective barrier into "something soft" [p. 113] and so on.

17. Quoted from Lynda Nead, *Myths of Sexuality: Representations of Women in Victorian Britain* (Oxford: Blackwell, 1988), p. 6. See further pp. 1–44.

18. Ibid., p. 36.

19. The recent literature on this topic is considerable, but among the most important work is that of Elaine Showalter, *The Female Malady: Women, Madness, and English Culture, 1830–1980* (New York: Pantheon Books, 1985). Showalter points out that a woman's erotic fantasies were considered symptomatic of clinical nymphomania, as was orgasmic excitement of any kind. For a briefer account see Showalter, "Victorian Women and Insanity," *Victorian Studies* 23 (1980), pp. 157–81; and Elizabeth Sheehan, "Victorian Clitoridectomy: Isaac Baker Brown and His Harmless Operative Procedure," *Medical Anthropology Newsletter* 12 (1981), pp. 9–15. See also Catherine Gallagher and Thomas Laqueur, eds., *The Making of the Modern Body: Sexuality and Society in the Nineteenth Century* (Berkeley and Los Angeles: University of California Press, 1987); and Mary Poovey, *Uneven Developments: The Ideological Work of Gender in Mid-Victorian England* (Chicago: University of Chicago Press, 1988).

20. Benson, *Women in Tolstoy,* p. 2.

21. The best formulation of this issue I know is Max Horkheimer and Theodor W. Adorno, *Dialectic of Enlightenment,* trans. John Cumming (New York: Continuum, 1972).

22. See Leppert, *Music and Image,* pp. 35–45.

23. See n. 9, above.

24. Leo Tolstoy, *What is Art? and Essays on Art,* trans. Aylmer Maude (London: Oxford University Press, 1930).

25. See Sander L. Gilman, *Disease and Representation: Images of Illness from Madness to AIDS* (Ithaca: Cornell University Press, 1988).

26. All passages quoted here are from Tolstoy, *What is Art?,* p. 222.

27. See also Dorothy Green, "'The Kreutzer Sonata': Tolstoy and Beethoven," *Melbourne Slavonic Studies* 1 (1967), pp. 11–23. To my knowledge this represents the only previous attempt to sort out the relation of Beethoven's music to the larger story; however, Green's intent, quite different from mine, is to suggest strong parallels between the formal structure and narratology of the novella and basic sonata procedure. I am not entirely convinced by her account, but it is often both smart and insightful. Thus with regard to Tolstoy's initially envisaging that the story would be read aloud, that is, be performed, she points out that, like music, it was "intended to make its appeal largely through the ear. The voice is the literary equivalent for the instruments; it has to carry the burden of the statement that Tolstoy reads, or hears, in the music" (p. 12).

28. My thanks to Lawrence Kramer who in a private communication noted,

> What's striking to me is the monumentality and unremitting intensity of the "concertante" sonata form as applied or imported into the salon medium of the violin sonata, suggesting an oratorical fury threatening to erupt amid polite conversation, or, more dangerously, the unsocialized energies latent within polite conversation. The strains of sublimation are still audible, deliberately, I think, in the second movement; the problem finale, composed originally for another sonata, is like a sudden shrug of compliance.

29. Once more, an insight from Lawrence Kramer, privately conveyed, which moves in a direction somewhat different from mine:

It's interesting to note that the erotic music that passes between Trukhachevsky and the wife is played only *after* the *Kreutzer* and that Pozdnyshev can remember it only in retrospect. His reaction to the sonata itself is to perceive it (less, perhaps, as the phallic display you describe, though there's a connection, than) as a vehicle of transcendence, of a spirituality quite inconsistent with the lust, *decolleté* and triviality of the drawing room. . . . Pozdnyshev's rage and resentment may thus come from his understanding, suggested specifically in the displaced erotic music and generally throughout the story, that this visionary experience of his can be generated only through the sleazy, illicit medium of music, the medium, above all, of the feminine and feminizing body. Hence, perhaps, a telling image: the dying wife lies on *his side* of the bed [p. 116].

30. Eve Kosofsky Sedgwick, *Between Men: English Literature and Male Homosocial Desire* (New York: Columbia University Press, 1985), pp. 1–2. Her study is based primarily on English novels published between 1750 and 1850 and thus complements the period of my own concerns.

31. See Leppert, *Music and Image,* pp. 168, 237 n. 2.

32. For a literary analogue see Carol Christ, "Victorian Masculinity and the Angel in the House," in *A Widening Sphere: Changing Roles of Victorian Women,* ed. Martha Vicinus (Bloomington: Indiana University Press, 1977), pp. 146–62. Christ examines a similar phenomenon in Coventry Patmore, "The Angel in the House" (see n. 35, below), and Tennyson, "The Princess," focusing on representations of masculinity that valorize male feminization. See also Richard Dellamora, *Masculine Desire: The Sexual Politics of Victorian Aestheticism* (Chapel Hill: University of North Carolina Press, 1990), which approaches the question in terms of homosexual desire.

33. See John Carl Flugel, *The Psychology of Clothes* (London: Hogarth Press, 1930), pp. 117–19; and Kaja Silverman, "Fragments of a Fashionable Discourse," in *Studies in Entertainment: Critical Approaches to Mass Culture,* ed. Tania Modleski (Bloomington: Indiana University Press, 1986), pp. 139–52.

34. The subject is undoubtedly closely related to the so-called New Woman phenomenon in late-Victorian England and America, on which see Susan P. Casteras, *Images of Victorian Womanhood in English Art* (London: Associated University Presses, 1987), pp. 144–46.

35. Thus William Acton, *The Functions and Disorders of the Reproductive Organs in Youth, in Adult Age, and in Advanced Life, Considered in Their Physiological, Social, and Psychological Relations,* 4th ed. (London, 1865), p. 114: The "perfect ideal of an English wife and mother [is] kind, considerate, self-sacrificing, and sensible, so pure-hearted as to be utterly ignorant of and averse to any sensual indulgence." The best known literary analogue to Acton's commonly held thesis is Coventry Patmore's epic-length poem celebrating domesticity, "The Angel in the House" (1854–56), which sold a quarter million copies in the last half of the century: "She is so perfect, true and pure, / Her virtue all virtue so endears, / That, often, when he thinks of her, / Life's meanness fills his eyes with tears" (quoted from the 1st ed., p. 45).

The bibliography concerning the construction of female sexuality in the nineteenth century is considerable, but among the most useful recent studies see Bram Dijkstra, *Idols of Perversity: Fantasies of Feminine Evil in Fin-de-Siècle Culture* (New York: Oxford University Press, 1986), fundamentally a visual study, whose principal contribution may be the encyclopedic range of the source material, if not necessarily the interpretations (the book is well indexed and provides access to subjects like the Medusa figure and woman as snake); Deborah Gorham, *The Victorian Girl and the Feminine Ideal* (Bloomington: Indiana University Press, 1982); Frank Mort, *Dangerous Sexualities: Medico-Moral Politics in England since 1830* (London: Routledge and Kegan Paul, 1987), especially pp. 77–85; Nead, *Myths of Sexuality,* focusing on visual representations of deviant female sexuality, the adulteress, and the prostitute; Cynthia Eagle Russett, *Sexual Science: The Victorian Construction of Womanhood* (Cambridge: Harvard University Press, 1989), concerning Anglo-American science on sexual and gender difference, the history of which parallels and depends on the social and moral philosophies regarding the inferiority of women: in general science held that "though she might not be evil she was most certainly flawed" (p. 74); Eric Trudgill, *Madonnas and Magdalens: The Origins and Development of Victorian Sexual Attitudes* (New York: Holmes and Meier, 1976); and Jeffrey Weeks, *Sex, Politics, and Society: The Regulation of Sexuality since 1800,* 2nd ed. (London: Longman, 1989). The best theoretical work I know concerning gender construction and its status as both a representation and a social relation is by Teresa de Lauretis. For a succinct statement of her thinking see "The Technology of Gender," in *Technologies of Gender: Essays on Theory, Film, and Fiction* (Bloomington: Indiana University Press, 1987), pp. 1–30.

36. See also Nina Auerbach, *Woman and the Demon: The Life of a Victorian Myth* (Cambridge: Harvard University Press, 1982), which takes up the question of the extra-domestic female in the Victorian imagination in literature, essays, letters, and memoirs as well as visual art. Auerbach recognizes "a vital Victorian mythology whose lovable woman is a silent and self-disinherited mutilate, the fullness of whose extraordinary and dangerous being might at any moment return through violence. The taboos that encased the Victorian woman contained buried tributes to her disruptive power" (p. 8). It is her disruptive power that Auerbach investigates. Concerning Rossetti's representation of "serpentine hands" see pp. 48–51. On the Medusa figure see further Mario Praz, *The Romantic Agony,* trans. Angus Davidson (Cleveland: Meridian Books, 1956), pp. 25–50; Pollock, *Vision and Difference,* p. 139; and Neil Hertz, "Medusa's Head: Male Hysteria under Political Pressure," *Representations* 4 (1983), pp. 27–54.

37. For more on this painting, by Sir John Everett Millais, see the exhibition catalogue, *The Pre-Raphaelites* (London: Tate Gallery/Harmondsworth: Penguin Books, 1984), no. 29, pp. 81–82.

38. For other examples of the tiff as a subject in Victorian painting, see Susan P. Casteras, "Down the Garden Path: Courtship Culture and Its Imagery in Victorian Painting," Ph.D. diss., Yale University, 1977, pp. 290–97, 570–71.

39. See E. D. Mackerness, *A Social History of English Music* (London: Routledge and Kegan Paul, 1964), pp. 172–80, 231–32; and, especially, Derek Scott, *The Singing Bourgeois: Songs of the Victorian Drawing Room and Parlour* (Milton Keynes: Open University Press, 1989).

40. See Chapter 6, n. 8, regarding a complementary view of male creativity among painters.

1. William Holman Hunt's *Awakening Conscience* is perhaps the most written-about English painting from its decade; indeed, few other Victorian pictures to the end of the nineteenth century have attracted as much scholarly attention—a description of the picture serves as the opening paragraph of the recent, rather sensational, study by Bram Dijkstra, *Idols of Perversity: Fantasies of Feminine Evil in Fin-de-Siècle Culture* (New York: Oxford University Press, 1986), p. 3. In addition to the sources cited throughout this essay I must mention one study that was not available to me: Anne J. d'Harnoncourt, *"The Awakening Conscience:* A Study in Moral Subject Matter in Pre-Raphaelite Paintings," master's thesis, Courtauld Institute of Art, University of London, 1967. On visual antecedents to this painting see Susan P. Casteras, "Down the Garden Path: Courtship Culture and Its Imagery in Victorian Painting," Ph.D. diss., Yale University, 1977, pp. 433–44.

2. Cf. Roland Barthes, "Diderot, Brecht, Eisenstein," *Image, Music, Text,* trans. Stephen Heath (New York: Hill and Wang, 1977), pp. 73–74, concerning what he calls "social gest": "It is a gesture or set of gestures (but never a gesticulation) in which a whole social situation can be read. Not every gest is social: there is nothing social in the movements a man makes in order to brush off a fly; but if this same man, poorly dressed, is struggling against guard-dogs, the gest becomes social."

3. Diana Holman-Hunt, *My Grandfather, His Wives and Loves* (New York: Norton, 1969), p. 113.

4. Michel Foucault, *The History of Sexuality,* vol. 1, *An Introduction,* trans. Robert Hurley (New York: Pantheon Books, 1978). On the general topic of prostitution, much researched, see Judith R. Walkowitz, *Prostitution and Victorian Society: Women, Class, and the State* (New York: Cambridge University Press, 1980); E. M. Sigsworth and T. J. Wyke, "A Study of Victorian Prostitution and Venereal Disease," in *Suffer and Be Still: Women in the Victorian Age,* ed. Martha Vicinus (Bloomington: Indiana University Press, 1973), pp. 77–99; Steven Marcus, *The Other Victorians: A Study of Sexuality and Pornography in Mid-Nineteenth-Century England* (New York: Basic Books, 1966).

5. Lise Vogel, "Fine Arts and Feminism: The Awakening Consciousness," in *Feminist Art Criticism: An Anthology,* ed. Arlene Raven, Cassandra Langer, and Joanna Frueh (Ann Arbor: UMI Research Press, 1988), p. 51: "In the milieu of the pre-Raphaelite painters, no real distinction existed between modeling and prostitution." Regarding Pre-Raphaelite photography and the sexual relationships involving artists' models see also p. 57. Hunt, as we know, did not behave in this manner. See also Holman-Hunt, *My Grandfather,* pp. 66–68.

6. Gay Daly, *Pre-Raphaelites in Love* (New York: Ticknor and Fields, 1989), p. 112.

7. Credit for the identification of Annie Miller as Hunt's model for *The Awakening Conscience* goes to Oswald Doughty, *A Victorian Romantic: Dante Gabriel Rossetti* (London: Muller, 1949), pp. 258–59. A great deal has recently been written about Annie Miller and her relationship to Holman Hunt, though much of it repeats from one text to another. Many of the details in this chapter are drawn from these studies. See especially Holman-Hunt, *My Grandfather,* the principal source of information; Daly, *Pre-Raphaelites in Love,*

pp. 101–08, 113–26, 132–37; Jan Marsh, *The Pre-Raphaelite Sisterhood* (New York: St. Martin's Press, 1985); G. H. Fleming, *That Ne'er Shall Meet Again: Rossetti, Millais, Hunt* (London: Joseph, 1971).

8. Holman-Hunt, *My Grandfather,* pp. 97–99, 113–14; and James H. Coombs et al., eds., *A Pre-Raphaelite Friendship: The Correspondence of William Holman Hunt and John Lucas Tupper* (Ann Arbor: UMI Research Press, 1986), p. 53 n. 1.

9. Regarding the slow deterioration of their relationship see Holman-Hunt, *My Grandfather,* pp. 173–80, 188–89, 194–210. Annie Miller died at age ninety in 1925, having spent her adult life financially secure, happily married to Sir Thomas Ranelagh Thomson, first cousin to Lord Ranelagh, to whom she had been, like her defaced self in *The Awakening Conscience,* mistress after leaving Hunt's employ-embrace. From Holman-Hunt, *My Grandfather,* pp. 228–29. Concerning her husband, see p. 166; see also pp. 223–29 and 245–49 regarding her blackmail of Hunt—at the instigation of her future husband! Regarding the blackmail see also the lucid commentary by Daly, *Pre-Raphaelites in Love,* pp. 135–37.

10. Daly, *Pre-Raphaelites in Love,* p. 135; on the relation between Hunt's "reputation for Christian purity" and the successful sale of his paintings, see p. 134.

11. Quoted in Jeremy Maas, *Holman Hunt and "The Light of the World"* (London: Scholar Press, 1984), p. 46.

12. Holman-Hunt, *My Grandfather,* p. 205.

13. Ibid.

14. See Georg Simmel, *The Philosophy of Money,* trans. Tom Bottomore and David Frisby (1900; reprint, London: Routledge and Kegan Paul, 1978), p. 383.

15. On the moral panic surrounding prostitution and its relation to political crises, see Lynn Nead, "The Magdalen in Modern Times: The Mythology of the Fallen Woman in Pre-Raphaelite Painting," in *Looking On: Images of Femininity in the Visual Arts and Media,* ed. Rosemary Betterton (London: Pandora, 1987), pp. 82–83.

16. See Richard Leppert, *Music and Image: Domesticity, Ideology, and Socio-Cultural Formation in Eighteenth-Century England* (Cambridge: Cambridge University Press, 1989), pp. 16–27.

17. See Jeffrey Weeks, *Sex, Politics, and Society: The Regulation of Sexuality since 1800,* 2nd ed. (London: Longman, 1989).

18. Marcus, *Other Victorians,* p. 159.

19. John Berkenhout, *A Volume of Letters from Dr Berkenhout to His Son at the University* (Cambridge, 1790), vol. 1, p. 189. I have further addressed this issue in *Music and Image,* pp. 22, 24, 127, 129.

20. Michel Foucault, *The History of Sexuality,* vol. 2: *The Use of Pleasure,* trans. Robert Hurley (New York: Vintage Books, 1990).

21. John Ruskin, "The Relation of Art to Morals," in *Lectures on Art, Lectures on Landscape, Aratra Pentelici,* vol. 14 of *The Complete Works* (New York: Thomas Y. Crowell, n.d.), p. 46. Concerning Ruskin's views on the use and moral value of art, see George P. Landow, *The Aesthetic and Critical Theories of John Ruskin* (Princeton: Princeton University Press, 1971), pp. 53–68. See also William J. Gatens, "John Ruskin and Music," *Victorian Studies* 30 (1986), pp. 77–97.

22. For a commentary on Ruskin's reading of Hunt's painting, see James Thompson, "Ruskin and Hunt's 'Awakening Conscience,'" *Victorian Institute Journal* 8 (1979), pp. 19–29.

23. Regarding the economic constitution of the Victorian middle class, including population tables and occupations, see Patricia Branca, *Silent Sisterhood: Middle Class Women in the Victorian Home* (Pittsburgh: Carnegie-Mellon University Press, 1975), pp. 38–45, and, for comparison, domestic servants' incomes, pp. 54–55. See also the excellent thorough study by Leonore Davidoff and Catherine Hall, *Family Fortunes: Men and Women of the English Middle Class, 1780–1850* (London: Hutchinson, 1987).

24. George P. Landow, *William Holman Hunt and Typological Symbolism* (London: Yale University Press for the Paul Mellon Centre for Studies in British Art, 1979), p. 48; Nead, "Magdalen in Modern Times," p. 89; and Caroline Arscott, "Employer, Husband, Spectator: Thomas Fairbairn's Commission of *The Awakening Conscience*," in *The Culture of Capital: Art, Power, and the Nineteenth-Century Middle Class,* ed. Janet Wolff and John Seed (Manchester: Manchester University Press, 1988), p. 186.

25. See Donald M. Lowe, *The History of Bourgeois Perception* (Chicago: University of Chicago Press, 1982), pp. 37–38.

26. For a fuller accounting of the myriad objects in the painting and their potential iconographical significance see Ronald Parkinson, "The Awakening Conscience and the Still Small Voice," in *The Tate Gallery Illustrated Biennial Report and Catalogue of Acquisitions {1976–1978}* (London: Tate Gallery Publications, 1978), p. 26; Susan P. Casteras, *Images of Victorian Womanhood in English Art* (London: Associated University Presses, 1987), pp. 140–42; and Landow, *Hunt and Typological Symbolism,* pp. 51–52.

27. Linda Nochlin, *Realism* (Harmondsworth: Penguin Books, 1971), p. 201; see also Nead, "Magdalen in Modern Times," p. 79.

28. William Holman Hunt, *Pre-Raphaelitism and the Pre-Raphaelite Brotherhood* (New York: Macmillan, 1905), vol. 1, p. 419.

29. Arscott, "Employer, Husband, Spectator," p. 181.

30. Hunt, *Pre-Raphaelitism,* vol. 1, p. 418.

31. Review of *The Awakening Conscience* published as part of a longer essay on the 1854 Royal Academy exhibition in *Athenaeum* (6 May 1854), pp. 559–61, and reprinted in John Charles Olmsted, ed., *Victorian Painting: Essays and Reviews,* vol. 2, *1849–1860* (New York: Garland, 1983), p. 289. On the problem of "reading" the picture, then and now, see the first-rate essay by Kate Flint, "Rereading *The Awakening Conscience* Rightly," in *Pre-Raphaelites Re-Viewed,* ed. Marcia Pointon (Manchester: Manchester University Press, 1989), pp. 45–65.

32. *Athenaeum* (6 May 1854), pp. 559–61, reprinted in Olmsted, *Victorian Painting,* vol. 2, p. 288.

33. From an 1856 exhibition review, quoted in Arscott, "Employer, Husband, Spectator," p. 185. Arscott provides a consistently brilliant reading of Annie Miller's face in *The Awakening Conscience,* pp. 180–84, focusing on psychoanalytic questions of scopophilia, the male gaze, and sexual desire. She points out that Ruskin's reading of the picture "converts the dangerous scopophilia offered by the picture into a safe sadistic voyeurism" (p. 184).

34. Judith Bronkhurst, "Fruits of a Connoisseur's Friendship: Sir Thomas Fairbairn and William Holman Hunt," *Burlington Magazine* 125 (October 1983), p. 588 n. 24.

35. [Bennett,] *Hunt,* p. 37. Holman-Hunt, *My Grandfather,* p. 134: "I think that Hunt did more than change the expression, I believe he scraped out most of the head, instead of overpainting. X-rays show nothing underneath. The new face does not resemble Annie Miller in the least." Hunt retouched the picture again in 1864, 1879–80, and finally 1886, though in these instances he apparently did not repaint the face of Annie Miller. See Bronkhurst, "Connoisseur's Friendship," pp. 588, 594–95; and the exhibition catalogue *The Pre-Raphaelites* (London: Tate Gallery/Harmondsworth: Penguin Books, 1984), no. 58, p. 120. See Hunt's own comments on the repainting in his *Pre-Raphaelitism,* vol. 1, p. 418 n. 1, which suggests that he reworked the face only once; avoiding Annie Miller's name, he acknowledges only that "the woman's head in its present condition is not exactly what it was when Ruskin described the picture."

36. Cf. Marcia Pointon, *Naked Authority: The Body in Western Painting, 1830–1908* (Cambridge: Cambridge University Press, 1990), p. 43, concerning Thomas Eakins's painting *The Gross Clinic.*

37. Julie F. Codell, "Expression over Beauty: Facial Expression, Body Language, and Circumstantiality in the Paintings of the Pre-Raphaelite Brotherhood," *Victorian Studies* 29 (1986), p. 273. For more on the massive interest of Victorians (including Hunt) in phrenology, physiognomy (both involved reading the body as a map of permanent character traits), and pathognomy (reading the body as a map of momentary emotion) and an interpretation of the central figure in *The Awakening Conscience,* see pp. 272–79. See also the excellent study by Mary Cowling, *The Artist as Anthropologist: The Representation of Type and Character in Victorian Art* (Cambridge: Cambridge University Press, 1989); and Patricia Magli, "The Face and the Soul," trans. Ughetta Lubin, in *Fragments for a History of the Human Body,* ed. Michel Feher (New York: Zone, 1989), vol. 2, pp. 86–127.

38. Hunt, *Pre-Raphaelitism,* vol. 1, p. 418. Regarding the early reception history of the painting see Fleming, *That Ne'er Shall Meet Again,* pp. 2–4; Holman-Hunt, *My Grandfather,* pp. 133–34; and especially Arscott, "Employer, Husband, Spectator," pp. 170–87, who provides a thoughtful, detailed account not only of Ruskin's gloss on the painting but also of the responses to his reading; she also reprints Ruskin's letter.

39. Janet Wolff and Caroline Arscott, "'Cultivated Capital': Patronage and Art in Nineteenth-Century Manchester and Leeds," *History Today* 37 (March 1987), pp. 22–28. See also Arscott, "Employer, Husband, Spectator," pp. 159–90.

40. Bronkhurst, "Connoisseur's Friendship," p. 586.

41. Ibid., p. 587. For additional biographical information see William Pole, ed., *The Life of Sir William Fairbairn . . . Partly Written by Himself* (London, 1877); and Arscott, "Employer, Husband, Spectator," pp. 162–63.

42. See Arscott, "Employer, Husband, Spectator," pp. 163–68.

43. On the subject of the fallen woman, much studied, see especially (1) Linda Nochlin, "Lost and *Found:* Once More the Fallen Woman," *Feminism and Art History: Questioning the Litany,* ed. Norma Broude and Mary D. Garrard (New York: Harper and Row, 1982), pp. 220–45. The subject of the fallen woman reached a peak in mid-nineteenth-century

England and "perhaps received its characteristic formulation in the circle of the Pre-Raphaelites and their friends. . . . [Indeed, it] interested Dante Gabriel Rossetti almost to the point of obsession" (p. 221). Nochlin's essay concerns Rossetti's painting *Found,* which she suggests "may be considered in some ways a paradoxically contradictory pendant" (p. 222) to Hunt's *Awakening Conscience;* (2) Nead, "Magdalen in Modern Times," pp. 73–92. This essay provides an excellent discussion of the "way in which paintings and other forms of cultural representation participated in the definition of sexual behaviour and 'respectability' during the nineteenth century" (p. 73); (3) Lynda Nead, *Myths of Sexuality: Representations of Women in Victorian Britain* (Oxford: Blackwell, 1988); (4) Helene E. Roberts, "Marriage, Redundancy, or Sin: The Painter's View of Women in the First Twenty-Five Years of Victoria's Reign," in *Suffer and Be Still: Women in the Victorian Age,* ed. Martha Vicinus (Bloomington: Indiana University Press, 1973), pp. 45–76; (5) Casteras, *Images of Victorian Womanhood,* pp. 131–43; and (6) Eric Trudgill, *Madonnas and Magdalens: The Origins and Development of Victorian Sexual Attitudes* (New York: Holmes and Meier, 1976), pp. 101–28, 277–306.

44. Bronkhurst, "Connoisseur's Friendship," p. 594. The painting is illustrated in color in Wolff and Arscott, "Cultivated Capital," p. 25. See also the discussion of the painting, pp. 27–28.

45. Bronkhurst, "Connoisseur's Frienship," p. 594.

46. Arscott, "Employer, Husband, Spectator," pp. 168–71, offers additional valuable insights in a comparison of the two paintings.

47. [Mary Bennett,] *William Holman Hunt* [exhibition catalogue] (Liverpool, Walker Art Gallery, 1969), p. 36.

48. Landow, *Hunt and Typological Symbolism,* p. 51.

49. See Hunt, *Pre-Raphaelitism,* vol. 2, pp. 429–30.

50. See [Bennett,] *Hunt,* p. 35, for the full texts; and Arscott, "Employer, Husband, Spectator," p. 178, for an interpretation of the verses. Hunt later disclaimed the scriptural passages printed in the Royal Academy catalogue; see Nochlin, "Lost and *Found,*" p. 244 n. 32.

51. Hunt, *Pre-Raphaelitism,* vol. 1, p. 430.

52. For more on the role of the piano in the home and the music played, see Derek Scott, *The Singing Bourgeois: Songs of the Victorian Drawing Room and Parlour* (Milton Keynes: Open University Press, 1989); and Mary Burgan, "Heroines at the Piano: Women and Music in Nineteenth-Century Fiction," *Victorian Studies* 30 (1986), pp. 51–76. From p. 51: "The sacrifice of her piano is one of the harshest elements of the woman's share in the economic disasters portrayed in nineteenth-century fiction. Without a piano, women with pretensions to gentility are deprived of the exercise of their special training, of any leading role in family recreation, and of one of their few legitimate channels for self-expression." Burgan has some excellent things to say about what she terms women's "demonic affinity with music" (p. 69). Danièle Pistone, *Le Piano dans la littérature française des origines jusque vers 1900* (Paris: Champion, 1975), has located references to the domestic piano in two thousand scenes in nineteenth-century novels.

53. Quoted in Michelle Perrot, ed., *A History of Private Life,* vol. 4, *From the Fires of*

Revolution to the Great War, trans. Arthur Goldhammer (Cambridge: Belknap Press of Harvard University Press, 1990), p. 531.

54. Ruskin in the *Times,* quoted in Hunt, *Pre-Raphaelitism,* vol. 1, p. 419.

55. See Dijkstra, *Idols of Perversity,* p. 65.

56. Peter Brooks, *The Melodramatic Imagination* (London: New Left Books, 1983); see also the discussion in Laura Mulvey, "Melodrama inside and outside the Home," in *Visual and Other Pleasures* (Bloomington: Indiana University Press, 1989), pp. 63–77.

57. Quoted from Flint, "Rereading *The Awakening Conscience* Rightly," p. 59.

58. For detailed information see Maas, *Holman Hunt and "The Light of the World,"* primarily a study of the later version painted between 1900 and 1904, especially the history of its exhibition tour and reception in Canada, Australia, New Zealand, and South Africa prior to its installation in St. Paul's Cathedral, London, where it has hung since 1908. See also Mark Roskill, "Holman Hunt's Differing Versions of *The Light of the World,"* *Victorian Studies* 6 (1962/63), pp. 329–42.

59. Hunt, *Pre-Raphaelitism,* vol. 2, p. 429. See further, re Hunt's intentions, George P. Landow, "Shadows Cast by *The Light of the World:* William Holman Hunt's Religious Paintings, 1893–1905," *Art Bulletin* 65 (1983), p. 481; the essay studies the impact of this painting on Hunt's life's work, and his virtual obsession with the subject of conversion and illumination.

60. Nina Auerbach, *Woman and the Demon: The Life of a Victorian Myth* (Cambridge: Harvard University Press, 1982), p. 77.

61. Codell, "Expression over Beauty," p. 264: the depiction of bodies in "transitional postures" is characteristic of Pre-Raphaelite Brotherhood art.

62. Holman-Hunt, *My Grandfather,* p. 98.

63. Marsh, *The Pre-Raphaelite Sisterhood,* p. 108.

64. Hunt, *Pre-Raphaelitism.* Principal references to the picture, so far as I can determine in this sprawling, unindexed two-volume book, are in vol. 1, pp. 347–48, 405, 418–19; vol. 2, pp. 428–31.

65. Remarks by Edward Clodd, published in his *Reminiscences,* p. 200, as quoted in Fleming, *That Ne'er Shall Meet Again,* p. 134.

66. Quoted in Hunt, *Pre-Raphaelitism,* vol. 1, p. 419.

67. Flint, "Reading *The Awakening Conscience* Rightly," p. 49.

68. Henry Noel Humphries, *The Origin and Progress of the Art of Writing,* 2nd ed. (London: Day and Son, 1855), p. 1.

69. Quoted in Vogel, "Fine Arts and Feminism," p. 21.

70. Giuseppe Verdi, *La Traviata,* act 3, English translation by Dale McAdoo (Angel Records: 3545 B/L, 1956), p. 14.

71. Scott, *Singing Bourgeois,* p. x. Regarding the success of Tom Moore, in whose collections "Oft, in the Stilly Night" appeared (without the comma in its title), see pp. 25–26. See also Maurice Disher, *Victorian Song: From Dive to Drawing Room* (London: Phoenix House, 1955); and Jacqueline S. Bratton, *The Victorian Popular Ballad* (Totowa, N.J.: Rowman and Littlefield, 1975).

72. See Jacques Attali, *Noise: The Political Economy of Music,* trans. Brian Massumi (Minneapolis: University of Minnesota Press, 1985), pp. 51–62, 77–81.

73. This matter is dealt with in detail throughout Leppert, *Music and Image.*

74. *The Poetical Works of Thomas Moore, Collected by Himself,* vol. 4, *Irish Melodies, National Airs, Sacred Songs* (London, 1853), pp. 167–68.

75. *Tennyson's Poetry: Authoritative Texts; Juvenilia and Early Responses; Criticism,* ed. Robert W. Hill, Jr. (New York: Norton, 1971), p. 114. For a good analysis of this poem see Graham Hough, "Tears, Idle Tears," *Hopkins Review* 4, no. 3 (1951), pp. 31–36.

76. Hunt, *Pre-Raphaelitism,* vol. 2, p. 429.

77. Roland Barthes, "Listening," in *The Responsibility of Forms: Critical Essays on Music, Art, and Representation,* trans. Richard Howard (New York: Hill and Wang, 1985), p. 255.

78. Kaja Silverman, *The Acoustic Mirror: The Female Voice in Psychoanalysis and Cinema* (Bloomington: Indiana University Press, 1988), p. 44; see also pp. 67–68. Cf. the chapter "Chant / Song," in David Appelbaum, *Voice* (Albany: State University of New York Press, 1990), pp. 85–97: "The sung voice introduces quantity. . . . Quantity in voice transmits the basal vibration of the body, calling an awareness of its condition and the condition of the world surrounding. Its *telos* is activation, address, and embodiment" (p. 94).

CHAPTER 9

1. All five of the six collections (of eight total) published during the composer's lifetime were dedicated to women. See Eric Werner, *Mendelssohn: A New Image of the Composer and His Age,* trans. Dika Newlin (London: Collier-Macmillian, 1963), p. 220; and Christa Jost, *Mendelssohns Lieder ohne Worte* (Tutzing: Schneider, 1988), pp. 55–63.

2. Wilfrid Blunt, *On Wings of Song: A Biography of Felix Mendelssohn* (New York: Scribner, 1974), p. 83.

3. Maurice J. E. Brown, "Songs without Words," and Karl-Heinz Köhler, "Mendelssohn(-Bartholdy), (Jacob Ludwig) Felix," *The New Grove Dictionary of Music and Musicians,* ed. Stanley Sadie (London: Macmillan, 1980), vol. 17, pp. 524–25; and vol. 12, p. 151.

4. This insight comes from Rose Rosengard Subotnik, *Developing Variations: Style and Ideology in Western Music* (Minneapolis: University of Minnesota Press, 1991), p. 148.

5. Roland Barthes, *S/Z: An Essay,* trans. Richard Miller (New York: Hill and Wang, 1974), p. 156. See also by Barthes, *The Pleasure of the Text,* trans. Richard Miller (New York: Hill and Wang, 1975), and *Writing Degree Zero,* trans. Annette Lavers and Colin Smith (New York: Hill and Wang, 1967).

6. Quoted in Heinrich Eduard Jacob, *Felix Mendelssohn and His Times,* trans. Richard Winston and Clara Winston (Englewood Cliffs, N.J.: Prentice Hall, 1963), pp. 185–86, which see for the full statement; and Herbert Kupferberg, *Felix Mendelssohn: His Life, His Family, His Music* (New York: Scribner, 1972), pp. 82–83.

7. Jacob, *Felix Mendelssohn and His Times,* p. 185. See also Jost, *Mendelssohns Lieder ohne Worte,* pp. 16–19, on this question.

8. Roland Barthes, "Twenty Key Words for Roland Barthes," in *The Grain of the Voice: Interviews, 1962–1980,* trans. Linda Coverdale (New York: Hill and Wang, 1985), p. 217.

9. See further Mark Johnson, *The Body in the Mind: The Bodily Basis of Meaning, Imagination, and Reason* (Chicago: University of Chicago Press, 1987).

10. Philip Radcliffe, *Mendelssohn* (London: Dent, 1954), pp. 81–86, cannot hear the "Songs without Words" except in feminine terms (in contrast to the implicit "masculinity" of Chopin and Schumann). Thus the second piece in Opus 62, later named "The Departure," "will always suggest to the present writer the exuberant chatter of Jane Austen's Miss Bates" (p. 84), though in the next breath Radcliffe notes that the last of the Gondola Songs is "curiously prophetic of certain things by Brahms," which I take as a claim that Radcliffe found in it a masculinity otherwise generally overwhelmed by Mendelssohn's "charm." The other descriptors he uses are consistently feminine: "serene," "cloistered," "attractive," "pleasant," "sickly." See further on these compositions Jacob, *Felix Mendelssohn and His Times,* pp. 186–90; Willi Kahl, "Zu Mendelssohns Liedern ohne Worte," *Zeitschrift für Musikwissenschaft* 3 (1920–21), pp. 459–69; Wolfgang Stresemann, *Eine Lanze für Felix Mendelssohn* (Berlin: Stapp, 1984), pp. 113–16; Louise H. Tischler and Hans Tischler, "Mendelssohn's Style: 'The Songs without Words,'" *Music Review* 8 (1947), pp. 256–73; Louise H. Tischler and Hans Tischler, "Mendelssohn's 'Songs without Words,'" *Musical Quarterly* 33 (1947), pp. 1–16; R. Larry Todd, "Piano Music Reformed: The Case of Felix Mendelssohn Bartholdy," *Nineteenth-Century Piano Music,* ed. R. Larry Todd (New York: Schirmer, 1990), pp. 192–99; Wulf Konold, *Felix Mendelssohn Bartholdy und seine Zeit* (n.p.: Laaber Verlag, 1984), pp. 256–66; and especially the major new study by Christa Jost, *Mendelssohns Lieder ohne Worte.*

11. Nina Auerbach, *Woman and the Demon: The Life of a Victorian Myth* (Cambridge: Harvard University Press, 1982), p. 8.

12. On Mendelssohn's considerable popularity in Victorian England, see Nicholas Temperley, "Mendelssohn's Influence on English Music," *Music and Letters* 43 (1962), pp. 224–33.

13. See Julia Kristeva, *Desire in Language: A Semiotic Approach to Literature and Art,* ed. Leon S. Roudiez, trans. Thomas Gora, Alice Jardine, and Leon S. Roudiez (New York: Columbia University Press, 1980), especially pp. 115–21 ("Science and Criticism: Music"), pp. 148–58 ("The Father, Love, and Banishment"), pp. 190–200 ("Shattering the Family"), and pp. 237–70 ("Motherhood according to Giovanni Bellini").

14. I use the word *homosocial* in accord with its coinage by Eve Kosofsky Sedgwick, *Between Men: English Literature and Male Homosocial Desire* (New York: Columbia University Press, 1985); see Chapter 7, n. 30, above.

15. Concerning Leighton's sexuality, see Leonée Ormond and Richard Ormond, *Lord Leighton* (New Haven: Yale University Press, 1975), p. 48, and on his relationship to Dorothy Dene, pp. 133–38.

16. See Chapter 6, n. 28, above.

17. Plato, *The Republic,* trans. A. D. Lindsay (New York: Dutton, 1957), p. 118 (Book III/411).

18. Allan Bloom, *The Closing of the American Mind: How Higher Education Has Failed*

Democracy and Impoverished the Souls of Today's Students (New York: Simon and Schuster, 1987), p. 73. In a similar vein see also Robert Pattison, *The Triumph of Vulgarity: Rock Music in the Mirror of Romanticism* (New York: Oxford University Press, 1987), of note to the extent that Pattison traces his subject to the nineteenth century: "Polite society takes the crude physical events of carnal existence and out of them makes love or has sex. The vulgarian screws or fucks" (p. 6). The undercurrent of this text's white paranoia is the supposed relation of rock to the black phallus. "Primitivism," high on Bloom's list of rock's socio-musical ailments, is much the culprit here as well. Pattison's account, however, is organized around song lyrics; he has little to say about sonority.

19. Bloom, *Closing of the American Mind,* pp. 79–80.

20. Ibid., p. 75.

21. For more on this painting see Stephen Jones, "Attic Attitudes: Leighton and Aesthetic Philosophy," in *Victorian Values: Personalities and Perspectives in Nineteenth-Century Society,* ed. Gordon Marsden (London: Longman, 1990), pp. 187–97. Regarding other of Leighton's representations of languid women, see Ormond and Ormond, *Lord Leighton,* pp. 129–32. For a more general account of this sort of representation in Victorian art see Susan P. Casteras, *Images of Victorian Womanhood in English Art* (London: Associated University Presses, 1987), pp. 159–64, and on Leighton, pp. 171, 177; Patrick Bade, *Femme Fatale: Images of Evil and Fascinating Women* (New York: Mayflower Books, 1979), pp. 6–15; and Fraser Harrison, *The Dark Angel: Aspects of Victorian Sexuality* (New York: Universe Books, 1978), pp. 28–38 and, concerning Leighton's career, with emphasis on his paintings of female nudes, pp. 74–88.

22. Kenneth Bendiner, *An Introduction to Victorian Painting* (New Haven: Yale University Press, 1985), p. 131. See further pp. 130–44 for an excellent account of this subject, commonplace in late Victorian painting. Concerning the fetishization of female physical weakness, see Lorna Duffin, "The Conspicuous Consumptive: Woman as an Invalid," in *The Nineteenth-Century Woman: Her Cultural and Physical World,* ed. Sara Delamont and Lorna Duffin (New York: Barnes and Noble, 1978), pp. 26–56.

23. See Auerbach, *Woman and the Demon,* pp. 42–43, who, commenting on Sleeping Beauty, notes that her sleep "told of terror as well as safety." Auerbach also discusses briefly George du Maurier's novel *Trilby,* pp. 17–21; Trilby, who becomes a great singer under the tutelage of her master Svengali, in essence overpowers him with the genius of her singing, enervating him, causing his fatal heart attack while he attempts to lead her to new musical heights. Auerbach notes that Trilby is portrayed as a virtual giantess who takes control of the novel. Du Maurier illustrated the text (some examples are reproduced by Auerbach), fixing her as a musical sight for the reader. "Her endowed voice is an accidental index of the multiplicity which allows her always to be a new incarnation of herself" (p. 18).

24. On the relation between domestic imagery and the public world of the nineteenth-century industrialist, see Chapter 8, nn. 23, 39.

25. Walter Pater, "The School of Giorgione," in *Walter Pater: Selected Works,* ed. Richard Aldington (Melbourne: William Heinemann, 1948), p. 271. Pater continues: "For while in all other kinds of art it is possible to distinguish the matter from the form, and

the understanding can always make this distinction, yet it is the constant effort of art to obliterate it."

The essay was first published in *Fortnightly Review,* October 1877. The contention over the production of an aesthetics of music in the nineteenth century, highly explosive, is well known in principle if not in detail. The best collections of primary materials currently available, accompanied by useful and lucid introductions, are Peter Le Huray and James Day, eds., *Music and Aesthetics in the Eighteenth and Early-Nineteenth Centuries* (Cambridge: Cambridge University Press, 1981); and Bojan Bujic, ed., *Music in European Thought, 1851–1912* (Cambridge: Cambridge University Press, 1988).

26. Pater, "The School of Giorgione," p. 273: "Art, then, is thus always striving to be independent of the mere intelligence, *to become a matter of pure perception, to get rid of its responsibilities to its subject or material*" (emphasis added).

27. Arthur Schopenhauer, *Die Welt als Wille und Vorstellung* (1819), excerpted in Le Huray and Day, *Music and Aesthetics,* p. 324. See further the discussion on Pater and Schopenhauer in Robert P. Morgan, "Secret Languages: The Roots of Musical Modernism," in *Modernism: Challenges and Perspectives,* ed. Monique Chefdor, Richardo Quinones, and Albert Wachtel (Urbana: University of Illinois Press, 1986), pp. 36–37.

28. Pater, "The School of Giorgione," p. 270.

29. To date the best theorization, however flawed, of the politics of sonoric silence and of sonoric political resistance is by Jacques Attali, *Noise: The Political Economy of Music,* trans. Brian Massumi (Minneapolis: University of Minnesota Press, 1985). Theorizations of resistance grow from two mutually opposed traditions. The first is the work of Theodor W. Adorno, concentrated mostly on a segment of the canonical classical repertoire, principally German (notably, some of the music of Beethoven and Schoenberg); for an introduction to his thought see *Introduction to the Sociology of Music,* trans. E. B. Ashton (New York: Continuum, 1976), and *Philosophy of Modern Music,* trans. Anne G. Mitchell and Wesley V. Blomster (New York: Continuum, 1985), which focuses on Schoenberg and, for Adorno, Schoenberg's nemesis, Stravinsky.

The second is the more recent work of scholars connected either to British Cultural Studies or American Studies on popular music, which largely rejects Adorno's scathing, undeniably mandarin, position regarding popular musical culture. Adorno's arguments on this score are best introduced in the chapter "The Culture Industry: Enlightenment as Mass Deception," in Max Horkheimer and Theodor W. Adorno, *Dialectic of Enlightenment,* trans. John Cumming (New York: Continuum, 1972), pp. 120–67. From the British Cultural Studies tradition see, for example, Simon Frith, *Sound Effects: Youth, Leisure, and the Politics of Rock 'n' Roll* (New York: Pantheon Books, 1981); from the American Studies group, George Lipsitz, *Time Passages: Collective Memory and American Popular Culture* (Minneapolis, University of Minnesota Press, 1990). Richard Leppert and George Lipsitz, "'Everybody's Lonesome for Somebody': Age, the Body, and Experience in the Music of Hank Williams," *Popular Music* 9 (1990), pp. 259–74, engages questions directly pertinent to this chapter as regards the body.

Finally, for work that goes beyond the boundaries of the West but nonetheless explicitly engages the cultural politics of Western colonialism and involves music, see John Blacking, *How Musical is Man?* (Seattle: University of Washington Press, 1973), which has a good deal to say about musico-political resistance on the part of the Venda of the Transvaal.

30. Pater, "The School of Giorgione," p. 279.

31. Ibid., p. 281.

32. Ibid., pp. 279–80.

33. Schopenhauer, *Die Welt als Wille und Vorstellung* (1819), excerpted in Le Huray and Day, *Music and Aesthetics,* p. 330.

34. See further, Attali, *Noise,* pp. 87–132; and also Kathi Meyer-Baer, *Music of the Spheres and the Dance of Death: Studies in Musical Iconology* (Princeton: Princeton University Press, 1970).

35. James McNeill Whistler's music personifications are well known, Albert Moore's less so, though Moore was a major figure in his day. His contribution was a preposterous painting called *A Quartet: A Painter's Tribute to the Art of Music, A.D. 1868,* a classical scene with a toga-clad male string quartet and an audience of three similarly bedecked women. Once again, to pay tribute to music required its simultaneous removal from history. The image is reproduced in Alfred Lys Baldry, *Albert Moore: His Life and Works* (London: George Bell and Sons, 1894), opposite p. 36; the original is now in a private New Zealand collection.

36. For more on this sort of imagery see Allen Staley, "The Condition of Music," *Art News Annual* 33 (1967), pp. 81–87.

37. Leighton had a considerable knowledge of and appreciation for music, regularly inviting professional performers to his house. The highlight of his home entertaining was an annual music party. See Ormond and Ormond, *Lord Leighton,* pp. 64–65.

38. Horkheimer and Adorno, *Dialectic of Enlightenment,* p. 230: "All objectification is a forgetting."

39. See further Albert Pomme de Mirimonde, "Les Sujets de musique dans la peinture Belge du XVIIIe siècle," *Jaarboek, Koninklijk Museum voor Schone Kunsten* (Antwerp, 1967), pp. 245–57; and also the exhibition catalogue, *Peter Jakob Horemans (1700–1776) Kurbayerischer Hofmaler* (Munich: Alte Pinakothek, 1974), which includes reproductions of two other paintings of this sort, plates 18–19. Regarding my Figures 98–99 see p. 33, no. 47; and p. 39, no. 73.

40. Attali, *Noise,* pp. 87–132, suggests that what he terms the stockpiling of music via technologies of recording has produced an ironic silence in the face of sonoric ubiquity. He errs significantly here by failing adequately to acknowledge that the availability of sounds, notably the sounds of other times and cultures, provides the opportunity for mediating our own sonoric practices and, hence, cultural relations. Attali's view on this matter is informed by Adorno's position on cultural standardization via mass culture. Regarding the general availability of art music and the considerable public and private audience for it in the nineteenth century—herein the irony of my use of the word *silence*—the work of William Weber is important. See especially his "Mass Culture and the Reshaping of

European Musical Taste, 1770–1870," *International Review of the Aesthetics and Sociology of Music* 8 (1977), pp. 5–22, and *Music and the Middle Class: The Social Structure of Concert Life in London, Paris, and Vienna* (New York: Holmes and Meier, 1975).

41. See Richard Leppert, *Music and Image: Domesticity, Ideology, and Socio-Cultural Formation in Eighteenth-Century England* (Cambridge: Cambridge University Press, 1989).

42. Kristeva, "The Novel as Polylogue," in *Desire in Language,* p. 179.

43. In his later life Khnopff in his studio preferred listening to music played on a piano situated on the floor below him. See Jeffrey W. Howe, *The Symbolist Art of Fernand Khnopff* (Ann Arbor: UMI Research Press, 1982), pp. 149–50; on this painting see also pp. 5–6, 121–22.

44. Roland Barthes, "Musica Practica," in *The Responsibility of Forms: Critical Essays on Music, Art, and Representation,* trans. Richard Howard (New York: Hill and Wang, 1985), p. 261.

45. Ibid.

46. Roland Barthes, "Loving Schumann," in *The Responsibility of Forms: Critical Essays on Music, Art, and Representation,* trans. Richard Howard (New York: Hill and Wang, 1985), p. 295.

47. Ibid., p. 298.

Acton, William. *The Functions and Disorders of the Reproductive Organs in Youth, in Adult Age, and in Advanced Life, Considered in Their Physiological, Social, and Psychological Relations.* 4th ed. London, 1865.

Adlam, Derek, and William J. Conner. "Pianoforte, 1,5." *The New Grove Dictionary of Music and Musicians.* Vol. 14, pp. 695–97.

Adlam, Derek, and Cyril Ehrlich. "Broadwood." *The New Grove Dictionary of Music and Musicians.* Vol. 3, pp. 324–25.

Adorno, Theodor W. *Aesthetic Theory.* Edited by Gretel Adorno and Rolf Tiedemann. Translated by C. Lenhardt. London: Routledge and Kegan Paul, 1984.

———. *Introduction to the Sociology of Music.* Translated by E. B. Ashton. New York: Continuum, 1976.

———. *Minima Moralia: Reflections from Damaged Life.* Translated by E. F. N. Jephcott. London: Verso, 1978.

———. *Philosophy of Modern Music.* Translated by Anne G. Mitchell and Wesley V. Blomster. New York: Continuum, 1985.

Alpers, Svetlana. *The Art of Describing: Dutch Art in the Seventeenth Century.* Chicago: University of Chicago Press, 1983.

Apel, Willi. *Gregorian Chant.* Bloomington: Indiana University Press, 1958.

Appelbaum, David. *Voice.* Albany: State University of New York Press, 1990.

Archer, John. *The Literature of British Domestic Architecture, 1715–1842.* Cambridge: MIT Press, 1985.

Archer, Mildred. *Company Drawings in the India Office Library.* London: Her Majesty's Stationery Office, 1972.

———. *India and British Portraiture, 1770–1825.* London: Sotheby Parke Bernet, 1979.

———. "'The Talented Baronet': Sir Charles D'Oyly and His Drawings of India." *Connoisseur* 175 (November 1970), pp. 173–81.

Archer, Mildred, and W. G. Archer. *Indian Painting for the British, 1770–1880*. London: Oxford University Press, 1955.

Arscott, Caroline. "Employer, Husband, Spectator: Thomas Fairbairn's Commission of *The Awakening Conscience*." In *The Culture of Capital: Art, Power, and the Nineteenth-Century Middle Class*, edited by Janet Wolff and John Seed, pp. 159–90. Manchester: Manchester University Press, 1988.

Atkinson, George F. *"Curry and Rice," on Forty Plates, or, the Ingredients of Social Life at "Our" Station in India*. London: Day and Son, c. 1856.

Attali, Jacques. *Noise: The Political Economy of Music*. Translated by Brian Massumi. Minneapolis: University of Minnesota Press, 1985.

Auerbach, Nina. *Woman and the Demon: The Life of a Victorian Myth*. Cambridge: Harvard University Press, 1982.

Ayars, Christine Merrick. *Contributions to the Art of Music in America by the Music Industries of Boston, 1640 to 1936*. New York: H. W. Wilson, 1937.

Bade, Patrick. *Femme Fatale: Images of Evil and Fascinating Women*. New York: Mayflower Books, 1979.

Bakhtin, Mikhail. *Rabelais and His World*. Translated by Helene Iswolsky. Bloomington: Indiana University Press, 1984.

Baldry, Alfred Lys. *Albert Moore: His Life and Works*. London: George Bell and Sons, 1894.

Ballstaedt, Andreas, and Tobias Widmaier. *Salonmusik: Zur Geschichte und Funktion einer bürgerlichen Musikpraxis*. Archiv für Musikwissenschaft, vol. 28. Stuttgart: Steiner, 1989.

Bangs, Lester. "James Taylor Marked for Death." In *Psychotic Reactions and Carburetor Dung*, edited by Greil Marcus, pp. 53–81. New York: Knopf, 1987.

Barrell, John. *The Dark Side of the Landscape: The Rural Poor in English Painting, 1730–1840*. Cambridge: Cambridge University Press, 1980.

Barthes, Roland. "Diderot, Brecht, Eisenstein." In *Image, Music, Text*. Translated by Stephen Heath, pp. 69–78. New York: Hill and Wang, 1977.

———. *The Pleasure of the Text*. Translated by Richard Miller. New York: Hill and Wang, 1975.

———. *The Responsibility of Forms: Critical Essays on Music, Art, and Representation*. Translated by Richard Howard. New York: Hill and Wang, 1985.

———. *S/Z: An Essay*. Translated by Richard Miller. New York: Hill and Wang, 1974.

———. "Twenty Key Words for Roland Barthes." In *The Grain of the Voice: Interviews, 1962–1980*. Translated by Linda Coverdale, pp. 205–32. New York: Hill and Wang, 1985.

———. *Writing Degree Zero*. Translated by Annette Lavers and Colin Smith. New York: Hill and Wang, 1967.

Bartram, Michael. *The Pre-Raphaelite Camera: Aspects of Victorian Photography*. Boston: Little, Brown, 1985.

Baumgart, Fritz. *Blumen Brueghel (Jan Brueghel d. Ä.): Leben und Werk*. Cologne, DuMont, 1978.

Bell, Leonard. "Artists and Empire: Victorian Representations of Subject People." *Art History* 5 (1982), pp. 73–86.

Bendiner, Kenneth. *An Introduction to Victorian Painting.* New Haven: Yale University Press, 1985.

Benjamin, Walter. *Moscow Diary.* Edited by Gary Smith. Translated by Richard Sieburth. Cambridge: Harvard University Press, 1986.

———. "Theses on the Philosophy of History." In *Illuminations.* Edited by Hannah Arendt. Translated by Harry Zohn, pp. 253–64. New York: Schocken Books, 1969.

———. *Ursprung des deutschen Trauerspiels.* Berlin: E. Rowohlt, 1927.

Bennett, John. *Letters to a Young Lady, on a Variety of Useful and Interesting Subjects Calculated to Improve the Heart, to Form the Manners, and Enlighten the Understanding.* 2 vols. Warrington, 1789.

[Bennett, Mary.] *William Holman Hunt* [exhibition catalogue]. Liverpool: Walker Art Gallery, 1969.

Benson, Ruth Crego. *Women in Tolstoy: The Ideal and the Erotic.* Urbana: University of Illinois Press, 1973.

Berger, John. "Painting and Time." In *The Sense of Sight,* edited by Lloyd Spencer, pp. 205–11. New York: Pantheon Books, 1985.

———. *Ways of Seeing.* Harmondsworth: Penguin Books, 1972.

Bergström, Ingvar. *Dutch Still-Life Painting in the Seventeenth Century.* Translated by Christina Hedström and Gerald Taylor. New York: T. Voseloff, 1956.

Berkenhout, John. *A Volume of Letters from Dr Berkenhout to His Son at the University.* 2 vols. Cambridge, 1790.

Bermingham, Ann. *Landscape and Ideology: The English Rustic Tradition, 1740–1860.* Berkeley and Los Angeles: University of California Press, 1986.

Bernt, Walther. *The Netherlandish Painters of the Seventeenth Century.* Translated by P. S. Falla. 3 vols., 3rd ed. London: Phaidon, 1970.

Blacking, John. *How Musical Is Man?* Seattle: University of Washington Press, 1973.

Blok, Petrus Johannes. *History of the People of the Netherlands.* 5 vols. Vol. 3, *The War with Spain.* Translated by Ruth Putnam. New York: Putnam, 1900.

Bloom, Allan. *The Closing of the American Mind: How Higher Education Has Failed Democracy and Impoverished the Souls of Today's Students.* New York: Simon and Schuster, 1987.

Blunt, Wilfrid. *On Wings of Song: A Biography of Felix Mendelssohn.* New York: Scribner, 1974.

Boalch, Donald Howard, and Peter Williams. "Kirckman." *The New Grove Dictionary of Music and Musicians.* Vol. 10, pp. 76–78.

———. "Shudi, Burkat." *The New Grove Dictionary of Music and Musicians.* Vol. 17, pp. 278–79.

Bocquet, Léon. *David Teniers.* Paris: Editions Nilsson, 1924.

Borel, France. *The Seduction of Venus: Artists and Models.* New York: Skira/Rizzoli, 1990.

Bourdieu, Pierre. *Distinction: A Social Critique of the Judgement of Taste.* Translated by Richard Nice. Cambridge: Harvard University Press, 1984.

Bower, Calvin. "Boethius." *The New Grove Dictionary of Music and Musicians.* Vol. 2, pp. 844–45.

Branca, Patricia. *Silent Sisterhood: Middle Class Women in the Victorian Home.* Pittsburgh: Carnegie-Mellon University Press, 1975.

Bratton, Jacqueline S. *The Victorian Popular Ballad.* Totowa, N.J.: Rowman and Littlefield, 1975.

Briggs, Asa. *Victorian Things.* Chicago: University of Chicago Press, 1988.

Bronkhurst, Judith. "Fruits of a Connoisseur's Friendship: Sir Thomas Fairbairn and William Holman Hunt." *Burlington Magazine* 125 (October 1983), pp. 586–95.

Brooks, Peter. *The Melodramatic Imagination.* London: New Left Books, 1983.

Brown, Maurice J. E. "Songs without Words." *The New Grove Dictionary of Music and Musicians.* Vol. 17, pp. 524–25.

Bryson, Norman. *Vision and Painting: The Logic of the Gaze.* New Haven: Yale University Press, 1983.

Buck-Morss, Susan. *The Origin of Negative Dialectics: Theodor W. Adorno, Walter Benjamin, and the Frankfurt Institute.* New York: Free Press, 1977.

Bujic, Bojan, ed. *Music in European Thought, 1851–1912.* Cambridge: Cambridge University Press, 1988.

Burgan, Mary. "Heroines at the Piano: Women and Music in Nineteenth-Century Fiction." *Victorian Studies* 30 (1986), pp. 51–76.

Burney, Charles. *A General History of Music, from the Earliest Ages to the Present Period.* 4 vols. 2nd ed. London, 1789.

Burton, Robert. *The Anatomy of Melancholy.* 1621. Reprint. New York: Da Capo, 1971.

Cadoux, Cecil John. *Philip of Spain and the Netherlands: An Essay on Moral Judgments in History.* N.p.: Archon Books, 1969.

Capellanus, Andreas. *The Art of Courtly Love.* Translated by John Jay Parray. New York: Norton, 1969.

Casteras, Susan P. "Down the Garden Path: Courtship Culture and Its Imagery in Victorian Painting." Ph.D. diss., Yale University, 1977.

————. *Images of Victorian Womanhood in English Art.* London: Associated University Presses, 1987.

Certeau, Michel de. *The Practice of Everyday Life.* Translated by Steven Rendall. Berkeley and Los Angeles: University of California Press, 1984.

Chapone, Hester. *Letters on Improvement of the Mind, Addressed to a Young Lady.* 2 vols. in 1. Hagerstown, Md., 1818–19.

Cherry, Deborah, and Griselda Pollock. "Woman as Sign in Pre-Raphaelite Literature: A Study of the Representation of Elizabeth Siddal." *Art History* 7 (1984), pp. 206–27.

Chirico, Robert F. "Some Reflections on Sound and Silence in the Visual Arts." *Arts Magazine* 56 (April 1982), pp. 101–05.

Christ, Carol. "Victorian Masculinity and the Angel in the House." In *A Widening Sphere: Changing Roles of Victorian Women,* edited by Martha Vicinus, pp. 146–62. Bloomington: Indiana University Press, 1977.

Clark, Timothy J. "Preliminaries to a Possible Treatment of *Olympia* in 1865." *Screen* 21 (1980), pp. 18–41.

Clements, Andrew. "Eccentric Pianos." In *The Book of the Piano,* edited by Dominic Gill, pp. 248–57. Ithaca: Cornell University Press, 1981.

Codell, Julie F. "Expression over Beauty: Facial Expression, Body Language, and Circumstantiality in the Paintings of the Pre-Raphaelite Brotherhood." *Victorian Studies* 29 (1986), pp. 255–90.

Cohn, Bernard S. "Representing Authority in Victorian India." In *The Invention of Tradition,* edited by Eric Hobsbawm and Terence Ranger, pp. 165–209. Cambridge: Cambridge University Press, 1983.

Collier, Jeremy. *Essays upon Several Moral Subjects. In Two Parts.* 2nd ed., corrected and enlarged. London, 1697.

Colt, C. F., with Antony Miall. *The Early Piano.* London: Stainer and Bell, 1981.

Coombs, James H., Anne M. Scott, George P. Landow, and Arnold A. Sanders, eds. *A Pre-Raphaelite Friendship: The Correspondence of William Holman Hunt and John Lucas Tupper.* Ann Arbor: UMI Research Press, 1986.

Corbin, Alain. *The Foul and the Fragrant: Odor and the French Social Imagination.* New York: Berg Publishers, 1986.

Coutagne, Henry. *Gaspard Duiffoproucart et les luthiers lyonnais du XVIe siècle.* Paris: Fischbacher, 1893.

Cowling, Mary. *The Artist as Anthropologist: The Representation of Type and Character in Victorian Art.* Cambridge: Cambridge University Press, 1989.

Curson, Henry. *The Theory of Sciences Illustrated; or the Grounds and Principles of the Seven Liberal Arts.* London, 1702.

Daly, Gay. *Pre-Raphaelites in Love.* New York: Ticknor and Fields, 1989.

Darrell, William. *A Gentleman Instructed in the Conduct of a Virtuous and Happy Life.* London, 1704.

Darwin, Erasmus. *A Plan for the Conduct of Female Education, in Boarding Schools, Private Families, and Public Seminaries.* Philadelphia, 1798.

Davidoff, Leonore, and Catherine Hall. *Family Fortunes: Men and Women of the English Middle Class, 1780–1850.* London: Hutchinson, 1987.

de Lauretis, Teresa. "The Technology of Gender." In *Technologies of Gender: Essays on Theory, Film, and Fiction,* pp. 1–30. Bloomington: Indiana University Press, 1987.

Dellamora, Richard. *Masculine Desire: The Sexual Politics of Victorian Aestheticism.* Chapel Hill: University of North Carolina Press, 1990.

Dennis, John. "Advancement and Reformation of Poetry." In *The Critical Works of John Dennis.* Edited by Edward Niles Hooker. 2 vols. Baltimore: Johns Hopkins Press, 1939–43.

———. *An Essay on Opera's after the Italian Manner, Which Are About to Be Establish'd on the English Stage: With Some Reflections on the Damage Which They May Bring to the Publick.* In *The Critical Works of John Dennis.* Edited by Edward Niles Hooker. 2 vols. Baltimore: Johns Hopkins Press, 1939–43.

Derrida, Jacques. *The Truth in Painting.* Translated by Geoff Bennington and Ian McLeod. Chicago: University of Chicago Press, 1987.

Dijck, Lucas van, and Ton Koopman. *Het klavecimbel in de Nederlandse kunst tot 1800. (The Harpsichord in Dutch Art before 1800)* (in English and Dutch). Zutphen: Walburg, 1987.

Dijkstra, Bram. *Idols of Perversity: Fantasies of Feminine Evil in Fin-de-Siècle Culture.* New York: Oxford University Press, 1986.

Disher, Maurice. *Victorian Song: From Dive to Drawing Room.* London: Phoenix House, 1955.

D'Oench, Ellen G. *The Conversation Piece: Arthur Devis and His Contemporaries* [exhibition catalogue]. New Haven: Yale Center for British Art, 1980.

Doughty, Oswald. *A Victorian Romantic: Dante Gabriel Rossetti.* London: Muller, 1949.

Duffin, Lorna. "The Conspicuous Consumptive: Woman as an Invalid." In *The Nineteenth-Century Woman: Her Cultural and Physical World,* edited by Sara Delamont and Lorna Duffin, pp. 26–56. New York: Barnes and Noble, 1978.

Durant, Alan. *Conditions of Music.* Albany: State University of New York Press, 1984.

———. "Improvisation in the Political Economy of Music." In *Music and the Politics of Culture,* edited by Christopher Norris, pp. 252–81. New York: St. Martin's Press, 1989.

Dussler, Luitpold. *Raphael: A Critical Catalogue of His Pictures, Wall-Paintings, and Tapestries.* Translated by Sebastian Cruft. London: Phaidon, 1971.

Dworkin, Andrea. *Intercourse.* New York: Free Press, 1987.

Edelstein, T. J. "'The Yellow-Haired Fiend'—Rossetti and the Sensational Novel." *Library Chronicle* 43 (1979), pp. 180–93.

Edwardes, Allen. *The Rape of India: A Biography of Robert Clive and a Sexual History of the Conquest of Hindustan.* New York: Julian Press, 1966.

Egan, David R., and Melinda A. Egan. *Leo Tolstoy: An Annotated Bibliography of English-Language Sources to 1978.* Metuchen, N.J.: Scarecrow Press, 1979.

Ehrlich, Cyril. *The Piano: A History.* London: Dent, 1976.

———. *Social Emulation and Industrial Progress—the Victorian Piano.* New Lecture Series, no. 82. Belfast: Queen's University, 1975.

Ertz, Klaus. *Jan Brueghel der Ältere (1568–1625): Die Gemälde, mit kritischem Oeuvrekatalog.* Cologne: DuMont, 1979.

Essex, John. *The Young Ladies Conduct: Or, Rules for Education, under Several Heads; with Instructions upon Dress, Both before and after Marriage. And Advice to Young Wives.* London, 1722.

Euterpe; or, Remarks on the Use and Abuse of Music, as a Part of Modern Education. London, c. 1778.

Fielding, Henry. *Tom Jones* [1750]. Edited by Sheridan Baker. New York: Norton, 1973.

Fink, Monika, Rainer Gstrein, and Günter Mössmer, eds. *Musica Privata: Die Rolle der Musik im privaten Leben (Festschrift für Walter Salmen).* Innsbruck: Helbling, 1991.

Fischer, Peter. *Music in Paintings of the Low Countries in the Sixteenth and Seventeenth Centuries.* Amsterdam: Swets, 1975.

Fishman, Jane Susannah. *Boerenverdriet: Violence between Peasants and Soldiers in Early Modern Netherlands Art.* Ann Arbor: UMI Research Press, 1982.

Fitzgerald, Penelope. *Edward Burne-Jones: A Biography.* London: Hamilton, 1975.

Fitzlyon, April. "Tolstoy, Lev Nikolayevich." *The New Grove Dictionary of Music and Musicians.* Vol. 19, pp. 31–32.

Fleming, G. H. *That Ne'er Shall Meet Again: Rossetti, Millais, Hunt.* London: Joseph, 1971.

Flint, Kate. "Rereading *The Awakening Conscience* Rightly." In *Pre-Raphaelites Re-Viewed*, edited by Marcia Pointon, pp. 45–65. Manchester: Manchester University Press, 1989.

Flugel, John Carl. *The Psychology of Clothes.* London: Hogarth Press, 1930.

Foster, William. "Additional Notes to British Artists in India, 1760–1820." *Walpole Society* 21 (1932–33), pp. 108–09.

———. "British Artists in India, 1760–1820." *Walpole Society* 19 (1930–31), pp. 1–88.

Foucault, Michel. *The Archaeology of Knowledge and the Discourse on Language.* Translated by A. M. Sheridan Smith. New York: Pantheon Books, 1972.

———. *Discipline and Punish: The Birth of the Prison.* Translated by Alan Sheridan. New York: Vintage Books, 1979.

———. *The History of Sexuality.* Vol. 1, *An Introduction.* Translated by Robert Hurley. New York: Pantheon Books, 1978.

———. *The History of Sexuality.* Vol. 2, *The Use of Pleasure.* Translated by Robert Hurley. New York: Vintage Books, 1990.

———. *The Order of Things: An Archaeology of the Human Sciences.* New York: Vintage Books, 1970.

Franits, Wayne E. J. *Paragons of Virtue: Women and Domesticity in Seventeenth-Century Dutch Art.* Cambridge: Cambridge University Press, forthcoming.

Frith, Simon. *Sound Effects: Youth, Leisure, and the Politics of Rock 'n' Roll.* New York: Pantheon Books, 1981.

Gallagher, Catherine, and Thomas Laqueur, eds. *The Making of the Modern Body: Sexuality and Society in the Nineteenth Century.* Berkeley and Los Angeles: University of California Press, 1987.

Gatens, William J. "John Ruskin and Music." *Victorian Studies* 30 (1986), pp. 77–97.

Germann, Sheridan. "Monsieur Doublet and His *Confrères:* The Harpsichord Decorators of Paris." *Early Music* 8 (1980), pp. 435–53; and 9 (1981), pp. 192–207.

Geyl, Pieter. *The Netherlands Divided (1609–1648).* Translated by S. T. Bindoff, in collaboration with Pieter Geyl. London: Williams and Norgate, 1936.

———. *The Revolt of the Netherlands (1555–1609).* 2nd ed. London: Ernest Benn, 1958.

Gilman, Sander L. "Black Bodies, White Bodies: Toward an Iconography of Female Sexuality in Late Nineteenth-Century Art, Medicine, and Literature." *Critical Inquiry* 12 (1985), pp. 204–42.

———. *Disease and Representation: Images of Illness from Madness to AIDS.* Ithaca: Cornell University Press, 1988.

Girdlestone, Cuthbert, Albert Cohen, and Mary Cyr, "Jean-Philippe Rameau." *The New Grove Dictionary of Music and Musicians.* Vol. 15, pp. 559–73.

Gleich, Clemens C. J. von. *Pianofortes uit de Lage Landen* (in English and Dutch). The Hague: Haags Gemeentemuseum in conjunction with Knuf, 1980.

Good, Edwin M. *Giraffes, Black Dragons, and Other Pianos: A Technological History from Christofori to the Modern Concert Grand.* Stanford: Stanford University Press, 1982.

Gorham, Deborah. *The Victorian Girl and the Feminine Ideal.* Bloomington: Indiana University Press, 1982.

Gramsci, Antonio. *An Antonio Gramsci Reader: Selected Writings, 1916–1935.* Edited by David Forgacs. New York: Schocken Books, 1988.

Green, Dorothy. "'The Kreutzer Sonata': Tolstoy and Beethoven." *Melbourne Slavonic Studies* 1 (1967), pp. 11–23.

Grocheo, Johannes de. *Concerning Music (De musica).* Translated by Albert Seay. 2nd ed. Colorado Springs: Colorado College Music Press, 1974.

Hall, James. *Dictionary of Subjects and Symbols in Art.* New York: Harper and Row, 1974.

Harding, Rosamond E. M. *The Piano-forte: Its History Traced to the Great Exhibition of 1851.* 1933. Reprint. New York: Da Capo, 1973.

Harnoncourt, Anne J. d'. "*The Awakening Conscience:* A Study in Moral Subject Matter in Pre-Raphaelite Paintings." Master's thesis, Courtauld Institute of Art, University of London, 1967.

Harrison, Fraser. *The Dark Angel: Aspects of Victorian Sexuality.* New York: Universe Books, 1978.

Harwood, Ian. "Tieffenbrucker," *The New Grove Dictionary of Musical Instruments.* Edited by Stanley Sadie. London: Macmillan, 1984. Vol. 3, pp. 583–84.

Hawkins, Sir John. *A General History of the Science and Practice of Music.* 2 vols. 1776. Reprint (facsimile of 1875 London edition). Graz: Akademische Druck und Verlagsanstalt, 1969.

Hayes, John. *The Drawings of Thomas Gainsborough.* London: Yale University Press, 1971.

———. *Thomas Gainsborough* [exhibition catalogue]. London: Tate Gallery, 1980.

Head, Raymond. "Corelli in Calcutta: Colonial Music-Making in India during the Seventeenth and Eighteenth Centuries." *Early Music* 13 (1985), pp. 548–53.

Hertz, Neil. "Medusa's Head: Male Hysteria under Political Pressure." *Representations* 4 (1983), pp. 27–54.

Hildebrandt, Dieter. *Pianoforte: A Social History of the Piano.* Translated by Harriet Goodman. New York: Braziller, 1988.

Hirt, Franz Josef. *Meisterwerke des Klavierbaus: Geschichte der Saitenklaviere von 1440 bis 1880.* Olten: Urs Graf-Verlag, 1955.

Hollander, Anne. *Seeing through Clothes.* New York: Penguin Books, 1978.

Hollis, Helen Rice. *The Piano: A Pictorial Account of Its Ancestry and Development.* New York: Hippocrene Books, 1975.

———. *Pianos in the Smithsonian Institution.* Smithsonian Studies in History and Technology, no. 27. Washington, D.C.: Smithsonian Institution Press, 1973.

Holman-Hunt, Diana. *My Grandfather, His Wives and Loves.* New York: Norton, 1969.

Home, Henry. *Loose Hints upon Education, Chiefly Concerning the Culture of the Heart.* Edinburgh and London, 1781.

Horkheimer, Max. *Critique of Instrumental Reason.* Translated by Matthew J. O'Connell and others. New York: Continuum, 1974.

Horkheimer, Max, and Theodor W. Adorno. *Dialectic of Enlightenment.* Translated by John Cumming. New York: Continuum, 1972.

Hough, Graham. "Tears, Idle Tears." *Hopkins Review* 4, no. 3 (1951), pp. 31–36.

Howe, Jeffrey W. *The Symbolist Art of Fernand Khnopff.* Ann Arbor: UMI Research Press, 1982.

Hubbard, Frank. *Three Centuries of Harpsichord Making.* Cambridge: Harvard University Press, 1965.

Hufstader, Alice Anderson. "Samuel Pepys, Inquisitive Amateur." *Musical Quarterly* 54 (1968), pp. 437–61.

Humphries, Henry Noel. *The Origin and Progress of the Art of Writing.* 2nd ed. London: Day and Son, 1855.

Hunt, William Holman. *Pre-Raphaelitism and the Pre-Raphaelite Brotherhood.* 2 vols. New York: Macmillan, 1905.

Jacob, Heinrich Eduard. *Felix Mendelssohn and His Times.* Translated by Richard Winston and Clara Winston. Englewood Cliffs, N.J.: Prentice Hall, 1963.

Jameson, Fredric. *Late Marxism: Adorno, or, the Persistence of the Dialectic.* London: Verso, 1990.

Jarrett, Derek. *England in the Age of Hogarth.* Frogmore, St. Albans, Hertfordshire: Paladin, 1976.

Jay, Martin. *Adorno.* Cambridge: Harvard University Press, 1984.

Johnson, Mark. *The Body in the Mind: The Bodily Basis of Meaning, Imagination, and Reason.* Chicago: University of Chicago Press, 1987.

Jones, Roger, and Nicholas Penny. *Raphael.* New Haven: Yale University Press, 1983.

Jones, Stephen. "Attic Attitudes: Leighton and Aesthetic Philosophy." In *Victorian Values: Personalities and Perspectives in Nineteenth-Century Society,* edited by Gordon Marsden, pp. 187–97. London: Longman, 1990.

Jongh, Eddy de. *Portretten van echt en trouw: Huwelijk en gezin in de Nederlandse kunst van de zeventiende eeuw* [exhibition catalogue]. Zwolle: Uitgeverij Waanders; and Haarlem: Frans Halsmuseum, 1986.

————. *Zinne- en minnebeelden in de schilderkunst van de zeventiende eeuw.* Antwerp: Openbare Kunstbezit in Vlaanderen, 1967.

Jost, Christa. *Mendelssohns Lieder ohne Worte.* Tutzing: Schneider, 1988.

Kahl, Willi. "Zu Mendelssohns Liedern ohne Worte." *Zeitschrift für Musikwissenschaft* 3 (1920–21), pp. 459–69.

Karpman, Ben. "*The Kreutzer Sonata:* A Problem in Latent Homosexuality and Castration." *Psychoanalytic Review* 25 (1938), pp. 20–48.

Kassler, Jamie Croy. *The Science of Music in Britain, 1714–1830: A Catalogue of Writings, Lectures, and Inventions.* 2 vols. New York: Garland, 1979.

Katalog der Sammlung alter Musikinstrumente. Vol. 1, *Saitenklaviere.* Vienna: Kunsthistorisches Museum [Neue Burg], 1966.

Kauffmann, Hans. "Die Fünfsinne in der niederländischen Malerei des 17. Jahrhunderts." In *Kunstgeschichtliche Studien: Festschrift für Dagobert Frey,* edited by Hans Tintelnot, pp. 133–57. Breslau: Gauverlag, 1943.

Keeble, John. *The Theory of Harmonics: Or, an Illustration of the Grecian Harmonica.* London, 1784.

Kincaid, Dennis. *British Social Life in India, 1608–1937.* London: G. Routledge and Sons, 1938.

King, Anthony. "The Bungalow." *Architectural Association Quarterly* 5 (1973), pp. 6–25.

Köhler, Karl-Heinz. "Mendelssohn(-Bartholdy), (Jacob Ludwig) Felix," *The New Grove Dictionary of Music and Musicians.* Vol. 12, pp. 135–59.

Konold, Wulf. *Felix Mendelssohn Bartholdy und seine Zeit.* N.p.: Laaber Verlag, 1984.

Kosinski, Dorothy M. *Orpheus in Nineteenth-Century Symbolism.* Ann Arbor: UMI Research Press, 1989.

Kramer, Lawrence. "Culture and Musical Hermeneutics: The Salome Complex." *Cambridge Opera Journal* 2 (1990), pp. 269–94.

———. *Music as Cultural Practice, 1800–1900.* Berkeley and Los Angeles: University of California Press, 1990.

Kren, Thomas. "Chi non vuol Baccho: Roeland van Laer's Burlesque Painting about Dutch Artists in Rome." *Simiolus* 11 (1980), pp. 63–80.

Kristeva, Julia. *Desire in Language: A Semiotic Approach to Literature and Art.* Edited by Leon S. Roudiez. Translated by Thomas Gora, Alice Jardine, and Leon S. Roudiez. New York: Columbia University Press, 1980.

Kupferberg, Herbert. *Felix Mendelssohn: His Life, His Family, His Music.* New York: Scribner, 1972.

Lambrechts-Douillez, Jeannine. "Documents Dealing with the Ruckers Family and Antwerp Harpsichord-building." In *Keyboard Instruments: Studies in Keyboard Organology,* edited by Edwin M. Ripin, pp. 37–41. Edinburgh: Edinburgh University Press, 1971.

Landow, George P. *The Aesthetic and Critical Theories of John Ruskin.* Princeton: Princeton University Press, 1971.

———. "Shadows Cast by *The Light of the World:* William Holman Hunt's Religious Paintings, 1893–1905." *Art Bulletin* 65 (1983), pp. 471–84.

———. *William Holman Hunt and Typological Symbolism.* London: Yale University Press for the Paul Mellon Centre for Studies in British Art, 1979.

Landwehr, John. *Emblem and Fable Books Printed in the Low Countries, 1542–1813: A Bibliography.* Utrecht: HES, 1988.

Layer, Adolf. "Tieffenbrucker." *Die Musik in Geschichte und Gegenwart.* Edited by Friedrich Blume. Vol. 13. Kassel and Basel: Bärenreiter, 1966, cols. 399–404.

Legrand, F.-C. *Les Peintres flamands de genre au XVIIe siècle.* Brussels: Editions Meddens, 1963.

Le Huray, Peter, and James Day, eds. *Music and Aesthetics in the Eighteenth and Early-Nineteenth Centuries.* Cambridge: Cambridge University Press, 1981.

Leppert, Richard. *Arcadia at Versailles: Noble Amateur Musicians and Their Musettes and Hurdy-Gurdies at the French Court (c. 1660–1789); a Visual Study.* Amsterdam: Swets, 1978.

———. "*Concert in a House:* Musical Iconography and Musical Thought." *Early Music* 7 (1979), pp. 3–17.

———. "David Teniers the Younger and the Image of Music," *Jaarboek, Koninklijk Museum voor Schone Kunsten* (Antwerp, 1978), pp. 63–155.

———. "Imagery, Musical Confrontation, and Cultural Difference in Early Eighteenth-Century London." *Early Music* 14 (1986), pp. 323–45.

———. "Men, Women, and Music at Home: The Influence of Cultural Values on Musical Life in Eighteenth-Century England." *Imago Musicae* 2 (1985), pp. 51–133.

———. *Music and Image: Domesticity, Ideology, and Socio-Cultural Formation in Eighteenth-Century England.* Cambridge: Cambridge University Press, 1989.

———. "Music Teachers of Upper-Class Amateur Musicians in Eighteenth-Century England." In *Music in the Classic Period: Essays in Honor of Barry S. Brook,* edited by Allan W. Atlas, pp. 133–58. New York: Pendragon, 1985.

———. *The Theme of Music in Flemish Paintings of the Seventeenth Century.* 2 vols. Munich and Salzburg: Musikverlag Emil Katzbichler, 1977.

Leppert, Richard, and George Lipsitz. "'Everybody's Lonesome for Somebody': Age, the Body, and Experience in the Music of Hank Williams." *Popular Music* 9 (1990), pp. 259–74.

Leppert, Richard, and Susan McClary, eds. *Music and Society: The Politics of Composition, Performance, and Reception.* Cambridge: Cambridge University Press, 1987.

Le Roy Ladurie, Emmanuel. *Carnival in Romans.* Translated by Mary Feeney. New York: Braziller, 1979.

Li, Chu-tsing. "The Five Senses in Art: An Analysis of Its Development in Northern Europe." Ph.D. diss., State University of Iowa, 1955.

Lippman, Edward A., ed. *Musical Aesthetics: A Historical Reader.* 2 vols. New York: Pendragon, 1986–88.

Lipsitz, George. *Time Passages: Collective Memory and American Popular Culture.* Minneapolis: University of Minnesota Press, 1990.

Loesser, Arthur. *Men, Women, and Pianos: A Social History.* New York: Simon and Schuster, 1954.

Lovejoy, Arthur O. "'Nature' as Aesthetic Norm." In *Essays in the History of Ideas,* pp. 69–77. Baltimore: Johns Hopkins Press, 1948.

Lowe, Donald M. *The History of Bourgeois Perception.* Chicago: University of Chicago Press, 1982.

Lütgendorff, Willibald Leo von. *Die Geigen und Lautenmacher vom Mittelalter bis zur Gegenwart.* 2 vols. Frankfurt am Main: Frankfurter Verlags-Anstalt, 1922.

Maas, Jeremy. *Holman Hunt and "The Light of the World."* London: Scholar Press, 1984.

Macaulay, Thomas Babington. *The Works of Lord Macaulay.* 12 vols. London, 1898.

McClary, Susan. "The Blasphemy of Talking Politics during Bach Year." In *Music and Society: The Politics of Composition, Performance, and Reception,* edited by Richard Leppert and Susan McClary, pp. 13–62. Cambridge: Cambridge University Press, 1987.

———. *Feminine Endings: Music, Gender, and Sexuality.* Minneapolis: University of Minnesota Press, 1991.

McGeary, Thomas. "Harpsichord Decoration—a Reflection of Renaissance Ideas about Music." *Explorations in Renaissance Culture* 6 (1980), pp. 1–27.

———. "Harpsichord Mottoes." *Journal of the American Musical Instrument Society* 7 (1981), pp. 5–35.

Mackerness, E. D. *A Social History of English Music.* London: Routledge and Kegan Paul, 1964.

Magli, Patricia. "The Face and the Soul." Translated by Ughetta Lubin. In *Fragments for a History of the Human Body,* edited by Michel Feher, vol. 2, pp. 86–127. New York: Zone, 1989.

Mahillon, Victor-Charles. *Catalogue descriptif et analytique du Musée instrumental (historique et technique) du Conservatoire royal de musique de Bruxelles.* 5 vols. Ghent: Ad. Hoste, 1893–1922. Reprint. Brussels: Les Amis de la Musique, 1978.

Mallalieu, H. L. *The Dictionary of British Watercolour Artists up to 1920.* N.p.: Antique Collector's Club, 1976.

Manchester, William. *Goodbye, Darkness: A Memoir of the Pacific War.* New York: Laurel, 1979.

Manners, Victoria, and G. C. Williamson. *John Zoffany, R.A., His Life and Works, 1735–1810.* London: John Lane, 1920.

Marcus, Steven. *The Other Victorians: A Study of Sexuality and Pornography in Mid-Nineteenth-Century England.* New York: Basic Books, 1966.

Marcuse, Herbert. "The Affirmative Character of Culture." In *Negations: Essays in Critical Theory.* Translated by Jeremy J. Shapiro, pp. 88–133. Boston: Beacon, 1968.

Marsh, Jan. *The Pre-Raphaelite Sisterhood.* New York: St. Martin's Press, 1985.

Marshall, Peter J. *Problems of Empire: Britain and India, 1757–1813.* London: Allen and Unwin, 1968.

Metcalf, Thomas R. "Architecture and the Representation of Empire: India, 1860–1910." *Representations* 6 (1984), pp. 37–65.

Meyer-Baer, Kathi. *Music of the Spheres and the Dance of Death: Studies in Musical Iconology.* Princeton: Princeton University Press, 1970.

Michel, Norman E. *Historical Pianos, Harpsichords, and Clavichords.* Pico Rivera, Calif.: N. E. Michel, 1970.

———. *Old Pianos.* Pico Rivera, Calif.: Privately printed, 1954.

Millar, Oliver. *Zoffany and His Tribuna.* London: Routledge and Kegan Paul, 1967.

Milner, James D. "Tilly Kettle." *Walpole Society* 15 (1926–27), pp. 47–103.

Mirimonde, Albert Pomme de. "Les 'Cabinets de musique.'" *Jaarboek, Koninklijk Museum voor Schone Kunsten* (Antwerp, 1966), pp. 141–78.

———. "Les Concerts des muses chez les maîtres du nord." *Gazette des beaux-arts,* 6th ser., vol. 64 (1964), pp. 253–84.

———. *L'Iconographie musicale sous les rois Bourbons: La Musique dans les arts plastiques (XVIIe–XVIIIe siècles),* La vie musicale en France sous les rois Bourbons, no. 22. Paris: Picard, 1975.

———. "Les Natures mortes à instruments de musique de Peter Boel." *Jaarboek, Koninklijk Museum voor Schone Kunsten* (Antwerp, 1964), pp. 107–43.

————. "Les Sujets de musique dans la peinture Belge du XVIIIe siècle." *Jaarboek, Koninklijk Museum voor Schone Kunsten* (Antwerp, 1967), pp. 245–57.

Moore, Thomas. *The Poetical Works of Thomas Moore, Collected by Himself.* Vol. 4, *Irish Melodies, National Airs, Sacred Songs.* London, 1853.

Morgan, Robert P. "Secret Languages: The Roots of Musical Modernism." In *Modernism: Challenges and Perspectives,* edited by Monique Chefdor, Richardo Quinones, and Albert Wachtel, pp. 33–53. Urbana: University of Illinois Press, 1986.

Morris, Robert. *Lectures on Architecture. Consisting of Rules Founded upon Harmonick and Arithmetical Proportions in Building.* London, 1734.

Mort, Frank. *Dangerous Sexualities: Medico-Moral Politics in England since 1830.* London: Routledge and Kegan Paul, 1987.

Mulvey, Laura. *Visual and Other Pleasures.* Bloomington: Indiana University Press, 1989.

Nead, Lynda. *Myths of Sexuality: Representations of Women in Victorian Britain.* Oxford: Blackwell, 1988.

Nead, Lynn. "The Magdalen in Modern Times: The Mythology of the Fallen Woman in Pre-Raphaelite Painting." In *Looking On: Images of Femininity in the Visual Arts and Media,* edited by Rosemary Betterton, pp. 73–92. London: Pandora, 1987.

Neubauer, John. *The Emancipation of Music from Language: Departure from Mimesis in Eighteenth-Century Aesthetics.* New Haven: Yale University Press, 1986.

The New Grove Dictionary of Music and Musicians. Edited by Stanley Sadie. 20 vols. London: Macmillan, 1980.

Nilsson, Sten. *European Architecture in India, 1750–1850.* Translated by Agnes George and Eleonore Zettersten. London: Faber, 1968.

Nochlin, Linda. "Lost and *Found:* Once More the Fallen Woman." In *Feminism and Art History: Questioning the Litany,* edited by Norma Broude and Mary D. Garrard, pp. 220–45. New York: Harper and Row, 1982.

————. *Realism.* Harmondsworth: Penguin Books, 1971.

Norton, Richard. *The History of Western Tonality: A Critical and Historical Perspective.* University Park: Pennsylvania State University Press, 1984.

O'Brien, Grant. *Ruckers: A Harpsichord and Virginal Building Tradition.* Cambridge: Cambridge University Press, 1990.

Olmsted, John Charles, ed. *Victorian Painting: Essays and Reviews.* 3 vols. New York: Garland, 1983.

Ormond, Leonée, and Richard Ormond. *Lord Leighton.* New Haven: Yale University Press, 1975.

Ormond, Richard. "George Chinnery and the Keswick Family." *Connoisseur* 175 (December 1970), pp. 245–55.

Palisca, Claude V. "Zarlino." *The New Grove Dictionary of Music and Musicians.* Vol. 20, pp. 646–49.

Parker, Geoffrey. *The Dutch Revolt.* Ithaca: Cornell University Press, 1977.

Parkinson, Ronald. "The Awakening Conscience and the Still Small Voice." In *The Tate Gallery Illustrated Biennial Report and Catalogue of Acquisitions {1976–1978},* pp. 21–29. London: Tate Gallery Publications, 1978.

Pater, Walter. "The School of Giorgione." In *Walter Pater: Selected Works*. Edited by Richard Aldington. Melbourne: William Heinemann, 1948.

Pattison, Robert. *The Triumph of Vulgarity: Rock Music in the Mirror of Romanticism*. New York: Oxford University Press, 1987.

Pavière, Sydney H. *The Devis Family of Painters*. Leigh-on-Sea: F. Lewis, 1950.

Pearson, R. *Eastern Interlude: A Social History of the European Community in Calcutta*. Calcutta: Thanker, Spink, 1954.

Perrot, Michelle, ed. *A History of Private Life*. Vol. 4, *From the Fires of Revolution to the Great War*. Translated by Arthur Goldhammer. Cambridge: Belknap Press of Harvard University Press, 1990.

Peter Jakob Horemans (1700–1776) Kurbayerischer Hofmaler [exhibition catalogue]. Munich: Alte Pinakothek, 1974.

Pevsner, Nikolaus. *The Englishness of English Art*. Harmondsworth: Penguin Books, 1964.

Philips, Peter. *Peter Philips: Select Italian Madrigals*. Transcribed and edited by John Steele. *Musica Britannica*, no. 29. London: Stainer and Bell, 1970.

Pistone, Danièle. *Le piano dans la littérature française des origines jusque vers 1900*. Paris: Champion, 1975.

Plato, *The Republic*. Translated by A. D. Lindsay. New York: Dutton, 1957.

Plumb, J. H. *England in the Eighteenth Century*. The Pelican History of England, no. 7. Harmondsworth: Penguin Books, 1950.

Pointon, Marcia. *Naked Authority: The Body in Western Painting, 1830–1908*. Cambridge: Cambridge University Press, 1990.

Pole, William, ed. *The Life of Sir William Fairbairn . . . Partly Written by Himself*. London, 1877.

The Polite Lady; or, a Course of Female Education. 2nd ed., corrected. London, 1769.

Pollock, Griselda. *Vision and Difference: Femininity, Feminism, and the Histories of Art*. London: Routledge, 1988.

Poovey, Mary. *Uneven Developments: The Ideological Work of Gender in Mid-Victorian England*. Chicago: University of Chicago Press, 1988.

Praz, Mario. *The Romantic Agony*. Translated by Angus Davidson. Cleveland: Meridian Books, 1956.

———. *Studies in Seventeenth-Century Imagery*. 2nd ed. Rome: Storia, 1964.

The Pre-Raphaelites [exhibition catalogue]. London: Tate Gallery / Harmondsworth: Penguin Books, 1984.

The Pre-Raphaelites and Their Circle in the National Gallery of Victoria [exhibition catalogue]. Melbourne: National Gallery of Victoria, 1978.

Radcliffe, Philip. *Mendelssohn*. London: Dent, 1954.

Raines, Robert. *Marcellus Laroon*. London: Routledge and Kegan Paul, 1966.

Rameau, Jean-Philippe. *Complete Theoretical Writings*. Edited by Erwin R. Jacobi. 6 vols. N.p.: American Institute of Musicology, 1968.

———. *Démonstration du principe de l'harmonie*. Paris, 1750.

———. *Treatise on Harmony*. Translated, with introduction and notes, by Philip Gossett. New York: Dover, 1971.

Réau, Louis. *Iconographie de l'art chrétien.* 3 vols. in 6. Paris: Presses Universitaires de France, 1955–59.

Renouf, Nicholas. *Musical Instruments in the Viennese Tradition: 1750–1850* [exhibition catalogue]. New Haven: Yale University Collection of Musical Instruments, 1981.

Reynolds, Graham. *Victorian Painting.* Rev. ed. New York: Harper and Row, 1987.

Ripin, Edwin M., et al. *The New Grove Piano.* The Grove Musical Instrument Series. Edited by Stanley Sadie. New York: Norton, 1988.

Roberts, Helene E. "Marriage, Redundancy, or Sin: The Painter's View of Women in the First Twenty-Five Years of Victoria's Reign." In *Suffer and Be Still: Women in the Victorian Age,* edited by Martha Vicinus, pp. 45–76. Bloomington: Indiana University Press, 1973.

Roell, Craig H. *The Piano in America, 1890–1940.* Chapel Hill: University of North Carolina Press, 1989.

Roskill, Mark. "Holman Hunt's Differing Versions of *The Light of the World.*" *Victorian Studies* 6 (1962/63), pp. 329–42.

Rueger, Christoph. *Musical Instruments and Their Decoration: Historical Gems of European Culture.* Translated by Peter Underwood. Cincinnati: Seven Hills Books, 1986.

Ruskin, John. "The Relation of Art to Morals." In *The Complete Works.* Vol. 14, *Lectures on Art, Lectures on Landscape, Aratra Pentelici.* New York: Thomas Y. Crowell, n.d.

Russell, Raymond. *Victoria and Albert Museum Catalogue of Musical Instruments.* Vol. 2, *Keyboard Instruments.* London: Her Majesty's Stationery Office, 1968.

The Russell Collection and Other Early Keyboard Instruments in Saint Cecilia's Hall, Edinburgh. Edinburgh: Edinburgh University Press, 1968.

Russett, Cynthia Eagle. *Sexual Science: The Victorian Construction of Womanhood.* Cambridge: Harvard University Press, 1989.

Russolo, Luigi. *The Art of Noises.* Monographs in Musicology, no. 6. Translated by Barclay Brown. New York: Pendragon, 1986.

Sachs, Curt. *World History of the Dance.* Translated by Bessie Schönberg. New York: Norton, 1937.

Said, Edward. *Orientalism.* New York: Vintage Books, 1978.

Salmen, Walter. Haus- und Kammermusik: Privates Musizieren im gesellschaftlichen Wandel zwischen *1600 und 1900.* Musikgeschichte in Bildern, vol. IV/3. Leipzig: Deutscher Verlag für Musik, 1969.

———. *Musikleben im 16. Jahrhundert.* Musikgeschichte in Bildern, vol. III/9. Leipzig: Deutscher Verlag für Musik, 1976.

Schama, Simon. *The Embarrassment of Riches: An Interpretation of Dutch Culture in the Golden Age.* New York: Knopf, 1987.

———. "Wives and Wantons: Versions of Womanhood in Seventeenth Century Dutch Art." *Oxford Art Journal* 3 (1980), pp. 5–13.

Schiebinger, Londa. "Skeletons in the Closet: The First Illustrations of the Female Skeleton in Eighteenth-Century Anatomy." *Representations* 14 (1986), pp. 42–82.

Scholes, Percy A. *The Great Doctor Burney: His Life, His Travels, His Works; His Family and His Friends.* 2 vols. Oxford: Oxford University Press, 1948.

Scott, Derek. *The Singing Bourgeois: Songs of the Victorian Drawing Room and Parlour*. Milton Keynes: Open University Press, 1989.

Sedgwick, Eve Kosofsky. *Between Men: English Literature and Male Homosocial Desire*. New York: Columbia University Press, 1985.

Sheehan, Elizabeth. "Victorian Clitoridectomy: Isaac Baker Brown and His Harmless Operative Procedure." *Medical Anthropology Newsletter* 12 (1981), pp. 9–15.

Shepherd, John. "Music and Male Hegemony." In *Music and Society: The Politics of Composition, Performance, and Reception,* edited by Richard Leppert and Susan McClary, pp. 151–72. Cambridge: Cambridge University Press, 1987.

————. *Music as Social Text*. Cambridge, U.K.: Polity, 1991.

Showalter, Elaine. *The Female Malady: Women, Madness, and English Culture, 1830–1980*. New York: Pantheon Books, 1985.

————. "Victorian Women and Insanity." *Victorian Studies* 23 (1980), pp. 157–81.

Sigsworth, E. M., and T. J. Wyke. "A Study of Victorian Prostitution and Venereal Disease." In *Suffer and Be Still: Women in the Victorian Age,* edited by Martha Vicinus, pp. 77–99. Bloomington: Indiana University Press, 1973.

Silverman, Kaja. *The Acoustic Mirror: The Female Voice in Psychoanalysis and Cinema*. Bloomington: Indiana University Press, 1988.

————. "Fragments of a Fashionable Discourse." In *Studies in Entertainment: Critical Approaches to Mass Culture,* edited by Tania Modleski, pp. 139–52. Bloomington: Indiana University Press, 1986.

Simmel, Georg. *The Philosophy of Money*. Translated by Tom Bottomore and David Frisby. 1900. Reprint. London: Routledge & Kegan Paul, 1978.

Sitwell, Sacheverell. *Conversation Pieces: A Survey of English Domestic Portraits and Their Painters*. 1936. Reprint. London: Batsford, 1969.

Skinner, William, comp. *The Belle Skinner Collection of Old Musical Instruments: A Descriptive Catalogue*. Privately printed, 1933.

Small, Christopher. *Music, Society, Education*. New York: Schirmer, 1980.

Smith, David R. "Courtesy and Its Discontents: Frans Hals's *Portrait of Isaac Massa and Beatrix van der Laen*." *Oud Holland* 100 (1986), pp. 2–34.

————. *Masks of Wedlock: Seventeenth-Century Dutch Marriage Portraiture*. Ann Arbor: UMI Research Press, 1982.

Spear, Thomas G. P. *The Nabobs: A Study of the Social Life of the English in Eighteenth Century India*. London: H. Milford, 1932.

Speth-Holteroff, Simone. *Les Peintres flamands de cabinets d'amateurs au XVIIe siècle*. Paris and Brussels: Elsevier, 1957.

Staley, Allen. "The Condition of Music." *Art News Annual* 33 (1967), pp. 81–87.

Stanhope, Philip Dormer. *Letters to His Son by the Earl of Chesterfield on the Fine Art of Becoming a Man of the World and a Gentleman*. Edited by Oliver H. G. Leigh. 2 vols. London: Navarre Society, 1926.

Steele, Valerie. *Fashion and Eroticism: Ideals of Feminine Beauty from the Victorian Era to the Jazz Age*. New York: Oxford University Press, 1985.

Stephens, J. E., ed. *Aubrey on Education: A Hitherto Unpublished Manuscript by the Author of "Brief Lives."* London: Routledge and Kegan Paul, 1972.

Stone, Lawrence. *The Family, Sex, and Marriage in England, 1500–1800.* Abridged ed. New York: Harper and Row, 1979.

Stresemann, Wolfgang. *Eine Lanze für Felix Mendelssohn.* Berlin: Stapp, 1984.

Strunk, Oliver, ed. *Source Readings in Music History: The Renaissance.* New York: Norton, 1965.

Stubbes, Philip. *Philip Stubbes's Anatomy of Abuses in England in Shakespeare's Youth, A.D. 1583.* Edited by Frederick J. Furnivall. 2 vols. London: New Shakespeare Society, 1877–82.

Subotnik, Rose Rosengard. *Developing Variations: Style and Ideology in Western Music.* Minneapolis: University of Minnesota Press, 1991.

———. "On Grounding Chopin." In *Music and Society: The Politics of Composition, Performance, and Reception,* edited by Richard Leppert and Susan McClary, pp. 105–31. Cambridge: Cambridge University Press, 1987.

Temperley, Nicholas. "London and the Piano, 1760–1860." *Musical Times* 129 (1988), pp. 289–93.

———. "The London Pianoforte School." *Musical Times* 126 (1985), pp. 25–27.

———. "Mendelssohn's Influence on English Music." *Music and Letters* 43 (1962), pp. 224–33.

Tennyson, Alfred Lord. *Tennyson's Poetry: Authoritative Texts; Juvenilia and Early Responses; Criticism.* Edited by Robert W. Hill, Jr. New York: Norton, 1971.

Theweleit, Klaus. *Male Fantasies.* Vol. 1, *Women, Floods, Bodies, History.* Translated by Stephen Conway, in collaboration with Erica Carter and Chris Turner. Minneapolis: University of Minnesota Press, 1987.

Thiel, P. J. J. van. "Marriage Symbolism in a Musical Party by Jan Miense Molenaar." *Simiolus* 2 (1967–68), pp. 90–99.

Thompson, Edward. *The Making of the Indian Princes.* London: Oxford University Press, 1943.

Thompson, Edward, and G. T. Garratt. *Rise and Fulfilment of British Rule in India.* London: Macmillan, 1934.

Thompson, James. "Ruskin and Hunt's 'Awakening Conscience.'" *Victorian Institute Journal* 8 (1979), pp. 19–29.

Tischler, Louise H., and Hans Tischler. "Mendelssohn's 'Songs without Words.'" *Musical Quarterly* 33 (1947), pp. 1–16.

———. "Mendelssohn's Style: 'The Songs without Words.'" *Music Review* 8 (1947), pp. 256–73.

Todd, R. Larry. "Piano Music Reformed: The Case of Felix Mendelssohn Bartholdy." In *Nineteenth-Century Piano Music,* edited by R. Larry Todd, pp. 178–220. New York: Schirmer, 1990.

Tolstoy, Leo. *The Kreutzer Sonata and Other Stories.* Translated by David McDuff. Harmondsworth: Penguin Books, 1985.

————. *What is Art? and Essays on Art.* Translated by Aylmer Maude. London: Oxford University Press, 1930.

Trudgill, Eric. *Madonnas and Magdalens: The Origins and Development of Victorian Sexual Attitudes.* New York: Holmes and Meier, 1976.

Velikovsky, I. "Tolstoy's Kreutzer Sonata and Unconscious Homosexuality." *Psychoanalytic Review* 24 (1937), pp. 18–25.

Verdi, Giuseppe. *La Traviata.* Italian translation by Dale McAdoo. Angel Records: 3545 B/L, 1956.

Verheyden, A. L. E. *Le Conseil des Troubles. Liste des condamnés (1567–1573).* Brussels: Palais des académies, 1961.

Vogel, Lise. "Fine Arts and Feminism: The Awakening Consciousness." In *Feminist Art Criticism: An Anthology,* edited by Arlene Raven, Cassandra Langer, and Joanna Frueh, pp. 21–57. Ann Arbor: UMI Research Press, 1988.

Volk, Mary Crawford. "Rubens in Madrid and the Decoration of the King's Summer Apartments." *Burlington Magazine* 123 (1981), pp. 513–25.

Wainwright, David. *Broadwood, by Appointment: A History.* London: Quiller, 1982.

————. *The Piano Makers.* London: Hutchinson, 1975.

Walkowitz, Judith R. *Prostitution and Victorian Society: Women, Class, and the State.* New York: Cambridge University Press, 1980.

Weber, William. "Mass Culture and the Reshaping of European Musical Taste, 1770–1870." *International Review of the Aesthetics and Sociology of Music* 8 (1977), pp. 5–22.

————. *Music and the Middle Class: The Social Structure of Concert Life in London, Paris, and Vienna.* New York: Holmes and Meier, 1975.

Webster, Mary. *Johan Zoffany, 1733–1810* [exhibition catalogue]. London: National Portrait Gallery, 1977.

Weeks, Jeffrey. *Sex, Politics, and Society: The Regulation of Sexuality since 1800.* 2nd ed. London: Longman, 1989.

Weiss, Piero, and Richard Taruskin, eds. *Music in the Western World: A History in Documents.* New York: Schirmer, 1984.

Werner, Eric. *Mendelssohn: A New Image of the Composer and His Age.* Translated by Dika Newlin. London: Collier-Macmillan, 1963.

Whitley, William T. *Artists and Their Friends in England, 1700–1799.* 2 vols. London: Medici Society, 1928.

The Whole Duty of a Woman, or a Guide to the Female Sex. From the Age of Sixteen to Sixty. 3rd ed. London, 1701.

Wier, Albert E. *The Piano: Its History, Makers, Players, and Music.* London: Longmans, Green, 1941.

Willetts, Pamela J. "Johann Andreas Stumpff, 1769–1846." *Musical Times* 118 (1977), pp. 29–32.

Williams, H. Noel. *Henry II: His Court and His Times.* London: Methuen, 1910.

Wilson, Michael I. "The Case of the Victorian Piano." *Victoria and Albert Museum Yearbook,* no. 3, pp. 133–53. London: Phaidon, 1972.

Winkelmann-Rhein, Gertraude. *The Paintings and Drawings of Jan "Flower" Bruegel.* Translated by Leonard Mins. New York: Harry N. Abrams, 1968.

Wittkower, Rudolf. *Gian Lorenzo Bernini: The Sculptor of the Roman Baroque.* 2nd ed. London: Phaidon, 1966.

Wolff, Janet, and Caroline Arscott. "'Cultivated Capital': Patronage and Art in Nineteenth-Century Manchester and Leeds." *History Today* 37 (March 1987), pp. 22–28.

Zarlino, Gioseffo. *Istituzioni armoniche* [1558]. Translated by Guy A. Marco and Claude V. Palisca. New Haven: Yale University Press, 1968.

INDEX

References to illustrations are printed in *italic* type. Titles of books are not indexed except for those few receiving detailed discussion; authors are indexed. Only significant references to persons and places are indexed.

307

Compositor:	G&S Typesetters
Text:	11/13 Garamond
Display:	Garamond
Printer:	Malloy Lithographing
Binder:	John H. Dekker & Sons